KU-782-079

Interpretations of AMERICAN LITERATURE

INTERPRETATIONS *of*

AMERICAN LITERATURE

EDITED BY

CHARLES FEIDELSON, Jr. *and* PAUL BRODTKORB, Jr.

OXFORD UNIVERSITY PRESS

LONDON   OXFORD   NEW YORK

OXFORD UNIVERSITY PRESS

Oxford   London   New York
Glasgow   Toronto   Melbourne   Wellington
Cape Town   Ibadan   Nairobi   Lusaka   Addis Ababa   Delhi
Bombay   Calcutta   Madras   Karachi   Lahore   Dacca
Kuala Lumpur   Hong Kong   Tokyo

Preface

This is a collection of interpretive essays on major works, major writers, and a few major strains of American literature. It is designed to serve the student and the inquiring reader as a running commentary on the basic texts.

In choosing essays for this volume, we have had a bias in favor of the contemporary: all these discussions are of relatively recent date; the earliest was first published in 1932, and most are from the 'fifties and 'forties. Usually (though by no means invariably) we have preferred less familiar and less easily available materials to selections that have been frequently reprinted or have already become critical classics. On the theory that arguments have an integrity that should be respected, we have tried as much as possible to avoid extracts from books and from articles too long to reprint.

But our main purpose has been to provide a series of substantial essays on substantial topics. We have not wished to emphasize any particular mode of interpretation; nor, on the other hand, have we attempted to illustrate the full range of methods and preoccupations in contemporary discussion of American writing. Primarily, we have had in mind the immediate needs of the student, who is presumably less interested in criticism as such than in particular

critiques that may help him to grasp particular literary facts—
works or writers or movements. We hope that the essays in this
volume will serve that end by posing questions of sufficient scope
and offering answers adequate to the questions asked.

CHARLES FEIDELSON, JR.

PAUL BRODTKORB, JR.

Yale University
April 1959

Table of Contents

Interpretations of AMERICAN LITERATURE

Hyatt Howe Waggoner

I

The Scarlet Letter

It is an interesting fact that Hawthorne's most widely read and admired novel is also the one that has inspired the most inconclusive debate about its meaning. *The Scarlet Letter* has been read as evidence of Hawthorne's "transcendentalism" and of his "Puritanism." It has been interpreted as a declaration in favor of feminism and as a half-hearted, and to that extent defective, statement of pragmatic modernism. Since Hawthorne was not a transcendentalist, a Puritan, or a feminist by any interpretation, however broad, of these terms, as even a slight acquaintance with his life and work is sufficient to show, the best thing to do with the first three of these interpretations is to dismiss them as clearly on the wrong track. As for the pragmatic reading, it is perhaps politic to wait and see. But it might be remarked now that it is hardly to be considered surprising that a reading conducted in terms of the variety of pragmatic liberalism fathered by Emerson, nourished by James, and matured by Dewey should find the novel worth only an A-minus.

Yet the very variety of the critical interpretations points to several conclusions, one of which surely is that if *The Scarlet Letter*

Reprinted by permission of the publishers from Hyatt Howe Waggoner, *Hawthorne: A Critical Study,* Cambridge, Mass.: The Belknap Press of Harvard University Press, Copyright, 1955, by The President and Fellows of Harvard College.

is allegory at all, it cannot be allegory of the older mode, with its clear-cut abstractions, for if it were, surely there would not be so much disagreement about its meaning. If it is rather a work of symbolism of the type Hawthorne made his own in the best of the tales, then we should expect that paraphrase will not be easy, and hasty paraphrase will not be rewarding.

II

In the three paragraphs of his opening chapter Hawthorne introduces the three chief symbols that will serve to give structure to the story on the thematic level, hints at the fourth, and starts two of the chief lines of imagery. The opening sentence suggests the darkness ("sad-colored," "gray"), the rigidity ("oak," "iron"), and the aspiration ("steeple-crowned") of the people "amongst whom religion and law were almost identical." Later sentences add "weatherstains," "a yet darker aspect," and "gloomy" to the suggestions already begun through color imagery. The closing words of the chapter make the metaphorical use of color explicit: Hawthorne hopes that a wild rose beside the prison door may serve "to symbolize some sweet moral blossom, that may be found along the track, or relieve the darkening close of a tale of human frailty and sorrow."

A large part of the opening chapter is allotted to this rose-bush and to some weeds that also grow beside the prison. Having learned to respect the economy with which Hawthorne worked in his tales, we should guess, even if we had not read beyond this first chapter, that these will turn out not to be merely "realistic" or "atmospheric" details. We should expect to meet them again, with expanded connotations. Actually, the flower and weed imagery is second in importance only to the color imagery in the novel. The more than thirty occasions on which it is subsequently found are not, like the even more frequent heart images, casual, or partly to be accounted for as stylistic mannerisms, the reflexes as it were of Hawthorne's style, but chief keys to the symbolic structure and intention of this work.

Finally, in addition to the Puritans themselves, the jail before which they stand, and the weeds and the rose, one other object, and only one, is mentioned in this first chapter. In the only generalized comment in a chapter otherwise devoted to objective description, Hawthorne tells us that "The founders of a new colony, whatever Utopia of human virtue and happiness they might originally project, have invariably recognized it among their earliest practical necessities to allot a portion of the virgin soil as a cemetery, and another as the site of a prison." The three climactic scenes of the novel take place before the scaffold in front of the prison. The cemetery, by contrast, remains in the background. We are not allowed to forget it, we learn that Chillingworth has a special interest in it, but we are not encouraged to make it the center of our attention until the end, when it moves into the foreground as the site of the tombstone with the strange inscription.

The cemetery, the prison, and the rose, with their associated values and the extensions of suggestion given them by the image patterns that intersect them, as the ugliest weeds are later discovered growing out of graves, suggest a symbolic pattern within which nearly everything that is most important in the novel may be placed. The cemetery and the prison are negative values, in some sense evils. The rose is a positive value, beautiful, in some sense a good. But the cemetery and the prison are not negative in the same sense: death, "the last great enemy," is a natural evil, resulting as some theologies would have it from moral evil but distinguished by coming to saint and sinner alike; the prison is a reminder of the present actuality of moral evil. Natural and moral evil, then, death and sin, are here suggested. The rose is "good" in the same sense in which the cemetery is an "evil": its beauty is neither moral nor immoral but is certainly a positive value. Like the beauty of a healthy child or an animal, it is the product not of choice but of necessity, of the laws of its being, so that it can be admired but not judged. Pearl, later in the story, is similarly immune from judgment. There is no strong suggestion of moral goodness in this first chapter, nor will there be in what is to follow. The cemetery and the weeds contrast with the rose, but only the suggestions of worship in the shape of the hats of the Puritans contrast with the prison, and those steeple-crowned hats are gray, a color which later takes on strongly negative associations.

Among the ideas implicit in the opening chapter, then, are, first, that the novel is to be concerned with the relationships of good and evil; second, that it will distinguish between two types of good and evil; and, third, that moral good will be less strongly felt than moral and natural evil. A symmetrical pattern is theoretically suggested here, and as we shall see, in the rest of the novel. But what is actually felt is an asymmetrical pattern, an imbalance, in which the shapes of moral and natural evil loom so large as to make it difficult to discern, or to "believe in" once we have discerned, the reality of moral goodness or redemption. The rose, in short, is finally not sufficient to relieve "the darkening close of a tale of human frailty and sorrow." The celestial radiance later seen gleaming from the white hair of Mr. Wilson is not sufficient either, nor the snowy innocence said to exist in the bosoms of certain maidens. In writing *The Scarlet Letter* Hawthorne let his genius takes its course, and death and sin turned out to be more convincing than life and goodness.

III

The extremes of Mr. Wilson's "light" and Chillingworth's "blackness" meet not only in the gray of Hester's dress and the Puritan hats, and in the indeterminate drabness of the Puritan clothing, but also in the ambiguous suggestions of red. Images of color, and of light and shade, are more numerous than any other images in the novel. Readers have always been aware that Hawthorne has used these images "artistically," and sometimes that he has used them "expressively"; yet precisely what they express and how they express it have never, even in the extended treatments of the subject, been adequately analyzed. Some of them Hawthorne makes explicitly symbolic, others seem obscurely to be so, while still others resist every effort at translation into abstract terms. Faced with this profusion and complexity of evidence, most commentators have wavered between the opinion that the color images are used "allegorically" and the even less discerning opinion that they are only in the vaguest sense, as realistic background, functional. Here, as on a number of other aspects of Hawthorne's work, criticism is forced to make something like a fresh start. I think it will prove useful as a preliminary to later analysis to distinguish among three ways in which images of color and light and shade appear in the novel.

There is, first, the pure sensory image used literally, not figuratively, though the literalness of its use will not destroy whatever intrinsic symbolic value it may have. Second, there is the

Literal- according to the primitive or verbal meaning, not figurative or metaphorical.

THE SCARLET LETTER   7

color or shade of light or darkness that must be taken literally but that also has explicit symbolic value. Finally, there is the image that has only, or chiefly, symbolic value, so that it cannot be taken literally. I shall call these pure, mixed, and drained images. It will be clear that this sort of classification cuts across other types of analysis, such as that which distinguishes between emphatic and casual imagery and that which seeks to isolate implicit paradox or distinguish types of ambiguity. The strategy here is intended to bring out the degree of "literalness" with which Hawthorne writes, and this matter in turn has an important bearing on the question of whether *The Scarlet Letter* is symbolism or allegory.

But first it must be clear that there is a real basis in the novel for making such distinctions—or that the data will lend themselves to such manipulation without forcing. A look at the first several chapters will be enough I think to give us an answer. Thus on the first page the grayness of the hats and the "weatherstains" of the jail are pure images, sense impressions to be taken quite literally. Only after we have become conscious of the part played by color in the tale are we apt to be aware of the appropriateness of these colors, though to be sure they may have had their effect on us before we became conscious of that effect. So likewise the "bright" morning sun and the "ruddy" cheeks of the spectators in the next chapter are first of all, and always fundamentally, to be understood in a perfectly literal sense. Again, the first time the scarlet letter is mentioned, the color image is pure: "On the breast of her gown, in fine red cloth, surrounded with an elaborate embroidery and fantastic flourishes of gold-thread, appeared the letter *A*."

Mixed images, on the other hand, have more than that suggestion of figurative extension that any image, however pure, will have: they may be said to *denote* both literal and figurative colors, so that in them the natural symbolism of color becomes explicit. The jail is "gloomy," that is, both physically and emotionally dark. The second time the letter is mentioned, its color has acquired a moral connotation from its context: Hester stood before the crowd with "desperate recklessness" while everyone looked at the sign of her ignominy, "that SCARLET LETTER." More clearly an example of this mixed type of image is the beadle's statement that here in this righteous colony "iniquity is dragged out into the sunshine": for Hester has just been brought from the literal darkness of the jail into the literal sunshine of the square, and this action is an example of "iniquity" which has been hidden or unknown being made public, brought into the (figurative) light. The speaker has meant his remark as a figure of speech, while the reader sees that it is literally appropriate too; there is a two-way movement, from the literal to the figurative, and from the figurative back to the literal, going on here and elsewhere in the color images in the novel. One final example in this preliminary survey of the mixed type of image: "his face darkened with some powerful emotion." Now powerful emotion may literally darken the face by flushing it, but here the symbolic effect of darkness, as that which is feared and evil, is also clear. This is the first reference to the "darkness" of Chillingworth.

The third or drained type of image is much less frequent than the other two. (There are ten times as many pure images as drained, and about twice as many mixed, according to my count.) On the first page we hear of the "black flower" of civilized society, a prison, and we realize that "black" is here figurative, for though the jail has been described as dark and weatherstained, it is not black in any literal sense. Again, in the last sentence of the first chapter we hear of the "darkening close" of the tale, and we read "darkening" to mean gloomy (in the emotional sense), sad. Finally, when the Reverend Mr. Wilson speaks to Hester of the "blackness" of her sin, the primary significance of the word, both for Hester and for the reader, is intensive and qualitative in a moral sense; the residue of literal meaning merely adds to the emotional overtones. Here, as in the "smile of dark and self-relying intelligence" displayed by Chillingworth, there is hardly any literal meaning left.

The colors presented in these three types of images are associated with natural good (beauty, health), moral and spiritual good (holiness), natural evil (ugliness, death), and moral evil (sin). With the exception of the yellow starch on the linen of Mistress Hibbins, in which I can discern only historical verisimilitude, all the colors in the novel, including yellow as used elsewhere, are associated with one or more natural or moral values, positive or negative. The most frequent colors are red in its several shades and black, pure or mixed, as in "gray" "shadowy," and "darksome." Red is ambiguous throughout, suggesting both sunlight and roses, on the one hand, and the traditional associations called up by "the scarlet woman" on the other. Pearl, a "natural" child, is dressed in red, Hester's letter is red, the roses are red, the bloom on healthy cheeks is red, and the glow in Chillingworth's eyes is thought to be red with the light of infernal fires. Black, dark gray, brown, all the darker shades, ordinarily suggest both natural and moral evil. Green and yellow are associated with natural good, with life and beauty.

Light is of various kinds. Sunlight suggests both truth and health. It is analogous to the spiritual Light of Revelation, which in Hawthorne's scheme of values should "illumine" nature, and to the light of grace. But there are also the "false light" of meteors and the "red light" of evil. Mr. Wilson, the most saintly of the Puritan ministers and the most sympathetic of the lesser characters, has "white" hair and light-colored ("gray") eyes, in marked contrast to the only colors assigned to Governor Bellingham, who has a "dark" feather and a "black" tunic. Thus too Dimmesdale, a mixed figure of lofty aspirations and base conduct, is seen as having a "white," lofty, and impending brow and "brown," melancholy eyes. Dressed in "black," he walks by choice in the "shadowy" bypaths. Hester is seen as red (her letter and her vivid complexion), gray (her dress), and black (her hair and eyes), the first two ambiguous in their associations, the last saved from being wholly negative by the glints of sunlight often seen in her hair. Pearl, though she has her mother's black hair and eyes, is usually seen as a flash of red and light: the "deep and vivid tints" of her "bright" complexion and "gorgeous robes" often throw an absolute circle of "radiance" around her. Chillingworth is compounded of shades of "darkness," except for the red, or reddish blue, glow thought to be seen in his eyes.

The relationships between the three types of images, the several colors, and their associated moral and natural values are highly complex, but I shall risk a few generalizations, the first of which is the most obvious. The use of colors in the novel is, as Leland Schubert has said, rhythmic, but it is more than that, for the rhythm is functional and expressive. In "The Interior of a Heart," for instance, there are twenty-two color images, all but two of which are black or white. The heart is Dimmesdale's, and Dimmesdale wavers between good and evil, we might almost say between the supernatural and the unnatural. It is conceptually right that he should be associated with both the radiance of Wilson and the darkness of Chillingworth. He is never associated with the greens and yellows and reds of sunlit nature.

Again, the chapter called "Hester at Her Needle" has eighteen color images, eleven of them red, seven black, dark, and white. Hester stands in an ambiguous position between Chillingworth and the white maidens, as Dimmesdale does between Chillingworth and Wilson, but she differs from him in her relation to nature. For a final example, on one page of "The Minister's Vigil," when the approach of Mr. Wilson and the threat of disclosure coincide, there are nine color images, eight of which are of light or whiteness. Recalling the beadle's earlier remark about the Puritan effort to drag iniquity out into the sunshine, in which light was associated with an uncharitable violation of the human heart, we become aware of what is sometimes obscured in discussions of Hawthorne: that color imagery is functional *in context.*

The most significant use of color in the novel is in the three key scenes, Hester on the scaffold with the infant Pearl, Dimmesdale with Hester and Pearl on the scaffold at midnight, and the three on the scaffold again at the end. In the first, Hester is dragged into the light and stands there "with the hot, mid-day sun burning down upon her face and lighting up its shame; with the scarlet letter of infamy on her breast. . ." In the second there is at first only the darkness of the "obscure night," which renders Dimmesdale's gesture ineffectual. Then two kinds of light appear. First there is the gleam of the lantern of the saintly Mr. Wilson, who appeared in his illuminated circle to be radiant with the "distant shine of the celestial city"; but Mr. Wilson's light does not reach Dimmesdale, who is thus "saved" by a narrow margin from disclosure. After Mr. Wilson's light recedes in the darkness, a meteor flames in the sky, making all visible, but in a "false" light, so that what Chillingworth sees by its aid is not true. Neither light in this scene accomplishes the necessary revelation. That is left for the final climactic scaffold scene, in which the three come together voluntarily in the light of the sun.

The second generalization I should like to suggest about the light and color images is this: their significance is enriched by the relations between the three types of images. In the first place, the pure images are so much the most numerous that they tend to establish, by sheer weight of repetition, the reading of the others. Where there is so much blackness, "gloomy" is bound to carry its physical as well as its emotional denotation. This becomes clearer when we compare the use of darkness in, say, *Dr. Grimshawe's Secret* with its use here. When in the later novel Redclyffe is said to exist in a darkened dream, we do not know quite what to make of it, for darkness has not been established as a motif in the novel. But when Governor Bellingham says that Pearl is "in the dark" concerning her soul, the expression means far more to the reader than that she is not, in the opinion of the governor, properly instructed: it calls up the whole range of colors, and the moral and other values attached to them, which the reader has absorbed by this time. We have another of those sudden expansions from image to symbol that is so conspicuous a feature of the novel.

In short, the marked predominance of pure images keeps the mixed and drained ones from losing force by becoming abstractly figurative, and this in turn is one of the reasons why the novel never becomes allegory. Though we must say that there is a struggle going on in the novel between the forces of darkness and of light, the preponderance of pure images keeps this struggle from becoming neatly dichotomous. When we read that Chillingworth had conceived "a new purpose, dark, it is true, if not guilty," we do not read this as a pleonasm, for darkness has acquired many associations beyond the guilt it may hide. Again, the "light" of the church is saved from being a mere figure for "the teaching of the church" by the fact that light has become associated with a cluster of positive values, both natural and moral, that cannot be translated adequately as "doctrine."

Finally, two drained images will illustrate the point. "The holy whiteness of the clergyman's good fame," in reference to Dimmesdale, draws a part of its meaning from the light constantly associated with Mr. Wilson and Christian Revelation, but another part from the false light of the meteor, which has only recently ceased to cast its distorting glare over the scene. And the smile that "flickered" over Chillingworth's face "so derisively" that the spectator could see his "blackness" " all the better for it" is also a false light which nevertheless may reveal some things truly, as the light of the meteor had revealed "the black, freshly turned earth" of the garden plots near the scaffold.

But the movement flows in another direction too, for the presence of the mixed and drained images underlines the symbolic value of the pure images. When Pearl, inspired by her mother's example, makes a letter out of eelgrass for her own breast, and Hester says that "the green letter, and on thy childish bosom, has no purport," we realize that the statement is true in several different senses: from Hester's point of view, the green letter has none of the "purport" that her own letter has, and she, of course, is preoccupied with just that kind of meaning; but from the reader's point of view, the greenness of the letter is an appropriate reminder of Pearl's association with nature. And when we see the Indians in the square on Election Day, the predominant reds and yellows of their barbaric finery and the black of their "snake-like" eyes carry associations with nature and with evil, but none at all with "celestial illumination." Like the weathered wood of the jail, the Indian costumes gather meaning from their context.

The point of my third generalization about the three types of images has perhaps already become sufficiently clear from what has been said, but it is so important that I should not like to let it rest on implication. The movement of the different colors back and forth between pure and drained images helps to keep what Hawthorne calls his "mesh of good and evil" a true mesh, with the strands intricately interwoven. Hawthorne usually presents a pure image first, establishing the sensed color, then expands it into a mixed image, exploring its connotations, then at last uses the color in a drained image that out of the total context of the novel would be bare and lifeless, or merely whimsical, but that in context is rich in the associations it has acquired along the way. But sometimes he reverses this process, and sometimes he jumbles the order, so that the colors are never completely fixed in the degree of their literalness or the extension of their symbolic values. When we read, for instance, of the "radiant halo" surrounding the head of Mr. Wilson as he walked through a "gloomy night of sin," the image that we should expect to be merely figurative, the "halo" of sanctity, turns out to be literal as well, for the light is shed by Mr. Wilson's lantern; and the one that we should at first expect to be literal—for we already know that it is a dark night, and as we start reading "this gloomy night . . ." we think we are getting a mere restatement of the darkness—turns out to be also figurative, forcing us to revise the reaction we had prepared.

The relations between the light and color images and their symbolic values are, then, neither static and schematized nor wholly free and arbitrary, but contextual within a general framework supplied by traditional patterns of color symbolism. The traditional associations of light and dark, for example, are apparently archetypal. Literature is filled with the darkness of death and sin and the light of life and goodness; and the common speech allows us to "throw light" upon a problem as often as we "explain" or "clarify" it. Perhaps the most nearly fixed in its symbolic values of all the colors in the novel is black. Yet even it is sometimes used ambiguously. Hester's black hair, that glistened so often in the sunlight before she covered it with a cap, and Pearl's "dark, glistening curls," so well set off by her scarlet costume, are examples. On the other hand, the red that runs through the book as a motif is almost always used ambiguously. Only a few examples, like the "red glare" in Chillingworth's eyes, are wholly clear, with one set of suggestions canceled out and another emphasized. The wild roses and the scarlet letter, Pearl's costume and her mother's complexion do not exhaust the possibilities. Chillingworth's light is thought to be a reflection of the infernal fires, but Pearl is also said to be a flame. When the forest, seeming to recognize a kindred spirit in Pearl, offers her partridgeberries "red as drops of blood" the gift carries with it memories not only of the rose bush but of the scarlet letter.

In short, red, black, gray, sunlight, firelight, and the less frequent green, yellow, blue, and purple are not simply descriptive of the setting and characters. In a very real sense they are themselves actors in the story that moves through and behind the story. Even in their absence they help to tell the tale. When we find that the most strongly and frequently presented colors are those most commonly associated with negative or ambiguous moral values, or with positive natural values, and that the light of positive moral and spiritual values is both less vivid and less frequent, we are not surprised. The first chapter prepared us for this, and Hawthorne's tales prepared us before that. Perhaps the largest generalization we may draw from a study of the approximately 425 light and color images is that Hawthorne conceived, but did not strongly feel, the possibility of escape from evil and the past.

IV

The "burdock, pigweed, apple-peru, and such unsightly vegetation" growing beside the prison, that "black flower of civilized society," where grass should have been, begin the flower and weed imagery, which, in some thirty images and extended analogies, reinforces and extends the implications of the imagery of color and light. Since these implications have already been drawn out, I shall simply call attention briefly to four relationships Hawthorne has set up.

First, and most clearly, the unnatural flowers and unsightly vegetation are aligned with moral evil, and with Chillingworth in particular. He too with his deformity is "unsightly." Low, dark, and ugly, he suggests to some people the notion that his step must wither the grass wherever he walks. The sun seems not to fall on him but to create "a circle of ominous shadow moving along with his deformity." It is natural enough then to find him explicitly associated with "deadly nightshade" and other types of "vegetable wickedness," to see him displaying a "dark, flabby leaf" found growing out of a grave, and to hear that prominent among the herbs he has gathered are some "black weeds" that have "sprung up out of a buried heart." When his evil work was done "he positively withered up, shriveled away . . . like an uprooted weed that lies wilting in the sun." Flower and weed imagery unites with light and color imagery to define Chillingworth's position as that of the chief sinner.

But Chillingworth is not the only one so aligned. Less emphatically, the Puritans themselves are associated with weeds and black flowers. The implications of color imagery first set up the association: as their "Puritanic gloom" increases in the second generation to "the blackest shade of Puritanism," we begin to see them as cousins to the "nightshade" and so are prepared for Pearl's pretense that the weeds she attacks in her solitary games are Puritan children. Accustomed to her apparently infallible instinct for the truth, we see in her game something more than childish imagination.

The second relationship deserving of note also starts in the first chapter. We recall Hawthorne's saying of the wild rose-bush in bloom beside the prison that he hoped it might "relieve the darkening close" of his tale. No "sweet moral blossom" plays any significant part in the main story, but the happy fortune of Pearl, related in the concluding chapter, does offer a contrast with the "frailty and sorrow" of the tale proper. Thus Pearl's final role is foreshadowed in the first chapter. But Hawthorne does not wait until the end to make this apparent. He constantly associates her not only with the scarlet letter on her mother's dress but with the red rose. The rose bears "delicate gems" and Pearl is the red-clad "gem" of her mother's bosom. Her flowerlike beauty is frequently underscored. And naturally so, for we are told that she had sprung, "a lovely and immortal flower," out of the "rank luxuriance" of a guilty passion.

The position thus defined is repeatedly emphasized. Pearl cries for a red rose in the governor's garden. She answers the catechetical question who made her by declaring that she had not been made at all but "had been plucked by her mother off the bush of wild roses that grew by the prison door." She decorates her hair with flowers, which are said to become her perfectly. She is reflected in the pool in "all the brilliant picturesqueness of her beauty, in its adornment of flowers." Her "flower-girdled and sunny image" has all the glory of a "bright flower." Pearl is a difficult child, capricious, unintentionally cruel, unfeeling in her demand for truth, but she has both the "naturalness" and the beauty of the rose, and like the rose she is a symbol of love and promise.

These are the associations Hawthorne most carefully elaborates, but there are two others worth noting briefly. Weeds or "black flowers" are on several occasions associated with Hester. The most striking instance of this occurs when Pearl pauses in the graveyard to pick "burrs" and arrange them "along the lines of the scarlet letter that decorated the maternal bosom, to which the burrs, as their nature was, tenaciously adhered." The burrs are like Pearl in acting according to nature, and what they suggest in their clinging cannot be wholly false. Hester implicitly acknowledges the truth of what the burrs have revealed when she suggests to Dimmesdale that they let the "black flower" of their love "blossom as it may."

But a more frequent and impressive association is set up between Hester and normal flowers. Even the badge of her shame, the token of her "guilty" love, is thus associated with natural beauty. The scarlet letter is related to the red rose from the very beginning. As Hester stands before her judges in the opening scenes, the sun shines on just two spots of vivid color in all that massed black, brown, and gray: on the rose and the letter, both red. The embroidery with which she decorates the letter further emphasizes the likeness, so that when Pearl throws flowers at her mother's badge and they hit the mark, we share her sense that this is appropriate. Burrs and flowers seem to have an affinity for Hester's letter. Hawthorne was too much of a Protestant to share the Catholic attitude toward "natural law": the imagery here suggests that moral law and nature's ways do not perfectly coincide, or run parallel on different levels; they cross, perhaps at something less than a right angle. At the point of their crossing the lovers' fate is determined. No reversal of the implied moral judgment is suggested when nature seems to rejoice at the reaffirmed love of the pair in the forest: "Such was the sympathy of Nature—that wild, heathen Nature of the forest, never subjugated to human law, nor illumined by higher truth—with the bliss of these two spirits! Love, whether newly born, or aroused from a death-like slumber, must always create a sunshine."

Hester's emblem, then, points to a love both good and bad. The ambiguity of her gray robes and dark glistening hair, her black eyes and bright complexion, is thus emphasized by the flower and weed imagery. As Chillingworth is associated with weeds, Pearl with flowers, and Dimmesdale with no natural growing thing at all, so Hester walks her ambiguous way between burdock and rose, neither of which is alone sufficient to define her nature and her position.

V

There are nearly twice as many heart images as there are flower and weed images, but with one exception Hawthorne insists upon them less. If they are in some respects even more revealing, we may guess that that is because they spring from Hawthorne's deepest concerns and most abiding insights, not from the top of his head but from his own heart. It is even more difficult to imagine Hawthorne's style stripped of its heart images than to picture

Dimmesdale without his hand over his heart. The minister's gesture is both consciously emblematic and a stylistic reflex.

But the heart imagery begins before we meet the minister. When Hester brings Pearl out of the dark "dungeon or . . . prison" we have veiled heart imagery, for the heart in Hawthorne is nearly as often a dungeon as it is a cavern or tomb. But this bringing out of the heart's secrets into the light is not voluntary, it is forced. It cannot then in Hawthorne's scheme of values be beneficial. One must "be true," but one cannot force others to be true. When the Puritans insist on "dragging" Hester into the public gaze—and get, clearly, a good deal of pleasure out of so doing— and then try to extort her secret from her, what they are doing constitutes an attempt at what Hawthorne calls elsewhere "a violation of the human heart"—the sin of Brand, Chillingworth, and other Hawthorne villains. To those who might be inclined to think that society has a right to do what the individual should not, Hawthorne has an answer, given in his comment on the stocks, that more common Puritan instrument for punishing by making the culprit publicly display his shame: "There can be no outrage, methinks, against our common nature,—whatever be the delinquencies of the individual,—no outrage more flagrant than to forbid the culprit to hide his face for shame."

The judges then stand in need of judgment. The Puritan people are here playing the role later played by Chillingworth. The heart imagery of the opening scenes establishes a tension that continues throughout the novel and is central to its meaning. That this interpretation does not constitute an overreading is suggested by the way light imagery reinforces heart imagery at this point: when we first see her, Hester's beauty shines out and makes a "halo," and Hawthorne says that to some she might have suggested an "image of the Divine Maternity." "The people's victim and life-long bond-slave," as Hawthorne calls her, is not sinless, but neither is she a sinner among the righteous. She is involved in a mesh of good and evil.

Many of the other uses of heart imagery are, as we should expect them to be, casual, almost incidental. They serve chiefly to keep us aware that we are here concerned finally with nothing less significant or permanent than the truths of the heart. Running reminders of the central heart images, they deepen and extend the reverberations of the action, sometimes into areas that defy analysis. The governor's mansion, for example, seems obscurely to be the heart of the Puritan rulers: behind a façade that glitters with fragments of broken glass, there is a suit of armor that reflects Hester's badge in magnified and distorted form. Despite the sunshine on the stucco walls, there would seem to be in this mansion an exaggerated consciousness of sin and almost no awareness of goodness, so that if we read this passage as a heart image we are reminded of "Young Goodman Brown."

Many of the others among the running heart images are clearer. The heart is a grave, in which corpses are buried. The heart is a chamber, in which the minister keeps his vigils in utter darkness; when Chillingworth enters the chamber, he is violating the heart. The heart is a hearth, in which one is wise to keep a fire. The heart is tomblike, or a niche in which images are set up and surrounded by curtains. The heart (or breast or bosom) is the place where the devil is most apt to set his mark. Of the fifty or so distinct heart images I have noted in the novel, most are of this order.

But those associated with Chillingworth are of special interest, for, along with the imagery of light and color and of weeds and flowers, they are the chief indications of his place in the scheme of values in the novel. What they do principally, of course, is once again to counter the judgment implied by the overt situation. Chillingworth, the "wronged" husband, does not cease to be the victim of injury when he strives "to go deep into his patient's bosom . . . like a treasure seeker in a dark cavern," but he makes it necessary to ask who is more greatly injured, he or the man who has "wronged" him. As the images continue the implication becomes clearer, so that, long before Dimmesdale has risen through his final act of honesty and courage, Chillingworth is seen as more sinning than sinned against, as more sinful even than the minister. "He now dug into the poor clergyman's heart, like a miner searching for gold; or rather, like a sexton delving into a grave . . ." He stole into the chamber of the heart like a thief and there turned over, without valuing, "many precious materials in the shape of high aspirations for the welfare of his race, warm love of souls, pure sentiments, natural piety, strengthened by thought and study, and illuminated by revelation." As he does so he imagines that his interest in what he finds is purely objective and disinterested, even scientific: "He had begun an investigation, as he imagined, with the severe and equal integrity of a judge, desirous only of truth, even as if the question involved no more than the air-drawn lines and figures of a geometrical problem, instead of human passions, and wrongs inflicted on himself." He is aided in his rationalization by the fact that his own heart is like a "cheerless habitation," cold in the absence of any household fire. But all the while it is becoming clearer that he is like Ethan Brand, who with "cold and remorseless purpose" conducted a psychological experiment on the heart of a young girl and "wasted, absorbed, and perhaps annihilated her soul, in the process."

Partly then as a result of the impact of the heart imagery, the reader feels his principal concern altered once again. First he was in suspense about the identity of Hester's partner in sin. Then, as that question begins to be answered, he wonders whether the minister will be publicly exposed and justice be done. But almost immediately, in "The Leech" and "The Leech and His Patient," he becomes concerned to have the minister escape somehow the persecutions of his tormentor. The central chapter on the relation between the two men, "The Leech and His Patient," begins and ends in heart imagery.

The most extended heart image is the forest scene. The forest in which Hester and Pearl take their walk has all the attributes common to normal human hearts in Hawthorne's work. It is black, mysterious, dismal, dim, gloomy, shadowy, obscure, and dreary. It is thought by the public to be where the Black Man meets his accomplices. It has in its depths a stream which as it mirrors the truth whispers "tales out of the heart of the old forest." But when Hester and Dimmesdale decide to follow the dictates of their hearts and, escaping man's law, live by nature, then "the wood's heart of mystery" becomes a "mystery of joy" and sunshine lights up the gloomy spot. In the four chapters concerned with this meeting, heart imagery plays a leading part, so that no analysis of the incident is likely to be adequate which does not take it into account.

VI

Probably the symbolism of the names of the characters is more important than the remaining patterns of imagery. Pearl, of course, gets her name from the "pearl of great price" used in St. Matthew to suggest the incomparable value of the hope of heaven. Hester's initial mood of bitter rebellion against her situation is clear in the naming of her child. And the other chief characters too have significant names. "Hester" is a modern form of "Esther"; and the Old Testament Esther is gifted with beauty, strength, and dignity. Courageous and loyal, she defends a weak and oppressed people. The obvious parallel between the two women contributes one more implication that Hester is to be seen as finally "in the right." And it offers another bit of evidence to those who like to stress the feminist implications of the novel, for we may see the "weaker sex" defended by Hester as but a variant of the weak people defended by Esther.

The minister's first name, Arthur, tends to suggest that devotion to a high ideal associated with King Arthur. It is at once descriptive and ironic as the name of Hester's partner in adultery. His last name falls naturally into two parts, with the root of the first part, "dim," suggesting both weakness and darkness, and the second part, "dale," suggesting, in its meaning of valley, the heart, of which Hawthorne is so frequently reminded by any hollow, opening, or cavity.

Finally, "Chillingworth" is also made up of two parts, the first of which suggests coldness and the second merit or worthiness. It is a name more transparently descriptive of this man than Dimmesdale is of the minister. For Chillingworth has, as he acknowledges to Hester, a cold heart, and his sin is one of the cold sins. Yet he was once a worthy man: decent, self-controlled, law-abiding, scholarly, "good" as the world tends to measure goodness, with nothing lacking except the most important thing of all, charity.

Names, then, are symbolic here, as they so frequently are in Hawthorne. There may be more name symbolism in the novel than I have indicated; there is certainly not less.

Of the other image patterns one of the most prominent is that of circles and chains. Considering the two as making up one pattern, since Hawthorne seems to think of them together, we find that each of the five times a circle or chain appears, it has the effect of increasing the guilt of the Puritan people and decreasing, or qualifying, Hester's. In the first few pages, for instance, we learn that the letter "had the effect of a spell, taking her out of the ordinary relations with humanity, and enclosing her in a sphere by herself." Hester then is in something like the position of Wake-field, who also was outside all "ordinary relations with humanity." But she has not chosen her fate, she has had it imposed upon her. The Puritan people who imposed it must be guilty of a very grave wrong indeed in Hawthorne's catalogue of sins. She is guilty of adultery, they of lack of charity. And since they had created "a sort of magic circle" around her, so that even in the crowd she was always alone, the reader can hardly blame her for casting away "the fragments of a broken chain" and thinking that "the world's law was no law for her mind." She had been literally forced into practicing Emerson's greatest virtue, self-reliance, in the isolation of her "magic circle of ignominy." No less excuse, in Hawthorne's world, would have exonerated her for breaking the connections in the "electric chain" of mutual sympathy and interdependence that should bind us together.

As circle and chain imagery is associated with Hester and helps to define her position, serpent imagery is associated with Chillingworth. At his first appearance we see a "writhing" horror "twisting" itself across his features. We are asked to visualize his figure as "low," a strange adjective surely if it means only "short," but appropriate to one who is said to "creep" along the ground. His ultimate transformation into a fiend should not take us by surprise if we have noted the snake imagery associated with him.

Another of Hawthorne's favorite image patterns, that of mirrors and pools that reflect, is used in the novel more prominently than the snake imagery, but with scattered rather than concentrated effect. The most telling instance is one we have already noted in passing in another connection: the reflection of Hester's letter in the polished suit of armor in the governor's house. The convex surface so magnifies and distorts the letter that she is quite obliterated by it: she is changed from a person to an abstraction, a walking sin.[1] Again the imagery connects the Puritan people and Chillingworth: compare his detached, "scientific" interest in Dimmesdale, not as a unique person but as an object to be investigated, with the Puritan view of Hester.

Unlike the curved mirror made by the armor, suited only to distort, natural mirrors, and especially those formed by water, whether of pools, streams, or fountains, normally tell the truth in Hawthorne, especially the hidden truth of the heart.[2] We may

presume that Dimmesdale saw something of the truth of his heart
when for protracted periods he stared at himself in the mirror
under the strongest possible light. And we may be sure that the
brook in the forest mirrors truths otherwise hidden as well as the
flowery beauty of Pearl. (Three chapters later it *becomes* a heart.)
Thus, whether distorted or "true," the revelations of the mirrors in
the novel are significant.

Finally, geometrical forms and patterns, the *shapes* of things,
seem to me to be quite consistently functional throughout. Clearest
are the images of the pointed arch, which draws the eye upward,
or the less concrete images of height, suggesting aspiration, piety, or
loftiness of purpose, and the low and twisted, suggesting evil. We
note the "steeple-crowned" hats in the first sentence, and Hawthorne reminds us of them again. They suggest, not only in their
obvious association with churches and so with worship but in the
intrinsic character of their shape, the lofty aspirations and devotion
to what was taken to be religious duty that conceived and created
the New England theocracy. Again, Dimmesdale is so presented
that the reader pictures him as tall and thin, in marked contrast
with Chillingworth, who is seen as "low," "twisted," and "deformed."

With these hints that whenever shape is prominent it is significant, we may be justified in seeing in the scarlet letter itself
something more than the first letter of *adultery,* something more
than the first letter of the alternative reading *angel* preferred finally
by some of the people: a design like that of steeples and the pointed
arches of Gothic "cathedrals," a shape leading the eye upward toward heavenly things: all nature seemed to rejoice when the lovers
reaffirmed in the forest a love that under different circumstances
would have taken a place very high among positive moral values.
That these implications do not "justify" adultery is clear. Hester's
scarlet letter remains as ambiguous in its implications as her social
position as outcast and sister of mercy, adulteress and light of the
sickroom. Hester remains, as Hawthorne might have said, a
"type" of those paradoxes of human nature that we have seen
earlier in Rappaccini's daughter.

VII

The Scarlet Letter is the most nearly static of all Hawthorne's novels.
There is very little external action. We can see one of the evidences
for this, and perhaps also one of the reasons for it, when we com-

pare the amount of space Hawthorne devotes to exposition and description with the amount he devotes to narration. It is likewise true, in a sense not yet fully explored, that on the deepest level of meaning the novel has only an ambiguous movement. But in between the surface and the depths movement is constant and complex, and it is in this middle area that the principal value of the work lies.

The movement may be conceived as being up and down the lines of natural and moral value, lines which, if they were to be represented in a diagram, should be conceived as crossing to form an *X*. Thus, most obviously, Hester's rise takes her from low on the line of moral value, a "scarlet woman" guilty of a sin black in the eyes of the Puritans, to a position not too remote from Mr. Wilson's, as she becomes a sister of mercy and the light of the sickroom: this when we measure by the yardstick of community approval. When we apply a standard of measurement less relativistic—and all but the most consistent ethical relativists will do so, consciously or unconsciously, thoughtfully or unthoughtfully—we are also likely to find that there has been a "rise." I suppose most of us will agree, whatever our religion or philosophy may be, that Hester has gained in stature and dignity by enduring and transcending suffering, and that she has grown in awareness of social responsibility. Like all tragic protagonists, she has demonstrated the dignity and potentialities of man, even in her defeat.

Dimmesdale is a more complicated, though less admirable and sympathetic, figure. He first descends from his original position as the saintly guide and inspiration of the godly to the position he occupies during the greater part of the novel as very nearly the worst of the sinners in his hypocrisy and cowardice, then reascends by his final act of courageous honesty to a position somewhere in between his reputation for light and his reality of darkness. He emerges at last, that is, into the light of day, if only dubiously into that shining from the celestial city. We cannot help feeling, I think, that if he had had any help he might have emerged from the darkness much sooner.

As for Chillingworth, he of course descends, but not to reascend. As in his injured pride and inhuman curiosity he devotes himself to prying into the minister's heart, whatever goodness had been his—which had always been negative, the mere absence of overt evil—disappears and pride moves into what had been a

natural science - the study of physical things as disting.
from mental or moral science.

24   INTERPRETATIONS OF AMERICAN LITERATURE

merely cold heart, prompting to revenge and displacing intellectual curiosity, which continues only as a rationalization, a "good" reason serving to distract attention from the real one. He becomes a moral monster who feeds only on another's torment, divorced wholly from the sources of life and goodness. He is eloquent testimony to the belief that Hawthorne shared with Shakespeare and Melville among others: that it is possible for man to make evil his good.

Thus the three principal characters move up and down the scale of moral values in a kind of counterpoint: Chillingworth clearly down, Hester ambiguously up, Dimmesdale in both directions, first down, then up, to end somewhere in the center. But this is not the end of the matter. Because there are obscure but real relationships, if only of analogy, between the moral and the natural (I am using "natural" in the sense of those aspects of existence studied by the natural sciences, which do not include the concept of freedom of choice among their working principles or their assumptions), because there are relations between the moral and the natural, the movements of the characters up and down the scale of moral values involve them in symbolic movements on the scale of natural values. The moral journeys are, in fact, as we have abundantly seen, largely suggested by physical imagery. Chillingworth becomes blacker and more twisted as he becomes more evil. Hester's beauty withers under the scorching brand, then momentarily reasserts itself in the forest scene, then disappears again. Dimmesdale becomes paler and walks more frequently in the shadow as his torment increases and his sin is multiplied.

But the moral changes are not simply made visible by the changes in the imagery: in their turn they require the visible changes and determine their direction. The outstanding example of this is of course Chillingworth's transformation. As we infer the potential evil in him from the snake imagery, the deformity, and the darkness associated with him when we first see him, so later his dedication to evil as his good suggests the "fancy" of the lurid flame in his eyes and the "notion" that it would be appropriate if he blasted the beauty of nature wherever he walked. So too the minister's moral journey suggests to the minds of the people both the red stigma which some think they see over his heart and the red *A* in the sky, with its ambiguous significance of angel or adultery. The total structure of the novel implies that the relation between fact and value is never simple: that neither is reducible to the other, yet that they are never wholly distinct.

All three of the chief characters, in short, exist on both of our crossed lines, the moral and the natural. They are seen in two perspectives, not identical but obscurely related. Pearl's situation, however, is somewhat different. She seems not to exist on the moral line at all. She is an object of natural beauty, a flower, a gem, instinctively trusted by the wild creatures of the forest. She is as incapable of deceit or dishonesty as nature itself, and at times as unsympathetic. She is not good or bad, because she is not responsible. Like the letter on her mother's breast, she is an emblem of sin. Like the red spot over the minister's heart, she is also a result of sin. But she is not herself a moral agent. Even when she torments her mother with her demands for the truth, or refuses to acknowledge the minister until he acknowledges them, she is not bad, she is merely natural. She is capricious with an animal's, or a small child's, lack of understanding of the human situation and consequent lack of responsiveness to emotions which it cannot understand.

Pearl is more than a picture of an intelligent and willful child drawn in part from Hawthorne's observations of his daughter Una: she is a symbol of what the human being would be if his situation were simplified by his existing on the natural plane only, as a creature. Hawthorne tells us that Pearl is potentially an immortal soul, but actually, at least before the "Conclusion," she seems more nearly a bird, a flower, or a ray of sunlight. Because of this "naturalness," this simplification, she can reach the patches of sunlight in the forest when Hester cannot: she is first cousin to the sunlight in moral neutrality as well as in brightness. From one point of view it seems curious that most readers find it harder to "believe in" Pearl than in any other major character in the book except perhaps in Chillingworth in his last stages, for Pearl is the only character drawn from Hawthorne's immediate experience with a living person. If the naturalistic aesthetic of the late nineteenth century were a correct description of the nature and processes of art, we should expect to find Pearl Hawthorne's most "real" character. That she is not (though it is easy to exaggerate her "unreality") is I suspect partly the result of the drastic simplification of life Hawthorne has here indulged in, in giving Pearl

existence only on the natural plane. He has surely exaggerated a
child's incapacity for moral action, its lack of involvement in the
demands of right and wrong, and so has produced in Pearl the only
important character in the book who constantly comes close to
being an abstraction. In creating Pearl, Hawthorne wrote partly
out of the currents of primitivism of his age, suppressing or refusing to extend his normal insights, much as he made an exception
to his convictions about the nature of the human heart when he
created his blonde maidens, who are equally hard to "believe in,"
and for rather similar reasons. Oversimplified conceptions of
experience cannot be made convincing.

Since "history" is created by the interaction of natural conditions and human choice, there is a significant sense in which
Pearl has no history in the story. She moves in and out of the foreground, a bright spot of color in a gloomy scene, serving to remind
Hester of her sin and the reader of the human condition by the
absence of one of its two poles in her being, but never becoming
herself fully human. In the final scaffold scene Hawthorne shows
us Pearl weeping for the first time and tells us that her tears "were
the pledge that she would grow up amid human joy and sorrow,
nor forever do battle with the world, but be a woman in it." In
the "Conclusion," when Hawthorne gives us a glimpse of the years
following the real end of his tale in the minister's confession, he
suggests that Pearl grew to happy womanhood abroad. If so, she
must have taken her place with Hester and Dimmesdale and
Chillingworth in the realm of moral values, making her history
and being made by it.

But the others, including the Puritan populace, have histories
and are involved in the larger movements of history created by all
of them together existing in nature as creatures and moral beings.
Hester might not have committed adultery had Chillingworth had
a warmer heart, or perhaps even had he been younger or less
deformed. He might not have fallen from a decent moral neutrality
to positive vice had she not first fallen. Hester is forced to become
stronger because the minister is so weak, and he gains strength by
contact with her strength when they meet again in the forest.
Chillingworth is stimulated by his victim's helplessness to greater
excesses of torment and sin, and the Puritan women around the
scaffold are stirred by Hester's youth and beauty to greater cruelty

than was implicit in their inquisition anyway. History as conceived in *The Scarlet Letter* is complex, dynamic, ambiguous; it is never static or abstractly linear, as both simple materialism and simple moralism tend to picture it. St. Paul's "We are members one of another" could be taken as a text to be illustrated by the histories of human hearts recounted in the novel.

Yet with all this complex movement on two planes, with all this richness, this density, of history, when we ask ourselves the final questions of meaning and value we find the movement indecisive or arrested in one direction, continuing clearly only in the other. The Puritan people and Chillingworth are condemned, but are Hester and Dimmesdale redeemed? It is significant in this connection that Pearl's growth into womanhood takes place after the end of the story proper. It is also significant that though Hester bore her suffering nobly, it is not clear that she ever repented; and that, though he indulged in several kinds of penance, it is possible to doubt that the minister ever did. The redemptive love and knowledge that worked the cure of Roderick Elliston in "Egotism" do not enter the picture here—though, to be sure, Elliston's was a less complicated case than Hester's and Dimmesdale's.

There is, then, despite Hester's rise, no certainty of final release from evil or of the kind of meaning to be found in tragedy, no well-grounded hope of escape from their sin for the sinners. The minister's dying words and the legend engraved on the tombstone both seem to me to make this clear. We recall the scene of the dance on the graves in "Alice Doane's Appeal." Here is a vision of history containing judgment but not mercy, condemnation but not forgiveness, sin and suffering but no remission, no "newness of life." If, as someone has suggested, the heraldic wording of the gravestone's inscription contains the possible suggestion that, just as the stigma of bastardy was wiped out by being emblazoned as the bar sinister on the noble escutcheon, so the sinfulness of the adultery was removed by being thus permanently acknowledged, the suggestion is surely not strongly supported by what has preceded. Hawthorne, in this respect a man of his age, never formulated his religious feelings and attitudes into any clear-cut theology. If he had done so, he might have been puzzled by the question of how central and significant a place to give to the Atonement.

In this final theological sense then the work is static. On the natural plane, beauty and ugliness, red rose and pigweed, equally exist with indisputable reality. But on the moral plane, only evil and suffering are really vivid and indisputable. Hawthorne's constant exception to his ordinary characterization of the human heart, the spotless, lily-like hearts of pure maidens, will hardly bear looking into. The light around Mr. Wilson's head shines too weakly to penetrate far into the surrounding gloom. And the only light into which Dimmesdale certainly emerges is the light of common day. The novel is structured around the metaphor of bringing the guilty secret from the black depths of the heart out into the light. But it is suggestive not only of what went on in his own heart but of the poverty both of the Puritanism of which he wrote and of the Unitarianism which Puritanism became and which Hawthorne knew at first hand that Hawthorne could conceive of the need but not the existence or the nature of any further step. After confession, what then? "No great wrong is ever undone." Surely being "true," the one moral among many, as Hawthorne tells us, that he chose to underscore, is not enough. *The Scarlet Letter* sprang from Hawthorne's heart, not from his head.

The dominant symbols, to return to the first chapter once more, are the cemetery, the prison, and the rose. The religious idealism suggested by the steeple-crowned hats is ineffective, positively perverted even, as the man of adamant's sincere piety was perverted by his fanaticism. The clearest tones in the book are the black of the prison and the weeds and the grave, and the redness of the letter and the rose, suggesting moral and natural evil and natural goodness, but not moral goodness. "On a field, sable, the letter A, gules." Of the literal and figurative light, one, the sunlight, is strong and positive, while the other, shining, as St. John tells us, from the Light of the World, falls fitfully and dimly over minor characters or is posited in mere speculative possibility.

The Scarlet Letter, then, like the majority of the best tales, suggests that Hawthorne's vision of death was a good deal stronger and more constant than his vision of life.[3] This is indeed, as Hawthorne calls it, a dark tale, and its mesh of good and evil is not equally strong in all its parts. Hawthorne was right in not wanting to be judged as a man solely by it, though I think he must have known, as we do, that it is his greatest book. For in it there is perfect charity, and a real, though defective, faith, but almost no hope. Unlike most of us today, Hawthorne was close enough to historic Christianity to know its main dogmas, even those he did not fully share. He preferred not to seem to be denying so central a part of the Christian Gospel as that men can be saved from their sins.

NOTES

1. See Yvor Winters, "Maule's Curse," *In Defense of Reason* (New York: William Morrow, 1947).

2. See Hawthorne's essay "Monsieur du Miroir" and Malcolm Cowley's "Hawthorne in the Looking Glass," *Sewanee Review,* October 1948.

3. W. Stacey Johnson has marshaled considerable evidence for the contrary view in his "Sin and Salvation in Hawthorne," *The Hibbert Journal,* October 1951. My comment on the argument of a part of this excellent article is that, while it is true that Hawthorne believed in the possibility of redemption, he did not "believe in it" in the same way, with the same kind of conviction, that he believed in sin and death.

II

Hawthorne as Poet

. . . What is one to conclude when faced with the account of Hawthorne in that admirable American work *The American People* (1949) by Professor H. B. Parkes? Here Hawthorne is characterized as

> a man of low emotional pressure who adopted throughout his life the role of an observer. Remaining always aloof from the world around him, he was able to record what he felt with a remarkable balance and detachment. . . . But since he lacked the compulsive drive of the writer who is himself the victim of conflict and must find a way of salvation, his work lacked force and energy. Carefully and delicately constructed, it was devoid of color and drama and almost passionless. Hawthorne's obsessing personal problem was his sense of isolation. He came to regard isolation as almost the root of all evil, and made it the theme of many of his stories. But Hawthorne's treatment of the subject was always too conscious and deliberate; he expressed it allegorically and not in symbols; and consequently he was unable to say anything about it that enlarges our understanding either of human nature or of the society in which Hawthorne lived.

This is in effect the account of Hawthorne that has always been in currency—stated for instance with more authority and more persuasively by Mr. Yvor Winters in the interesting essay "Maule's Curse, or Hawthorne and the Problem of Allegory,"

From *The Sewanee Review*, Vol. LIX, 1951, pp. 180–205. Copyright 1951 by the University of the South. Reprinted by permission of the publisher and author.

where, though he claims that *The Scarlet Letter* is "faultless, in
scheme and detail; it is one of the chief masterpieces of English
prose," yet he classifies it as "pure allegory," and dismisses all
"Hawthorne's sketches and short stories [as] at best slight performances." Even Henry James, whose monograph on Hawthorne is
felt, and was clearly intended, to be the tribute of an artist to the
predecessor from whom he inherits, even James demurs at what
he calls "allegory, quite one of the lighter exercises of the imagination." But it is clear that James is deploring Hawthorne's
merely fanciful pieces; he exempts the works "redolent of a rich
imagination." The standard account relegates Hawthorne along
with Bunyan to an inferior class of writer who depends for his effects on "allegory," something mechanical and inferior, as Dr.
Johnson implied when he wrote "allegory is perhaps one of the
most pleasing vehicles of instruction." But when James wrote
"Hawthorne is perpetually looking for images which shall place
themselves in picturesque correspondence with the spiritual facts
with which he is concerned, and of course the search is of the very
essence of poetry," he admits, however inadequately, that Hawthorne's intention is a poetic one, nothing less. Similarly, in general acceptance Hawthorne is a "delicate" writer, but when he is
praised for his "delicacy" it is intended to stamp his art as something minor. I should prefer to have the purity of his writing
noted instead. Nor is the epithet "charming," selected by Henry
James, appropriate.

The account, as endorsed by Mr. Parkes, contrives to be un-
just to Hawthorne's object and to ignore the very nature of his art.
Hawthorne's less interesting work bulks large, no doubt, but it is
easily cut free from what is his essential contribution to American
literature. The essential Hawthorne—and he seems to me a great
genius, the creator of a literary tradition as well as a wonderfully
original and accomplished artist—is the author of *Young Goodman
Brown, The Maypole of Merry Mount, My Kinsman Major Molineux, The
Snow-Image, The Blithedale Romance, The Scarlet Letter,* and of a
number of sketches and less pregnant stories associated with these
works such as *The Gray Champion, Main Street, Old News, Endicott of
the Red Cross, The Artist of the Beautiful.* This work is not comparable with the productions of the eighteenth-century "allegorical"
essayists nor is it in the manner of Spenser, Milton, or Bunyan—

whom of course it can be seen he has not merely studied but assimilated. The first batch of works I specified is essentially dramatic, its use of language is poetic, and it is symbolic, and richly so, as is the dramatic poet's. In fact I should suggest that Hawthorne can have gone to school with no one but Shakespeare for his inspiration and model.[1] Mr. Wilson Knight's approach to Shakespeare's tragedies—each play an expanded metaphor—is a cue for the method of rightly apprehending these works of Hawthorne's, where the "symbol" is the thing itself, with no separable paraphrasable meaning as in an allegory: the language is directly evocative. Rereading this work, one is certainly not conscious of a limited and devitalized talent employing a simple-minded pedestrian technique; one is constantly struck by fresh subtleties of organization, of intention, expression and feeling, of original psychological insight and a new minting of terms to convey it, as well as of a predominantly dramatic construction. . . .

The aspect of Hawthorne that I want to stress as the important one, decisive for American literature, and to be found most convincingly in the works I specified, is this: that he was the critic and interpreter of American cultural history and thereby the finder and creator of a literary tradition from which sprang Henry James on the one hand and Melville on the other. I find it impossible to follow Mr. Parkes's argument[2] that "what is lacking in [Hawthorne's] framework of experience is any sense of society as a kind of organic whole to which the individual belongs and in which he has his appointed place. And lacking the notion of social continuity and tradition, [he] lacks also the corresponding metaphysical conception of the natural universe as an ordered unity which harmonizes with human ideals."[3] It is precisely those problems, the relation of the individual to society, the way in which a distinctively American society developed and how it came to have a tradition of its own, the relation of the creative writer to the earlier nineteenth-century American community, and his function and how he could contrive to exercise it—the exploration of these questions and the communication in literary art of his findings—that are his claim to importance. It is true that he is most successful in treating pre-Revolutionary America, but that, after all, is, as he saw it, the decisive period, and *The Blithedale Romance* is the finest test of his dictum in *Old News* that "All philosophy that

would abstract mankind from the present is no more than words."
As I see it, Hawthorne's sense of being part of the contemporary
America could be expressed only in concern for its evolution—he
needed to see how it had come about, and by discovering what
America had, culturally speaking, started from and with, to find
what choices had faced his countrymen and what they had had to
sacrifice in order to create that distinctive "organic whole." He
was very conscious of the nature of his work; he asserted that to
be the function of every great writer, as when in *The Old Manse*
he wrote: "A work of genius is but the newspaper of a century, or
perchance of a hundred centuries." [Indeed, in some sketches,
such as *Old News,* we can see the half-way stage between the news-
papers and the work of genius; these sketches have a function like
that of the *Letters* of Jane Austen in the evolution of her novels.]
And he prepared himself for the task by study, though Providence
had furnished him with an eminently usable private Past, in the
history of his own family, which epitomized the earlier phases of
New England history; this vividly stylized the social history of
Colonial America, provided him with a personal mythology, and
gave him an emotional stake in the past, a private key to tradition. We know that his first pieces which he later burnt in despair
of getting published were called *Seven Tales of My Native Land.*
Though he was the very opposite of a Dreiser (whom Mr. Parkes
backs in contrast) yet I should choose to describe Hawthorne as a
sociological novelist in effect, employing a poetic technique which
communicates instead of stating his findings. The just comparison
with *The Scarlet Letter* is not *The Pilgrim's Progress* but *Anna Karenina,*
which in theme and technique it seems to me astonishingly to resemble. This brings up again the objection cited above that "Remaining always aloof from the world around him, he was able to
record what he felt with a remarkable balance and detachment,
but lacked the compulsive drive of the writer who is himself the
victim of conflict and must find a way of salvation." There is disguised here a romantic assumption about the Artist. We surely
recognize, equally in the Shakespeare of the great tragedies and
Measure for Measure, in Henry James in his novels and *nouvelles,* and
in the Tolstoy of *Anna* (as opposed to the Tolstoy of *Resurrection*)
that "remarkable balance and detachment" which is indispensable
to the greatest achievement of literary art. Like these artists Haw-

thorne in his best work is offering in dramatic form an analysis of a complex situation in which he sides with no one party but is imaginatively present in each, having created each to represent a facet of the total experience he is concerned to communicate. The analysis and the synthesis help us to find our own "way of salvation" (not a form of words I should have chosen). . . .

The Maypole of Merry Mount is an early work bearing obvious signs of immaturity but it also shows great originality, and it is a root work, proving that Hawthorne had laid the foundations of much later successes, notably *The Scarlet Letter* and *The Blithedale Romance,* in his beginnings almost. It proves also that he decided in his youth on his characteristic technique. We notice that it is essentially a poetic technique: the opening is almost too deliberately poetic in rhythm and word-order. But once the convention has been established in the first two paragraphs, he relaxes and proceeds less artificially. We are, or should be, struck in this early piece by the mastery Hawthorne achieves in a new form of prose art, by the skill with which he manages to convey ironic inflexions and to control transitions from one layer of meaning to another, and by which he turns, as it was to become his great distinction to do, history into myth and anecdote into parable. The essential if not the greatest Hawthorne had so soon found himself.

The tale originally had a sub-title: "A Parable," and in a few prefatory sentences Hawthorne wrote that "the curious history of the early settlement of Mount Wollaston, or Merry Mount" furnishes "an admirable foundation for a philosophic romance"— we see his decision to take for his own from the start the associations of "romance" and not of "novel" or some such term suggesting a disingenuous connection between fiction and daily life. He continued: "In the slight sketch here attempted the facts, recorded on the grave pages of our New England annalists, have wrought themselves, almost spontaneously, into a sort of allegory." If an allegory (unfortunate word), it is a "sort" that no experience of *The Faerie Queen* and *The Pilgrim's Progress* can prepare us for. Its distinctive quality is its use of symbols to convey meaning, and a boldness of imagination and stylization which while drawing on life does not hesitate to rearrange facts and even violate history in that interest. The outline of the historically insignificant Merry

Mount affair, whether as recorded by the Puritan historian Governor Bradford or so very differently by the protagonist Thomas Morton in his entertaining *New England Canaan,* was a godsend to Hawthorne, who saw in it a means of precipitating his own reactions to his forefathers' choice. While Hawthorne's imagination was historical in a large sense, he was never an imaginative recreator of the romantic past, a historical novelist: he had always from the first very clearly in view the *criticism* of the past. The past was his peculiar concern since it was the source of his present. He always works through the external forms of a society to its essence and its origin. He felt that the significance of early America lay in the conflict between the Puritans who became New England and thus America, and the non-Puritans who were, to him, merely the English in America and whom he partly with triumph but partly also with anguish sees as being cast out (here is a source of conflict). He saw this process as a symbolic recurring struggle, an endless drama that he recorded in a series of works—*The Maypole, My Kinsman Major Molineux, Endicott of the Red Cross, The Gray Champion, The Scarlet Letter, The Blithedale Romance,* among others—that together form something that it would not be fanciful to describe as a ritual drama reminding us of, for instance, the Norse Edda. If his artistic medium is primitive, his intention is not. It is a kind of spiritual and cultural casting-up of accounts: what was lost and what gained, what sacrificed to create what? he is perpetually asking, and showing.

Perhaps the American Puritans, who must if so have had none of the humane qualities of Bunyan and his class that make *Pilgrim's Progress* so pleasing—perhaps those who emigrated were more intensively intolerant than those who remained at home, or perhaps the persecuting aspect of their way of life was peculiarly present to Hawthorne because of the witch-hanging judge and the Quaker-whipping Major among his ancestors. But the essential truth Hawthorne rightly seized on, that the decisive minority set themselves in absolute hostility to the immemorial culture of the English folk with its Catholic and ultimately pagan roots, preserved in song and dance, festivals and superstitions, and especially the rites and dramatic practices of which the May-Day ceremonies were the key. Morton did rear a Maypole at Merry Mount and the fanatic Governor Endicott did indeed (but only after Morton had been seized and shipped home) visit the settlement and have the abominable tree cut down. Moreover the early theologians and historians had dramatized in their writings the elements of the scene in scriptural and theological terms. But this theological myth Hawthorne adapted to convey subtle and often ironic meanings, just as he freely adapts the historical facts. Morton was actually as well as ideally a High Churchman of good birth, a Royalist and deliberately anti-Puritan, but the object of his settlement was profitable trading with the Indians. Having none of the Puritans' conviction of the damned state of the savages, he made friends with them. Thus Hawthorne could make these settlers embody the old way of living as opposed to the new. He starts with the Maypole as the symbol of the pagan religion for "what chiefly characterized the colonists of Merry Mount was their veneration for the Maypole. It has made their true history a poet's tale." A living tree, "venerated" for it is the center of life and changes with the seasons, it is now on the festival of Midsummer's Eve hung with roses, "some that had been gathered in the sunniest spots of the forest and others, of still richer blush, which the colonists had reared from English seed." Here we have the earliest use of one of Hawthorne's chief symbols, the rose, and we notice that the native wild rose and the cultivated rose carried as seed from England (with generations of grafting and cultivation behind it) are in process of being mingled at Merry Mount. Round the tree the worshippers of the natural religion are figured with extraordinary vitality of imagination: "Gothic monsters, though perhaps of Grecian ancestry," the animal-masked figures of mythology and primitive art (man as wolf, bear, stag and he-goat); "And, almost as wondrous, stood a real bear of the dark forest, lending each of his fore-paws to the grasp of a human hand, and as ready for the dance as any in that circle. His inferior nature rose half-way to meet his companions as they stooped"; "the Salvage Man, well known in heraldry, hairy as a baboon and girdled with green leaves"; Indians real and counterfeit. The harmony between man and beast and nature that was once recognized by a religious ritual could hardly be more poetically conjured up. Then the youth and maiden who represent the May Lord and Lady are shown; they are about to be permanently as well as ritually married, by an English priest who wears also "a chaplet of the native vine-leaves." Later on he is named by Endicott as "Blackstone," though Hawthorne protects himself against the fact that the historic Blaxton had nothing to do with Merry Mount by an equivocal footnote: Blackstone here represents a poetic license which Hawthorne is perfectly justified in taking. Blackstone, who is similarly imported into *The Scarlet Letter* in a key passage, was actually not a High Churchman nor "a clerk of Oxford" as he declares in *The Maypole,* but like most New England divines a Cambridge man and anti-Episcopalian. But he must be of Oxford because Hawthorne needs him to represent Catholicism and Royalism, to complete the culture-complex of Merry Mount, which has been shown in every other respect to be ancient, harmonious and traditional, a chain of life from the dim past, from the tree and animal upwards, all tolerated and respected as part of the natural and right order. The reader is expected to take the reference to the historical Blaxton, who like Endicott and Ann Hutchinson, among others, become in Hawthorne's art cultural heroes. How eminently adapted for Hawthorne's purpose he was is seen in this account by the historian of *The Colonial Period of American History:*

> The Rev. William Blaxton, M.A. Emmanuel College, Cambridge, removed to the western slope of Shawmut peninsula [Beacon Hill] where, near an excellent spring, he built a house, planted an orchard, raised apples, and cultivated a vegetable garden. Leaving Boston in 1635, disillusioned because of the intolerance of the Puritan magistrates, he went southward saying as he departed, "I came from England because I did not like the Lord Bishops, but I cannot join with you because I would not be under the Lord Brethren." He too wanted to worship God in his own way.

He represents, among other things, the crowning, the unPuritan virtue of tolerance, one of Hawthorne's main positives. Without what he stands for the dance and drama round the Maypole and the whole pagan year-cycle of "hereditary pastimes" would be negligible in comparison with the Christian culture even of the Puritans.

Meanwhile a band of Puritans in hiding are watching the scene. To them the masquers and their comrades are like "those devils and ruined souls with whom their superstitions peopled the black wilderness." For

> Unfortunately there were men in the new world, of a sterner faith

than these Maypole worshippers. Not far from Merry Mount was a
settlement of Puritans, most dismal wretches, who said their prayers
before daylight, and then wrought in the forest or the cornfield, till
evening made it prayer time again.

This, to judge by the "most dismal wretches," is to be discounted
by the reader as probably the prejudiced view of the Maypole
worshippers, just as to the Puritans the others appear to be "the
crew of Comus." But if so persuaded, we are brought up short by
a characteristic taut statement about the Puritans, shocking both
in its literal and allegorical implications, that immediately follows:
"Their weapons were always at hand to shoot down the straggling
savage." At Merry Mount we have seen a life where the "savage,"
without and within the human breast, is accepted as part of life.
Hawthorne continues in the same tone:

> When they met in conclave, it was never to keep up the old English
> mirth, but to hear sermons three hours long, or to proclaim bounties
> on the heads of wolves and the scalps of Indians. Their festivals were
> fast days, and their chief pastime the singing of psalms. Woe to the
> youth or maiden who did but dream of a dance! The selectman nodded
> to the constable; and there sat the light-heeled reprobate in the stock;
> or if he danced, it was round the whipping-post, which might be
> termed the Puritan Maypole.

The practices of the Puritan are described as being a horrible
parody of those of the Maypole worshipers, a deliberate offense
against the spirit of Life. The force of the cunning phrase "to pro-
claim bounties on the heads of wolves and the scalps of Indians,"
charged with a sense of the inhumanity that leveled the Indian
with the wolf, should not be overlooked.

I need not continue to analyze and quote in detail, I hope,
to demonstrate the success of the kind of literary art Hawthorne
has here created, but I want to note a few more of his total effects,
by way of prelude to his later work. We have seen and felt what
the religion of the old order was. We find ourselves then inescapably faced by Hawthorne with the question: And what did the
Puritans worship? We are left in no doubt as to Hawthorne's
answer: Force. Hawthorne had realized that religion is a matter
of symbols, and his choice of appropriate symbols is not at all
simple-minded. The Maypole worshipers are not, it turns out, to
be accepted without qualification. They have another symbolic

quality attached to them, they are "silken"—"Sworn triflers of a life-time, they would not venture among the sober truths of life, not even to be truly blest." Everyone was "gay" at Merry Mount, but what really was "the quality of their mirth"? "Once, it is said, they were seen following a flower-decked corpse, with merriment and festive music, to his grave. But did the dead man laugh?" We have been rounded on as in the passage about the Puritans. Hawthorne is preparing a more complex whole for us, and preparing us to receive it. The term for the Puritans corresponding to "silken" for the settlers is "iron." We find it immediately after the passage quoted above where their practices are described as systematically inhumane. A party comes "toiling through the difficult woods, each with a horse-load of iron armour to burden his footsteps." A little later they are "men of iron," and when they surround and overpower the Maypole-worshipers their leader is revealed as iron all through: "So stern was the energy of his aspect, that the whole man, visage, frame and soul, seemed wrought of iron, gifted with life and thought, yet all of one substance with his headpiece and breastplate. It was the Puritan of Puritans; it was Endicott himself." He cuts down the Maypole with his sword, which he rests on while deciding the fate of the May Lord and Lady, and "with his own gauntleted hand" he finally crowns them with the wreath of mingled roses from the ruin of the Maypole. The associations of iron are all brought into play, suggesting the rigid system which burdens life, the metal that makes man militant and ultimately inhuman, and it is spiritually the sign of heaviness and gloom, opposed in every way to the associations of lightness—silken, sunny, gay and mirthful, used for the followers of the old way of life. The iron imagery is finally concentrated in the doom brought on New England by the Puritans' victory at Merry Mount: "It was a deed of prophecy. As the moral gloom of the world overpowers systematic gaiety. . . ." The armor in *Endicott of the Red Cross* and *The Scarlet Letter* has more extensive meanings too.

The Puritans' religion is expressed in their rites—acts of persecution, oppression and cruelty. Endicott and his followers pass sentence on "the heathen crew." Their tame bear is to be shot— "I suspect witchcraft in the beast," says the leader, and even the "long glossy curls" on the May Lord's head must be cut. "Crop it forthwith, and that in the true pumpkin-shell fashion"—the brutal denial of personal dignity and natural comeliness is indicated with striking economy. The language of Bunyan is made to sound very differently in these mouths; Hawthorne, a master of language, has many such resources at his command. But Hawthorne's total meaning is very complex and his last word is not by any means a simple condemnation. While the Merry Mount way of life embodies something essential that is lacking in the Puritans', making theirs appear ugly and inhuman, yet Hawthorne's point is that in the New World the old way could be only an imported artifice; New England, he deeply felt, could never be a mere reproduction of the Old. The fairies, as John Wilson says in *The Scarlet Letter,* were left behind in old England with Catholicism. And Hawthorne implies that the outlook of Merry Mount is not consonant with the realities of life in the New World, or the new phase of the world anywhere perhaps. The Puritans may be odious but they have a secret which is a better thing than the religion of the nature and humanity. The May Lord and Lady, at Endicott's command, leave their Paradise—the reference to Adam and Eve driven from the Garden is unmistakable, as others to Milton in this tale—and there is a general suggestion that the "choice" imposed on New England is like that made by Adam and Eve, they sacrifice bliss for something more arduous and better worth having. Hawthorne has no doubt that the May Lord and Lady enter into a finer bond in Christian marriage than they could otherwise have known as symbolic figures in a fertility rite. Nevertheless though their future is "blessed" it is not pleasant or gracious. Hawthorne felt acutely the wrong the Lord Brethren had done to the Blaxtons, typified by the doings of an Endicott. The close parallel between the Merry Mount drama and the corresponding conflict in Milton's poem between the Brothers and the followers of Comus must be intentional—there are explicit references—and intended by Hawthorne as a criticism of Milton's presentment of the case. Virtue and Vice are a simple-minded division in Milton's *Comus,* however his symbolism may be interpreted. In Hawthorne's view that contest was quite other than a matter of Right and Wrong; his Puritans are an ironic comment on Milton's cause and case. Hawthorne's rendering shows two partial truths or qualified goods set in regrettable opposition. What Hawthorne implies is that it was a disaster for New England that they could not be reconciled. Hawthorne is both subtler and wiser than Milton, and his poem, unlike Milton's, is really dramatic and embodies a genuine cultural and spiritual conflict. Milton is a Puritan and Hawthorne is not; to Hawthorne, Milton is a man of iron. Hawthorne is seen explicitly the unwilling heir of the Puritans, and their indignant critic, in a fine passage in *Main Street* which ends "Let us thank God for having given us such ancestors; and let each successive generation thank him not less fervently, for being one step further from them in the march of ages."

Just as the rose, the flower that symbolizes human grace and whose beauty is essentially something cultivated, the product of long training—just as the rose is used from *The Maypole* onwards, so the concept of the iron man becomes basic thereafter. The meaning is expounded in a remarkable section of *Main Street* which concludes:

> All was well, so long as their lamps were freshly kindled at the heavenly flame. After a while, however, whether in their time or their children's, these lamps began to burn more dimly, or with a less genuine lustre; and then it might be seen how hard, cold and confined, was their system,—how like an iron cage was that which they called Liberty.

I believe the image was taken by Hawthorne, consciously or unconsciously, from Bunyan; it may be remembered that in the Interpreter's House Christian is shown a Man in an Iron Cage as an awful warning of what a true Christian should never be. Now Bunyan's Man in an Iron Cage exemplified Despair. I have mentioned also that "Blackstone" recurs in *The Scarlet Letter* in an almost mystically poetic context. In fact, these writings of Hawthorne's, to yield all they offer, must be studied as a whole, as a poet's works are, each illuminating and strengthening the rest. This is not the case with the fictions of any English nineteenth-century novelist. Perhaps this makes my point that Hawthorne needs a quite other approach from the one we commonly make to a novelist. His recurrent drama is a poet's vision of the meaning of his world, and it is communicated by poetic means.

Young Goodman Brown, visibly a much later and more practiced work than the last, is also more powerful and more closely knit than anything else of Hawthorne's with the possible exception of the very complex and ambitious *Major Molineux*. It lends itself to much the same kind of analysis, that is, demands the same approach, as has been already outlined, and is even more unmistakably a prose poem. If its content has reminded literary critics of *Macbeth* and the Walpurgisnacht of *Faust,* that is unfortunate, for the relevant point is that Young Goodman Brown is Everyman in seventeenth-century New England—the title as usual giving the clue. He is the son of the Old Goodman Brown, that is, the Old Adam (or Adam the First as he is called in Bunyan), and recently wedded to Faith. We must note that every word is significant in the opening sentence: "Young Goodman Brown came forth at sunset into the street of Salem Village; but put his head back, after crossing the threshold, to exchange a parting kiss with his young wife." She begs him to "put off his journey until sunrise," but he declares he cannot: "My journey, as thou callest it, forth and back again, must needs be done 'twixt now and sunrise." It is a journey he takes under compulsion, and it should not escape us that she tries to stop him because she is under a similar compulsion to go on a "journey" herself—"*She* talks of dreams, too," Young Goodman Brown reflects as he leaves her. The journey each must take alone, in dread, at night, is the journey away from home and the community, from conscious, everyday social life, to the wilderness where the hidden self satisfies, or is forced to realize, its subconscious fears and promptings in sleep. We take that journey with him into the awful forest. We note the division, which is to be the basis of *The Scarlet Letter,* between the town (where the minister rules) and the forest (where the Black Man reigns). From his pious home and Faith Young Goodman Brown reluctantly wanders back into the desert, meeting as he expects one who "bears a considerable resemblance to him. They might have been taken for father and son." He resists as best he can until he is made to realize to his surprise and horror that his father had gone on that journey before him, and sees many respected neighbours indeed pass him to the trysting-place. At first, confident in the appearance of virtue in the daily life of his fellows, he retorts indignantly: "My father never went into the woods on such an errand, nor his father before him. We have been a race of honest men and good Christians since the days of the martyrs." "We are a people of prayer, and good works to boot, and abide no such wickedness." The sinister likeness of his grandfather is able to convince him otherwise, though "the arguments seemed rather to spring up in the bosom of his auditor than to be suggested by" the Devil. We feel how an accumulation of unconscious doubts about the "saints" precipitates Young Goodman Brown's conviction of universal sinfulness. As he loses his belief in the reality of virtue in others the scene grows increasingly sinister until the road "vanished at length, leaving him in the heart of the dark wilderness, still rushing onward with the instinct that guides mortal man to evil. The whole forest was peopled with frightful sounds—the creaking of the trees, the howling of the wild beasts, and the yell of Indians." We see Hawthorne making timely use of the traditional Puritan association of trees, animals, and Indians as the hostile powers, allies of the fiend.

> But he was himself the chief horror of the scene, and shrank not from its other horrors.
> "Ha! ha! ha!" roared Goodman Brown when the wind laughed at him. "Let us hear which will laugh loudest. Think not to frighten me with your deviltry. Come witch, come wizard, come Indian pow-wow, come devil himself, and here comes Goodman Brown. You may as well fear him as he fear you." In truth, all through the haunted forest there could be nothing more frightful than the figure of Goodman Brown.

The nightmare poetry gathers volume and power as he approaches the flaming center of the forest, but Hawthorne's poetic imagination is as different as possible from Poe's—there is no touch of the Gothic horrors one might anticipate. When Goodman Brown ends his journey he finds his whole world, even the elders and ministers, assembled to worship at the devil's altar; he and his Faith are only the latest to be received into the communion of the lost.

When Young Goodman Brown returns to Salem Village with the morning light, "staring around him like a bewildered man," his eyes have been opened to the true nature of his fellowmen, that is, human nature; he inescapably knows that what he suspected of himself is true of all men. He must live with that knowledge, and he is thenceforward a man of gloom, the Man in the Iron Cage, a Calvinist indeed. What Hawthorne has given us is not an allegory, and not an ambiguous problem-story (we are not to ask: Was it an actual Satanic experience or only a dream?).

Hawthorne has made a dramatic poem of the Calvinist experience in New England. The unfailing tact with which the experience is evoked subjectively, in the most impressive concrete terms, is a subordinate proof of genius. I should prefer to stress the wonderful control of local and total rhythm, which never falters or slackens, and rises from the quiet but impressive opening to its poetic climax in the superb and moving finale, which I should have liked to quote in full. It ends "they carved no hopeful verse upon his tombstone; for his dying hour was gloom."

Hawthorne has imaginatively recreated for the reader that Calvinist sense of sin, that theory which did in actuality shape the early social and spiritual history of New England. But in Hawthorne, by a wonderful feat of transmutation, it has no religious significance, it is as a psychological state that it is explored. Young Goodman Brown's Faith is not faith in Christ but faith in human beings, and losing it he is doomed to isolation forever. . . .

In this tale Hawthorne achieved a considerable contribution toward the comprehensive masterpiece he was to produce in *The Scarlet Letter,* for the tale is partially taken up into the later romance.

In his introduction to a volume of tales brought out in 1851 but mostly written much earlier Hawthorne, then in his prime as an artist, with *The Scarlet Letter* a year behind him, confessed that he was "disposed to quarrel with the earlier sketches," most of all "because they come so nearly up to the standard of the best that I can achieve now." As one of the earlier sketches in his collection was *My Kinsman Major Molineux* (1831), he might justly have felt that he was never to achieve anything better.

Ideally it should be preceded by a reading of the three studies collected under the title *Old News,* which give the historical background and are clearly the fruit of work preparatory for *Major Molineux.* This remarkable tale might have been less commonly overlooked or misunderstood if it had had a sub-title, such as Hawthorne often provided by way of a hint. It could do with some such explanatory sub-title as "America Comes of Age." But though if a naturalistic story is looked for the reader would be left merely puzzled, the tale lends itself readily to comprehension as a poetic parable in dramatic form, and the opening paragraph as usual clearly explains the situation and furnishes the required clue. We are in the age which was preparing the colonies for the War of Independence and we are made to take part in a dramatic precipitation of, or prophetic forecast of, the rejection of England that was to occur in fact much later.

The actual tale begins by describing a country-bred youth coming to town, starting with the significant sentence: "It was near nine o'clock of a moonlight evening, when a boat crossed the ferry with a single passenger." The sturdy pious youth Robin, the son of the typical farmer-clergyman, represents the young America; he has *left his home* in the village in the woods and crossing by the *ferry, alone, at nightfall,* reaches the little metropolis of a New England port—that is, the contemporary scene where the historic future will be decided. He arrives poor but hopeful, confidently anticipating help in making his fortune from "my kinsman Major Molineux," the reiteration of the phrase being an important contribution to the total effect. The kinsman is Hawthorne's and ours (if we are Americans) as well as Robin's, and his name suggests both his military and aristocratic status. Robin explains much later in the tale that his father and the Major are brother's sons— that is, one brother had stayed in England and the other left to colonize New England. Their children, the next generation, represented by Robin's father and the Major, had kept on friendly terms and the rich Major, representative in New England of the British civil and military rule and keeping "great pomp," was in a position to patronize his poor country cousin. We do not get this straightforward account in the tale, of course, we have to unravel it for ourselves, for the presentation of the theme is entirely dramatic and we have to identify our consciousness with the protagonist Robin. The essential information is revealed only when we have ourselves experienced for some time the same bewilderment as poor Robin, who cannot understand why his request to be directed to the house of his kinsman is met by the various types of citizen with suspicion, with contempt, with anger, with disgust, with sneers, or with laughter. In fact, Robin has arrived at a critical moment in his kinsman's history. The colonists—with considerable skill and economy Hawthorne represents all ranks and classes of the states in this dream-town—have secretly planned to throw off British rule, or at any rate to rid themselves of Major Molineux, a symbolic action which, performed in the street outside the church at midnight and before the innocent eyes of the mystified youth, takes the form of something between a pageant and a ritual drama, disguised in the emotional logic of a dream. As a dream it has a far greater emotional pull than actuality could have. Hawthorne never anywhere surpassed this tale (written when he was not more than twenty-seven) in dramatic power, in control of tone, pace, and tension, and in something more wonderful, the creation of a suspension between the fullest consciousness of meaning and the emotional incoherence of dreaming. How this is achieved and for what purpose can be seen only by a careful examination of the last half of the tale, but I will quote as sparingly as possible.

Until this point, precisely the middle of the work, no departure from the everyday normal has been necessary, though we have been wrought to a state of exasperation which is ready for working on. And Hawthorne now introduces another note:

> He now roamed desperately, and at random, through the town, almost ready to believe that a spell was on him, like that by which a wizard of his country had once kept three pursuers wandering, a whole winter night, within twenty paces of the cottage which they sought. The streets lay before him, strange and desolate, and the lights were extinguished in almost every house. Twice, however, little parties of men, among whom Robin distinguished individuals in outlandish attire, came hurrying along; but though on both occasions they paused to address him, such intercourse did not at all enlighten his perplexity. They did but utter a few words in some language of which Robin knew nothing, and perceiving his inability to answer, bestowed a curse upon him in plain English, and hastened away. Finally, the lad determined to knock at the door of every mansion, trusting that perseverance would overcome the fatality that had hitherto thwarted him. Firm in this resolve, he was passing beneath the walls of a church, which formed the corner of two streets, when, as he turned into the shade of its steeple, he encountered a bulky stranger, muffled in a cloak. The man was proceeding with the speed of earnest business, but Robin planted himself full before him, holding the oak cudgel with both hands across his body, as a bar to further passage.
>
> "Halt, honest man, and answer me a question," said he, very resolutely. "Tell me, this instant, whereabouts is the dwelling of my kinsman, Major Molineux!"
>
> . . . The stranger, instead of attempting to force his passage, stepped back into the moonlight, unmuffled his face, and stared full into that of Robin.
>
> "Watch here an hour, and Major Molineux will pass by," said he.

Robin gazed with dismay and astonishment on the unprecedented physiognomy of the speaker. The forehead with its double prominence, the broad hooked nose, the shaggy eyebrow, and fiery eyes, were those which he had noticed at the inn, but the man's complexion had undergone a singular, or, more properly, a two-fold change. One side of the face blazed an intense red, while the other was black as midnight, the division line being in the broad bridge of the nose; and a mouth which seemed to extend from ear to ear was black or red, in contrast to the color of the cheek. The effect was as if two individual devils, a fiend of fire and a fiend of darkness, had united themselves to form this infernal visage. The stranger grinned in Robin's face, muffled his parti-colored features, and was out of sight in a moment.

The stranger, whose unearthly appearance we were prepared for by the "individuals in outlandish attire" speaking in a code—for as we realize later they were obviously conspirators demanding from Robin a password he could not furnish, but they help to increase the nightmare atmosphere—is shown by his face to be something more than a man in disguise. The tension is being screwed up to the pitch needed for the approaching climax of the drama: this is not a man like the others but a Janus-like fiend of fire and darkness, that is, we presently learn, "war personified" in its dual aspects of Death and Destruction. But it is not just a personification, it is a symbol with emotional repercussions which passes through a series of suggestive forms. The account of its features at first: "The forehead with its double prominence, the broad hooked nose" etc. suggests Punch and so also the grotesque associations of puppet-show farce. The division of the face into black and red implies the conventional get-up of the jester, and indeed he "grinned in Robin's face" before he "muffled his parti-colored features." At this point Robin, carrying the reader with him, having "consumed a few moments in philosophical speculation upon the species of man who had just left him," is able to "settle this point shrewdly, rationally and satisfactorily." He and we are of course deceived in our complacency. He falls into a drowse by sending his thoughts "to imagine how that evening of ambiguity and weariness had been spent in his father's household." This actually completes his bewilderment—"Am I here or there?" he cries, "But still his mind kept vibrating between fancy and reality."

Now, so prepared, we hear the murmur that becomes a confused medley of voices and shouts as it approaches, turning into "frequent bursts from many instruments of discord, and a wild and confused laughter filled up the intervals." "The antipodes of music" heralds "a mighty stream of people" led by a single horseman whom Robin recognizes as the eerie stranger in a fresh avatar. With the "rough music" that in Old England was traditionally used to drive undesirable characters out of the community, by the red glare of torches and with "War personified" as their leader, the citizens of America, with Indians in their train and cheered on by their women, are symbolically if proleptically casting out the English ruler. The nightmare impression reaches its climax: "In his train were wild figures in the Indian dress, and many fantastic shapes without a model, giving the whole march a visionary air, as if a dream had broken forth from some feverish brain, and were sweeping visibly through the midnight streets. . . . 'The double-faced fellow has his eye upon me' muttered Robin, with an indefinite but uncomfortable idea that he was himself to bear a part in the pageantry."

It seems indeed that the pageant has been brought to this place for Robin's benefit.

> A moment more, and the leader thundered a command to halt: the trumpets vomited a horrid breath, and then held their peace; the shouts and laughter of the people died away, and there remained only a universal hum, allied to silence. Right before Robin's eyes was an uncovered cart. There the torches blazed the brightest, there the moon shone out like day, and there, in tar-and-feathery dignity, sat his kinsman Major Molineux!
>
> He was an elderly man, of large and majestic person, and strong, square features, betokening a steady soul; but steady as it was, his enemies had found means to shake it. His face was pale as death, and far more ghastly; the broad forehead was contracted in his agony, so that his eyebrows formed one grizzled line; his eyes were red and wild, and the foam hung white upon his quivering lip. His whole frame was agitated by a quick and continual tremor, which his pride strove to quell, even in those circumstances of overwhelming humiliation. But perhaps the bitterest pang of all was when his eyes met those of Robin; for he evidently knew him on the instant, as the youth stood witnessing the foul disgrace of a head grown gray in honor. They stared at each other in silence, and Robin's knees shook, and his hair bristled, with a mixture of pity and terror.

The pageant is thus seen to represent a tragedy and is felt by us as such; it arouses in Robin the appropriate blend of emotions—

the classical "pity and terror." But Hawthorne has by some inspiration—for how could he have known except intuitively of the origins of tragedy in ritual drama?—gone back to the type of action that fathered Tragedy. Just as the "War personified" suggests an idol or a human representative of the god, so does the other terrible figure "in tar-and-feathery dignity" in the cart. We seem to be spectators at that most primitive of all dramatic representations, the conquest of the old king by the new.

If the story had ended here, on this note, it would have been remarkable enough, but Hawthorne has an almost incredible consummation to follow. I mean incredible in being so subtly achieved with such mastery of tone. From being a spectator at a tragedy, Robin has to fulfill his premonitions of having "to bear a part in the pageantry" himself. He is drawn into the emotional vortex and comes to share the reactions of the participants. He has felt intimately the dreadful degradation of his English kinsman, but now he is seized with the excitement of the victors, his fellow-countrymen, and sees their triumph as his own—"a perception of tremendous ridicule in the whole scene affected him with a sort of mental inebriety." Drunk with success the whole town roars in a frenzy of laughter, and Robin's shout joins theirs and is the loudest. Then in a sudden calm that follows this orgy "the procession resumed its march. On they went, like fiends that throng in mockery around some dead potentate, mighty no more, but majestic still in his agony." We are left in the silent street, brought back into the world of problems in which the tale opened. Robin still has to settle with reality and decide his future, the future of his generation. He asks to be shown the way back to the ferry: "I begin to grow weary of a town life" he says to the townsman who has stayed behind to note his reactions. But his new friend replies: "Some few days hence, if you wish it, I will speed you on your journey. Or, if you prefer to remain with us, perhaps, as you are a shrewd youth, you may rise in the world without the help of your kinsman, Major Molineux."

Hawthorne has been blamed for failing to provide a "solution" and for not being optimistic as a good American should be, but it seems to me that here, as in *The Maypole*, he ends in reasonable, sober hopefulness for the future of life. Provided we recognize the facts and fully comprehend the positions, we can cope with it, if not master it, he implies. Declining to be, perhaps incapable of being, a naturalistic novelist, he was true to his best perceptions of his genius when he did the work of a dramatic poet, the interpreter and radical critic of the society which had produced him and for whose benefit he expressed his insight in a unique literature.

NOTES

1. I find support for this in "Our Old Home": "Shakespeare has surface beneath surface, to an immeasurable depth. . . . There is no exhausting the various interpretation of his symbols."

2. "Poe, Hawthorne, Melville: An Essay in Sociological Criticism," *Partisan Review,* Feb., 1949.

3. This naïve demand should be measured against this passage from *Hawthorne's Last Phase* (E. H. Davidson, 1949): "The rare springtime beauty of the English scene struck him more forcibly than it could the ordinary tourist, for it represented to him the perfect balance between man and nature. This balance was conspicuously absent in the untamed forests of the U.S., where man was busily engaged in subduing nature and dominating a continent. 'It is only an American who can fell it," Hawthorne wrote."

Darrel Abel

A Key to The House of Usher

By common consent, the most characteristic of Poe's "arabesque" tales is "The Fall of the House of Usher." It is usually admired for its "atmosphere" and for its exquisitely artificial manipulation of Gothic claptrap and décor, but careful reading reveals admirable method in the author's use of things generally regarded by his readers as mere decorative properties. . . .

I

Too much of the horror of the tale has usually been attributed to its setting superficially considered. But the setting does have a double importance, descriptive and symbolic. It first operates descriptively, as suggestively appropriate and picturesque background for the unfolding of events. It later operates symbolically: certain features of the setting assume an ominous animism and function; they become important active elements instead of mere static backdrop.

Descriptively the setting has two uses: to suggest a mood to the observer which makes him properly receptive to the horrible ideas which grow in his mind during the action; and to supply details which reinforce, but do not produce, those ideas.

From *University of Toronto Quarterly*, Vol. XVIII,, January 1949, pp. 176–185. Copyright 1949 by the University of Toronto Press. Reprinted by permission of the publisher and author.

The qualities of the setting are remoteness, decadence, horrible gloom. Remoteness (and loss of feature) is suggested by details of outline, dimension, and vista. Decadence is suggested by details of the death or decrepitude of normal human and vegetable existences and constructions, and by the growth of morbid and parasitic human and vegetable existences, as well as by the surging sentience of inorganism. Gloom and despair are suggested by sombre and listless details of colour and motion (at climactic points, lurid colour and violent action erupt with startling effect from this sombre listlessness). The narrator points out in the opening passage of the tale that the gloom which invested the domain of Usher was not sublime and pleasurable (which would have made it an expression of "supernal beauty" in Poe's opinion), but was sinister and vaguely terrible.

Five persons figure in the tale, but the interest centres exclusively in one—Roderick Usher. The narrator is uncharacterized, undescribed, even unnamed. (I shall call him Anthropos, for convenient reference.) In fact, he is a mere point of view for the reader to occupy, but he does lend the reader some acute, though not individualizing, faculties: five keen senses which shrewdly perceive actual physical circumstances; a sixth sense of vague and indescribable realities behind the physical and apparent; a clever faculty of rational interpretation of sensible phenomena; and finally, a sceptical and matter-of-fact propensity to mistrust intuitional apprehensions and to seek natural and rational explanations. In short, he is an habitual naturalist resisting urgent convictions of the preternatural.

The doctor and valet are not realized as characters; they are less impressive than the furniture; and Anthropos sees each only once and briefly. No duties requiring the attendance of other persons are mentioned, so our attention is never for a moment diverted from Roderick Usher. His sister Madeline's place in the story can best be explained in connection with comment on Usher himself.

The action of the story is comparatively slight; the energetic symbolism, to be discussed later, accomplishes more. Anthropos arrives at the House of Usher, and is conducted into the presence of his host. Usher has invited Anthropos, a friend of his schooldays, in the hope that a renewal of their association will assist him to throw off a morbid depression of spirits which has affected his health. Anthropos is shocked at the ghastly infirmity of his friend. He learns that Madeline, Roderick's twin and the only other living Usher, is near death from a mysterious malady which baffles her physicians. Presently she dies and Roderick Usher, fearing that the doctors who had been so fascinated by the pathology of the case might steal her body from the grave, places it in a sealed coffin in a subterranean vault under the House of Usher. Anthropos assists in this labour.

Immediately there is an observable increase in the nervous apprehensiveness of Roderick Usher. He finds partial relief from his agitation in the painting of horribly vague abstract pictures and in the improvisation of wild tunes to the accompaniment of his "speaking guitar." For seven or eight days his apprehensiveness increases and steadily communicates itself to Anthropos as well, so that, at the end of that time, a night arrives when Anthropos' state of vague alarm prevents his going to sleep. Usher enters and shows him through the window that, although the night is heavily clouded, the House of Usher's environs are strangely illuminated. Anthropos endeavours, not very judiciously, to calm him by reading aloud from a romance that might have come from the library of Don Quixote. At points of suspense in this romance, marked by description of loud noises, Anthropos fancies that he hears similar sounds below him in the House of Usher. Roderick Usher's manner, during this reading, is inattentive and wildly preoccupied; at the noisy climax of the romance Usher melodramatically shrieks that the noises outside had actually been those of his sister breaking out of the coffin in which she had been sealed alive. The door bursts open; Madeline appears and, falling forward dead in her gory shroud, carries Roderick Usher likewise dead to the floor beneath her. Anthropos rushes from the House of Usher, turning in his flight to view its shattering collapse into the gloomy tarn beneath it. How these events become invested with horror can only be understood by discerning the meanings which the symbolism of the tale conveys into them.

II

Roderick Usher is himself a symbol—of isolation, and of a concentration of vitality so introverted that it utterly destroys itself. He is physically isolated. Anthropos reaches the House of Usher after a whole's day's journey "through a singularly dreary tract of country" that is recognizably the same sort of domain-beyond-reality as that traversed by Childe Roland and his medieval prototypes. Arrived at the mansion, he is conducted to Usher's "studio" "through many dark and intricate passages." And there "the eye struggled in vain to reach the remoter angles of the chamber" in which his host received him.

Usher is psychologically isolated. Although he has invited his former "boon companion" to visit and support him in this moral crisis, clearly there has never been any conviviality in his nature. "His reserve had always been habitual and excessive," and he has now evidently become more singular, preoccupied, and aloof than before. "For many years, he had never ventured forth" from the gloomy House of Usher, wherein "he was enchained by certain superstitious impressions." ("Superstitious" is the sceptical judgment of Anthropos.) Thus, although his seclusion had probably once been voluntary, it is now inescapable. His sister Madeline does not relieve his isolation; paradoxically, she intensifies it, for they are twins whose "striking similitude" and "sympathies of a scarcely intelligible nature" eliminate that margin of difference which is necessary to social relationship between persons. They are not two persons, but one consciousness in two bodies, each mirroring the other, intensifying the introversion of the family character. Further, no collateral branches of the family survive; all the life of the Ushers is flickering to extinction in these feeble representatives. Therefore no wonder that Anthropos cannot connect his host's appearance "with any idea of a simple humanity."

The isolation and concentration of the vitalities of the Ushers had brought about the decay of the line. Formerly the family energies had found magnificently varied expression: "His very ancient family had been noted, time out of mind, for a peculiar sensibility of temperament; displaying itself, through long ages, in many works of exalted art, and manifested, of late, in repeated deeds of munificent yet unobtrusive charity, as well as in a passionate devotion to the intricacies, perhaps even more than to the orthodox and easily recognizable beauties, of musical science." For all the splendid flowering of this "peculiar sensibility," its devotion to intricacies was a fatal weakness; in tending inward to more hidden channels of expression, the family sensibility had become in its current representative morbidity introverted from lack of proper object and exercise, and its only flowers were flowers of evil. It was fretting Roderick Usher to death: "He suffered much from a morbid acuteness of the senses; the most insipid food was alone endurable; he could wear only garments of a certain texture; the odors of all flowers were oppressive; his eyes were tortured by even a faint light; and there were but peculiar sounds, and these from stringed instruments, which did not inspire him with horror." These specifications detail the hyper-acuity but progressive desuetude of his five senses. The sum of things which these five senses convey to a man is the sum of physical life; the relinquishment of their use is the relinquishment of life itself. The hyper-acuity of Roderick Usher's senses was caused by the introverted concentration of the family energies; the inhibition of his senses was caused by the physical and psychological isolation of Usher. It is noteworthy that the only willing use he makes of his senses is a morbid one—not to sustain and positively experience life, but to project his "distempered ideality" on canvas and in music. This morbid use of faculties which ought to sustain and express life shows that, as Life progressively loses its hold on Roderick Usher, Death as steadily asserts its empery over him. The central action and symbolism of the tale dramatize this contest between Life and Death for the possession of Roderick Usher.

III

Some of the non-human symbols of the tale are, as has been mentioned, features of the physical setting which detach themselves from the merely picturesque ensemble of background particulars and assume symbolical meaning as the tale unfolds. They have what might be called an historical function; they symbolize what has been and is. The remaining symbols are created by the "distempered ideality" of Roderick Usher as the narrative progresses. These have prophetic significance; they symbolize what is becoming and what will be. The symbols which Usher creates, however, flow from the same dark source as the evil in symbols which exist independently of Usher: that evil is merely channelled through his artistic sensibility to find bold new expression.

All the symbols express the opposition of Life-Reason to Death-Madness. Most of them are mixed manifestations of those two existences; more precisely, they show ascendant evil encroaching upon decadent good. On the Life-Reason side are ranged the heavenly, natural, organic, harmonious, featured, active qualities of things. Against them are ranged the subterranean, subnatural, inorganic, inharmonious, vague or featureless, passive qualities of things. Although most of the symbols show the encroachment of Death-Madness on Life-Reason, two symbols show absolute evil triumphant, with no commixture of good even in decay. One of these is the tarn, a physically permanent feature of the setting; the other is Roderick Usher's ghastly abstract painting, an impromptu expression of the evil which has mastered his sensibility. There are no symbols of absolute good.

The House of Usher is the most conspicuous symbol in the tale. It displays all the qualities (listed above) of Life-Reason, corrupted and threatened by Death-Madness. It stands under the clouded heavens, but it is significantly related to the subterranean by the zigzag crack which extends from its roof (the most heavenward part of the house) to the tarn. The trees about it connect it with nature, but they are all dead, blasted by the preternatural evil of the place; the only living vegetation consists of "rank sedges" (no doubt nourished by the tarn), and fungi growing from the roof, the most heavenward part. The house is also a symbol of the organic and harmonious because it expresses human thought and design, but the structure is crazy, threatened not only by the ominous, zigzag, scarcely discernible fissure, but also by the perilous decrepitude of its constituent materials, which maintained their coherency in a way that looked almost miraculous to Anthropos: "No portion of the masonry had fallen; and there appeared to be a wild inconsistency between its still perfect adaptation of parts, and the crumbling condition of the individual stones." In the interior of the house, the furnishings seemed no longer to express the ordered living of human creatures: "The general furniture was profuse, comfortless, antique, and tattered. Many books and musical instruments lay scattered about, but failed to give any vitality to the scene." That is, the human life it expressed was not ordered and full, but scattered and tattered. The "eyelike windows," the most conspicuous feature of the house, looked vacant from without, and from within were seen to be "altogether inaccessible"; they admitted only "feeble gleams of encrimsoned light." Life and motion within the house were nearly extinct. "An air of stern, deep, and irredeemable gloom hung over and pervaded all."

Roderick Usher resembles his house. It is unnecessary to point out the ways in which a human being is normally an expression of Life-Reason—of heavenly, natural, organic, harmonious, featured, and active qualities. The Death-Madness opposites to these qualities are manifested in interesting correspondences between the physical appearance of Usher and that of his house. The zigzag crack in the house, and the "inconsistency" between its decayed materials and intact structure, are like the difficultly maintained composure of Usher. Anthropos declares: "In the manner of my friend I was at once struck with an incoherence—an *inconsistency* [my italics]; and I soon found this to arise from a series of feeble and futile struggles to overcome an habitual trepidancy—an excessive nervous agitation." The "minute fungi . . . hanging in a fine tangled web-work from the eaves" of the house have their curious counterpart, as a symbol of morbid vitality, in the hair of Usher, "of a more than web-like softness and tenuity . . . [which, as it] had been suffered to grow all unheeded, . . . floated rather than fell about the face, [so that] I could not, even with an effort, connect its Arabesque expression with any idea of simple humanity." (We are reminded of the hair reputed to grow so luxuriantly out of the heads of inhumed corpses.) Usher's organic existence and sanity seem threatened: his "cadaverousness of complexion" is conspicuous; and he not only attributes sentience to vegetable things, but also to "the kingdom of inorganization" which he evidently feels to be assuming domination over him. His most conspicuous feature was "an eye large, liquid, and luminous beyond comparison"; after Madeline Usher's death, Anthropos observes that "the luminousness of his eye had utterly gone out." It was thus assimilated to the "vacant eyelike windows" of his house. And the active qualities of Usher were also fading. We have noticed that his malady was a combined hyper-acuity and inhibition of function of the five senses which maintain life and mind. Altogether, the fabric of Usher, like that of his house, exhibited a "specious totality."

The only other important mixed symbol is Usher's song of the "Haunted Palace." It is largely a contrast of before and after. Be-

fore the palace was assailed by "evil things, in robes of sorrow," it
had "reared its head" grandly under the heavens:

> Never seraph spread a pinion
> Over fabric half so fair!

It displayed several of the characteristics of Life-Reason. But after
the assult of "evil things," the Death-Madness qualities are
triumphant. Order is destroyed; instead of

> Spirits moving musically
> To a lute's well-tuned law,

within the palace are to be seen

> Vast forms that move fantastically
> To a discordant melody.

Instead of a "troop of Echoes" flowing and sparkling through the
"fair palace door," "a hideous throng rush out for ever" through
the "pale door" "like a rapid ghastly river." Reason has toppled
from its throne, and this song intimated to Anthropos "a full consciousness on the part of Usher of the tottering of his lofty reason
upon her throne." The perceptible fading of bright features in the
palace is like the fading of the features and vitality of both Usher
and his house.

The principal symbols of decrepit Life-Reason having been
explicated, it remains to comment on the two symbols of ascendant
Death-Madness—the tarn, and Roderick Usher's madly abstract
painting. These show the same qualities that we have seen evilly
encroaching upon the Life-Reason symbols, but these qualities are
here unmitigated by any hint or reminiscence of Life-Reason. The
juxtaposition of the tarn-house symbols is crucial; the zig-zag fissure
in the house is an index to the source of the evil which eventually
overwhelms the Ushers. The tarn is an outlet of a subterranean
realm; on the surface of the earth this realm disputes dominion
with the powers of heaven and wins. This subnatural realm manifests itself in the miasma that rises from the tarn. "About the
mansion and the whole domain there hung an atmosphere peculiar
to themselves and their immediate vicinity—an atmosphere which
had no affinity with the air of heaven, but which had reeked up
from the decayed trees, and the gray wall, and the silent tarn—a
pestilent and mystic vapor, dull, sluggish, faintly discernible, and

leaden-hued." This upward-reeking effluvium has its counterpart in the "distempered ideality" of Usher while he is producing his mad compositions after the death of Madeline: they are products of "a mind from which darkness, as if an inherent positive quality, poured forth upon all objects of the moral and physical universe in one unceasing radiation of gloom."

"Radiation of gloom" is as interesting an idea as "darkness visible." It reminds us that another mark of this emanation of evil was lurid illumination. The feeble gleams of light that entered Usher's studio were encrimsoned. The "luminous windows" of the "radiant palace" became the "red-litten windows" of the "haunted palace." Oddly, even Usher's mad music is described in a visual figure as having a "sulphureous lustre." On the catastrophic last night of the House of Usher, the environs are at first illuminated, not by any celestial luminaries, but by the "unnatural light of a faintly luminous and distinctly visible gaseous [so our matter-of-fact Anthropos] exhalation which hung about and enshrouded the mansion." And finally, the collapse of the house is melodramatically spot-lighted by "the full, setting, and blood-red moon, which now shone vividly through that once barely perceptible fissure."

Roderick Usher's dread of the "kingdom of inorganization" as a really sentient order of existence reminds us of the animate inanimation of the tarn. Activity and harmony are really related qualities; harmony is an agreeable coincidence of motions. The tarn's absolute stillness is the negation of these qualities. Water is a universal and immemorial symbol of life; this dead water is thus a symbol of Death-in-Life. It lies "unruffled" from the first, and when at last the House of Usher topples thunderously into it, to the noisy accompaniment of Nature in tumult, its waters close "sullenly and silently over the fragments." This horrid inactivity is the condition toward which Usher is tending when he finds the exercise of his senses intolerable.

The tarn is as featureless as any visible thing can be; its blackness, "unruffled lustre," and silence are like the painted "vaguenesses" at which Anthropos shuddered "the more thrillingly" because he shuddered "not knowing why." Here are blank horrors, with only enough suggestion of feature to set the imagination fearfully to work.

This leads us to the only remaining symbol of importance,

Usher's terrible painting. It is more horrible than the "Haunted Palace" because, whereas the song described the lost but regretted state of lovely Life and Reason, the painting depicts Death-Madness horribly regnant, with no reminiscence of Life and Reason. The scene pictured is subterranean (Madeline's coffin was deposited in a suggestively similar vault): "Certain accessory points of the design served well to convey the idea that this excavation lay at an exceeding depth below the surface of the earth." It is preternaturally lurid: "No torch or other artificial source of light was discernible; yet a flood of intense rays rolled throughout, and bathed the whole in a ghastly and inappropriate splendor." The picture shows a lifeless scene without features—"smooth, white, and without interruption or device."

Before these remarks on the symbolism of the tale are concluded, some notice should be taken of the part which musical symbols play in it. Poe uses his favorite heart-lute image, from Béranger, as a motto:

> Son coeur est un luth suspendu;
> Sîtot qu'on le touche il résonne.

The "lute's well-tuned law" symbolizes ideal order in the "radiant palace," and the whole of that song is an explicit musical metaphor for derangement of intellect. For Poe, music was the highest as well as the most rational expression of the intelligence, and string music was quintessential music (wherefore Usher's jangled intellect can endure only string music). Time out of mind, music has symbolized celestial order. His conception was not far from that expressed in Dryden's "Song for St. Cecilia's Day," with "The diapason closing full in Man." The derangement of human reason, then, "sweet bells jangled out of tune and harsh," cannot be better expressed than in a musical figure.

IV

I have thus tediously but by no means exhaustively exposed the filaments of symbol in "The Fall of the House of Usher" to show how much of its effect depends on the artfully inconspicuous iteration and reiteration of identical suggestions which could not operate so unobtrusively in any other way. Human actions in the story are of much less importance, but one or two events deserve notice. The depositing of Madeline's coffin in the underground vault provides Anthropos with an opportunity to compare the appearance of Roderick and Madeline Usher. She had on her face and bosom "the mockery of a faint blush" and on her lips "that suspiciously lingering smile . . . which is so terrible in death." In contrast, the "cadaverousness of complexion" of Roderick Usher had been repeatedly remarked. Thus is indicated how nearly triumphant Death is in the Ushers from the moment when Anthropos first enters the house, how scarcely perceptible is the difference between a live Usher and a dead one. Consequently, Madeline's rising up from her coffin to claim her brother for death really suggests that he had mistakenly and perversely lingered among the living, that the similitude of life in an Usher was merely morbid animation. He needed only to cross a shadowy line to yield himself up to Madness and Death.

The night of catastrophe, then, witnessed this transition. The reading of "The Mad Trist" shows a mechanical, not a symbolical, correspondence between Usher's ruin and external things; it is the only piece of superimposed and unfunctional trumpery in the tale, though it does serve, perhaps, to explain and justify the suspenseful doubt and surprise of Anthropos when he hears the weird sounds of Madeline's ghastly up-rising. The storm which rages outside is not a supernatural storm, but a tumult of natural elements impotently opposing the silent and sullen powers which in that hour assert dominion over the House of Usher and draw it into their Plutonian depths.

The tragedy of Roderick Usher was not merely his fatal introversion, but his too-late realization of his own doom, the ineffectuality of his effort to re-establish connection with life by summoning to him the person most his friend. When at last he shrieks "Madman!" at this presumably sane friend, he crosses the borderline between sanity and madness. In a moment he dies in melodramatic circumstances, and immediately thereafter is carried into the tarn by the culminatingly symbolical collapse of his house.

V

It is expedient to review the impressions of Anthropos the determined doubter, who leaves the domain of Usher with a sense of supernatural fatality accomplished. Throughout the tale he scrupulously tries to find rational explanations for the horrors which agitate him. He explains his depression of spirits when he first views the House of Usher by reference to the gloomy combination of "very simple natural objects." That the tarn deepened this depression he accounted for psychologically: "The consciousness of the rapid increase of my superstition—for why should I not so term it?—served mainly to accelerate the increase itself." In the house he is puzzled to account for the fact that, although the furniture is all of a sort to which he has been accustomed throughout his life, it has an "unfamiliar" effect of gloom; and it is difficult for him to connect any "idea of simple humanity" with Usher's ghastly appearance, although he dutifully tries. He tells us that Usher "admitted" that his "superstitious impressions in regard to the dwelling which he tenanted" might be traced to "a more natural and far more palpable origin" than the malign sentience which he attributed to the place, that is to his grief at his sister's hopeless illness. The music which Usher composes during his bereavement is characterized by his common-sensible friend as distempered and perverted, and Usher himself is called a hypochondriac. The limited tolerance of Usher for sound is described in Anthropos' medical jargon as "a morbid condition of the auditory nerve." Usher's conviction of the sentience of the "kingdom of inorganization" is regarded by his friend as a pertinacious but not altogether novel delusion. Usher's agitation is partly ascribed to the influence of the fantastic literature which he reads. The sounds which interrupt the reading of "The Mad Trist" are, Anthropos thinks (before the apparition of Madeline changes his opinion), hallucinations prompted by the wild story and his own state of excited suggestibility. The lurid, upward-streaming illumination of the environs of the House of Usher on the night of catastrophe is explained as a natural phenomenon—a "gaseous exhalation." And, if we wish, we can attribute the stupendously shattering collapse of the ancient House of Usher itself to merely physical and natural causes—the violent thrust of the storm against its frail fabric and almost dilapidated structure. But, significantly, our matter-of-fact Anthropos does not suggest any natural explanation; he merely flees "aghast." . . .

Edward H. Davidson

IV

The Tale as Allegory

Poe has often been cited for his detestation of allegory and for his pungent remarks on the "heresy of the didactic." These comments must be taken several ways: in their own time and context they were Poe's rejection of the tale as "simply moral"—that attitude which made art into science, religion, morality, and anything else the artist may cover. He was attacking a view very common in his day and one especially noticeable in fiction or the prose tale which, ever since the eighteenth century, was a suspect form anyway. The tale had to assume that it was a narrative and then everything else too; Cooper, the outstanding novelist or tale-teller in Poe's day, was careful to include those lessons, moral saws, or outright sermons in the mouths of his moral mouthpieces like Natty Bumppo; and Hawthorne, as Poe himself quite corectly pointed out, had a tendency to lapse into allegory and thereby reduce and delimit those imaginative exercises which, with the purity of his "tone," made the Hawthorne tale itself an act of the imagination. Poe's war was, therefore, on the necessity of the tale to be allegorical and to be moral. The other direction of Poe's attack on allegory was no doubt more personal. He himself could not write "alle-

Reprinted by permission of the publishers from Edward Hutchins Davidson, *Poe: A Critical Study,* Cambridge, Mass.: The Belknap Press of Harvard University Press, Copyright, 1957, by The President and Fellows of Harvard College.

gories"; he could not do that work which was so remunerative in
the gift annuals and in the periodicals. They were merely sneers at
a profitable commodity in the literary marketplace.

Yet Poe was an allegorist in spite of himself. An allegory was
a means whereby his creative imagination undertook to solve certain problems of its own mind and art; they were ways of reducing reality to determinate and logical outlines. Together they
formed a significant group—perhaps the most considerable dem-
onstrations of Poe's art as it came closest to a consideration of the
religious, social, political, and imaginative worlds in which it lived.
They were ways of making a fractured and dismembered world
obtain some form; for, truly speaking, Poe's world was utterly dis-
organized not only because Poe himself saw the world that way
but also because his world was that way. We might well consider
these tales as a group and analyze a few representative examples
under a set of provisional hypotheses.

Poe's allegorical narratives might conveniently be examined
under two major themes, one religious, the other social and political. The first, if it can be measured by the number of tales which
were written around essentially religious subjects, probably occupied a larger space in his art and thought; the second is, however, of importance, if for no other reason than that it marks one
more way by which Poe rejected the real world around him and
set up a fictive, symbolic range of experience and expression. The
"destructive tendency" was operative in both; it had more subjects and more ranges in the religious dimension than it had in the
social and political.

II

Poe belonged to a select, though not unusual, group of writers in
America, or in the world for that matter. It is a group which
could exist at any time and in any place; it numbered in the nineteenth century such writers as Hawthorne, Melville, Emily Dickinson, and Henry Adams. One mark which characterized all these
writers is that they came at a time when a once-powerful religion
was in decline; yet this decline left "a detritus of pieties, strong assumptions, which afford a particularly fortunate condition for certain kinds of literature."[1] The "condition" was one which offered

strong religious motives for thought and action but which exacted no requirement that the writers themselves adhere to any religious belief; yet all the while they were free to investigate and dramatize religious themes with a clarity which, to some extent, is denied the believer. Hawthorne's *Scarlet Letter* is a superb inquiry into the Puritan mind; it operates on basic Puritan dogmas of sin and regeneration—yet there is not the slightest indication that these codes and dogmas had any prescription for Hawthorne or for the times in which Hawthorne lived. A *Scarlet Letter* was impossible in the age of Cotton Mather; a *Scarlet Letter* was inevitable in the times of Melville and Whitman because men in New England still adhered to the whole program of sin and regeneration as set forth in Hawthorne's novel—and yet the heart of a once-great religion had gone out of their life. Hawthorne's generation, which was Poe's, was either struggling toward another religious formulation or in the act of losing the old.

In New England, the religious detritus was exhibited in a clash between soul and intellect (as it had been from the time of Jonathan Edwards to William Ellery Channing); intellect no doubt won the struggle, but while the struggle was going on, it was acutely dramatized in the nineteenth century by the clash between business and morality: morality was itself part of the running-down of a powerful religious impulse that had been on the wane ever since Franklin had penned the easy morality of Poor Richard. Throughout this tension the churches in New England and the best minds all the way through Horace Bushnell to Josiah Royce posited the final power of the percipient self; yet all the while the practical mind of New England was emphasizing and placing all its code of salvation on the humanly willed product of man's hands.

In the South, on the other hand, the decline of a religious force was not so precipitate or apparent. Especially in Virginia, where there had been for two centuries only one church, religion had too long been the support of the status quo ever to force an issue or to raise the dramatic specter of doubt. The church, in sum, was the final sanctification of the whole southern code of morals, slavery, politics, love, oratory, war, daily living, even of a pseudo-Greek revival in architecture; to break away from the church meant a total break with society itself—or, to put the matter conversely, to break with society spelled a permanent rift with the dominant religious mind of Virginia.

The church or religion in the South sanctified all of men's activities and put its benediction on all man's expressions except one—the arts; the church in Virginia had nothing to say or do for the arts except to encourage a weak classicism and an amiable sense of the deep past. The church had been sufficiently disestablished not to interfere in men's lives; yet religion was so much a part of the equipment of a Virginian that he could not personally get along very well without it. Religion offered no drama, no antagonisms, no tension; it did offer a set of wordly prescriptions. The church in the South never suffered from the attacks of Unitarians or Quakers or even the hell-fire Methodists simply because it had so long acclimated itself to the very air men breathed; however, to reject the church and its worldly-wise teachings was to make one virtually an outcast from what was the accepted mode of conduct and belief in the first half of the nineteenth century.

Yet far beyond the edge of this world of observed pieties were the camp meetings, the Negro prayers and songs, and the torch-lit revivals among lonely people on the frontier. Every southerner heard these wild voices in some strange cacophony which did not fit his experience in the white man's settled world. As one listened, these songs were the one poignant expression of a religion for the desolate and lost and not for the comfortable and accepted. Stephen Foster and other pseudo-folklorists domesticated those songs for the consumption of the circumspect; yet somewhere beyond the churches of Richmond a boy like Poe must have heard the uncontrolled wail of those whom his society regarded as trash and as lost.

These matters are conjectural only because we do not have the evidence which links Poe's home and early life with the tales he wrote when he became a man. This evidence could not be supplied, for Poe or any man, because it is part of the imaginative sediment a sensitive boy takes with him into manhood and can never tell where he got it. The best we can do is not to engage in suspect psychoanalysis of Poe the boy or Poe the man but to inquire into representative short stories which Poe wrote at the height of his career and see how the decline and loss of a once-strong religious motive helped to produce the *outré* situations and the half-demented human beings who are products of a curious and inquiring religious temper.

III

One of the primary marks of a writer whose imagination might be regarded as religious but whose temper has long removed him from any doctrinal or dogmatic religious content is that, whether poet or tale-teller, he becomes his own god, his own supreme maker of visions, prophecies, and parables. Yet all the while the baffling character of these projections is that they have no apparent relationship to any body of truth or revelation. They are, to put it another way, not anti- or pro-Christian; they are simply not Christian nor even pagan; they have, if such things can be, the character of being a wholly invented simulacrum of a religious action and faith. In this respect, to play god was one of the favorite excursions of the romantic mind: Shelley engaged in the adventure so far that he invented a universe of Idea which, in an instant, he could destroy; and Keats's private pleasure-dome of aesthetic dimension had all the requisites of a profound religious experience, while Keats himself was his own god and demon. In the end, the religious mind of the Romantics became demonic because it was ultimately destructive of what it had created.

Poe's assumption of the role of god took a form not quite typical of poets or imaginative seers in the nineteenth century but one characteristic of the spell-binders and projectors of new thought in that age. His role takes him into a religious primitivism, that is, back to the primary revelation or to the original moment when the revelation was given, just as Protestant enthusiasts have longed for a return to Apostolic times and to a re-creation of the true gospel as it was initially revealed by the Messiah. In another way, however, Poe is typical of certain expressions of the Romantic mind: his religious premise is essentially anti-intellectual and anti-ritualistic; he would return to the pure religion before it became contaminated by priestcraft and bell-ringing. Or, to state a corollary, he looks forward to the final Apocalypse, to the utter destruction of all things wherein the god finally achieves his justice or gets his awful revenge on the wicked.

In such an early tale as "The Conversation of Eiros and

Charmion" (1839) we have this vision of the last day. A comet, in accordance with all the words of "the biblical prophecies," came within range of the earth and, by "a total extraction of the nitrogen" around the earth, rendered the air so combustible that the world was destroyed in one massive, blinding flash—"the entire fulfilment," Poe as vision-maker insists, "in all their minute and terrible details, of the fiery and horror-inspiring denunciations of the prophecies of the Holy Book."[2] We are not too far from the Puritan Wigglesworth's *Day of Doom* or the horrendous threats hurled against the damned by nineteenth-century evangelists.

Yet Poe's apocalyptic visions were not intended as denunciations; they were meant to be rationalizations or scientific expositions of what might be considered proved religious fact. In "The Colloquy of Monos and Una" (1841) the idea turns on not the end of the world as an inevitable fact in the logistics of nature but on the death of a single human being as a "swoon" or transfer from one form of perception to another. Monos, or the fractured and many-sided human being, passes through the three phases of being which, as we shall see, marked the upward progress toward personal fulfillment in Poe's hierarchy of insight: Monos proceeds through the physical or sensual, then through the intellectual ("a mental pendulous sensation"), and finally into pure spiritual being from which, the body having been resolved to dust, the mind and imagination can move, beyond "Place and Time."[3]

Poe's religious inquiry began, therefore, with simplicities. He took creation either back to its primal origin or forward to its ultimate consummation. Like religious myth-makers of long ago, he felt free to create his own cosmos in any form that suited him and to give it any function necessary to its fulfillment. Thus death was denied in the mere "swoon" from one stage of perception to the next, as in "The Colloquy of Monos and Una"; or he was privileged to evolve a universe in which all its atomic structures served only those purposes and intentions which he as god-player ordained. It was, in short, a child's magic world, and hardly religious at all; for it had no room for evil and no condition of tragedy; no souls were lost and none was saved. But it was at such an utter remove from the conventionalized religious world in which Poe moved that it seemed like a revenge on what, in its own terms, was a rigid and institutionalized body of thought and belief. Poe's universe in imagination was at least spaceless and timeless in contrast to the easy temporality of the church in Richmond, or Philadelphia, or New York.

This universe of Poe's is not merely a spaceless and timeless cosmos; people do inhabit it; yet they do not exist in it on the simple level of morality and belief that one might expect in such a primal world as Poe imagined. Poe's nightmare universe is one in which the world itself either just began or just finished but the people in it are condemned to live as if they are in some long after-time of belief and morality. They exist very like the South Sea islanders Melville found on Nukaheva: they live by a rigid code of the taboo, but they have long lost any notion of what the code means. They are forced to belive and exist for reasons that have long ceased to have any meaning. No one understands or can interpret, in this moral region of Poe's lost souls, why he must be punished; yet the penalty for any moral infraction is frightful and all the more terrifying because no one had enforced it and no one knows why it must be administered. The punishment comes not from a church, a law, or even from society: it comes from some inner compulsion of the evil-doer himself who suffers from what Poe otherwise terms "perversity": he must do evil, and yet he wants to be punished and to suffer. Thus he has willed his crime, and he wills his retribution.

These characters are themselves god-players. In "The Tell-Tale Heart" the narrator assumes the right to do away with the old man whose one "eye, with a film over it," becomes an object of loathing to him. It is not so much an old man that he kills as it is the "Evil Eye"; but this god-player made the mistake of thinking it was an eye which was so vexatious; all the while it was a sound, the beating of the old man's heart, which kept pounding in the murderer's ears after the man was dead. The police who made a routine investigation are not ministers of justice; they are mere expressions of the narrator's compulsion to unmask and destroy himself by finally admitting the crime he had committed. In this respect the god easily passes into the devil and becomes his maker and slayer both.

"The Black Cat" (1843) is even more pointedly addressed to this theme "of perverseness . . . this unfathomable longing of the soul *to vex itself*—to offer violence to its own nature—to do wrong for the wrong's sake only." The sins the protagonist committed were so "deadly" that his "immortal soul" would be placed "even beyond the reach of the infinite mercy of the Most Merciful and Most Terrible God." When the criminal had reached the completion of his iniquity and had walled up the body of his dead wife, he had, of a necessity beyond his comprehension, buried alive the cat which would betray and condemn him. No other god but the self as god can wreak such vengeance as when the criminal is his own judge and executioner.

In these ways, therefore, Poe removed all moral and religious considerations as far as possible from any social code or body of religious warrants. This method was not so much an overt attack on the society of his day as it was his tacit assumption that a moral and social code had so little cogency that he would have to discover or invent a rationale of existence as remote as possible from it. The otherwise baffling tale, "The Man of the Crowd," (1840) is a consideration of man's abandonment of the moral prescription within which he is supposed to live. We have the modern metropolis and a man so typical as to be almost an Everyman; we never know, however, whether this Man is an individual who cannot bear to be alone or whether he is, in reality, the narrator and protagonist of the story in a cringing, fearsome guise that the narrator will not admit even to himself. That the Man is some embodiment of evil in the modern world which has long lost any belief in evil is suggested by "an expression . . . never seen before, . . . the pictorial incarnations of the fiend." This nameless and almost faceless Man may be several things: he could be that human being who really has no inner being at all; the horror he faces is that he might be thrust into the private world of mind or spirit; if such an event were to happen to him, he would go mad of desperation and loneliness. The other matter of interest in "The Man of the Crowd" is that we can never be sure whether we are following a mere Man or whether we are pursuing the narrator himself, who is so terrified of admitting who or what he is that he projects himself into this desperate and wholly imagined fugitive. It is interesting to note that the "I" is never at a loss to follow the Man through the darkest byways of a vast metropolis; and he knows the Man so well that he can easily see through "a rent in a closely-buttoned and evidently second-hand *roquelaire* which enveloped him" and gave him "a glimpse both of a diamond and of a dagger." Whoever or whatever he is, the Man is the lost soul which never knows it is lost. He is, like Hawthorne's Wakefield, an "outcast of the universe," one who has somehow taken a single step awry and has thereafter lost any sense of belonging to the human and material worlds.

If the subject of "The Man of the Crowd" concerns the inability of a Man either to belong in a world of evil or to acknowledge to himself that he is one of "the Crowd" which is the world, the tale does not seek out these ideas in the Man himself. As so frequently happens in Poe's writing, inner moods and ideas are consistently externalized; the city itself, the labyrinthian streets, the noise and garish colors—these are the pictorial and frenzied manifestations of states of mind which would presuppose that the world is a mirrored chiaroscuro of the human psyche. Yet what Poe was further attempting to suggest was that whatever has happened to the Man or whatever he has done is a monotonous repetition of the crime of the human race: its implacable indifference to suffering, its bland ignorance that evil exists at all. The Man is, however, an outcast because he does suffer and because he wants to discover some similitude to his suffering among the millions who swirl about him.

If there is a moral system in these stories, it is nebulous indeed. Poe consistently attacked the Utilitarians of his day, with their idea of "happiness" and "the greatest good to the greatest number."[4] Yet, while he could not locate the moral sense in mankind itself, he was unwilling to make the individual responsible. Even more interestingly, he did not consider that the universe itself was God's primary mistake or the outward manifestation of a cosmic tragedy; for him "the invisible spheres" were not "formed in fright." Evil or good is each man's right and his willing; each one saves or damns himself. But the ultimate reason why man chooses or wills one or the other is far beyond anyone's knowing; the sinner is compulsively driven by some motive to be malignant, by some maggot in the brain which he cannot anticipate or understand but the penalty of which he is more than willing to suffer. This need to do evil Poe placed in the idea of "perversity," man's tendency to act "for the reason that he should not." The "assurance of the wrong or error of any action," Poe continued, "is often the one unconquerable *force* which impels us, and alone impels us to its prosecution. Nor will the overwhelming tendency to do wrong for wrong's sake admit of analysis, or resolution into ulterior elements. It is a radical, a primitive impulse—elementary." Here then was the rationale for man's moral system and the answer to his bewildering actions which, in so many crimes, went diametrically against any Utilitarian theory of man's willing and seeking his own happiness or the greatest happiness to the greatest number.

Poe was content to lodge this faculty in man alone and apparently leave him a moral freak in the world of mind and God. Yet this "principle, the antagonist of bliss," is, however, similarly found in the universe itself: what man is, as a fractured and disjointed being, is but a miniature of imperfection and dispersion in the cosmic order. By a curious variation on the myth of Adam and Eve, Poe demonstrated that man had willed his own degradation; the earth had suffered the fatal flaw, and throughout the rest of the world's time-span this condition of evil and suffering steadily worsens. Owing to this defect in man and in the universe, "the world will never see . . . that full extent of triumphant execution, in the richer domains of art, of which the human nature is absolutely capable." Evil and suffering have become, therefore, the capacity and measure of man to feel and know: moral sensitivity is not an act or even a thought but the knowledge all the while that pain is the basis for life and death is the only release from this grotesque condition of "perversity," or man's determination to hurt and destroy himself. Thus the Poe protagonists so eagerly will their own deaths; they must plunge into "the common vortex of unhappiness which yawns for those of pre-eminent endowments"; only in death can they find release and peace.

Each character in Poe's moral inquiries is his own moral arbiter, lodged in a total moral anarchy. Society has invented law and justice, but these are mere illusion and exact no true penalty. The Poe hero or villain is never in revolt against them, as the Romantic hero so frequently is; the Poe hero acts as if the laws of society had never even existed. The moral drama is, however, all the more terrifying because it has no rules and no reason for bringing about the end that eventually comes. It is not even a comfortably deterministic moral scheme in which whatever happens must happen; it is a moral world of an inscrutable calculus in which any one of an infinite number of results might occur.

This, then, so far as it can be sketched with any consistency, is Poe's moral cosmology, a universe of such individualism that virtually every atom has its own right and rule to exist. Within it is, of course, lodged man; but man is himself, in an almost Shakespearean way, a mirror of the universe, or the universe is a macrocosmic extension of man. The universal metaphysic is tripartite: body, mind, and soul. Every element and form in the cosmos, as Poe had suggested in "Al Aaraaf," is constituted so that it has three separate organisms and functions at the same time that these three parts are intricately interrelated to form the one and the many, the "monos" and the "una" of a universal design. Poe's final exploration of this subject was *Eureka*, written in the last years of his life.

However inexact Poe was in his outline of the tripartite organization of the material universe, he was quite explicit concerning man: man is a being formed of three separate and yet interacting forms, body, mind, and spirit. The transitions between them are so slight as sometimes to be almost indistinguishable; they form the one total "machine" that is the complete human being; they also constitute absolutely distinct functions and even parts of the human organism, and one may become, as we shall see, hypertrophied or atrophied at the expense of the other. The sources and bases for these ideas have been sufficiently well explored that we need not consider them here; suffice to say, this scheme of the human being was derived from the popular psychology of Andrew Combe and Spurzheim early in the nineteenth century. Poe was content to assume that all of his readers were so well aware of it that he did not need to go into explanatory detail; several of his noteworthy moral investigations of men are, however, built around this psychology of the tripartite organization and functioning of man.[5]

The normal, healthy human being is one in whom these three faculties are in balance; none dominates the other. But in the mysterious and chaotic condition of the universe, which is itself a duplicate of man's state of being, anything at any moment may occur in order to tip the human psyche either way, into sanity or into madness. And like the universe, the human organism, so

delicately is it made and so intricately adjusted are its parts, can
be turned in an instant into any one of an infinite number of possible
conditions or states. The mind itself, the second or midway faculty of
reason and direction, has no power to control either its own condition or the responses of the body and the soul; its only capacity is
to speculate on whatever state of being it finds itself in at a particular moment. Neither the body nor the soul has this power: the
body functions only as brute, insensitive existence; the soul, with
only rare moments of perception, has the power of penetrating far
beyond the limits of this sensual existence; chiefly the soul sleeps
or is moribund.

In "The Fall of the House of Usher" (1839) we have an early
exposition, and one of the best, of this psychic drama, a summary
of Poe's ideas and method of investigating the self in disintegration.[6] The story was a study of the tripartite division and identity
of the self. It was, to go even further, an attempted demonstration
of the theory that spirit is extended through and animating all
matter, a theory confirmed by the books which Poe, and Usher,
had read: Swedenborg's *Heaven and Hell,* Campanella's *City of the
Sun,* and Robert Flud's *Chiromancy,* to name only a few listed in the
narrative, all of which consider the material world as manifestation
of the spiritual. From the opening sentence of the story we have
the point-for-point identification of the external world with the
human constitution. The House is the total human being, its three
parts functioning as one; the outside construction of the house is
like the body; the dark tarn is a mirror or the mind which can
"image . . . a strange fancy," almost "a dream." The "barely perceptible fissure" which extended "from the roof of the building . . .
until it became lost in the sullen waters of the tarn" is the fatal
dislocation or fracture which, as the story develops, destroys the
whole psychic being of which the house is the outward manifestation.

Turning now from the material to the human realms, we find
that the tripartite division of the faculties is even more clearly
evidenced. Usher represents the mind or intellectual aspect of the
total being: ". . . the character of his face had been at all times
remarkable. A cadaverousness of complexion; an eye large, liquid,
and luminous beyond comparison; lips somewhat thin and very
pallid but of a surpassingly beautiful curve; . . . a finely moulded

chin, speaking, in its want of prominence, of a want of moral energy." Madeline is the sensual or physical side of this psyche: they are identical twins (Poe ignores, and so may we, the fact that identical twins cannot be of differing sex); her name is derived from Saint Mary Magdala, which means "tower"; therefore she is the lady of the house.[7]

The tale is a study of the total disintegration of a complex human being, not in any one of the three aspects of body, mind, and soul, but in all three together. Roderick Usher suffers from the diseased mind which has too long abstracted and absented itself from physical reality; in fact, the physical world, and even the physical side of himself, fills him with such repugnance that he can maintain his unique world or self of the mind only by destroying his twin sister or the physical side of himself. Madeline sickens from some mortal disease and, when she is presumed dead, is buried in the subterranean family vaults or in a place as far remote as possible from the place of aesthetic delight wherein the mind of Roderick lives. Yet Madeline is not dead; she returns from the coffin and in one convulsive motion brings her brother to his death: the body and the mind thus die together. Very shortly afterward the House collapses, for it has all the while represented the total being of this complex body-mind relation which Poe had studied in the symbolic guise of a brother and sister relationship: "and the deep and dark tarn . . . closed sullenly and silently over the fragments of the 'House of Usher.'"

One of the curiosities of Poe's tale is that, while we have a study not only of the interrelationship of mind and body in the psychic life of a human being but also of the rapid disintegration of that being when one aspect of the self becomes hypertrophied, we have a narrative of presumed psychological inquiry with everything presented, as it were, "outside." We know no more of Roderick or of Madeline, or of the narrator for that matter, at the end than we knew at the beginning. The method is entirely pictorial, as though external objects and the configuration of the intricate material world could themselves assume a psychic dimension: not only is the material world an outward demonstration of some inner and cosmic drama but it is at every moment exhibiting that drama more strikingly than can the human actors. The two realms, material and immaterial, coexist in such exquisite balance that one can be read as a precise synecdoche of the other. The convulsive aspect of Poe's writing becomes nowhere better appararent than in his method of making the physical world of nature experience the drama more intensely than can any human being.

Another tale in which this theory of the multiple character of the self is treated is "William Wilson" (1840). In "The Fall of the House of Usher" the being of Roderick in its vital body-mind condition suffered complete deterioration and death; in "William Wilson" we have the converse theme of the nature of the self in its desperate necessity to preserve itself; in that act of self-preservation Wilson is not the prey to outward circumstances nor does he abstract himself from them, as did Usher. William Wilson is the clever man of the world who, however, in order to succeed in the world, must destroy an essential part of himself, his soul or spirit.[8]

At almost every point "William Wilson" poses a different question from that set forth in "The Fall of the House of Usher." The central problem of "William Wilson" is the nature of self-identity: is the self born isolated and alone, as was the early theme of "Usher," or is it permissively designed to order is own way in the world? From the beginning Wilson is endowed with freedom; as a child, he says, "My voice was a household law; and at an age when few children have abandoned their leading-strings, I was left to the guidance of my own will." This is not mere childish petulance and willfulness; it is, we are informed, a "hereditary temper" which makes impossible any submission to control. For a time the young Wilson is confined within the "iron" control of Dr. Bransby's school—it is interesting to note the images of iron and rigidity in the description of the school itself and of the narrowly confined lives of the students; but all the while this boy is living with only his mind to guide him. Society and religion have no force over him; and even the whispering voice of another boy also named William Wilson is not really a moral conscience (for conscience depends on some spiritual determinant in order to have any force at all) but is merely another being in the moral wilderness of Wilson's life. He is his own moral arbiter in a world wherein the only criterion is success; for no action of Wilson, not the cheating at cards nor even the attempted seduction of the Duke di Broglio's wife, is really bad; it is simply a failure in some materialistic ordering of the world which rewards success and punishes failure. Wilson is a moral incompetent and Utilitarian who assumes that the cosmic design is as materialistic as he is; the awful revenge comes when the realm of spirit, whose existence he has more and more denied, overcomes and destroys him.

Wilson also makes a progress down the ladder of private being. He begins as a complex body-mind-spirit whose first exercises are expressions of that total self in the games, studies, and prayers at Dr. Bransby's school. He is early able to hear his conscience or spirit breathing and speaking to him; he even makes a nightly visit to that other side of himself in order to be certain that it exists. Then he moves downward into the mind-side of himself: his cleverness in cheating and in impressing his fellows makes him for a time a success, until finally he is unmasked as cheating at cards. Thereafter he moves from the rational or mind elements to the merely physical when, in the last action of the tale, he tries to effect a seduction which would be almost a rape. Then the body and spiritual aspects of Wilson have become so far separated that one can exist only at the expense of the other; and Wilson, as a being, destroys himself.

In this psychic drama it is interesting to note that, unlike "Usher," none of the elements of the inner self is dramatized outwardly until Wilson stands appalled before a mirror that gives back to him what he really is. The reason for this incapacity in Wilson to find anything in the world which is an extension of himself is not that such extensions and manifestations do not exist but that Wilson so lives by the anarchy of his own private godlike will that he is only his own mirror and manifestation. Usher saw around him the infinite interrelations of the self and the world outside; he lived in such terror that his private mind-being might be destroyed that he created the outer protective shell or the House. Wilson, on the other hand, is the Romantic individualist for whom the world is nothing but the externalization of the self: at any instant what the self wills the world must become; his journey to extinction is only a few thousand miles shorter than that of Captain Ahab, who had to go from New Bedford to the central Pacific before he too was annihilated.

"The Cask of Amontillado," coming in 1846 toward the end of Poe's mastery of the short-story form, is the tale of another nameless "I" who has the power of moving downward from his mind or intellectual being and into his brute or physical self and then of returning again to his intellectual being with his total self-hood unimpaired. It is as though one might separate the physical aspect from the mind and then restore at will the harmony again. But this "I" has one power which was denied to Usher, Wilson, and others: he is from the beginning master, even god, of his cir-cumstances: "I must not only punish," he ruminates, "but punish with impunity. A wrong is unredressed when retribution overtakes its redresser. It is equally unredressed," he concludes, "when the avenger fails to make himself felt as such to him who has done the wrong." The tale delineates the mastery which the controlling self, when it concentrates all its energies in one of its three faculties, can obtain and maintain over the world around it. The "I" does not function as a mind; we never know what has made him hate Fortunato nor are we aware that he has ever laid out any plan to effect his revenge. All we know is that we descend into the brute world "during the supreme madness of the carnival season," and there, in motley and drunkenness, we watch Montresor play on Fortunato's weakness—his connoisseurship of wines, his jealousy of a rival Luchesi, and his indifference to the evil effects of the nitre in the subterranean depths. There is nothing intellectual here; everything is mad and improvisatory—and Montresor succeeds just so far as he is able to adapt himself to a mad, improvisatory world. In short, he descends from one faculty to another and then returns to his former condition, all the while having suffered no detection from society or the world around him. The other protagonists destroyed themselves because they could not com-pletely dissociate one faculty from another; Montresor is the rare example in Poe's studies of the variable self who succeeds because he could, for a time, live in distinctly separate functions.

"The Cask of Amontillado" raises, however, another question pertaining to the multiple character of the self, a question which has been implicit throughout Poe's other studies of this theme. There is no verifiable consistency in any of these treatments of the human will and behavior; no one character is very much like any other and no single motive or action has very much relation to others. The fracture or dislocation of human faculties is different every time such an event occurs. The only permission Poe may have for such a curious psychology of human behavior is the apparent conviction he had that life consists of the disjunction of sides of the self: various elements in the human psyche or being are forever at war with each other; tragedy is always present because, in the inevitable bifurcation, one element is bound to obtain control and thereby exert such dominance that the human being is separated not only from the normal condition of a balanced selfhood but from his fellows and from the world around him. The Poe protagonist, in another respect, is compulsively driven toward death because, if life is the condition of fatal separation of the human body, mind, and spirit, death or what-ever afterlife there may be is the unification of these faculties. The narrator of "The Tell-Tale Heart," who suffers and commits a crime because of the excess of emotion over intelligence, is impelled to give himself up and pay the death penalty because he may thereby return to full selfhood or primal being. Death is the com-pletion of the life cycle; it restores that totality of being with which one began existence or which one might have had in some prior existence but which, in the inevitable chaos of this earthly life, is more and more destroyed. The tragedy (if it is a tragedy) of the Poe heroes is that they suffer from a war between their own faculties, body and mind, or mind and soul; and once that struggle has be-gun, it ends only with death. This disease of being is the enormous distension of any one perception or faculty at the expense of the others; and the Poe protagonists nearly all have in common the death-wish: at the end the tripartite self is able to realize its total selfhood. In death comes the full comprehension toward which Poe had moved in the poems but which he could more artfully treat, as process and intellectual activity, in the short stories.

Religiously, therefore, Poe postulated that mind is the only reality; physical nature is the total, unrelieved chaos of natural forms which, if they ever had design, have long been condemned to insensitivity in the general decay of the world. Man is forever lodged in this dualism, the double worlds of nature and of mind. The only way the mind can make order out of nature is either to make nature a total illusion of the mind, as in "The Fall of the House of Usher," or else to conceive of nature as the demonstra-tion of *a* mind, perhaps some other mind, and then trace the natural world back to some primal order which coexisted with the beginning of time; this task of tracing backward Poe assumed in *Eureka*. In the short stories of his middle and late career he resolved the problem in the death of the mind and its return to its own presumed condition of unity.

In a sense, Poe's poetic career declined as he more and more renounced or destroyed the natural world and sought ways for the imagination to go beyond or, as it were, into the limitless regions of thought which are the domain only of poetic inquiry. His short-story writing career developed and his mind matured, on the other hand, the more he sought ways for the creative imagination to come to some terms with the real or phenomenal world outside. Yet he could not help wavering in his purpose: by turns he asserted the insane condition of the natural world and the accompanying insanity of the human mind; again, he formulated some inter-action between mind and reality as the mind struggled for full awareness; and, still again, he established the primacy of the mind as the only knower and doer, as capable of knowing only its own experience and ideas.

Poe was too much a child of the eighteenth century not to abandon the rationally ordered universe without a struggle. Yet he was well aware that the new science of his own day was steadily undermining the sense-world of the Enlightenment—his own curious fumbling between Leibniz's monads and Kantian ideal forms displays this tension. The psychology of Hartley and the popular phrenology of Combe and Spurzheim, much as they emphasized the rational interaction of object and mind, steadily moved in the direction of the mind's capacity to know only itself and its private ideas and to reduce the world more and more to an illusion.

Poe's moral and religious ideas, for all their presumed ration-ality and coherence, are anti-rationalistic. If the only reality is mind, then reality slips away and distorts its shapes. The strangely disorganizing, even destructive, element in Poe's mind and writing was that he posited an organic world which had evolved from some primal, generative idea but that he was never able to account for man as having a vital, creative place in it. He had the choice of an invariable, deterministic world somehow existing apart from man or of the mind of man as itself a pure determinism whose specu-lations had nothing to do with external reality. He could subscribe to neither view, and thus he was left with a moral system which somehow granted to man the right to create his own moral anarchy and suffer as a result of it. Man's rule cannot be nature's, and man's mind is the reflector and initiator of no order other than its own. Melville and Poe are both crises in this dislocation of man: they both put the final moral responsibility on man, but the measure and degree of that responsibility are no longer capable of any assessment by any standard man has so far discovered.

Like Melville too, Poe had not made the major transition which the later nineteenth century would make, namely, that of lifting the burden of moral responsibility from the individual and imposing it on society. Poe's moral world was the "agony" of men who are morally responsible but who have somehow lost all awareness of and any reason for their responsibility. Guilt and evil are all the more appalling because they exist in the ever-worsening condition of the world, and yet no one is to blame. Men are forced to exist in this drama of terror and death as though there were some long-enduring and consistent regimen of action and judgment; all the while, however, they must improvise on the moment whatever is their action and moral justification. Roderick Usher, William Wilson, the man in the crowd, Montresor in "The Cask of Amontillado"—all these and others comport themselves and are necessarily judged as though there were a massive tradition or morality behind them, but they have themselves never known what it was. They are like Kafka's man in *The Trial* who never knows the charges contained in his indictment.

Here was one more in a central intellectual problem of the nineteenth century. Every time it occurred it took a different form. Gerard Manley Hopkins, a Catholic, could live in his own agony world and rely on a solid body of dogma and religious refreshment; his emotions and his mind pulled him in two directions at once. Emily Dickinson had long lost hold on the Puritan-Protestant world into which she was born, and yet she could use all the phrases and formalisms of that faith as the vocabulary of her own invented world. Melville renounced faith and yet was unable to accept science; Mark Twain tried to grasp science and was unable to let faith go. Poe, for his part, tried to swallow the new science whole and make it a substitute for the ritualized and dying faith in which he was reared. But what he thought was "science" was, after all, only his own private reconstruction of reality, not a system, not a logic, not even a moral scheme. It was a continued act of will which attempted to make reasonable a wholly irrational world. Thus "reality" and man's good and evil were not a science or an order at all but an imaginative construct; whatever moral or religious system there was must be contained only within a single knowing mind which faced a different situation every time it had a thought. . . .

NOTES

1. Lionel Trilling, *The Liberal Imagination* (New York, 1950), p. 300. This discussion of religion in the pre-Civil War South leans heavily on W. J. Cash, *The Mind of the South* (New York, 1954), pp. 65–70, 89–93.

2. *Works,* IV, 5, 8. Mr. Allen Tate has considered at length these apocalyptical tales; see "The Angelic Imagination: Poe and the Power of Words," *Kenyon Rev.,* XIV (Summer, 1952), 455–75.

3. See *Works,* IV, 200–212.

4. The most pointed of Poe's attacks on the Utilitarians are in the tale "Mellonta Tauta," 1849 (see *Works,* VI, 201–5) and in *Eureka, Works,* XVI, 188–95. . . .

5. For this popular version of the "science of mind" or psychology in Poe's day, see Edward Hungerford, "Poe and Phrenology," *Amer. Lit.,* II (November 1930), 209–31.

6. Two months before Poe's "Usher" was printed in *Burton's Gentleman's Magazine* there appeared a short article entitled "An Opinion on Dreams"; though unsigned, it was from the hand of a certain Horace Binney Wallace, known to Poe only as "William Landor." Wallace argued that the reason nothing had hitherto been known about dreams was that there had never been a correct distinction made between Mind and Soul. "I believe," Wallace went on, "man to be in himself a *Trinity,* viz. *Mind, Body,* and *Soul.*" Then he made a distinction between "dreams," which are of the mind and "proceed partly from the supernatural, and partly from natural causes," and "visions," which are of the soul and are "immaterial . . . alone." "Thus *three* portions of the *one* man seem to be most essentially different, in this way; that the body often sleeps, the mind occasionally, the Soul never." The mind is situated, therefore, at center mediating between the two opposites, body and Soul. The Soul is continually reporting its "visions" to the mind which, in turn, though it remembers only a small fraction of them after sleeping, is still the only link between those two opposing faculties, the body and the soul. If the mind were not forgetful and so much subject to the sleepy control of the body, then we should all be aware of the illuminations and revelations which have come so vividly to saints and mystics—and sometimes to writers and poets. [H. B. Wallace], "An Opinion on Dreams," *Burton's,* V(August 1839), 105. This identification was first made by T. O. Mabbott, "Poe's Vaults," *N & Q,* no. 198 (December 1953), 542–3. The critical writing on "The Fall of the House of Usher" has always been stimulating; in recent years it has become almost

an arena for critical warfare. Of the many pieces in this debate, the following are perhaps the most stimulating: Darrel Abel, "A Key to the House of Usher," *Univ. of Toronto Rev.*, XVIII (January 1949), 176–85; and D. H. Lawrence, *Studies in Classic American Literature* (New York, 1923), pp. 110–16.

7. Further suggestive relationships between the House and the inhabitants thereof are ably treated by Maurice Beebe, "The Fall of the House of Pyncheon," *Nineteenth-Century Fiction*, XI (July 1956), 4–6.

8. The source for "William Wilson" is Washington Irving's "An Unwritten Drama of Lord Byron," which appeared in *The Gift: A Christmas and New Year's Present* (Philadelphia, 1836), pp. 166–71; the volume also contained a reprint of Poe's "Manuscript Found in a Bottle." In a letter to Irving, dated October 12, 1839, which has recently come to light, Poe acknowledged this debt; see John Ostrom, "Supplement to *The Letters of Poe*," *Amer. Lit.*, XXIV (November 1952), 360.

John Parke

V

Seven Moby-Dicks

"Hark ye yet again,—the little lower layer."

—AHAB

Moby-Dick has been justly and sufficiently acclaimed as a peerless saga of physical adventure, appealing to young and old just like any other good yarn. Its external action takes place in a world of athletic heroism, the kind of man's world that many girls at one time or another and all boys fervently wish to enter. It is filled with boasting talk, odd characters, rough deeds, alarums, accidents, mysteries, and narrow escapes. The exciting paradox of the fragility of men's bodies and the sturdiness of their ingenuities is vividly present; and the technical descriptions—of the process of killing a whale, for instance—with their robustly metaphoric picturization and their hallmark of cleanly observant intimacy with materials and elements, arouse the most imaginative sort of manipulative interest. Merely as marine exposition the book is expert; merely as action narrative the story is a good one, as the frequent appearance of "The Chase" in anthologies and school readers attests.

But let us descend one layer. Mere good narrative or exposition is exhaustible. Even those readers least disposed or equipped to interpret *Moby-Dick* metaphorically often feel its power as some-

From *The New England Quarterly,* Vol. XXVIII, 1955, pp. 319–38. Copyright 1955 by *The New England Quarterly.* Reprinted by permission of the managing editor.

thing strange and haunting. This phenomenon did not escape critical notice even prior to the Melville renaissance of the 1920's; Melville's version of the old struggle with the sea and monsters simply seems to excel as a producer of what might be called the spiritual sensation of marine adventure. For here the sea and the universe are perhaps most unconquerable (and does man not tire of "conquests" over nature at last?). Here civilized insulation from the cosmos is least purchasable; the very fierceness with which it is scorned should challenge the creeping spirit of the most troglodytic reader. "The Lee Shore," an early heroic chapter, sets this spiritual tone (if Chapter I has not already), vigorously lifting the adventure story to a supraphysical level; and though from here on the central narrative and theme go in a morally oblique direction (or does Bulkington? and would *he* have bent to Ahab's will?), this "six-inch chapter" is as it were a harmonic which vibrates again and again throughout the book, particularly in relation to the landlessness of Ahab, and the crew's gradual involvement in it, on the one hand, and the far-voyaging speculations of the narrator-adventurer on the other. And when the majesty of the antagonist whale, or the alluring terror of the putative drop from masthead to water, is dramatized against such a background of material observation, we surely have adventure writing of the highest order, even as we do in the fight with Grendel's mother or the escape from Circe.

But leaving behind that self-limiting view which is pleased to regard *Moby-Dick* as a mere physical adventure story with a certain exotic spiritual tonality, we can proceed to discover next a sort of emblem-story of man and nature, in which are revealed certain accumulated meanings of an age-long struggle. Several generations of readers have seen in these emblems, the more obvious ones at least, what man does to nature and nature to man—the imprint left on each by the other. At times, as in the descriptions of Flask's pugnacity concerning whales or of Moby Dick's accumulated tangle of barbs and line, they are presented in fairly literal terms—so literal, in fact, that the reader predisposed to literalness will contend, again, that they are nothing more than what they seem. At other times, as with the albatross, the mat-weaving, or the final vignette of the flag, the hammer, and the bird, they are in more figurative, and hence more suggestive and extendible, terms. (We except here the more dramatic metaphors or symbolic constructions which relate directly to dynamic aspects of the theme, such as Ishmael's hallucination at the helm when he gazes into the nocturnal try-works, or Ahab's magnetizing of the needle.) These symbolic vignettes, often explicitly—even heavily—interpreted by the author, were Melville's delight; indeed, he had a connoisseur's penchant for them. This is held against him by readers unreceptive to the central symbolism of *Moby-Dick;* and if the subject-matter exclusive of strict narration consisted largely of a heavy sprinkling of unrelated emblematic tableaux, they would have solid grounds for objection. But such is not the case. The various symbols, static and otherwise, do indeed "add up"; they are, ultimately, part of the tissue of drama and inner theme. These latter elements must now be dealt with on their own proper level.

For Ahab's wound and mania, the preternatural Fedallah, Starbuck's tense and ambivalent relation to his captain, the prophetic soliloquies, Pip, and the "Whiteness of the Whale"—these are entities of another sort. When we examine the complicated moral drama, with the much disputed theme—that "hideous and intolerable allegory" which Melville more than half facetiously disavowed—we are indeed working on a much "lower layer," or series of layers. In the story of Ahab and his crew, and the one articulate antagonist, Starbuck, we discover a grimly joined inner battle, a searing and terrible symbolic representation of a profound conflict in the soul of man. There is no mistaking Melville's intent so to generalize. There is only the necessary search for applicability.

As with *Hamlet,* where three hundred years have not sufficed for the emergence of a definitive thematic interpretation, we have here a host of contenders for authoritative explication. This can mean one of two things: that the text, due to confusion in concept or execution, is at fault; or that, as a sort of master metaphor, it embodies an archetypal situation capable of a considerable variation of perfectly relevant responses or "meanings." Of course, this state of affairs always produces at some time a school of critics whose compulsion is to debunk all symbolic interpretations and to deny all levels of meaning in the work except the "factual" or phenomenal. It is our privilege to ignore these dogmatic skeptics and to assume, pending close examination, that the second alternative above fairly describes the novel. It is our further privilege to work for as specific an interpretation as possible according to our own lights, in the hope that all thoughtful contributions to an understanding of the work may enrich the experience of its readers, whether or not final agreement is yet—or ever—possible.

The primary and indisputable fact of the inner drama is that Captain Ahab had been led to attribute deliberation ("inscrutable malignity") on the part of the universe against himself. Thereafter, instead of minding his whaling business prudently, as Starbuck or any good Quaker would, he conjured up a soul's antagonist in The Whale. With this phantasm he then had to do unceasing battle, magnifying it to the proportions of a life-usurping fetish, until its power over his soul destroyed him, just as the actual whale sank his ship and left him to drown. This inner human destruction is the core of the drama, as two utterances by Ahab at the denouement show: "For the third time my soul's ship starts upon this voyage, Starbuck;" and finally:

Oh, now I feel my topmost greatness lies in my topmost grief. Ho, ho! from all your furthest bounds, pour ye now in, ye bold billows of my whole foregone life, and top this one piled comber of my death! Towards thee I roll, thou all-destroying but unconquering whale; to the last I grapple with thee; from hell's heart I stab at thee; for hate's sake I spit my last breath at thee. Sink all coffins and all hearses to one common pool! and since neither can be mine, let me then tow to pieces, while still chasing thee, though tied to thee, thou damned whale! *Thus,* I give up the spear!

Now, what brought about this titanic nemesis? What is at issue in the conflict within the particular man Ahab, and between him and Starbuck? What is Melville's "mighty theme" for which the drama serves as vehicle? What is the archetypal situation?

The title points to The Whale as chief protagonist, not to Ahab; The Whale was there before Ahab, and outlived him, so we had best find out about it. Moby Dick, with his ambivalent whiteness, his solitariness, his mildness and transient fury, his ubiquitousness and his scars, is, as more than one critic has suggested, the noumenon of nature itself—a comprehensive dynamic symbol for the whole immense, riddling, uncaring cosmos in which man finds himself nurtured, stunned, challenged, and (if he choose and can) at home. The *uncaringness* is the point. A significant part of the thematic framework of the book is the strong auctorial suggestion that the universe is neutral and unpurposeful in terms of human values and purposes. From this it follows that man's adaptation to the universe, to the limitations, opportunities, and destiny (favorable or otherwise) with which it presents him, shapes his whole concept of it.

For, if external nature simply does not concern itself with man's destiny, the malevolence or benevolence he attributes to it is obviously a mere projection of his own hate or love, fear or faith. But if he believes it malevolent—i.e., cannot accept whatever is accorded him of fate—and attacks it, it will prove malevolent, or prove to seem so, and expertly accommodate him in his own undoing—either physically, or inwardly through upheaval in his own nature, or both. Melville drives home this neutrality of nature in the chapter on The Whale's mysterious whiteness, where the ambivalence (to man) is marvelously exhibited through countless and ageless instances: the evil white and the beneficent white in man's vision, but always the irresistible white, the dazzling summit of all colors, the emblem of his most intense spiritual energy. The energy, in man and outside him, is impersonal and neutral; it is man personally or collectively who, by free choice or inward compulsion, turns it to destructive or creative ends in himself and so sees it in malevolent or benevolent aspects outside him.

It is further evident that man in this universe is equipped to observe, marvel, deduce; that he can minutely and partially manipulate, deflect, exploit; but that he can not influence the power of created life at its source; and, strangely, that he cannot even attempt this with impunity. The mighty Whale is content to let Ahab and other men live, so long as they do not seek power over the principle of nature itself, the "phantom of life"; so long as they attack only whales and not The Great Whale of the Universe.

> "Oh! Ahab," cried Starbuck, "not too late is it, even now, the third day, to desist. See! Moby Dick seeks thee not. It is thou, thou, that madly seekest him!"

Consider normal man (Starbuck), rational and sane, submitting his heart and his behavior not only to those natural forces far beyond his control but to a traditional *ethos*, acknowledging both his relatedness and his obligation to his kind (Ahab can not endure obligation: "Cursed be . . . mortal inter-indebtedness . . ."). Encountering the raw power of physical nature, he can maintain his livelihood and his equanimity by ingenuity, patience, submission to necessity, and the fulfilment of his sense of responsibility. But let some traumatic experience or historical upheaval upset his sense of cosmic and social proportion, his humanity, and his proper respect toward immensity and careless omnipotence; above all, let him then indulge in vindictiveness toward that which is incapable of charity, justice, and premeditated animosity alike, and he is lost. His presumption ("I'd strike the sun if it insulted me"), violating a law of his own nature, will ignite a conflict in his soul so abrasive that he will gradually wear away a lung and half a heart (yet possibly become great in the process—". . . all mortal greatness is but disease," says Melville; the trauma is perhaps the grain which stings the pearl into being); he will become an unconsciously eager victim of a catastrophe which will seem to him in his phantasm the working of a purposeful external vengeance.

So with Ahab. In him nature's mold has cracked, and so the universe seems to have turned against him. As in the opening of *King Lear,* the loyal and wholly human man (Kent, Starbuck) is impotent; the runaway fragment holds mad sway. What such a desperate man, who would be whole and reign within himself, has then to contend with is something in the nature of an autonomous complex: Ahab's "purpose, by its own sheer inveteracy of will, forced itself against gods and devils into a kind of self-assumed, independent being of its own." Now, the conflict between Ahab and Starbuck is the direct reflection of this conflict within Ahab; Starbuck submits to an *ethos,* a job, and an emotional responsibility to his family, accepting any disproportion "between his just deserts and what he gets"; Ahab, on the other hand, profoundly sensitive enough to have been hurt by life, identifying his whole being with an injured part that will not heal, and rationalizing his consequent derangement, sets himself up above the *ethos,* denies his obligations and his human feeling, and opposes his personal conscious will to destiny. And this, of course, is the *hubris;* over-simplified, it is the sin of pride. Here is a basic thematic interpretation.

But again, "the little lower layer." More than the pride of a particular man is involved, both initially and ultimately, and more than trauma. Melville's intention was not nearly so simple, and part of the novel's durable fascination is the fact that the *hubris* is less readily apparent, in its precise nature, than the nemesis. In fact, it is both deeply subtle and extremely complex.

Mankind itself (all races and important nationalities are represented in the crew of the *Pequod*) is fatefully embarked on a pursuit which is, as we have seen, a titanically malicious attack on nature itself. (Ahab's malice is partly intellectual—more of that anon—while the crew's is blindly instinctive.) Now, while it is of course fitting, or at least traditional, that hazardous expeditions are for men, the absence of women and their influence from the crew and, generally speaking, from the story, may be taken as symbolic. For not merely humanity (the moral quality) is left ashore, but the specific feminine principle of relatedness, of nurturing, of instinctive affection, is implicitly and expressly denied. Even the comradeship of Ishmael and Queequeg, so intimate in the early chapters, is dropped. Pip, the most defenseless and lovable creature imaginable, is deranged by being abandoned in the water and is later agonized by the crew's denial of the security which he needs and which, paradoxically, it becomes Ahab's particular joy to give him. Ahab cancels his ties with his new wife and babe. Masculinity is isolated; life is unbalanced. Only Starbuck, among the active characters, remains whole, despite his limitations, and truly human—that is, both masculine and potentially feminine.

The denouement is thus made psychologically inevitable, since self-mutilation can result only in disaster; Melville hints at it many times in advance. The sexless, inhuman symbol Fedallah (identified with the devil, for he casts no shadow) is an early harbinger of what is to come. From the moment of embarkation at Nantucket there is an insidious presence and a tension on board, manifested in all sorts of external omens and symbols; these are a sort of ground bass for the gradual revelation of the core of evil in Ahab's soliloquies, colloquies, and actions.

Vast destructive powers are loosed as Ahab and the opposing forces converge; despite the integrity and sanity and (in normal human measure) the considerable strength of Starbuck, despite his protests to the captain, despite Ahab's intense struggle with himself and his long surviving ability to feel sympathy and pain, the captain totally rejects his instincts, casts off his humanity, even the tool of his craft of navigation; he resolves on his own destruction. As his mania gathers the support of all his faculties, his fervor and his will catch up all the other men (but Starbuck) in a great bonfire of destructive energy. All values are inverted—note Ishmael's sense of psychic inversion in "The Try-Works"; there are no laws to hold to when man sets himself to wreak vengeance on the nameless phantom life itself, on the universe, on himself. And, inevitably, all is lost in the grand debacle of such a paranoiac orgy.

Justice poetic enough, and righteous enough even for the orthodox Christian of Melville's day. The sins of pride and self-mutilation are fittingly punished. May we not now sum up the theme and extend it to a universal moral? Ahab's intellectual presumption, his denial of humanity, his identification of his entire personality with his injured pride and towering conscious will, is in every one of us who seeks knowledge of all mysteries, who seeks total power over circumstance, and who would refuse submission to the law of personal integration, who would reject that which is greater than personality and beyond the human. This it is to be a renegade. The dramatization of the issue is, of course, out of all proportion to our individual variant experiences; but that is precisely why it so affects us. It is as if one of our own little inward battles against superpersonal necessity were projected on a screen in dimensions and social ramifications a thousand times beyond the scope of our insignificance. *Moby-Dick* is a huge nightmare of ourselves at war with fate and the universe, one which we would do well to contemplate—Americans particularly, who have yet, in all their scientific plundering and tinkering, to learn respect for nature and the cosmos, for life and death, and for themselves.

But, once more, the situation is not so simple. There is another "lower layer." For Ahab voluntarily and deliberately places himself outside the pale of Christendom; *and yet he dies a hero of a sort.* Renegade though he is, it is he, not Starbuck, who excites our admiration and our vicarious participation, and is meant to. Starbuck is by contrast simply too human, too normally proportioned. ("Thou art but too good a fellow, Starbuck," says Ahab.) Let us consider Ahab as a hero, and let us see the way in which Melville presents him to us.

Just as Hawthorne's too masculine Ethan Brand embodies the destructive aspect of the pride of knowledge, Ahab, in our initial oversimplification, embodies the pride of will. He must overcome destiny. But he is presented far more effectively than Hawthorne's character, with far more of revelation, for Melville is magnanimous and daring enough to force us to admire Ahab and to pity him, to make us feel the pull of his electric leadership, to have us see for ourselves what it is to become exalted and then overwhelmed in the identification with maimed and self-maimed, vengeful masculinity. ("I, Ishmael, was one of that crew; my shouts had gone up with the rest. . . .") In the Hawthorne tale (as in many of his others) it is hard for us to embed the author's implied judgment very deep in our feeling, however much we may intellectually agree, for the protagonist is too black and furtive, too repugnant, too pitiless toward himself, for us to see readily in him a reflection of any part of ourselves. But Ahab, figurehead of the independent mind, scorning to reconcile himself to a fate he can neither control nor avoid, much less understand; Prometheus-like refusing (in Elizabethan rhetoric!) to acknowledge the everlasting superiority of the cosmic forces concentrated against his brittleness like an immense, careless army; above all, knowing his own madness, his pain, and his humanity: this is irresistible. Though we quit and condemn his presumptuous folly at last, even as Ishmael escapes the wreck of the *Pequod,* we do so with intimate knowledge and with profit; for Melville, instead of reading us a homily, has made us participants. If nothing else in the book will do it, the titanic pathos of the "Sunset" chapter, or the heartrending gibberish of Pip (Lear's fool's descendant), or the tremendous climactic antiphony of "The Symphony," will implicate us in pity for the part of ourselves that has been wrenched from us in the magnificently demented Ahab. Perhaps not even Lear, who cracks too easily and whose fault is so much more trivial, can stir us so.

For Ahab is tragic, not just pathetic or grotesque. He has the courage to face what he fears, the inner nemesis he knows he has prepared for himself; and he finds he must constantly fight his own humanity to keep that courage. The sacrifice is not easy. This is made especially convincing in the two chapters last named above. At the same time that he misdirects his great spiritual energies to a suicidal as well as homicidal end, he becomes fully, painfully aware of what he has sacrificed in himself and in others. (His ordering Starbuck to keep to the ship at the end is profoundly humane as well as self-propitiatory.) If he is not finally master of himself or of the situation he finds himself in, not able to balance values and create himself anew at his death, he at least has the courage and far exceeds the vision of Milton's Satan, who has been more than sufficiently admired as a "tragic hero." And if, like Conrad's Kurtz, he dies unreconstructed despite his at times prayerful awareness of the moral and psychic horror in which he has become involved, he has the decency to outlive his moment of pause and to die unself-forgiving and with harness on his back. Satan's end is repulsive, Kurtz's pathetic; Ahab's, though like the others' morally repugnant, is paradoxically magnificent. The ambivalence, as in *Macbeth,* makes this a doubly stirring, if disconcerting, denouement for modern readers.

Now, the nature of the theme on this sixth layer will become evident if we examine the situation which calls forth heroic action. This tragedy is neither Aristotelian nor, in the Elizabethan sense, personally or politically ethical, nor, in the Thomas Hardy sense, psychologically deterministic. Ahab's downfall carries with it far more than the undoing of one man and his accomplices. The tone of the ending, to take one of the many indications, is epically grand and out of all proportion to Ahab's immediate significance as a mere individual. It does indeed, in spite of Melville's scornful disclaimer, suggest an allegory of man in a historical predicament.

The plain fact is that Melville, in dealing with the problem of fate, is doing so completely outside the Christian frame of reference. "I have written a wicked book, and feel spotless as a lamb," he wrote Hawthorne after finishing *Moby-Dick.* His depiction of a *universe both godless and purposeless* was, and he knew it, in effect a blasphemy from the point of view of orthodoxy and transcendentalism alike. The shock upon his contemporary public (if they had widely understood) could be compared to the effect that Robinson Jeffers' theology might have had upon Queen Victoria.

Now we see why Melville left his hero unredeemed and apparently uncondemned (note the final helplessness of the godly Starbuck), dying in a black destructive fury of pride and negation —yet, paradoxically, still heroic. For Ahab's tragic predicament is the result of his own heroic temper and special personality *plus* this philosophical or theological condition: the removal of God and Providence from the universe. If the universe is ethically ungov-

erned and purposeless, the apparent corollary is the absence of
any principle of fatal justice, and so the stultification of human
ethical norms and social laws. No wonder Ahab sought his own
death and met it with a curse! No wonder Melville felt socially
"guilty," for he was cutting himself loose from all the bulwarks of
ethical and theological thought familiar and normal in his day.
He was heading into a dangerous open sea, and he knew it.

Interestingly enough, the process seems to have begun during
the writing of the book. In the early chapters, before Ishmael and
Queequeg reach Nantucket, there are no eschatological under-
tones, and the frame of reference is specifically Protestant: both
Father Mapple's austere but genuine kindliness and evangelism,
and the brotherly rapport between the self-respecting New Englander and the pagan harpooneer embody this. All is black and
white. But these are points of departure only, for we soon move on
into an already senile, partly blasphemous world of Quaker commercialism at Nantucket, which in its decadence is threatened by
Elijah's prophecy and the mysterious embarkation of the apostate
Ahab's boat crew. Next Bulkington, the unaffiliated man of pure,
unquestioning spirituality, is swept overboard at the start of the
voyage (how isolated he would have been among the *Pequod's*
crew!). Then the comradeship of Ishmael and Queequeg is quietly
dropped, as Ishmael becomes less a character and more a device;
and the whole focus of the book ("WHALING VOYAGE BY
ONE ISHMAEL"?) seems to change as Melville becomes caught
up in an immense superpersonal theme.

Ultimately, in *Moby-Dick,* we find ourselves involved in a sort
of apocalypse: "This is the way the world ends." (At least there's
a bang to it in nineteenth-century America!) This, Melville's
prophetic intuition seems to tell him, is the only at-present-
conceivable result of the collision between the wayward spirit and
intellect of man (with all his inherited ideals of justice) and the
un-Providential, unjudicial, uncaring universe empty of God. Note
that Melville wastes no love upon his steadfast Christian, Starbuck: the mate is, in the moral climate of the story, an anachronism:
he lives on, secure and unshakable, in a world whose illusions are
irreparably shattered for Ahab. When Starbuck at the height of
the typhoon says, "God, God is against thee, old man, . . ." and the
superstitious crew falter before the corposants, we can only laugh,

not at the fear but at the terms in which it is articulated by the mate; for the poetry has converted us already to Ahab's fierce animism, as our identification with him (so carefully and gradually developed by Melville) had previously made us atheists. Though we cannot but respect Starbuck's uprightness, his humanitarian goodness, his steadfastness, we can only scorn his prosaic mildness beside the splendid vigor of Ahab.

True, Ahab is a fated loser; even at his most admirable, when he is struggling most awarely and most feelingly to preside over his own experience and salvage his soul, he is damned. Melville never lets us forget or doubt this. He carries his personal doom with him, and loves it, for in a collapsing moral creation its grandeur is all he is left. But, *natural* laws are still in operation: Ahab, by the nature of his reaction to the void with which his time, his misfortune, and his personal disposition confront him, seals his own fate. Hate still does not, cannot, triumph over nature, but over the hater at last; Moby Dick goes free, immortal, and essentially invulnerable, while Captain Ahab and his accomplices are unmercifully drowned. As Lewis Mumford has said, Ahab "becomes the image of the thing he hates; he has lost his humanity in the very act of vindicating it."

If he is heroic, it is because of his intellectual and spiritual fortitude as a mere human being in confronting chaos—physical, ethical, metaphysical chaos, the long displaced but never extinguished old deity of the myths. How, indeed, when God and the comforting concepts of Providence, divine justice, and salvation are lost, does man reconcile himself to his fate? Ahab, born into the story scarred and godless, most nakedly exposed to the apparent nihilism of the universe, faces this challenge alone. The others do not see it; he is their superior. The fact that from the outset he takes a course which dooms him to frustration and madness makes him no less heroic, and no less pitiable. Finding in the cosmos indifference, injustice, even (apparently) total depravity, he determines to make it bow to his personal need for revenge—an attempt at restoration of order—or know the reason why. It is a blind, typically human reaction, stirring because of the preterhuman stature and intellectual power of the man who embodies it, and because of his abiding sense of alternatives. The fact that his personality is still inadequate to embrace a resolution that is not self-destructive suggests Melville, the prophet's, terror before the looming problem—and his courage in revealing its direct and present threat.

Having progressed through so many levels of interpretation to this exposition of a theological allegory, we might think we had reached the full depth, the quintessence, of Melville's "mighty theme." This, indeed, is as mighty as the story of Job himself: the confrontation of chaos by man—Chaos, the old of the Mediterranean, so frighteningly depicted by Milton as waiting, though in abeyance, outside the framework of the created universe, where he waits still, no doubt, for modern man, beyond the crumbling pale of the Christian citadel and the evaporating heavenly city of rationalism, close beneath the flimsy suburban scaffolding of scientific relativism. But, "Hark ye yet again . . . " there is more.

The chaos, says Melville, is not merely around man; it is in him. For, after the dissipation of the Christian theology, the heart of man is still found to be literally writhing with evil. In fact, the evil in man is the cause of the apparent outer chaos ("Moby Dick seeks thee not . . ."). Perhaps our author would have liked to be a humanist; but his insight into human nature would not let him! For, in one telling passage (buttressed by many others), he indisputably objectifies and points up for us the eternal problem of human evil and man's bewilderment before it as the basis of Ahab's preoccupation and therefore as the inmost core of the book's theme:

> The White Whale swam before him as the monomaniac incarnation of all those malicious agencies which some deep men feel eating in them. . . . That intangible malignity which has been from the beginning . . . deliriously transferring its idea to the abhorred white whale, he pitted himself, all mutilated, against it. . . . all the subtle demonisms of life and thought; all evil, to crazy Ahab, were visibly personified and made practically assailable in Moby Dick. He piled upon the whale's white hump the sum of all the general rage and hate felt by his whole race from Adam down; and then, as if his chest had been a mortar, he burst his hot heart's shell upon it.

Moby-Dick, then, is ultimately a study of evil. But what sort of evil? What is Melville's notion of evil? Evil's first apparent manifestation (or so it is interpreted by Ahab) is the White Whale's mutilation of his leg. But the *Pequod* meets an English whaler whose captain has had his arm torn off by the same whale; this man is not maddened, nor does he regard the event as more than a perfectly natural, though fearful, accident incurred in the routine business of whaling. His sensible conclusion is that, as far as he and his men are concerned, this particular whale is best let alone. Now, Ahab, a deeper man by far, is obsessed not only with what seems the injustice of the excruciating treatment accorded him (he was delirious for days after the accident, and convalescent for months); he is obsessed too, as we have seen, with the notion of hidden forces in the universe. More than this, he is a sinisterly marked man, with a long, livid, probably congenital scar (an emblem, surely, of original sin); with a record of blasphemy and certain peculiar, darkly violent deeds; with a series of evil prophecies hanging over him; and with the given name of an idolatrous and savage king.

All this is fittingly suggestive preparation for the complete deliverance of Ahab's soul to evil through obsession and revenge. But his motive for revenge is not simple, not merely wicked. His quest for Moby Dick is in part a metaphysical one, for he is *in revolt against the existence of evil itself.* His vindictiveness, blind as it is, and motivated by personal hurt, is nevertheless against the eternal fact of evil. He thinks "the invisible spheres were formed in fright," feels his burden is that of all mankind (". . . as though I were Adam, staggering beneath the piled centuries since Paradise"), thinks the White Whale either the "principal" or the agent of all evil. He, Ahab, is evil, Melville seems to say (through Starbuck and Ahab both), because he seeks to overthrow the established order of dualistic human creation; and yet he is admirable, for he has gone over to evil not merely, like Faustus, for purposes of self-gratification, but in angry and misguided protest against its existence and its ravages in him.

What inevitably happens is that, in casting himself as the race-hero opposing the existence of the principle of evil, he but projects his own evil outward ("deliriously transferring its idea to the abhorred white whale") and so becomes all the more its avatar and its prey. He would "strike through the mask" of the visible object (the agent of evil), hoping there to find the key to the riddle. His occasional suspicion ("Sometimes I think there's naught beyond") that this will not result in any discovery whatsoever, and so not in an effective revenge, deters him not at all, though it drives him ever in upon himself as his fatal hour approaches, till, near the end, he does see the working of evil in himself—and yet dies its avowed agent. For he is mad; he is "madness maddened," quite conscious of his own derangement, and obsessed with it. The final, terrifying chaos, then, is that which he discovers within himself as his vestigial sanity contemplates his madness and its futility, as he admits his incomprehension of the thing that has driven him to irreparable folly and has lost him his very identity ("Is Ahab, Ahab?"):

> "What is it, what nameless, inscrutable, unearthly thing is it [the very language used earlier to describe evil]; what cozening, hidden lord and master, and cruel, remorseless emperor commands me; that against all natural lovings and longings, I so keep pushing, and crowding, and jamming myself on all the time? . . ."

Here is raised even the question of whether man, this proud and splendid aristocrat of the spirit, is indeed a free agent; Ahab, having at other times defied all the gods and called them cricket players, having assumed and never doubted that he could have made himself lord of creation, now turns (in "The Symphony") from Edmund's flouting, free-will cynicism to Gloucester's craven determinism: "By heaven, man, we are turned round and round in this world, like yonder windlass, and Fate is the handspike." He is not captain of his soul after all.

Ahab knows, then, everything about his predicament except its cause in himself—and so its solution. He feels the cause to be an immemorial curse visited upon all men. An exile from Christendom, he yet perceives and abhors the existence of evil. Worse still, he resists it; he will not come to terms with it. He wishes it could simply be swept away, or covered over: "Man, in the ideal, is so noble and so sparkling, such a grand and glowing creature, that over any ignominious blemish in him all his fellows should run to throw their costliest robes." But the dark side (which cannot be concealed) cannot be explained or avoided, either. And the most maddening thing of all about it—this is a constant refrain throughout the book—is the deceptive way it lurks beneath a smiling and lovely exterior. ("These temporary apprehensions, so vague but so awful, derived a wondrous potency from the contrasting serenity of the weather. . . ." ". . . Fate is the handspike. And all the time, lo! that smiling sky, and this unsounded sea!" And on the very morning of the last terrible day of The Chase—

> "What a lovely day again! were it a new-made world, and made for a summer-house to the angels, and this morning the first of its throwing open to them, a fairer day could not dawn upon that world.")

Ahab's tragedy (and, on this final level, the book's theme) is, then, his inability to locate and objectify evil in himself, or to accept it and deal with it prudently as part of the entire created world, and so to *grow* despite it and because of it; it is his own fated indenture to evil while he seeks to destroy it, and his more and more precise knowledge of what is happening to him. It is the magnificence and yet the futility of his attempt. "I know that of me, which thou knowest not of thyself, oh, thou omnipotent," he cries to the great impersonal spirit of fire which he acknowledges as his maker and which, as its individualized creation, he defies. He defies his paternal maker, light, because, discovering his own dual nature (he says he never knew his mother), he has revolted and leagued himself now with darkness (the unrecognized mother-symbol, standing here for a regressive identification, which is of course what supplies the destructive energy). Then, "I am darkness leaping out of light," and "cursed be all the things that cast man's eyes aloft to that heaven, whose live vividness but scorches him. . . ." "So far gone am I in the dark side of earth, that its other side, the theoretic bright one, seems but uncertain twilight to me." And at his death, the magnificent line—as great and moving in its utter verbal simplicity, and yet as fraught with complex resignation as Edgar's "Ripeness is all": "I turn my body from the sun"—a line whose full and exact significance has been specifically constellated in advance by his own apostrophe to the dying whale in Chapter CXVI.

Ahab is no Faustus. He always has a choice. Many are the times he backslides; the tension between humanity and will is constantly active. Pip, the piteous embodiment of warmly instinctive human nature, of all that Ahab must tread on in himself, acts several times as the unwitting touchstone of that humanity. "Hands off from that holiness!" But, "There is that in thee, poor lad, which I feel too curing to my malady . . . and for this hunt, my malady becomes my most desired health." Starbuck too again

and again is the foil and the polar opposite; and once Ahab even
finds it good to feel dependence on human aid, for when the
White Whale has crushed his ivory leg in the "Second Day," he
exclaims while half hanging on the shoulder of his chief mate,
"Aye aye, Starbuck, 'tis sweet to lean sometimes . . . and would
old Ahab had leaned oftener than he has." And just once, in "The
Symphony," "Ahab dropped a tear into the sea; nor did all the
Pacific contain such wealth as that one wee drop."

He must remain, for the brooding Melville apparently and
for us, a symbol of that independent spirit and will which, scorning all "lovely leewardings," pushes off from the haven of all
creeds to confront an ultimate chaos in the human soul; admirable,
perhaps, beyond all flawed heroes (Bulkington was too simple an
embodiment—pure essence, he was fit only for deification) in his
energy and his courage, but condemned to split at last on the rock
of evil, the very thing he willed out of existence; fated—and
magnificently, agonizingly willing—to become the pawn (no, the
prince, the king) of evil in consequence of his misguided revolt, to
lose his identity in the end because he sought to exalt it against
the immutable principles of its creation.

Here is our many-layered theme—a Protean archetype indeed! The physical adventure, the spiritual exaltation of hazardous
voyaging, the interaction of husbandmen and nature, are there as
fresh and valid as ever. The pride and retribution thesis still
stands, and the nemesis of self-mutilation through the exalting of
will at the expense of instinct. On the metaphysical level, however,
chaos, even if thought of only as externally cosmic, is an old, old
image of man's, the adversary of all enshrined deities; it confrontation by man is fit matter for grand tragedy. But as an
internal moral and emotional predicament the chaos of evil and
idealism and madness in the individual is certainly the most compelling phase of the archetype, and the one which evokes more
and deeper echoes than any other.

For Melville's grand implication seems to be that all attempts
to resist or deny evil, no matter how they are rationalized, are
maddeningly futile. Christianity may be gone, he says in effect,
but evil is here to stay; no use trying to idealize it out of existence,
or conceal it with "costliest robes" or annihilate it by main

strength of will and resentment. It will abide and elude; and it must be reckoned with. It is in us, even the deepest of us. Melville cites no text; he preaches no sermon on this head; he merely enunciates as best he can the critical moral predicament which his prophetic imagination apprehends.

Part of the extendibility of Melville's theme on this final level, of course, is due to the fact that he was truly prophetic, both in the sense of apprehending an incipient but suppressed conflict and dilemma of his own day (which only Hawthorne among his American contemporaries honestly confronted in his writings), and in the sense that historically the full reckoning with the problem was yet to come—*and just such an ill-starred solution was to be attempted* by modern man, who has tried philosophically and pragmatically to dismiss the notion of evil.

The problem has been with us now so long that there are many who have lost the capacity to be terrified by it; if an ever richer general response to this tragic novel can help us today or tomorrow to grasp and hold the reality of evil in our imagination, the book will have served as high a human purpose as any less "wicked" book in a time of more stable values. And if Ahab is to be the last of the race of great literary heroes (fittingly embodying the evil of evils and the highest spiritual splendor of man), why, even in the decline of our culture our pleasure in reading *Moby-Dick,* mixed with pain in a true purgation, will come in large part from our sense of participation in the magnificence and the richly deserved doom.

How it could be avoided. Melville does not tell us. Could we tell him?

R. W. Short

VI

Melville as Symbolist

A revaluation of Melville, at least in such brief compass as this, must concern itself principally with *Moby-Dick,* all the later works being but lesser fishes swimming in the wake of the great leviathan. Also, a revaluation must be something like a capstone of prior valuations, rather than a *novum organum,* Melville's later work having enjoyed frequent and penetrating criticism for more than a quarter of a century. Indeed, it has proved difficult for anyone with a grain of sympathy to write wholly in vain about Melville. His whole work has the quality, not only of attracting comment, but of drawing the commentator into a study of its heart and meaning. In this it resembles the picture hanging in the Spouter-Inn:

> A boggy, soggy, squitchy picture truly, enough to drive a nervous man distracted. Yet was there a sort of indefinite, half-attained, unimaginable sublimity about it that fairly froze you to it, till you involuntarily took an oath with yourself to find out what that marvelous painting meant.[1]

The simplest sort of reader senses that *Moby-Dick* is more than a whaling tale; that *Mardi, Pierre, The Confidence Man, Billy Budd,*

From *The University of Kansas City Review,* Vol. XV, 1948, pp. 38–46. Copyright 1948 by The University of Kansas City. Reprinted by permission of the publisher and author.

Benito Cereno, and the other short pieces are reservoirs of significance; and even the laziest reader wants to make some pursuit of the mysteries. Here lies the essential Melville problem. If we can reduce to general terms both quest and goal, we shall understand why none of the interpreters, even of the contradictory ones, has been wholly wrong; and why to most of us Melville's meaning seems so near and at the same time so remote.

II

Many of the writers on Melville have to some degree dealt with his work, especially *Moby-Dick,* as allegory. Let us consider the extent to which this approach is justified.

One standing in the Spouter-Inn before the marvelous painting, (which prefigures *Moby-Dick*) would be thus affected:

> Ever and anon a bright, but, alas, deceptive idea would dart you through.—It's the Black Sea in a midnight gale.—It's the unnatural combat of the four primal elements.—It's a blasted heath.—It's a Hyperborean winter scene.—It's the breaking-up of the ice-bound stream of Time. But at last all these fancies yielded to that one portentous something in the picture's midst. *That* once found out, and all the rest were plain. But stop; does it not bear a faint resemblance to a gigantic fish? even the great leviathan himself?

The deceptive fancies of the gazer resemble allegorical meanings; he is discouraged from accepting them. They lead to the core of the picture's meaning, but we must not mistake them for the core, though the temptation to do so is strong. Even as signposts, their existence is contingent upon the reality of the core itself—the gigantic fish which in its own meaning comprises the host of particular fancies. In short, the allegorical approach doesn't work. The doubloon that Ahab nailed to the mast carries a similar message. The members of the crew kept finding various allegorical meanings in it, until Stubb, keenly observant though deficient in imagination, finally concluded: "There's another rendering now; but still one text. All sorts of men in one kind of world, you see." We remember also the error of mad Gabriel, "in his gibbering insanity, pronouncing the White Whale to be no less a being than the Shaker God incarnated." Mad Gabriel's identification of Moby Dick was too specific, none the less an error for being "inspired." His error further reminds us of the error of the skeptical landsmen, who "might scout at Moby Dick as a monstrous fable, or still worse and more detestable, a hideous and intolerable allegory."

On the other hand, Willard Thorpe quotes Melville's letter to Mrs. Hawthorne:

> I had some vague idea while writing it [*Moby-Dick*] that the whole book was susceptible of an allegorical construction, and also that parts of it were—but the specialty of many of the particular subordinate allegories were first revealed to me after reading Mr. Hawthorne's letter, which without citing any particular examples, yet intimated the part-and-parcel allegoricalness of the whole.[2]

Taken with the citations from the book itself, this letter, written after the book was completed, seems to confuse the issue, or at least to suggest that Melville was himself confused as to the nature of his work. If so, his confusion was merely terminological, for the work itself indicates a precise, rather than a confused, state of affairs.

Allegory probably meant to Melville either the positive parallelisms of Bunyan (like his own use of the quadrant and other "particular subordinate allegories") or the vaguely felt intimations common in Hawthorne, Browning, and Tennyson, where the reader may decode to his own taste and no harm done. Let us be clear that Melville neither intended nor achieved either of these types. What he did intend, he lacked critical vocabulary to define, for the critics of the mid-nineteenth century wrote intelligibly of allegory and realism, but falteringly if at all of varieties of symbolism or use of myth, the language of Melville's artistic strategy.

Strict allegory is essentially rationalistic; when it exists, faith has passed over into dogma, the department where everything has one and only one name. Even though allegory may co-exist with mysticism, it is, especially as an artistic method, opposed to non-rational experience and battens upon doctrine, or some other codification of experience. Thus to a certain type of mind allegory seems to deal with experience less directly than symbolism. In a passage later to be quoted, Melville says of the "original [symbolical] character" that it is like a Drummond light "raying away from itself"—in other words, it seeks affinities in the furtherest rings of experience, whereas the allegorical figure aims at analysis and differentiation. Spenser's Red Cross Knight, Holiness, is a concept from experience strained through doctrine and studied apart from Truth, Wisdom, Prudence, and other virtues. Though Spenser intended Prince Arthur to represent magnanimity, the composite of the virtues, he found very little use for him. In his allegorical treatment, the separate functions, Artegal, Britomart, Guyon, are distillations achieved by the rational intelligence, and as such, fully occupy the spotlight.

On this point, after arguing that Melville was weak in creating characters, R. P. Blackmur writes:

> This is, if you like, the mode of allegory—the highest form of the putative imagination, in which, things are *said* but need not be *shown* to be other than they seem, and thus hardly require to *be* much of anything. But successful allegory—*La Vita Nuova* and *Pilgrim's Progress*— requires the preliminary possession of a complete and stable body of belief appropriate to the theme in hand. Melville was not so equipped; neither was Hawthorne; neither was anyone in nineteenth century America or since.[3]

Professor Blackmur, of course, speaks truly of allegory and of Melville's incapacity for allegory on the order of Dante and Bunyan. Although *Moby-Dick* does employ unnaturalistic methods in the attempt to render experiential values, it is not allegory in this sense. We shall not however judge Melville finally incapable until we have compared his accomplishment with his own method, granting meanwhile that his method was different from Bunyan's and willing to find the same true of his accomplishment.

In another connection, Professor Blackmur quotes an important passage from *Pierre:*

> For the more and the more that he wrote, and the deeper and deeper that he dived, Pierre saw the everlasting elusiveness of Truth; the universal lurking insincerity of even the greatest and purest written thoughts.

Certainly Melville, like Pierre, wished to avoid even the highest kind of insincerity, which in his case was the insincerity imposed by the inevitable exclusiveness of both art and doctrine. If truth is the totality of experience, both Dante and Bunyan had double handicaps—as artists and as dogmatists. For example, when Christian thrust his clinging family behind him, he made a choice which simplified his problems, as it did his experience, by exclusion.[4] Bunyan's division of humanity into Christian, Worldly Wiseman, and so on, implies that truth can be reached only if the division be maintained. Ahab, Starbuck, and the rest of the crew are also parts of humanity, rather than autonomous beings, but gathered together in the *Pequod* they make up an implicit whole; they are indivisible humanity, the protagonist, actualized only in the reader and the writer, and symbolized in Bulkington, the man who does not appear.

Naturally Melville is anti-doctrinal, for in his view doctrine must be a simplification, and hence an insincerity. Calvinism, transcendentalism, naturalism, supernaturalism, these are all excerpts from experience which will be contained in any full account of experience, like one's first explanations of the Spouter-Inn picture or like mad Gabriel's dogmatic explanation of Moby Dick; but these excerpts must not be identified as the whole. "Aye, chance, freewill, and necessity—nowise incompatible—all interweavingly working together." In a sense, then, symbolism of Melville's brand may subsume allegory; and this is why even the most rigidly schematic interpretations of *Moby-Dick, Pierre, Billy Budd, The Confidence Man, Mardi,* and *Benito Cereno* bring the reader some profit.

III

"*Moby-Dick,*" writes E. M. Forster, "is full of meanings: its meaning is a different problem. It is wrong to turn the *Delight* or the coffin into symbols, because even if the symbolism is correct, it silences the book."[5] Clearly, Mr. Forster means symbols of an allegorical, or precise, nature; his is a happy way of saying that when *a* meaning is attached to the symbols, the Drummond light stops revolving.

In the face of Professor Blackmur's essay, "The Craft of Herman Melville," the most penetrating essay on Melville I have read, it would be folly to claim that *Moby-Dick* fully overcomes the "insincerity" devolving upon him as a practitioner of art. The struggle is titanic, the accomplishment uneven. In every chapter we mark the presence of apparently incongruous materials and methods. A major incongruity, however,—that between Melville's rendition of things and of characters—besteads the author's symbolism to a degree that checks, if it does not silence, criticism.

Let Captain Ahab have the first word. "All visible objects, man, are but as pasteboard masks." Beneath these masks, of course, lie the true realities. Melville's business will be with these realities, if he can get to them, and he will not very often try to forward this business by pretending that the objects represent anything but themselves. When he does so pretend, as with the sad ship named *Delight,* or the quadrant, the pretence will have the nature of a shorthand note on experience, rather than of his more characteristic exploration of experience. Ordinarily he will not mean the tiller to represent the *Old Testament* and the sails the *New Testament;* nevertheless, as tiller and sails grow involved in the complex myth, they will develop certain symbolic potentialities, and these will be the realities beneath the masks.

In his arrogance, Ahab called the masks "pasteboard"; we find the surfaces tougher. This toughness in the physical rind of objects—harpoons, ropes, porpoises, waves—resists our effort to penetrate their depths; and even when we think we have got through, they never surrender their stubborn identity in the physical world. So, in the swirling world of the *Pequod,* we cling to solid nails and pitchpoles as Ishmael clung to the unsinkable coffin. This seems to be their purpose. We are reminded of Marlow's fixation in *The Heart of Darkness,* when, closed round by waves of evil, he set his heart and mind on "rivets." Like Conrad's rivets, Melville's incredible wealth of things preserves our contact with the simple certainties of reality; we should not try too hard to interpret them. He himself was surprised when Hawthorne suggested that they might be consistently interpreted, and his surprise lacked enthusiasm. The symbolical potentials develop dynamically with the story, and it is questionable if they are retroactive; if for instance the connotations of the rope which binds Fedallah to his fate and hangs Captain Ahab in Chapter CXXXV should carry back to the rope as described in Chapter LX. The deeper realities of the things come to us naturally, without ratiocination, by their vitality, and they help to lead us to the great leviathan; as Professor Thorp has put it: "It is by means of the energy in this external story that its allegorical significance is, in Ahab's word, 'shoved' near us."[6]

This treatment of physical objects is very different from Melville's treatment of persons. Where the first is at least superficially realistic, the latter is consistently and deliberately fantastic. His practice is just the opposite of Shakespeare's, whose convincingly real characters move through environments of abandoned romanticism—ghosts, witches, monsters, bears, fairies, stagey battles and phony situations. Not to mention *Billy Budd,* even *Bartleby the Scrivener* and *The Confidence Man* have homely, concrete settings; the material circumstances of *Benito Cereno* and *The Encantadas* are more exotic, but even the exoticism in these pieces is justified by a wealth of credible detail. Only *Pierre,* the least successful of the latter works, has a background in which we do not put immediate trust. On the grocer's scales, these stages weigh more than the characters who perform upon them.

Nevertheless, it is wrong to impute the unreality of Melville's characters wholly to the maladroit dodges he often uses apparently to preserve their unreality, dodges principally relating to their speech, as the bombastic echoes of the worst aspects of blank verse in Milton, Shakespeare, and minor Jacobean tragedy; the imitation of the Jacobean masque in Chapter XL of *Moby-Dick* ("Midnight, Forecastle"); the painful soliloquies; and the embarrassing dialects. There is little speech as direct as this:

> "What do ye do when ye see a whale, men?"
> "Sing out for him" . . .
> "Good! . . . And what do ye next, men?"
> "Lower away, and after him!"

But there is much in tune with this:

> "Oh, God, to sail with such a heathen crew that have small touch of human mothers in them!"

In *The Confidence Man,* Melville described the kind of character we find in his works:

> Furthermore, if we consider, what is popularly held to entitle characters in fiction to being deemed original, is but something personal—confined to itself. The character sheds not its characteristic on its surroundings, whereas, the original character, essentially such, is like a revolving Drummond light, raying away from itself all round it—everything is lit by it, everything starts to it (mark how it is with Hamlet), so that, in certain minds, there follows upon the adequate conception of such a character, an effect, in its way, akin to that which in Genesis attends upon the beginnings of things.

There is a hint of Ahab in the contempt with which Melville dismisses the quality, "something personal—confined to itself," that most writers strive for and most readers hunger for in fictional character portrayal. Melville wants his characters to be "original" in the sense that Adam, Eve, and Satan were original in the Garden of Eden. In this type, his clearest creations are probably Claggart and Billy Budd, the one original evil and the other original innocence. Certainly Claggart and Billy Budd ray out from themselves, shedding concentric rings of light upon the values of their universe: their ship and shipmates, the mutiny, the navy, the world of men in general, and the realm of good and evil. Melville, however, realistically recognizes that the effect of such characters will be felt only by "certain minds," who will have achieved an "adequate conception" of them. Furthermore, not all the originals are as simple as Claggart and Billy Budd; there will be originals of knowledge, of practicality, of brute nature, of whatever human essence or "characteristic" may in life lie beneath the pasteboard mask. And in a given character these essences may be mixed, as (to give them a name) sympathy and law are combined in Captain Vere. The characters of Melville, then, often have a certain complexity, but one thing they do not have; to continue in Ahab's term, they do not have, even at best, a firmly rendered, consistently maintained pasteboard mask. Their nearly naked essences function organically in their own world, but would shiver and evaporate in the company of Shakespeare's men and women.

Let us not too rashly conclude that Melville ætherialized his characters through incapacity. For in spite of their sometimes painful unreality, they have dignity and impressiveness. The reason is this: though their unreality is often emphasized by clumsy means, they are so rendered in accord with a firm clear purpose, and they derive artistic stature from their service to this purpose. They may be outside the human community, but they are not outside the organization of the work of art.

Even though we agree that Hamlet is a greater work of art than *Moby-Dick*, we must see that it has had, in one respect, a less favorable critical history. Whereas the reader of *Moby-Dick* at once asks himself the crucial question, "What does the work mean?"— the reader of *Hamlet* has too often been lured off into a subordinate quest, the elusive problem of personality presented by **Ham-let** the character. The typical critique of *Hamlet* is a study of Hamlet, with a ridiculously inadequate treatment of *the play,* and that usually in terms of Hamlet.

Both Melville and Shakespeare were concerned with elements of experience behind the immediate fog of physical reality. Like other writers with this concern, they needed a myth-world; that is, a world wherein the strict dogma of probability could be relaxed, for daily life cold-shoulders life's problems as snobbishly as art conceals art. Almost overrich, Shakespeare in the middle plays colonized his myth-world with wonderfully expressive, psycholog-ically motivated beings.[7] In *Moby-Dick* only the things are real, though we notice the lack of real people only as an afterthought. The characters have the fluidity, the essentially symbolical quality, the abstraction from probability and individual crochet, appropri-ate to their own myth-world. If Shakespeare illuminates reality by showing the struggles of real persons in a myth-world, where the problems are more nakedly revealed than in a naturalistic world, Melville's characters more pliantly serve the myth; he chose the less dangerous course of preserving contact with physical reality by bearing down on rivets. The counter-danger he ran was that of failing to make a conquest of his reader. The chance he took can be measured by the fact that in his works the reader must supply the function of real person at grips with ultimate values.

Symbolistic artists differ greatly from each other, in method as well as purpose. Melville's habit as symbolist, judging from his later works, resembled Blake's as described by Mark Schorer in his *William Blake:*

> Blake's habit of mind may be described, in the sense of C. E. Douglas, as apocalyptic, "thinking visually. The Apocalyptist thinks in pictures, not 'true' in themselves, but indicative of the truth which lies behind." The difference is that between ideas which come to the poet in the form of images and images in which the poet later discovers ideas. Intellect and sense are fused in both methods, but the control in the first is exercised by intellect, in the second by sense. The first method results in a relatively systematic arrangement of images within the poem, the second, in a kaleidoscopic lack of arrangement, if it is a poem of any length. The second method is characteristic of Blake.[8]

The voyage of the *Pequod* is therefore a voyage of discovery in the seas of experience for the writer as well as for the reader. Melville perhaps began with little more than the strong feeling that the whaling industry teemed with potential symbols, which if explored might lead to the leviathan itself, that is, to the meaning of the leviathan—which "maketh a path to shine after him" like the monarch of all Drummond lights. With studied detail he presented the host of subordinate images—hooks, yards, trying vats, and stripping rigs—images of unfamiliar objects he had to make the reader visualize clearly if some of them were later to become small moons of light. These images, then, formed a frame in which he gradually made out his picture. As the picture grew, the images themselves began to reveal their essential (symbolic) meanings, but so gradually that one cannot say whether these meanings make the growing picture or are drawn from it. In this world of dense reality, humanity, more abruptly symbolized, tries to assert itself. The trial and catastrophic failure compose the tragedy; unlike most riddling tragedies, terror settles down as the meanings ray out toward the overwhelming ambiguity of the leviathan.

IV

Melville's method, then, allows his symbols to accumulate meanings in the course of their use, as they knock about in his myth-world, and so a single meaning attached to them often has at least a partial validity. Allegorical interpretation of a medieval or puritanic sort, however, defeats the larger aspect of the work, for Melville's view of reality is a more oriental view, based upon a sense of the ultimate interdependence, rather than the isolation, of experiential units. By devices which serve his ends, even though they involve a considerable dehumanization of his characters, he makes his symbols blur through one another and take shape at that vanishing point where the one and the many become indivisible. His structure suggests a hierarchical arrangement of the interfused symbols, like Milton's arrangement of celestial beings in *Paradise Lost,* an arrangement difficult to justify in rationalistic (allegorical) language. Ahab contains all the qualities of his crew; but it cannot be said that the individuals of the crew contain all the qualities of Ahab, even as potentialities. And Ahab contains in tentative, frangible form all the qualities a mere "human" can contain of Moby Dick.

In the preface to *The Great Wall of China,* Edwin Muir writes of Kafka's *The Castle* and *The Trial* that "in temper, in plan, in execution, they are heroic, and only to be compared, among modern works of fiction, with Herman Melville's *Moby-Dick*."[9] Mr. Muir has a good case. We have seen a single work of Kafka's interpreted as Calvinistic, Judaistic, and Freudian, and have felt that none of these interpretations excludes the others. Mr. Muir might also have found this basic similiarity in Thomas Mann's writing. The reader will recall that Mann began *The Magic Mountain* as a diatribe against the views of his brother, but under his hands the symbols blossomed toward a meaning that subsumed his brother's position in much the same way *The Trial* and *Moby-Dick* subsume various systematizations of experience. These writers, like Dostoevski, engaged in a Nietzschean quest for values lying on the thither side of reason and beyond good and evil. Their words tend toward the accumulative of *ur*-symbol.

One sees that the movement of the book *Moby-Dick*, which corresponds to the search of the *Pequod* for the white whale, is irresistibly toward an *ur*-symbol, where beginnings and ends flow together; and the movement concludes, as does the search, with the confrontation of Moby Dick. What then is Moby Dick?

Obviously Melville believed, here as elsewhere, that the ultimate realm of man's exploration is the realm of good and evil. Moby Dick, as the goal of man's desiring, stands as *ur*-symbol in the apex of the problem. He contains all possibilities, at least all that Melville intuitively grasped. Therefore he is evil, though he is not Evil; and he is evil only from the human point of view, which though limited is still of consequence to us. Moby Dick is all that critics have called him, and more, for this is a paramount case of a whole greater than the sum of its parts. Too few of the critics have accepted the unmistakable statement of moral ambivalence in the famous chapter "The Whiteness of the Whale," a statement supported throughout the work by subordinate ironies. We might say that Moby Dick is God. Melville would doubtless have objected to this ascription because of the name's doctrinal adhesions. Nevertheless we cannot long imagine that Moby Dick is God's antagonist; embrace him we must, though optimism dies in the effort.

That the emphasis rests so heavily upon evil may perhaps be taken to imply a residue of American Calvinism in Melville, though it is his freedom from dogmatic considerations that permits him to locate it in his master-symbol. One of the weaknesses of our puritanical faith was its inability to draw a sharp imaginative distinction between good and evil. Nothing but doctrine separated the two. Hester Prynne and the reader are justly perplexed to know which is good, the fruit of the scarlet letter or the fruit of Dimmesdale's God; doctrine flutters down like *deus ex machina* to decide the issue. The Mathers and Edwards solved the problem in the same unsatisfactory way. Thus in the imagination Calvinism tottered on the brink of devil-worship. Melville removed the doctrinal dividing line between good and evil, while retaining the familiar Calvinistic emphasis upon the latter.

Mr. Forster has strongly felt and aptly expressed the essential meaning of Moby Dick's symbolism: "Melville—after the initial roughness of his realism—reaches straight back into the universal, to a blackness and sadness so transcending our own that they are undistinguishable from glory." The white whale, as a matter of fact, finds a parallel in Mr. Forster's *Passage to India*. In this book, the Marabar caves correspond to Moby Dick in description (as far as caves and whales can be described in similar terms) and function. In the caves, too, evil holds its habitation, and all human sounds, of love or lust, violence or doctrine, lose their identity in a common vacuous echo, or to put it differently, they join in a silence which is the blend of all noises.

Apparently Melville fully comprehended the unorthodoxy of his vision of the place of evil in ultimate values. This would explain the comment he made at the completion of *Moby-Dick:* "I have written an evil book, and feel as spotless as the lamb."[10] The reaction was appropriately ambiguous and symbolic.

NOTES

1. *Moby Dick, or the Whale,* ed. Willard Thorp, Oxford University Press, 1947, p. 12. All quotations of *Moby-Dick* have been taken from this edition.

2. *Herman Melville,* by Willard Thorp, American Book Company, 1938, p. lxxiin.

3. *The Expense of Greatness,* Arrow Editions, 1940, p. 148.

4. Starbuck and Ahab, it will be remembered, yearned for their families.

5. *Aspects of the Novel,* Harcourt, Brace & Co., 1927, p. 203.

6. *Herman Melville,* p. lxxii.

7. An interesting study might be made of the way Shakespeare drifted toward the practice here imputed to Melville, in the last three plays.

8. Henry Holt & Co., 1946, p. 11.

9. Schoken Books, 1946, p. xiv.

10. Quoted by Raymond Weaver, *Moby-Dick,* The Modern Library, 1926, p. v.

Perry Miller

VII

From Edwards to Emerson

Ralph Waldo Emerson believed that every man has an inward and immediate access to that Being for whom he found the word "God" inadequate and whom he preferred to designate as the "Over-Soul." He believed that this Over-Soul, this dread universal essence, which is beauty, love, wisdom, and power all in one, is present in Nature and throughout Nature. Consequently Emerson, and the young transcendentalists of New England with him, could look with complacence upon certain prospects which our less transcendental generation beholds with misgiving:

> If the red slayer thinks he slays,
>   Or if the slain think he is slain,
> They know not well the subtle ways
>   I keep, and pass, and turn again.

Life was exciting in Massachusetts of the 1830's and '40's; abolitionists were mobbed, and for a time Mr. Emerson was a dangerous radical; Dr. Webster committed an ingenious murder; but by and large, young men were not called upon to confront possible slaughter unless they elected to travel the Oregon Trail, and the only scholar who did that was definitely not a transcendentalist. Thus it seems today that Emerson ran no great risk in asserting

From *The New England Quarterly,* Vol. XIII, 1940, pp. 589–617. Copyright 1940 by *The New England Quarterly.* Reprinted by permission of the managing editor.

that should he ever be bayoneted he would fall by his own hand disguised in another uniform, that because all men participate in the Over-Soul those who shoot and those who are shot prove to be identical, that in the realm of the transcendental there is nothing to choose between eating and being eaten.

It is hardly surprising that the present generation, those who are called upon to serve not merely as doubters and the doubt but also as slayers and slain, greet the serene pronouncements of Brahma with cries of dissent. Professors somewhat nervously explain to unsympathetic undergraduates that of course these theories are not the real Emerson, much less the real Thoreau. They were importations, not native American growths. They came from Germany, through Coleridge; they were extracted from imperfect translations of the Hindu scriptures, misunderstood and extravagantly embraced by Yankees who ought to have known better—and who fortunately in some moments did know better, for whenever Emerson and Parker and Thoreau looked upon the mill towns or the conflict of classes they could perceive a few realities through the haze of their transcendentalism. They were but transcendental north-north-west; when the wind was southerly they knew the difference between Beacon Hill and South Boston. I suppose that many who now read Emerson, and surely all who endeavor to read Bronson Alcott, are put off by the "philosophy." The doctrines of the Over-Soul, correspondence, and compensation seem nowadays to add up to shallow optimism and insufferable smugness. Contemporary criticism reflects this distaste, and would lead us to prize these men, if at all, for their incidental remarks, their shrewd observations upon society, art, manners, or the weather, while we put aside their premises and their conclusions, the ideas to which they devoted their principal energies, as notions too utterly fantastic to be any longer taken seriously.

Fortunately, no one is compelled to take them seriously. We are not required to persuade ourselves the next time we venture into the woods that we may become, as Emerson said we might, transparent eyeballs, and that thereupon all disagreeable appearances—"swine, spiders, snakes, pests, madhouses, prisons, enemies" —shall vanish and be no more seen. These afflictions have not proved temporary or illusory to many, or the compensations always obvious. But whether such ideas are or are not intelligible to

us, there remains the question of whence they came. Where did
Emerson, Alcott, Thoreau, and Margaret Fuller find this pantheism
which they preached in varying degrees, which the Harvard faculty
and most Boston businessmen found both disconcerting and con-
temptible? Was New England's transcendentalism wholly Germanic
or Hindu in origin? Is there any sense, even though a loose one,
in which we can say that this particular blossom in the flowering
of New England had its roots in the soil? Was it foolishly trans-
planted from some desert where it had better been left to blush
unseen? Emerson becomes most vivid to us when he is inscribing
his pungent remarks upon the depression of 1837, and Thoreau in
his grim comments upon the American blitzkrieg against Mexico.
But our age has a tendency, when dealing with figures of the past,
to amputate whatever we find irrelevant from what the past itself
considered the body of its teaching. Certain fragments may be
kept alive in the critical test tubes of the Great Tradition, while
the rest is shoveled off to potter's field. The question of how much
in the transcendental philosophy emerged out of the American
background, of how much of it was not appropriated from foreign
sources, is a question that concerns the entire American tradition,
with which and in which we still must work. Although the metaphysic of the Over-Soul, of self-reliance, and of compensation is
not one to which we can easily subscribe, yet if the particular formulations achieved by Emerson and Thoreau, Parker and Ripley,
were restatements of a native disposition rather than amateur
versions of *The Critique of Pure Reason*, then we who must also re-
formulate our traditions may find their philosophy meaningful, if
not for what it held, at least for whence they got it.

Among the tenets of transcendentalism is one which today
excites the minimum of our sympathy, which declared truth to be
forever and everywhere one and the same, and all ideas to be one
idea, all religions the same religion, all poets singers of the same
music of the same spheres, chanting eternally the recurrent theme.
We have become certain, on the contrary, that ideas are born in
time and place, that they spring from specific environments, that
they express the force of societies and classes, that they are generated by power relations. We are impatient with an undiscrim-
inating eclecticism which merges the Bhagavad-Gita, Robert
Herrick, Saadi, Swedenborg, Plotinus, and Confucius into one

monotonous iteration. Emerson found a positive pleasure—which he called "the most modern joy"—in extracting all *time* from the verses of Chaucer, Marvell, and Dryden, and so concluded that one nature wrote all the good books and one nature could read them. The bad books, one infers, were written by fragmentary individuals temporarily out of touch with the Over-Soul, and are bad because they do partake of their age and nation. "There is such equality and identity both of judgment and point of view in the narrative that it is plainly the work of one all-seeing, all-hearing gentleman." We have labored to restore the historical time to Chaucer and Dryden; we do not find it at all plain that they were mouthpieces of one all-seeing agency, and we are sure that if there is any such universal agent he certainly is not a gentleman. We are exasperated with Emerson's tedious habit of seeing everything *sub specie aeternitatis*. When we find him writing in 1872, just before his mind and memory began that retreat into the Over-Soul which makes his last years so pathetic, that while in our day we have witnessed great revolutions in religion we do not therefore lose faith "in the eternal pillars which we so differently name, but cannot choose but see their identity in all healthy souls," we are ready to agree heartily with Walt Whitman, who growled that Emerson showed no signs of adapting himself to new times, but had "about the same attitude as twenty-five or thirty years ago," and that he himself was "utterly tired of these scholarly things." We may become even more tired of scholarly things when we find that from the very beginning Emerson conceived the movement which we call transcendentalism as one more expression of the benign gentleman who previously had spoken in the persons of Socrates and Zoroaster, Mohammed and Buddha, Shakespeare and St. Paul. He does not assist our quest for native origins, indeed for any origins which we are prepared to credit, when he says in 1842, in the Boston Masonic Temple, that transcendentalism is a "Saturnalia of Faith," an age-old way of thinking which, falling upon Roman times, made Stoic philosophers; falling on despotic times, made Catos and Brutuses; on Popish times, made Protestants; "on prelatical times, made Puritans and Quakers; and falling on Unitarian and commercial times, makes the peculiar shades of Idealism which we know." Were we to take him at his word, and agree that he himself was a

Stoic revisiting the glimpses of the moon, and that Henry Thoreau was Cato redivivus, we might then decide that both of them could fetch the shades of their idealism from ancient Rome or, if they wished, from Timbuktu, and that they would bear at best only an incidental relation to the American scene. We might conclude with the luckless San Francisco journalist, assigned the task of reporting an Emerson lecture, who wrote, "All left the church feeling that an elegant tribute had been paid to the Creative genius of the First Cause," but we should not perceive that any compliments had been paid to the intellectual history of New England.

Still, to take Emerson literally is often hazardous. We may allow him his Stoics, his Catos and Brutuses, for rhetorical embellishment. He is coming closer home, however, when he comes to Puritans and Quakers, to Unitarian and commercial times. Whether he intended it or not, this particular sequence constitutes in little an intellectual and social history of New England: first Puritans and Quakers, then Unitarians and commercial times, and now transcendentalists! Emerson contended that when poets spoke out of the transcendental Reason, which knows the eternal correspondence of things, rather than out of the shortsighted Understanding—which dwells slavishly in the present, the expedient, and the customary, and thinks in terms of history, economics, and institutions—they builded better than they knew. When they were ravished by the imagination, which makes every dull fact an emblem of the spirit, and were not held earthbound by the fancy, which knows only the surfaces of things, they brought their creations from no vain or shallow thought. Yet he did not intend ever to dispense with the understanding and the fancy, to forget the customary and the institutional—as witness his constant concern with "manners." He would not raise the siege of his hencoop to march away to a pretended siege of Babylon; though he was not conspicuously successful with a shovel in his garden, he was never, like Elizabeth Peabody, so entirely subjective as to walk straight into a tree because "I saw it, but I did not realize it." Could it be, therefore, that while his reason was dreaming among the Upanishads, and his imagination reveling with Swedenborg, his understanding perceived that on the plain of material causation the transcendentalism of New England had some connection with New England experience, and that his fancy, which remained at home with the customary and with history, guided this choice of words? Did these lower faculties contrive, by that cunning which distinguishes them from reason and imagination in the very moment when transcendentalism was being proclaimed a saturnalia of faith, that there should appear a cryptic suggestion that it betokened less an Oriental ecstasy and more a natural reaction of some descendants of Puritans and Quakers to Unitarian and commercial times?

I have called Emerson mystical and pantheistical. These are difficult adjectives; we might conveniently begin with Webster's dictionary, which declares mysticism to be the doctrine that the ultimate nature of reality or of the divine essence may be known by an immediate insight. The connotations of pantheism are infinite, but in general a pantheist holds that the universe itself is God, or that God is the combined forces and laws manifested in the existing universe, that God is, in short, both the slayer and the slain. Emerson and the others might qualify their doctrine, but when Professor Andrews Norton read that in the woods "I become a transparent eyeball; I am nothing, I see all; the currents of the Universal Being circulate through me; I am part or particle of God," in his forthright fashion he could not help perceiving that this was both mysticism and pantheism, and so attacking it as "the latest form of infidelity."

Could we go back to the Puritans whom Emerson adduced as his predecessors, and ask the Emersons and Ripleys, not to mention the Winthrops, Cottons, and Mathers, of the seventeenth century whether the eyeball passage was infidelity, there would be no doubt about the answer. They too might call it the "latest" form of infidelity, for in the first years of New England Winthrop and Cotton had very bitter experience with a similar doctrine. Our wonder is that they did not have more. To our minds, no longer at home in the fine distinctions of theology, it might seem that from the Calvinist doctrine of regeneration, from the theory that a regenerate soul receives an influx of divine spirit, and is joined to God by a direct infusion of His grace, we might deduce the possibility of receiving all instruction immediately from the indwelling spirit, through an inward communication which is essentially mystical. Such was exactly the deduction of Mistress Anne Hutchinson, for which she was expelled into Rhode Island.

It was exactly the conclusion of the Quakers, who added that every man was naturally susceptible to this inward communication, that he did not need a special and supernatural dispensation. Quakers also were cast into Rhode Island or, if they refused to stay there, hanged on Boston Common. Emerson, descendant of Puritans, found the descendants of Quakers "a sublime class of speculators," and wrote in 1835 that they had been the most explicit teachers "of the highest article to which human faith soars [,] the strict union of the willing soul to God & so the soul's access at all times to a verdict upon every question which the opinion of all mankind cannot shake & which the opinion of all mankind cannot confirm." But his ancestors had held that while the soul does indeed have an access to God, it receives from the spirit no verdict upon any question, only a dutiful disposition to accept the verdict confirmed by Scripture, by authority, and by logic. As Roger Clap remarked, both Anne Hutchinson and the Quakers "would talk of the Spirit, and of revelations by the Spirit without the Word, . . . of the Light within them, rejecting the holy Scripture"; and the Puritan minister declared that the errors of the Antinomians, "like strong wine, make men's judgements reel and stagger, who are drunken therwith." The more one studies the history of Puritan New England, the more astonished he becomes at the amount of reeling and staggering there was in it.

These seventeenth-century "infidels" were more interested in enlarging the soul's access to God from within than in exploring the possibilities of an access from without, from nature. But if we, in our interrogation of the shades of Puritans, were to ask them whether there exists a spirit that rolls through all things and propels all things, whose dwelling is the light of setting suns, and the round ocean, and the mind of man, a spirit from whom we should learn to be disturbed by the joy of elevated thoughts, the Puritans would feel at once that we needed looking after. They would concede that the visible universe is the handiwork of God, that He governs it and is present in the flight of every sparrow, the fall of every stone, the rising and setting of suns, in the tempests of the round ocean. "Who set those candles, those torches of heaven, on the table? Who hung out those lanterns in heaven to enlighten a dark world?" asked the preacher, informing his flock that although we do not see God in nature, yet in it His finger is con-

stantly evident. The textbook of theology used at Harvard told
New England students that every creature would return into nothing if God did not uphold it—"the very cessation of Divine con-
servation, would without any other operation presently reduce
every Creature into nothing." In regard of His essence, said
Thomas Hooker, God is in all places alike, He is in all creatures
and beyond them, "hee is excluded *out* of no place, included *in* no
place." But it did not follow that the universe, though created by
God and sustained by His continuous presence, was God Himself.
We were not to go to nature and, by surrendering to the stream of
natural forces, derive from it our elevated thoughts. We were not
to become nothing and let the currents of Universal Being circulate through us. Whatever difficulties were involved in explaining
that the universe is the work of God but that we do not meet God
face to face in the universe, Puritan theologians knew that the distinction must be maintained, lest excitable Yankees reel and
stagger with another error which they would pretend was an elevated thought. The difficulties of explanation were so great that
the preachers often avoided the issue, declaring, "this is but a
curious question: therefore I will leave it," or remarking that the
Lord fills both heaven and earth, yet He is not in the world as the
soul is in the body, "but in an incomprehensible manner, which
we cannot expresse to you." Thomas Shepard in Cambridge tried
to be more explicit: the Godhead, he said, is common to everything and every man, even to the most wicked man, "nay, to the
vilest creature in the world." The same power that made a blade
of grass made also the angels, but grass and angels are not
the same substance, and so the spirit of God which is in the setting
sun and the round ocean is not the same manifestation which He
puts forth as a special and "supernatural" grace in the regenerate
soul. "There comes another spirit upon us, which common men
have not." This other spirit teaches us, not elevated thoughts, but
how to submit our corrupt thoughts to the rule of Scripture, to the
law and the gospel as expounded at Harvard College and by
Harvard graduates.

The reason for Puritan opposition to these ideas is not far to
seek. The Renaissance mind—which was still a medieval mind—
remembered that for fifteen hundred years Christian thinkers had
striven to conceive of the relation of God to the world in such a

fashion that the transcendence of God should not be called in question, that while God was presented as the creator and governor of the world, He would always be something other than the world itself. Both mysticism and pantheism, in whatever form, identified Him with nature, made Him over in the image of man, interpreted Him in the terms either of human intuitions or of human perceptions, made Him one with the forces of psychology or of matter. The Renaissance produced a number of eccentrics who broached these dangerous ideas—Giordano Bruno, for instance, who was burned at the stake by a sentence which Catholics and Calvinists alike found just. The Puritans carried to New England the historic convictions of Christian orthodoxy, and in America found an added incentive for maintaining them intact. Puritanism was not merely a religious creed and a theology, it was also a program for society. We go to New England, said John Winthrop, to establish a due form of government, both civil and ecclesiastical, under the rule of law and Scripture. It was to be a medieval society of status, with every man in his place and a place for every man; it was to be no utopia of rugged individualists and transcendental freethinkers. But if Anne Hutchinson was correct, and if men could hear the voice of God within themselves, or if they could go into the woods and feel the currents of Universal Being circulate through them—in either event they would pay little heed to governors and ministers. The New England tradition commenced with a clear understanding that both mysticism and pantheism were heretical, and also with a frank admission that such ideas were dangerous to society, that men who imbibed noxious errors from an inner voice or from the presence of God in the natural landscape would reel and stagger through the streets of Boston and disturb the civil peace.

Yet from the works of the most orthodox of Calvinists we can perceive that the Puritans had good cause to be apprehensive lest mystical or pantheistical conclusions arise out of their premises. Anne Hutchinson and the Quakers commenced as Calvinists; from the idea of regeneration they drew, with what seemed to them impeccable logic, the idea that God imparted His teaching directly to the individual spirit. With equal ease others could deduce from the doctrines of divine creation and providence the idea that God was immanent in nature. The point might be put thus: there was in Puritanism a piety, a religious passion, the sense of an inward communication and of the divine symbolism of nature. One side of the Puritan nature hungered for these excitements; certain of its appetites desired these satisfactions and therefore found delight and ecstasy in the doctrines of regeneration and providence. But in Puritanism there was also another side, an ideal of social conformity, of law and order, of regulation and control. At the core of the theology there was an indestructible element which was mystical, and a feeling for the universe which was almost pantheistic; but there was also a social code demanding obedience to external law, a code to which good people voluntarily conformed and to which bad people should be made to conform. It aimed at propriety and decency, the virtues of middle-class respectability, self-control, thrift, and dignity, at a discipline of the emotions. It demanded, as Winthrop informed the citizens of Massachusetts Bay in 1645, that men forbear to exercise the liberty they had by nature, the freedom to do anything they chose, and having entered into society thereafter, devote themselves to doing only that which the authorities defined as intrinsically "good, just and honest." The New England tradition contained a dual heritage, the heritage of the troubled spirit and the heritage of wordly caution and social conservatism. It gave with one hand what it took away with the other: it taught men that God is present to their intuitions and in the beauty and terror of nature, but it disciplined them into subjecting their intuitions to the wisdom of society and their impressions of nature to the standards of decorum.

In the eighteenth century, certain sections of New England, or certain persons, grew wealthy. It can hardly be a coincidence that among those who were acquiring the rewards of industry and commerce there should be progressively developed the second part of the heritage, the tradition of reason and criticism, and that among them the tradition of emotion and ecstasy should dwindle. Even though a few of the clergy, like Jonathan Mayhew and Lemuel Briant, were moving faster than their congregations, yet in Boston and Salem, the centers of shipping and banking, ministers preached rationality rather than dogma, the Newtonian universe and the sensational psychology rather than providence and innate depravity. The back country, the Connecticut Valley, burst into flame with the Great Awakening of the 1740's; but the massive Charles Chauncy, minister at the First Church, the successor of John Cotton, declared that "the passionate discovery" of divine love is not a good evidence of election. "The surest and most substantial Proof is, *Obedience to the Commandments of God,* and the *stronger* the Love, the more uniform, steady and pleasant will be this *Obedience.*" Religion is of the understanding as well as of the affections, and when the emotions are stressed at the expense of reason, "it can't be but People should run into Disorders." In his ponderous way, Chauncy was here indulging in Yankee understatement. During the Awakening the people of the back country ran into more than disorders; they gave the most extravagant exhibition of staggering and reeling that New England had yet beheld. Chauncy was aroused, not merely because he disapproved of displays of emotion, but because the whole society seemed in danger when persons who made a high pretense to religion displayed it in their conduct "as something wild and fanciful." On the contrary, he stoutly insisted, true religion is sober and well-behaved; as it is taught in the Bible, "it approves itself to the Understanding and Conscience, . . . and is in the best Manner calculated to promote the Good of Mankind." The transformation of this segment of Puritanism from a piety to an ethic, from a religious faith to a social code, was here completed, although an explicit break with the formal theology was yet to come.

Charles Chauncy had already split the Puritan heritage. Emerson tells that Chauncy, going into his pulpit for the Thursday lecture (people at that time came all the way from Salem to hear him), was informed that a little boy had fallen into Frog Pond and drowned. Requested to improve the occasion,

> the doctor was much distressed, and in his prayer he hesitated, he tried to make soft approaches, he prayed for Harvard College, he prayed for the schools, he implored the Divine Being "to—to—to bless to them all the boy that was this morning drowned in Frog Pond."

But Jonathan Edwards felt an ardency of soul which he knew not how to express, a desire "to lie in the dust, and to be full of Christ alone; to love him with a holy and pure love; to trust in him; to live upon him; to serve and follow him; and to be perfectly sanctified and made pure, with a divine and heavenly purity." To one who conceived the highest function of religion to be the promotion

of the good of mankind, Jonathan Edwards stood guilty of foment-
ing disorders. Chauncy blamed Edwards for inciting the populace,
and was pleased when the congregation at Northampton, refusing
to measure up to the standards of sanctification demanded by Edwards, banished him into the wilderness of Stockbridge. Edwards,
though he was distressed over the disorders of the Awakening,
would never grant that a concern for the good of mankind
should take precedence over the desire to be perfectly sanctified
and made pure. In his exile at Stockbridge he wrote the great
tracts which have secured his fame for all time, the magnificent
studies of the freedom of the will, of the nature of true virtue, of
the purpose of God in creating the universe, in which Chauncy
and Harvard College were refuted; in which, though still in the
language of logic and systematic theology, the other half of the
Puritan heritage—the sense of God's overwhelming presence in
the soul and in nature—once more found perfect expression.

   Though the treatises on the will and on virtue are the
more impressive performances, for our purposes the eloquent *Dissertation Concerning the End for which God Created the World* is the
more relevant, if only because when he came to this question
Edwards was forced to reply specifically to the scientific rationalism toward which Chauncy and Harvard College were tending.
He had, therefore, to make even more explicit than did the earlier
divines the doctrines which verged upon both mysticism and
pantheism, the doctrines of inward communication and of the divine in nature. It was not enough for Edwards to say, as John
Cotton had done, that God created the world out of nothing to
show His glory; rationalists in Boston could reply that God's glory
was manisfested in the orderly machine of Newtonian physics, and
that a man glorified God in such a world by going about his rational business: real estate, the triangular trade, or the manufac-
ture of rum out of smuggled molasses. God did not create the
world, said Edwards, merely to exhibit His glory; He did not
create it out of nothing simply to show that He could: He who is
Himself the source of all being, the substance of all life, created
the world out of Himself by a diffusion of Himself into time and
space. He made the world, not by sitting outside and above it, by
modeling it as a child models sand, but by an extension of Himself, by taking upon Himself the forms of stones and trees and of

man. He created without any ulterior object in view, neither for
His glory nor for His power, but for the pure joy of self-expression,
as an artist creates beauty for the love of beauty. God does
not need a world or the worship of man; He is perfect in Himself.
If He bothers to create, it is out of the fullness of His own nature,
the overflowing virtue that is in Him. Edwards did not use my
simile of the artist; his way of saying it was, "The disposition to
communicate himself, or diffuse his own fulness, which we must
conceive of as being originally in God as a perfection of his nature, was what moved him to create the world," but we may still
employ the simile because Edwards invested his God with the sub-
blime egotism of a very great artist. God created by the laws of
His own nature, with no thought of doing good for anybody or for
mankind, with no didactic purpose, for no other reason but the joy
of creativeness. "It is a regard to himself that disposes him to diffuse and communicate himself. It is such a delight in his own internal fulness and glory, that disposes him to an abundant effusion
and emanation of that glory."

Edwards was much too skilled in the historic problems of
theology to lose sight of the distinction between God and the world
or to fuse them into one substance, to blur the all-important
doctrine of the divine transcendence. He forced into his system
every safeguard against identifying the inward experience of the
saint with the Deity Himself, or of God with nature. Nevertheless,
assuming, as we have some right to assume, that what subsequent
generations find to be a hidden or potential implication in a
thought is a part of that thought, we may venture to feel that
Edwards was particularly careful to hold in check the mystical
and pantheistical tendencies of his teaching because he himself
was so apt to become a mystic and a pantheist. The imagery in
which a great thinker expresses his sense of things is often more
revealing than his explicit contentions, and Edwards betrays the
nature of his insight when he uses as the symbol of God's relation
to the world the metaphor that has perennially been invoked by
mystics, the metaphor of light and of the sun:

> And [it] is fitly compared to an effulgence or emanation of light from
> a luminary, by which this glory of God is abundantly represented in
> Scripture. Light is the external expression, exhibition and manifestation
> of the excellency of the luminary, of the sun for instance: it is the

abundant, extensive emanation and communication of the fulness of the sun to innumerable beings that partake of it. It is by this that the sun itself is seen, and his glory beheld, and all other things are discovered; it is by a participation of this communication from the sun, that surrounding objects receive all their lustre, beauty and brightness. It is by this that all nature is quickened and receives life, comfort, and joy.

Here is the respect that makes Edwards great among theologians, and here in fact he strained theology to the breaking point. Holding himself by brute will power within the forms of ancient Calvinism, he filled those forms with a new and throbbing spirit. Beneath the dogmas of the old theology he discovered a different cosmos from that of the seventeenth century, a dynamic world, filled with the presence of God, quickened with divine life, pervaded with joy and ecstasy. With this insight he turned to combat the rationalism of Boston, to argue that man cannot live by Newtonian schemes and mathematical calculations, but only by surrender to the will of God, by reflecting back the beauty of God as a jewel gives back the light of the sun. But another result of Edward's doctrine, one which he would denounce to the nethermost circle of Hell but which is implicit in the texture, if not in the logic, of his thought, could very easily be what we have called mysticism or pantheism, or both. If God is diffused through nature, and the substance of man is the substance of God, then it may follow that man is divine, that nature is the garment of the Over-Soul, that man must be self-reliant, and that when he goes into the woods the currents of Being will indeed circulate through him. All that prevented this deduction was the orthodox theology, supposedly derived from the Word of God, which taught that God and nature are not one, that man is corrupt and his self-reliance is reliance on evil. But take away the theology, remove this overlying stone of dogma from the wellsprings of Puritan conviction, and both nature and man become divine.

We know that Edwards failed to revitalize Calvinism. He tried to fill the old bottles with new wine, yet none but himself could savor the vintage. Meanwhile, in the circles where Chauncy had begun to reëducate the New England taste, there developed, by a very gradual process, a rejection of the Westminster Confession, indeed of all theology, and at last emerged the Unitarian

churches. Unitarianism was entirely different wine from any that
had ever been pressed from the grapes of Calvinism, and in entirely new bottles, which the merchants of Boston found much to their
liking. It was a pure, white, dry claret that went well with dinners
served by the Harvard Corporation, but it was mild and was
guaranteed not to send them home reeling and staggering. As
William Ellery Channing declared, to contemplate the horrors of
New England's ancestral creed is "a consideration singularly fitted
to teach us tolerant views of error, and to enjoin caution and
sobriety."

In Unitarianism one half of the New England tradition—that
which inculcated caution and sobriety—definitely cast off all allegiance to the other. The ideal of decorum, of law and self-control,
was institutionalized. Though Unitarianism was "liberal" in theology, it was generally conservative in its social thinking and in its
metaphysics. Even Channing, who strove always to avoid controversy
and to appear "mild and amiable," was still more of an enthusiast
than those he supplied with ideas, as was proved when almost
alone among Unitarian divines he spoke out against slavery. He
frequently found himself thwarted by the suavity of Unitarian
breeding. In his effort to establish a literary society in Boston, he
repaired, as Emerson tells the story, to the home of Dr. John
Collins Warren, where

> he found a well-chosen assembly of gentlemen variously distinguished;
> there was mutual greeting and introduction, and they were chatting
> agreeably on indifferent matters and drawing gently towards their
> great expectation, when a side-door opened, the whole company
> streamed in to an oyster supper, crowned by excellent wines; and so
> ended the first attempt to establish aesthetic society in Boston.

But if the strain in the New England tradition which flowered so
agreeably in the home of Dr. Warren, the quality that made for
reason and breeding and good suppers, found itself happily
divorced from enthusiasm and perfectly enshrined in the liberal
profession of Unitarianism, what of the other strain? What of the
mysticism, the hunger of the soul, the sense of divine emanation in
man and in nature, which had been so important an element in
the Puritan character? Had it died out of New England? Was it to
live, if at all, forever caged and confined in the prison house of
Calvinism? Could it be asserted only by another Edwards in an-

other treatise on the will and a new dissertation on the end for which God created the universe? Andover Seminary was, of course, turning out treatises and dissertations, and there were many New Englanders outside of Boston who were still untouched by Unitarianism. But for those who had been "liberated" by Channing and Norton, who could no longer express their desires in the language of a creed that had been shown to be outworn, Calvinism was dead. Unitarianism rolled away the heavy stone of dogma that had sealed up the mystical springs in the New England character; as far as most Unitarians were concerned, the stone could now be lifted with safety, because to them the code of caution and sobriety, nourished on oyster suppers, would serve quite as well as the old doctrines of original sin and divine transcendence to prevent mankind from reeling and staggering in freedom. But for those in whom the old springs were still living, the removal of the theological stopper might mean a welling up and an overflowing of long suppressed desires. And if these desires could no longer be satisfied in theology, toward what objects would they now be turned? If they could no longer be expressed in the language of supernatural regeneration and divine sovereignty, in what language were they to be described?

The answer was not long forthcoming. If the inherent mysticism, the ingrained pantheism, of certain Yankees could not be stated in the old terms, it could be couched in the new terms of transcendental idealism, of Platonism, of Swedenborg, of "Tintern Abbey" and the Bhagavad-Gita, in the eclectic and polyglot speech of the Over-Soul, in "Brahma," in "Self-Reliance," in *Nature*. The children of Puritans could no longer say that the visible fabric of nature was quickened and made joyful by a diffusion of the fullness of God, but they could recapture the Edwardsean vision by saying, "Nature can only be conceived as existing to a universal and not to a particular end; to a universe of ends, and not to one,—a work of *ecstasy,* to be represented by a circular movement, as intention might be signified by a straight line of definite length." But in this case the circular conception enjoyed one great advantage—so it seemed at the time— that it had not possessed for Edwards: the new generation of ecstatics had learned from Channing and Norton, from the prophets of intention and the straight line of definite length, that men did not need to grovel in the dust. They did not have to throw themselves on the ground, as did Edwards, with a sense of their own unworthiness; they could say without trepidation that no concept of the understanding, no utilitarian consideration for the good of mankind, could account for any man's existence, that there was no further reason than *"so it was to be."* Overtones of the seventeenth century become distinctly audible when Emerson declares, "The *royal* reason, the Grace of God, seems the only description of our multiform but ever identical fact," and the force of his heredity is manifest when he must go on to say, having mentioned the grace of God, "There is the incoming or the receding of God," and as Edwards also would have said, "we can show neither how nor why." In the face of this awful and arbitrary power, the Puritan had been forced to conclude that man was empty and insignificant, and account for its recedings on the hypothesis of innate depravity. Emerson does not deny that such reflections are in order; when we view the fact of the inexplicable recedings "from the platform of action," when we see men left high and dry without the grace of God, we see "Self-accusation, remorse, and the didactic morals of self-denial and strife with sin"; but our enlightenment, our liberation from the sterile dogmas of Calvinism, enables us also to view the fact from "the platform of intellection," and in this view "there is nothing for us but praise and wonder." The ecstasy and the vision which Calvinists knew only in the moment of vocation, the passing of which left them agonizingly aware of depravity and sin, could become the permanent joy of those who had put aside the conception of depravity, and the moments between could be filled no longer with self-accusation but with praise and wonder. Unitarianism had stripped off the dogmas, and Emerson was free to celebrate purely and simply the presence of God in the soul and in nature, the pure metaphysical essence of the New England tradition. If he could no longer publish it as orthodoxy, he could speak it fearlessly as the very latest form of infidelity.

At this point there might legitimately be raised a question whether my argument is anything more than obscurantism. Do words like "New England tradition" and "Puritan heritage" mean anything concrete and tangible? Do they "explain" anything? Do habits of thought persist in a society as acquired characteristics, and by what mysterious alchemy are they transmitted in the blood stream? I am as guilty as Emerson himself if I treat ideas as a self-contained rhetoric, forgetting that they are, as we are now discovering, weapons, the weapons of classes and interests, a masquerade of power relations.

Yet Emerson, transcendental though he was, could see in his own ideas a certain relation to society. In his imagination transcendentalism was a saturnalia of faith, but in his fancy it was a reaction against Unitarianism and in his understanding a revulsion against commercialism. We can improve his hint by remarking the obvious connection between the growth of rationalism in New England and the history of eighteenth-century capitalism. Once the Unitarian apologists had renounced the Westminster Confession, they attacked Calvinism not merely as irrational but as a species of pantheism, and in their eyes this charge was sufficient condemnation in itself. Calvinism, said Channing, robs the mind of self-determining force and makes men passive recipients of the universal force:

> It is a striking fact that the philosophy which teaches that matter is an inert substance, and that God is the force which pervades it, has led men to question whether any such thing as matter exists. . . . Without a free power in man, he is nothing. The divine agent within him is every thing, Man acts only in show. He is a phenomenal existence, under which the One Infinite Power is manifested; and is this much better than Pantheism?

One does not have to be too prone to economic interpretation in order to perceive that there was a connection between the Unitarian insistence that matter is substance and not shadow, that men are self-determining agents and not passive recipients of Infinite Power, and the practical interests of the society in which Unitarianism flourished. Pantheism was not a marketable commodity on State Street, and merchants could most successfully conduct their business if they were not required to lie in the dust and desire to be full of the divine agent within.

Hence the words "New England tradition" and "Puritan heritage" can be shown to have some concrete meaning when applied to the gradual evolution of Unitarianism out of the seventeenth-century background; there is a continuity both social and intellectual. But what of the young men and young women, many of them born and reared in circles in which, Channing said,

"Society is going forward in intelligence and charity," who in their very adolescence instinctively turned their intelligence and even their charity against this liberalism, and sought instead the strange and uncharitable gods of transcendentalism? Why should Emerson and Margaret Fuller, almost from their first reflective moments, have cried out for a philosophy which would reassure them that matter is the shadow and spirit the substance, that man acts by an influx of power—why should they deliberately return to the bondage from which Channing had delivered them? Even before he entered the divinity school Emerson was looking askance at Unitarianism, writing in his twentieth year to his southern friend, John Boynton Hill, that for all the flood of genius and knowledge being poured out from Boston pulpits, the light of Christianity was lost: "An exemplary Christian of today, and even a Minister, is content to be just such a man as was a good Roman in the days of Circero." Andrews Norton would not have been distressed over his observation, but young Emerson was. "Presbyterianism & Calvinism at the South," he wrote, "at least make Christianity a more real & tangible system and give it some novelties which were worth unfolding to the ignorance of men." Thus much, but no more, he could say for "orthodoxy": "When I have been to Cambridge & studied Divinity, I will tell you whether I can make out for myself any better system than Luther or Calvin, or the *liberal besoms* of modern days." The "Divinity School Address" was forecast in these youthful lines, and Emerson the man declared what the boy had divined when he ridiculed the "pale negations" of Unitarianism, called it an "icehouse," and spoke of "the corpse-cold Unitarianism of Harvard College and Brattle Street." Margaret Fuller thrilled to the epistle of John read from a Unitarian pulpit: "Every one that loveth is born of God, and knoweth God," but she shuddered as the preacher straightway rose up "to deny mysteries, to deny second birth, to deny influx, and to renounce the sovereign gift of insight, for the sake of what he deemed a *'rational'* exercise of will." This Unitarianism, she argued in her journal, has had its place, but the time has now come for reinterpreting old dogmas: "For one I would now preach the Holy Ghost as zealously as they have been preaching Man, and faith instead of the understanding, and mysticism instead &c—." And there, characteristically enough, she remarks, "But why go on?"

A complete answer to the question of motives is probably not possible as yet. Why Waldo and Margaret in the 1820's and '30's should instinctively have revolted against a creed that had at last been perfected as the ideology of their own group, of respectable, prosperous, middle-class Boston and Cambridge—why these youngsters, who by all the laws of economic determinism ought to have been the white-headed children of Unitarianism, elected to become transcendental black sheep, cannot be decided until we know more about the period than has been told in *The Flowering of New England* and more about the nature of social change in general. The personal matter is obviously of crucial importance. The characters of the transcendentalists account for their having become transcendental; still two facts of a more historical nature seem to me worth considering in the effort to answer our question.

The emergence of Unitarianism out of Calvinism was a very gradual, almost an imperceptible, process. One can hardly say at what point rationalists in eastern Massachusetts ceased to be Calvinists, for they were forced to organize into a separate church only after the development of their thought was completed. Consequently, although young men and women in Boston might be, like Waldo and Margaret, the children of rationalists, all about them the society still bore the impress of Calvinism: the theological break had come, but not the cultural. In a thousand ways the forms of society were still those determined by the ancient orthodoxy, piously observed by persons who no longer believed in the creed. We do not need to posit some magical transmission of Puritanism from the seventeenth to the nineteenth century in order to account for the fact that these children of Unitarians felt emotionally starved and spiritually undernourished. In 1859 James Cabot sent Emerson *The Life of Trust*, a crude narrative by one George Muller of his personal conversations with the Lord, which Cabot expected Emerson to enjoy as another instance of man's communion with the Over-Soul, which probably seemed to Cabot no more crackbrained than many of the books Emerson admired. Emerson returned the volume, accompanied by a vigorous rebuke to Cabot for occupying himself with such trash:

> I sometimes think that you & your coevals missed much that I & mine found: for Calvinism was still robust & effective on life & character in all the people who surrounded my childhood, & gave a deep religious tinge to manners & conversation. I doubt the race is now

extinct, & certainly no sentiment has taken its place on the new generation,—none as pervasive & controlling. But they were a high tragic school, & found much of their own belief in the grander traits of the Greek mythology,—Nemesis, the Fates, & the Eumenides, and, I am sure, would have raised an eyebrow at this pistareen Providence of . . . George Muller.

At least two members of the high tragic school Emerson knew intimately and has sympathetically described for us—his step-grandfather, the Reverend Ezra Ripley, and his aunt, Mary Moody Emerson. Miss Emerson put the essence of the Puritan aesthetic into one short sentence: "How insipid is fiction to a mind touched with immortal views!" Speaking as a Calvinist, she anticipated Max Weber's discovery that the Protestant ethic fathered the spirit of capitalism, in the pungent observation, "I respect in a rich man the order of Providence." Emerson said that her journal "marks the precise time when the power of the old creed yielded to the influence of modern science and humanity"; still in her the old creed never so far yielded its power to the influence of modern humanity but that she could declare, with a finality granted only to those who have grasped the doctrine of divine sovereignty, "I was never patient with the faults of the good." When Thomas Cholmondeley once suggested to Emerson that many of his ideas were similar to those of Calvinism, Emerson broke in with irritation, "I see you are speaking of something which had a meaning once, but is now grown obsolete. Those words formerly stood for something, and the world got good from them, but not now." The old creed would no longer serve, but there had been power in it, a power conspicuously absent from the pale negations of Unitarianism. At this distance in time, we forget that Emerson was in a position fully to appreciate what the obsolete words had formerly stood for, and we are betrayed by the novelty of his vocabulary, which seems to have no relation to the jargon of Calvinism, into overlooking a fact of which he was always aware—the great debt owed by his generation "to that old religion which, in the childhood of most of us, still dwelt like a sabbath morning in the country of New England, teaching privation, self-denial and sorrow!" The retarded tempo of the change in New England, extending through the eighteenth into the nineteenth century, makes comprehensible why young Unitarians had enough contact with the past to receive from it a religious standard by which to condemn the pallid and unexciting liberalism of Unitarianism.

Finally, we do well to remember that what we call the transcendental movement was not an isolated phenomenon in nineteenth-century New England. As Professor Whicher has remarked, "Liberal ideas came slowly to the Connecticut Valley." They came slowly also to Andover Theological Seminary. But slowly they came, and again undermined Calvinist orthodoxies as they had undermined orthodoxy in eighteenth-century Boston; and again they liberated a succession of New Englanders from the Westminster Confession, but they did not convert them into rationalists and Unitarians. Like Emerson, when other New Englanders were brought to ask themselves, "And what is to replace for us the piety of that race?" they preferred to bask "in the great morning which rises forever out of the eastern sea" rather than to rest content with mere liberation. "I stand here to say, Let us worship the mighty and transcendent Soul"—but not the good of mankind! Over and again the rational attack upon Calvinism served only to release energies which then sought for new forms of expression in directions entirely opposite to rationalism. Some, like Sylvester Judd, revolted against the Calvinism of the Connecticut Valley, went into Unitarianism, and then came under the spell of Emerson's transcendentalist tuition. Others, late in the century, sought out new heresies, not those of transcendentalism, but interesting parallels and analogues. Out of Andover came Harriet Beecher Stowe, lovingly but firmly underlining the emotional restrictions of Calvinism in *The Minister's Wooing* and *Oldtown Folks,* while she herself left the grim faith at last for the ritualism of the Church of England. Out of Andover also came Elizabeth Stuart Phelps in feverish revolt against the hard logic of her father and grandfather, preaching instead the emotionalism of *Gates Ajar.* In Connecticut, Horace Bushnell, reacting against the dry intellectualism of Nathaniel Taylor's Calvinism just as Margaret Fuller had reacted a decade earlier against the dry rationalism of Norton's Unitarianism, read Coleridge with an avidity equal to hers and Emerson's, and by 1849 found the answer to his religious quest, as he himself said, "after all his thought and study, not as something reasoned out, but as an inspiration—a revelation from the mind of God himself." He published the revelation in a book, the very title of which tells the whole story, *Nature and the Supernatural To-gether Constituting One System of God,* wherein was preached anew the immanence of God in nature: "God is the spiritual reality of which nature is the manifestation." With this publication the latest—and yet the oldest—form of New England infidelity stalked in the citadel of orthodoxy, and Calvinism itself was, as it were, transcendentalized. At Amherst, Emily Dickinson's mental climate, in the Gilded Age, was still Emerson's; the break-up of Calvinism came later there than in Boston, but when it had come the poems of Emily Dickinson were filled with "Emersonian echoes," echoes which Professor Whicher wisely declines to point out because, as he says, resemblances in Emerson, Thoreau, Parker, and Emily Dickinson are not evidences of borrowings one from another, but their common response to the spirit of the time, even though the spirit reached Emily Dickinson a little later in time than it did Emerson and Thoreau. "Their work," he says, "was in various ways a fulfillment of the finer energies of a Puritanism that was discarding the husks of dogma." From the time of Edwards to that of Emerson, the husks of Puritanism were being discarded, but the energies of many Puritans were not yet diverted—they could not be diverted—from a passionate search of the soul and of nature, from the quest to which Calvinism had devoted them. These New Englanders—a few here and there—turned aside from the doctrines of sin and predestination, and thereupon sought with renewed fervor for the accents of the Holy Ghost in their own hearts and in woods and mountains. But now that the restraining hand of theology was withdrawn, there was nothing to prevent them, as there had been everything to prevent Edwards, from identifying their intuitions with the voice of God, or from fusing God and nature into the one substance of the transcendental imagination. Mystics were no longer inhibited by dogma. They were free to carry on the ancient New England propensity for reeling and staggering with new opinions. They could give themselves over, unrestrainedly, to becoming transparent eyeballs and debauches of dew.

Richard P. Adams

VIII

Emerson and the Organic Metaphor

The importance of the organic metaphor in Emerson's thinking and writing has been increasingly recognized in recent years. The formerly prevalent notion that Emerson was a great writer in spite of obvious faults and in the absence of most of the familiar virtues, that as a thinker he was rescued from his own contradictions only by some unexplainable, perhaps mystical, consistency in his character, has been forced into the background, though it still persists in many people's minds and in some published criticism.[1] It has been progressively corrected by such investigations as those of Henry D. Gray, Norman Foerster, Joseph Warren Beach, F. O. Matthiessen, Robert E. Spiller, Vivian C. Hopkins, and Sherman Paul, in which the romantic origins of Emerson's thought and art are explored, and in which organic theories are increasingly used to explain his meanings and to evaluate his aesthetic achievements.[2] I should like to carry this line of inquiry a little further, because I believe that Emerson should be placed more wholly in the romantic tradition than he has yet been, and that his importance depends on a more fundamental, consistent, and logical use than he has yet been shown to have made of the organic principle, which is one of the central concepts of romantic philosophy.[3]

From *Publications of the Modern Language Association*, Vol. LXIX, 1954, pp. 117–30. Reprinted by permission of the executive secretary of the Modern Language Association of America.

Let me begin by making some distinctions between the organic and the two most important other ways of looking at the universe which were available to Emerson in the 1820's. The first of these was formism, which has descended from Platonic idealism and which is mainly to be found in the humanistic tradition. Younger, but vastly more popular, was mechanism, characteristic of the "new philosophy" of science which had disturbed and then defeated the humanists in the seventeenth century and which has pretty much dominated mass thinking ever since. Because Emerson hated mechanism from the start, his problem was to find some more effective means of fighting it than those used unsuccessfully by the humanists. Like most romantics, he adopted the organic rather than the formistic theory, although he did not emphasize the differences between the two, perhaps because he did not see them very clearly and perhaps partly because he felt that the common antipathy to mechanism was more important. The distinction is none the less real.

When I suggest that Emerson was an organicist, I mean that he did not habitually think of the universe as a copy of ideal reality or form, in the Platonic manner, or as a vast self-regulating machine, in the manner of eighteenth-century scientific rationalists, but that he thought of it as if it were like a living plant or animal. Two crucial differences may be seen between this way of thinking and the others: first, that change, in the tradition of romantic organicism, is a good thing because it implies growth, or the quality of life, which is not inherent in the assumptions of either scientific mechanism or Platonic idealism; second, that organicism is more strongly synthetic than either of the others. A mechanist is inclined to feel that things can be best understood if they are separated into their component parts, and if each observed effect is assigned its proper cause. A formist also is likely to insist on the importance of distinctions, because each prototypical idea, being eternally itself, is different from every other idea. An organicist, however, tends to concentrate, often with a rather mystical air, on the wholeness of the whole, reluctant to analyze at all, maintaining with Wordsworth that "We murder to dissect," or with Blake that the atoms and particles into which the physicists divide the world "Are sands upon the Red Sea shore,/Where Israel's tents do shine so bright."

Reluctance to separate things can be a weakness, and roman-

tic writers who use this kind of thinking are sometimes vulnerable
to the favorite criticism of humanists, that their treatment blurs
the basic distinctions. However, organicism derives its greatest advantages from this same synthetic tendency. Alfred N. Whitehead
has sharply criticized the scheme of mechanistic materialism on the
ground that it gives "no reason in the nature of things why portions of material should have any physical relations to each other,"
and he favors "the abandonment of the traditional scientific materialism, and the substitution of an alternative doctrine of organism,"[4] citing the romantic nature poetry of Wordsworth and
others as a practical source of ideas for scientists today.

   Historically, then, the role of organicism would seem to be
that it offers a possible means of transcending the mechanistic difficulty in showing relationships, a problem that humanistic idealism does not solve. The way that organicists have of concentrating
on functional relations has in fact proved useful in many practical
activities, from architecture to the synthesis of rubber, as well as in
the fine arts and in metaphysics.

   If there were or could be such a thing as a perfect organicist,
Emerson was certainly not one. However, his most eloquent statements of belief are often remarkably similar to some of the best
descriptions of the organic theory available today. Let us consider,
for example, the following passage by Stephen C. Pepper:

> Organicism . . . is the world hypothesis that stresses the internal
> relatedness or coherence of things. It is impressed with the manner in
> which observations at first apparently unconnected turn out to be
> closely related, and with the fact that as knowledge progresses it be-
> comes more systematized. It conceives the value of our knowledge as
> proportional to the degree of integration it has attained, and comes to
> identify value with integration in all spheres. Value in the sphere of
> knowledge is integration of judgments; in the sphere of ethics, it is in-
> tegration of acts; in the sphere of art, it is integration of feelings. Finally,
> it conceives all of these as contained in a total integration of existence
> or reality.[5]

Organicism, by this account, is not concerned with ideal forms or
categorical distinctions, like formism, or with analysis of causes
and effects, like mechanism. Its aim is to realize the ultimate
organization of all things in a unity which includes them as they
are, a harmonious relationship of human experience with all the
processes of nature, or the universe.

   Now let us compare Emerson's familiar and justly famous

passage concerning the influence of nature on the scholar's mind
in the Phi Beta Kappa Address of 1837, "The American Scholar":

> Far too as her splendors shine, system on system shooting like rays, up-
> ward, downward, without centre, without circumference,—in the mass
> and in the particle, Nature hastens to render account of herself to the
> mind. Classification begins. To the young mind every thing is individ-
> ual, stands by itself. By and by, it finds how to join two things and see
> in them one nature; then three, then three thousand; and so, tyrannized
> over by its own unifying instinct, it goes on tying things together, di-
> minishing anomalies, discovering roots running under ground whereby
> contrary and remote things cohere and flower out from one stem. . . .
> The ambitious soul sits down before each refractory fact; one after
> another reduces all strange constitutions, all new powers, to their class
> and their law, and goes on forever to animate the last fibre of organiza-
> tion, the outskirts of nature, by insight.
>
> Thus to him, to this schoolboy under the bending dome of day, is
> suggested that he and it proceed from one root; one is leaf and one is
> flower; relation, sympathy, stirring in every vein (1, 85–86).[6]

Here Emerson is obviously in close agreement with the main tenet
of organicism as Pepper defines it, that the important thing to discover is not causes or archetypal ideas but relatedness, and his account of the progress of knowledge is the same, that it is a continuous integration of one fact with another, leading toward a total
integration of the universe. He takes pains to repudiate the formistic belief that each fact is a thing in itself, and he makes it
perfectly clear, especially in his final image, that he derives his
formula from the basic metaphor of the living plant.[7] This metaphor embodies the concept of progressive relatedness and ultimate
unity in which a great many romantic writers, especially those of
the more positive sort, appear to believe.[8]

There is a great deal of spadework still to be done on the
origins and development of this idea, especially in Germany,
whence it seems to have come to this country and to Emerson
chiefly by way of England and France. But this paper is not a
study of influences. How much Emerson's treatment of the organic
principle may have been conditioned by his reading I am not prepared to say, beyond a suggestion that whatever foreign seeds of
organic thought fell into his mind struck fertile ground there, and
very soon found themselves at home. Like anyone of independent
spirit, he chose his influences; they were not thrust upon him.

They helped him do what he wanted to do and would have done, though doubtless with greater effort and smaller success, without them.

The ideas were not brand new to him in 1837. He had used organic formulations in sermons as early as 1830,[9] a striking example occurring in the sermon on "Self and Others" first preached on 12 January 1831, where he praised "the perfection of that web of relations to all beings into which your own lot is woven," and made it very clear, in defining brotherhood, that the relations he meant were derived from the organic metaphor. As children of God, he said, "We live but in him, as the leaf lives in the tree. . . . We shall be parts of God, as the hand is part of the body, if only the hand had a will."[10] Like Whitman, Emerson simmered for a considerable time before coming to a boil, with the publication of *Nature* in 1836. And even *Nature*, the first really literary announcement of his theme, was not as strong as it might have been.

Nature has always seemed to me, in spite of its many brilliant passages, a fundamentally unsatisfactory piece of work. However, for that reason, an examination of it yields important clues to Emerson's difficulty in arriving at a coherent statement of his thoughts and beliefs. Its lack of unity may be explainable partly by the peristence of the sermon structure, with its firstly, secondly, and so on, which is poorly suited to the subject. But a more important reason, it seems to me, is that its language also fails to assimilate the organic idea which it struggles to express.

One reason for both these weaknesses may be that the strategy of the book was determined too early, before Emerson had gained a clear understanding of the gospel he wanted to preach. In a sermon on "Summer," first delivered on 14 June 1829, he had discussed nature under four headings very like the first four he was to use in 1836: first, the utilitarian function of plants in assimilating nutritious elements from the earth and making them fit for human sustenance ("Commodity"); second, the beauty of nature, which is not necessary for our physical welfare and must therefore be "to give pleasure" to our souls ("Beauty"); third, the correspondence between us and nature which makes everything in it "an emblem, a hieroglyphic," and a means of communicating the soul's truth among men ("Language"); and fourth, a moral influence admonishing us to do our duty as well as the plants do theirs ("Discipline").[11] On 6 January 1832, when he put down in his journal an outline of a book he thought of writing, he used a somewhat similar list of topics (II, 445).[12] And, when he finally began the work, at the end of his first European trip in September 1833, he was obviously still committed to the same general scheme. In these four headings, and more especially in the three he added, "Idealism," "Spirit," and "Prospects," he established only partly, and then in fragments, the desired sense of harmony with the world. His point of view was not steady enough; it shifted uncomfortably and unpredictably between something like Platonic idealism and something like romantic organicism, doing justice to neither.

The same awkwardness may be seen in the slight but irritating inappropriateness of diction that permeates the essay, especially in the chapter on "Language," where Emerson tried to make use of the Swedenborgian doctrine of correspondence, the theory that the world objectifies the mind of God and therefore also the similarly formed, though smaller, mind of man. The Swedenborgian correspondence, with its one-to-one ratio of idea and object, is not the same thing as the organic theory of functional and universal relationship, as Emerson himself later pointed out (*Works,* IV, 121). His eclectic use of it in *Nature* was as a steppingstone to the pure organic idea for which he had not yet mastered an effective vocabulary.

The essay itself seems less like a stepping-stone than a stumbling-block in Emerson's career; the last of his apprentice exercises rather than the first of his mature works; a thing that had to be done before he could do something better, to be put behind him before he could go ahead. It belongs to 1829 more than to 1836, and its publication represents a clearing up and clearing away of Emerson's accounts with his teachers and his own journals to that point, and brings him up to date. It is partly for that reason, I suspect, that when the pressure of the Phi Beta Kappa invitation was applied he was ready, though not without difficulty and worrying delays, to say more cogently what he thought in 1837.

"The American Scholar" seems to me in fact the best of Emerson's efforts to present his whole view in a single work. It is superior to *Nature* in many ways, but the important point for this study is that its consistency of tone and consecutiveness of argument are largely due to the fact that the organic metaphor is dominant from the first paragraph, which appeals for an American culture offering "something better than the exertions of mechanical skill," to the last, which calls on American scholars "to yield that peculiar fruit which each man was created to bear . . ." (*Works*, I, 81, 115). The central point, on which the whole essay depends, is that the social body of humanity is properly "One Man," in contrast to the present state of society, "in which the members have suffered amputation from the trunk, and strut about so many walking monsters,—a good finger, a neck, a stomach, an elbow, but never a man" (I, 82–83). That is, the organic wholeness of humanity and of individual men has been destroyed by mechanical specialization. And again, in an image parallel to those used in the sermon "Self and Others," mankind is compared to the fingers of a hand, which ought to cooperate in the functional unity of the organ to which they belong.

A striking feature of "The American Scholar" is the emphasis repeatedly placed on the principle of change, progression, and orginality implied in the metaphor of the living organism. The scholar, Emerson insists, cannot be content with merely assimilating other men's ideas; he must go on to create his own. He must be the publisher of living, contemporary truth, never merely the parrot of dead thoughts from the past. The object of knowledge is not a static, absolute ideal but a growing body, and the scholar who understands its character and his own "shall look forward to an ever expanding knowledge as to a becoming creator" (I, 86). He will be an original force in a changing world, which yet has finally a total unity of organization. It is the business of Man Thinking to understand, and the business of all mankind to act in harmony with the movement toward, this final unity. The great eloquence of the essay seems to derive largely from the fact that Emerson for a happy moment forgot the goal in his enthusiasm for the dynamic quality of the drive itself, the sense of creative activity resulting from original thinking in terms of the organic metaphor.

However, having made in this address one of the finest presentations of the organic idea yet published, Emerson found that he had not left all his troubles and doubts behind, but had exchanged one set of difficulties for another which was the more perplexing, as well as the more challenging, because it was new. It is still new, and some of the same difficulties are, as Whitehead has shown, among the crucial problems of philosophy in our own day,[13] though a century of progress in thinking about them enables us to gauge Emerson's failures, as well as his achievements, more accurately, perhaps, than Emerson could do. Some of his difficulties were caused by the historical situation, and these have been more or less outgrown and left behind. Others were caused by the nature of organicism itself, which, like any other philosophical system, has its gaps and weaknesses; these are still with us. And some, as might be expected, were due to Emerson's own peculiarities in applying organic theory to the business of thinking and writing; these offer the best and perhaps the only legitimate foothold for adverse criticism of his work.

The historical difficulty, that of newness, can be most easily seen in the heavy borrowings that Emerson, like Coleridge, levied on the language and apparently to some extent on the thinking of writers belonging to the formistic tradition of Platonic idealism, particularly the English humanists of the seventeenth century. In such men as Cudworth, More, Taylor, Hooker, Burnet, Herbert, Herrick, Donne, Jonson, Milton, and even Bacon and Newton, Emerson found, or thought he found, some of his strongest, most available predecessors and allies in the fight against mechanistic materialism.[14] As I have tried to indicate, their ideas were not really the same as his, and their language, when he borrowed it, was likely to prove inappropriate, though he had some justification in feeling that it offered the nearest practicable equivalent, at the time, for what he wanted to say. The strategy sometimes succeeded; an old term carefully redefined, such as Coleridge's kidnapped "Reason," might be used with telling effect. The result was less happy when Emerson, without giving his reader adequate notice, adopted the word "classification" or the word "law" from the older tradition and used it to mean the establishment of organic relationships between ideas, as he did for example in the passage quoted from "The American Scholar." Any reasonably careful examination will show, I think, that Emerson used Platonic, neo-Platonic, and sometimes mystical language to express ideas which are really neither Platonic, neo-Platonic, nor mystical. Plato, as critics have been coming more clearly to recognize, was only Emerson's ally, not his countryman, much less his ancestor.

The difficulty in the nature of organicism itself is that it contains a logical contradiction. Its most obvious weakness, as Pepper points out ((pp. 280–283), is the mutual incompatibility of what he calls its progressive and its ideal categories, that is, its dynamic and its static aspects. The organicist sees the world in two ways. In everyday experience it is a various and changing complex of phenomena, which he believes to be real in spite of the fragmentary and often irreconcilable appearances which it presents. But at the same time it is ultimately an integration (or, as Emerson would say, using the term in its original sense, an "organization") of everything in a unity which is not temporal, or various, or changing, and in which all fragments are related and all superficial inconsistencies reconciled. He may be tempted to suppose that the timeless unity is the real aspect and that experience seems fragmentary only because of his inability to comprehend the final unity; but he is really neither a dualistic nor a monistic idealist. He believes in the seamless continuity of all things, and he feels that material and temporal appearances are not false, or different from the ultimate reality, but parts of it. This reality, of course, does not consist of norms or patterns but is the single principle of organization that makes creation a universe instead of a multiverse. Stated crudely, the difficulty lies in believing that the universe really changes, but that it really does not change, a paradox which disappears in the image of the living tree but which is hard to resolve in any discursive treatment of the metaphor and its implications.

Emerson was aware of this problem and acutely conscious of his inability to solve it, as several passages in his journals and published works indicate. His best method of treating it was to make the inconsistency itself serve him in the dialectic movement of his thinking. "By obeying each thought frankly," he maintained, "by harping, or, if you will, pounding on each string, we learn at last its power. By the same obedience to other thoughts we learn theirs, and then comes some reasonable hope of harmonizing them" (*Works*, VI, 4). Or, more broadly, as he remarked later, "I might suggest that he who contents himself with dotting a fragmentary curve, recording only what facts he has observed, without attempting to arrange them within one outline, follows a system also,—a system as grand as any other, though he does not interfere with its vast curves by prematurely forcing them into a circle or ellipse . . ." (XII, 11–12). Emerson held, as an organicist will, that ultimately the relations between the apparently incompatible facts of experience were always there. Many of us are not capable of that belief, but if we are not, we can still respect Emerson's method, thus described, as a coherent and logical way of thinking, with characteristic virtues and uses, as well as limitations, like any other. It is not a closed system, but, as he says, it is a grand one, and it goes a long way, for me, toward explaining the larger consistency that most critics have sensed, without being able to account for it very well, in Emerson's work.

Weaknesses caused by the historical situation and by the inherent qualities of the doctrine can easily be forgiven; certain other weaknesses, which seem to be caused by Emerson's defective handling of the doctrine, must be counted as faults in his work. The most obvious of these probably lies in his cosmic optimism, which nearly all critics agree was often too easy. His statements were not always or even usually so carefully balanced and qualified as the one just cited. He tended to move too far toward the pole of unity and to ignore too much of our commonly frustrating and sometimes tragic experience of the confused, weltering world we live in. He knew about pain and poverty, love and hate, good and evil, accident and luck, and madness and ecstasy; but we sometimes feel, as he sometimes did, that he was not enough involved in them, that they did not have enough to do with his faith or his manner of arriving at it. We are too often asked to take his optimism straight, without the sense of its having been earned, and at such times we are likely to sympathize with objections made by Melville and Hawthorne, among others, to his enthusiastic, if not reckless, celebrations of the perfection of the universe. Cosmic optimism can be logically grounded on the premise that all things and events are ultimately organized in perfect unity, but it is a unity that we cannot see, and that Emerson cannot show us.

The fundamental tendency of the mind, according to him, and certainly it seems true of his mind, is to reduce all things to one law; and this tendency he felt to be right as well as inevitable. He was capable of saying, if not always of believing, that the "methodizing mind meets no resistance in its attempts." Moreover, he maintained, "It is necessary to suppose that every hose in Nature fits every hydrant; so only is combination, chemistry, vegetation, animation, intellection possible. Without identity at base, chaos must be forever" (*Works*, XII, 20). Faced with such a whole hog as that, a reader may well be excused for taking none. However, it is this belief which explains not only Emerson's optimism but all or nearly all of the difficult, paradoxical, daringly metaphorical, or at first glance apparently mystical passages in his works. It accounts for his feeling that every truth or partial truth, followed far enough, reaches identity with all other visions or versions of truth; that, if any man seems to disagree, "he only uses a different vocabulary from yours; it comes to the same thing" (*Journals*, II, 522); and "that if Buddah, Confucius, Socrates, Boehmen, George Fox, should meet they would perfectly understand and confirm each other's word."[15] It also supports his risky assertion in "Self-Reliance" that the farther we push our individual development, whatever direction it takes, the nearer we will come to comprehending the universal values. All these contentions are in some sense true, or at least reasonable, if we accept the assumptions that Emerson grounded on the organic metaphor; but most of us, having reservations about those premises, cannot wholly agree with his more extreme conclusions.

Another very frequent and cogent objection to Emerson's work is the pragmatic one that his essays and poems lack the organic unity that he aimed at in his thinking. F. O. Matthiessen, for example, says that "Emerson's writing was only too liable to exemplify the consequences of what he deemed the prevailing thought of his century, its reassertion of the Heraclitean doctrine of the Flowing" (p. 69). Matthiessen's objection is valid, if it can be grounded on the doctrine that the dynamism of romantic thought, properly understood, is not a flowing but a growing; not a featureless flux but the development of an organic structure with a strong though not rigid inner logic and an unbounded but not incoherent shape. Emerson's language, when he used the Heraclitean metaphor, as he did continually, betrayed his insecure grasp of the significantly different metaphor of the living plant. And his writings generally betrayed his insufficient appreciation of the fact that in an organic work of art there is just as great need for a tightly knit complex of inner functional relations as there is in a classical work for what we more familiarly know as form.

Most of the critics who have tried to defend Emerson against this objection have had to make so many concessions and reservations, and their comments have amounted to such faint praise, that the defense has fallen rather flat. Matthiessen, going out of his way to present a favorable explication of "Days" (which he does very convincingly), seems to abandon the rest of the canon to Heraclitean wateriness (pp. 59–64). W. T. Harris, writing in 1882, found a Coleridgean organic unity in "The Sphynx," "Each and All," "Uriel," *Nature, English Traits,* and "Experience," but not in other works, such as "The Over-Soul" and "Spiritual Laws," which he said only stated and did not develop their themes.[16] Walter Blair and Clarence Faust, though they intimate that other works might be defended, confine their discussion to "Art," "The Poet," "Each and All," and "Threnody."[17] These observations indicate, rightly enough I think, that Emerson created very few individual works which can be said to have anything like the organic unity which the New Critics and their predecessors in the romantic tradition have taught us to expect. Nevertheless I believe that Emerson was a great writer, and therefore that something remains to be explained.

The most promising approach that I have seen to such an explanation was first suggested by Harris in an article in 1884, in which he expanded and specified his previous discussion of unity in Emerson's work, using terms more nearly in harmony with his own predilection for the Hegelian system. Besides the Coleridgean organic unity which he had previously discussed, and which he now limited to works of "literary art" (that is, poems), he discovered in Emerson's prose essays a "dialectic unity" which was "an unfolding of the subject according to its natural growth in experience."[18] The words "unfolding" and "growth" make this look like a kind of unity that might be considered both logical and organic, which I am inclined to think it is. Harris went on to show in detail how Emerson had arrived at this unity in the essay "Experience," and to make a very good case for his successful practice of a dialectic method in his composition generally. Blair and Faust, adopting Harris' hint, have suggested a dialectic quality in Emerson's structural use of the "twice bisected line" of Plato, to whom Emerson himself ascribed a dialectic method in philosophy. And, most recently, Sherman Paul (pp. 117–118), building on both these studies, has attributed the same kind of dialectic unity very convincingly to the first series of *Essays* and to *The Conduct of Life*.

It seems to me that the twice bisected line, which implies a fourfold hierarchy of values corresponding to "conjecture, faith, understanding, reason" (*Works*, IV, 69), marks the course of a blind alley, and that Emerson explains his own method, if not Plato's, better when he abandons that rather stiff and geometric analogy and says that Plato "represents the privilege of the intellect, the power, namely, of carrying up every fact to successive platforms and so disclosing in every fact a germ of expansion," adding that such "expansions are organic" (IV, 81–82). With that reservation, I should like to see Harris' method of analysis applied still more widely to Emerson's work.

As Emerson indicated in "The American Scholar," his usual practice was to take the scattered facts of experience and try to establish relations among them, without any forcing or rearrangement. Sometimes he went about it, limiting himself more or less closely to one point of view, by beginning with the crudest considerations he could think of and working up to the highest and rarest abstractions of the organic idea. In *Nature*, for example, he started from "Commodity" and went through "Beauty," "Language," and "Discipline" to arrive at "Idealism," "Spirit," and "Prospects." Similarly, in *The Conduct of Life*, he began with "Fate," "Power," and "Wealth," proceeded by a somewhat wandering course through "Culture," "Behavior," "Worship," and "Considerations by the Way," and reached his climax in "Beauty" and "Illusions." At other times he attempted a larger scope by moving back and forth, or up and down, from statements of diversity to declarations of unity and back again to diversity. The first series of *Essays* might be so arranged, roughly, if we were to classify "History" and "Self-Reliance" under the heading of diversity; "Compensation" and "Spiritual Laws" under unity; "Love," "Friendship," "Prudence," and "Heroism" under practical experience, or diversity again; and "The Over-Soul," "Circles," "Intellect," and "Art" under ideal integration, or unity. A complete analysis would of course reveal many further complexities in the structure of the book, but some such main lines as these would probably persist.

It must be admitted, as a defect, that in some individual essays Emerson seems to have begun by assuming the final unity as his premise and forcing it on the facts of experience in such a way as to do them violence; for example, in "Compensation" or "Circles." But these were not published as separate works by Emerson, and to discuss them without some correcting reference to "History" or "Prudence" in the same series is to misrepresent his range of thought.

The real difficulty in the first *Essays,* and in most of Emerson's work, is to find a middle between the extremes. His own simile of the dotted curve is appropriate; there are gaps, perhaps in his thinking, certainly in his writing, left unfilled. Melville's simile in *Moby Dick,* that the chapters of a book grow as the branches and twigs of a tree from its trunk, is more in harmony with what Emerson was driving at. It seems to me, in fact, that not only Melville but other novelists such as Henry James, who was careful to let his stories grow from the smallest possible germs of thought, or Faulkner, whose Yoknapatawpha chronicles appear to have developed from an almost invisible seed in *Soldier's Pay* to the marvellous jungle of his later works, have practiced Emerson's method more consistently, and to better effect, than he was able to do himself. He was at his best, I feel, in such a work as "Experience," where he admitted most liberally the confused and contradictory character of human life and refrained from building on it any further in the direction of unity than the nature of his materials permitted.

Emerson's feeling, however, was somewhat different from mine, and his application of the organic theory was made from another point of view. He believed, as he explained in *Nature,* that "The standard of beauty is the entire circuit of natural forms,— the totality of nature. . . . Nothing is quite beautiful alone; nothing but is beautiful in the whole" (i, 23–24).[19] Or, as he said with even more emphasis in "Each and All," beauty for him was an attribute of the whole universe and could not exist or be satisfactorily embodied, any more than truth could, in any separate fragment. Every true perception of beauty therefore depended on the whole context, the universe, in which every object had its one proper place, and out of which it could not be seen without distortion and ugliness. Any attempt to create a separately complete representation of either beauty or truth would be an almost sacrilegious wrenching at the universal fabric. Emerson's works, then, may be said to have been intended as glimpses of this and that aspect of the macrocosm in its whole vastness, however imperfectly seen, rather than as microcosmically complete and perfect organisms in themselves. For that reason, if for no other, the individual works are likely to lack the very qualities of structural relatedness, wholeness, and unity which Emerson considered the most important attributes of the universal reality.

Emerson's defects, then, when they are not the defects of his time and of the inherent nature of his ideas, may fairly be called the defects of his qualities; and, when all is said, they are minor. It we look at the whole body of his work from as near as we can come to his own point of view, remembering that he always aimed at the universal rather than at any particular unity, and that the relation between his various statements is usually organic in the progressive, or dialectic, rather than in any static sense, we can see that his philosophy and his art have a consistency which need not be referred to his character but which inheres fundamentally in the organic metaphor and which is often most present in the tension and dynamic balance of his most contradictory pronouncements. Historically, though he was by no means our greatest literary artist, he was perhaps the most important thinker and writer we have had, the first to make our declaration of cultural independence effective, and the chief pioneer of romanticism (that is to say, of modern thought and art) in this country. We can well afford to forgive him his structural weaknesses and his excessive optimism, which was never merely sentimental, as some critics have assumed. And we owe it to ourselves, if not to Emerson, to remember that we are where we are in the world's culture today partly because we have his high, stooping shoulders to stand upon.

NOTES

1. This view is characteristic of most of the earlier, more generally humanistic writers such as Arnold, Brownell, John Jay Chapman, Stuart P. Sherman, and John S. Harrison; and it seems fairly pervasive, though not so dominant, in Foerster, Matthiessen, and others whose appreciation of the organic principle is stronger but not always accurate.

2. Gray, *Emerson: A Statement of New England Transcendentalism as Expressed in the Philosophy of Its Chief Exponent* (Stanford, 1917); Foerster, "Emerson on the Organic Prin-

ciple in Art," *PMLA,* XLI (March 1926), 193–208, and *American Criticism* (Boston, 1928), pp. 52–110; Beach, *The Concept of Nature in Nineteenth-Century English Poetry* (New York, 1936), pp. 336–69; Matthiessen, *American Renaissance* (New York, 1946); Spiller, "Ralph Waldo Emerson," *Literary History of the United States,* ed. Spiller et al. (New York, 1948), I, 358–87; Hopkins, *Spires of Form: A Study of Emerson's Aesthetic Theory* (Cambridge, Mass., 1951); and Paul, *Emerson's Angle of Vision: Man and Nature in American Experience* (Cambridge, Mass., 1952).

3. See Arthur O. Lovejoy, *The Great Chain of Being* (Cambridge, Mass., 1936), pp. 242–333; Meyer Abrams, "Archetypal Analogies in the Language of Criticism," *Univ. of Toronto Quart.,* XVIII (July 1949), 313–27; Morse Peckham, "Toward a Theory of Romanticism," *PMLA,* LXVI (March 1951), 5–23; and my "Romanticism and the American Renaissance," *AL,* XXIII (Jan. 1952), 419–32.

4. *Science and the Modern World* (New York, 1925), pp. 104, 112.

5. Pepper, *The Basis of Criticism in the Arts* (Cambridge, Mass., 1945), p. 74. My discussion of the differences between organicism, formism, and mechanism is based largely on Pepper's *World Hypotheses* (Berkeley, 1948).

6. *The Complete Works of Ralph Waldo Emerson,* ed. Edward Waldo Emerson (Boston, 1903–4), 12 vols.

7. For a full discussion of organicism and its root metaphor, see Pepper, *World Hypotheses,* pp. 280–314.

8. Cf. Peckham, op. cit. (n. 3).

9. Kenneth W. Cameron, *Emerson the Essayist* (Raleigh, N.C., 1945), I, 166. Cameron emphasizes Emerson's debt to Coleridge on pp. 162–99.

10. *Young Emerson Speaks,* ed. Arthur S. McGiffert, Jr. (Boston, 1938), pp. 128, 132.

11. Ibid., pp. 43–5.

12. *Journals of Ralph Waldo Emerson,* ed. Edward Waldo Emerson and Waldo Emerson Forbes (Boston, 1909–14), 10 vols.

13. See Whitehead, op. cit.; also Suzanne K. Langer, *Philosophy in a New Key* (Cambridge, Mass., 1942).

14. See especially Matthiessen, pp. 100–132, and J. Russell Roberts, "Emerson's Debt to the Seventeenth Century," *AL,* XXI (Nov. 1949), 298–310.

15. *Uncollected Lectures of Ralph Waldo Emerson,* ed. Clarence F. Gohdes (New York, 1932), p. 53.

16. "Ralph Waldo Emerson," *Atlantic,* L (Aug. 1882), 238–52. Matthiessen, p. 68, also singles out "The Over-Soul" for special dispraise.

17. "Emerson's Literary Method," *MP,* XLII (Nov. 1944), 79–95.

18. "The Dialectic Unity in Emerson's Prose," *Jour. of Speculative Philos.,* XVIII (April 1884), 195. (This paper was first delivered as a lecture at the Concord School of Philosophy in the summer of 1882.)

19. Cf. XII, 217–18, where Emerson credits this idea to Moritz.

Stephen E. Whicher

IX

Emerson's Tragic Sense

•

There is something enigmatic about most American authors. Poe, Hawthorne, Melville, Thoreau, Whitman, Mark Twain, Emily Dickinson, Henry Adams, Henry James, Frost, Faulkner—each has his secret space, his halls of Thermes, his figure in the carpet, which is felt most strongly in his best work and yet eludes definition. Sometimes it is quite opposed to what its possessor thinks he is or wants to be: for example, Hawthorne, envying Trollope his sunshine and his sales, whose best story was "positively hell-fired"; or Whitman, affirmer of life, whose poetry is never more powerful than when it treats of death; Poe, who liked to think himself icily logical and who wrote best from a haunted fantasy; Mark Twain, professional joker and amateur pessimist; or Frost, tough and humorous individualist, whose best poems are often his saddest. Generally this is linked with an obscure fear or grief, even despair: American literature, closely read, can seem one of the least hopeful of literatures.

To all this, Emerson, representative American author that he is, is no exception. The more we know him, the less we know him. He can be summed up in a formula only by those who know their own minds better than his. We hear his grand, assuring words, but

From *The American Scholar*, Vol. XXII, Summer 1953, pp. 285–92. Copyright 1953 by *The American Scholar*. Reprinted by permission of the author and periodical.

where is the man who speaks them? We know the part he played so well; we feel his powerful charm: we do not know the player. He is, finally, impenetrable, for all his forty-odd volumes.

Yet no man can write so much and so honestly and not reveal himself in some measure. We can see enough to sense in him an unusually large gap, even a contradiction, between his teachings and his experience. He taught self-reliance and felt self-distrust, worshipped reality and knew illusion, proclaimed freedom and submitted to fate. No one has expected more of man; few have found him less competent. There is an Emersonian tragedy and an Emersonian sense of tragedy, and we begin to know him when we feel their presence underlying his impressive confidence.

Of course I must stress the word "Emersonian" here. As Mark Van Doren has remarked, "Emerson had no theory of tragedy," unless to deny its existence is a theory. His oblivion can be prodigious.

> The soul will not know either deformity or pain. If, in the hours of clear reason, we should speak the severest truth, we should say that we had never made a sacrifice. In these hours the mind seems so great, that nothing can be taken from us that seems much. All loss, all pain, is particular; the universe remains to the heart unhurt. Neither vexations nor calamities abate our trust. No man ever stated his griefs as lightly as he might.

As he explained in his lecture on "The Tragic," the man who is grounded in the divine life will transcend suffering in a flight to a region "whereunto these passionate clouds of sorrow cannot rise."

Such transcendence of suffering is one of the great historic answers to tragedy and commands respect. To be valid, however, it must "cost not less than everything." Emerson seems to pay no such price. When, in the same lecture on "The Tragic," he tells the "tender American girl," horrified at reading of the transatlantic slave trade, that these crucifixions were not horrid to the obtuse and barbarous blacks who underwent them, "but only a little worse than the old sufferings," we wonder if he paid anything at all for his peace. The only coin in which we can discharge our debt to suffering is attention to it, but Emerson seems to evade this obligation.

Yet this chilling idealism is not simple insensitivity. Emerson is teaching his tested secret of insulation from calamity: Live in the Soul. His famous assertion in *Experience* of the unreality of his devastating grief for his son is an impressive illustration of the necessity he was under to protect, at whatever human cost, his hard-won security. Yeats has said somewhere that we begin to live when we have conceived life as tragedy. The opposite was true of Emerson. Only as he refused to conceive life as tragedy could he find the courage to live.

By denying man's fate, however, Emerson did not escape it. His urgent need to deny it shows that his confidence was more precarious than he would admit. Who has not felt the insistence, the over-insistence, in such radical claims to freedom and power as *Self-Reliance?*

> Trust thyself: every heart vibrates to that iron string. Accept the place the divine providence has found for you, the society of your contemporaries, the connection of events. Great men have always done so, and confided themselves childlike to the genius of their age, betraying their perception that the absolutely trustworthy was seated at their heart, working through their hands, predominating in all their being. And we are now men, and must accept in the highest mind the same transcendent destiny; and not minors and invalids in a protected corner, not cowards fleeing before a revolution, but guides, redeemers, and benefactors, obeying the Almighty effort, and advancing on Chaos and the Dark.

What speaks here is self-*dis*trust, a distrust so pervasive that it must find an "absolutely trustworthy" seated at the heart before it can trust at all. Self-reliance, in the oft-cited phrase, is God-reliance, and therefore not self-reliance. Contrast the accent of a genuine individualist like Ibsen: "The strongest man in the world is he who stands most alone." Or recall a truly self-reliant American: "It was about this time I conceiv'd the bold and arduous project of arriving at moral perfection. I wish'd to live without committing any fault at any time; I would conquer all that either natural inclination, custom, or company might lead me into. As I knew, or thought I knew, what was right and wrong, I did not see why I might not always do the one and avoid the other. . . . For this purpose I therefore contrived the following method. . . ." The free and easy assurance of Franklin is just what is missing in Emerson.

Certainly the first thirty years or so showed no great self-trust. A tubercular, like many in his family (two brothers died of the disease), he was engaged throughout his twenties in a serious battle of life and death in which he was not at all sure of winning. With his poor health went a disheartening self-criticism. He imagined he was incurably idle and self-indulgent, without force or worldly competence, constrained in the company of others, unresponsive in his affections. Though his early journals often show a manly courage and good sense, the dominant mood is a sense of impotence. He lacks all power to realize his larger ambitions and feels himself drifting, sometimes in humiliation, sometimes in wry amusement, before the inexorable flowing of time. He was the servant more than the master of his fate, he found in 1824; and later, in the depths of his illness, it seemed to him that he shaped his fortunes not at all. In all his life, he wrote, he obeyed a strong necessity.

The electrifying release of power brought to him by the amazing discovery, the start of his proper career, that God was within his own soul is understandable only against this early—indeed, this lifelong submission to a strong necessity. His subjection bred a longing for self-direction, all the stronger for his underlying sense of its impossibility. The force of his transcendental faith, and its almost willful extravagance, sprang from his need to throw off, against all probability and common sense, his annihilating dependence. He welcomed the paradoxical doctrine that "God dwells in thee" with uncritical delight, as the solution to all the doubts that oppressed him, and rushed in a Saturnalia of faith to spell out its revolutionary consequences for the solitary soul:

> . . . The world is nothing, the man is all; . . . in yourself slumbers the whole of Reason; it is for you to know all, it is for you to dare all. . . .
> . . . The height, the deity of man is, to be self-sustained, to need no gift, no foreign force. . . . All that you call the world is the shadow of that substance which you are, the perpetual creation of the powers of thought, of those that are dependent and of those that are independent of your will. . . . You think me the child of my circumstances: I make my circumstance. . . .
> . . . Every rational creature has all nature for his dowry and estate. It is his, if he will. He may divest himself of it; he may creep into a corner, and abdicate his kingdom, as most men do, but he is entitled to the world by his constitution. . . .

Yet this proclamation of the kingdom of man was always what he soon came to call it, a romance. He retained a common-sense awareness (and so retains our respect) that experience did not support it. Not merely were all manipular attempts to realize his kingdom premature and futile. The Power within, from which all capacity stemmed, was itself wayward. The individual relying on it was a mere pipe for a divine energy that came and went as it willed. With this hidden life within him, man was no longer hopeless, but he was still helpless. "I would gladly," Emerson wrote at the age of forty-one, ". . . allow the most to the will of man, but I have set my heart on honesty in this chapter, and I can see nothing at last, in success or failure, than more or less of vital force supplied from the Eternal."

When Emerson wrote *The American Scholar,* seven years earlier, his imagination had kindled to a blaze at the thought of the divine power latent in the soul. Give way to it, let it act, and the conversion of the world will follow. As this millennial enthusiasm inevitably waned, the old helplessness it had contradicted emerged unaltered from the flames. The result was a head-on clash of belief and fact. His vision of man as he might be only intensified the plight of man as he was. Something resembling the Fall of Man, which he had so ringingly denied, reappears in his pages.

It is not sin now that troubles him, but "the incompetency of power." One may accuse Providence of a certain parsimony.

> It has shown the heaven and earth to every child, and filled him with a desire for the whole; a desire raging, infinite; a hunger, as of space to be filled with planets; a cry of famine, as of devils for souls. Then for the satisfaction,—to each man is administered a single drop, a bead of dew of vital power, *per day,*—a cup as large as space, and one drop of the water of life in it. Each man woke in the morning with an appetite that could eat the solar system like a cake; a spirit for action and passion without bounds; he could lay his hand on the morning star; he could try conclusions with gravitation or chemistry; but, on the first motion to prove his strength,—hands, feet, senses, gave way, and would not serve him. He was an emperor deserted by his states, and left to whistle by himself, or thrust into a mob of emperors, all whistling: and still the sirens sang, "The attractions are proportioned to the destinies." In every house, in the heart of each maiden and of each boy, in the soul of the soaring saint, this chasm is found,—between the largest promise of ideal power and the shabby experience.

This chasm is the Emersonian tragedy, a tragedy of incapacity. Man's reach must exceed his grasp, of course; that is not tragic. Emerson's chasm cuts deeper: between a vision that claims all power now, and an experience that finds none. Emerson's thought of the self was split between a total Yes and a total No, which could not coexist, could not be reconciled, and yet were both true. "Alas for this infirm faith, this will not strenuous, this vast ebb of a vast flow! I am God in nature; I am a weed by the wall."

There is an Emersonian skepticism as well as an Emersonian faith. Of the seven "lords of life" he distinguishes in his key essay, *Experience,* five are principles of weakness. A man is slave to his moods and his temperament, swept like a bubble down the stream of time, blinded and drugged with illusion, the captive of his senses—in a word, the creature of a strong necessity. To be sure, the God is a native of the bleak rocks of his isolation, and can at any moment surprise and cheer him with new glimpses of reality. But for all this miraculous consolation, he has no will or force of his own; self-reliant is precisely what he can never be. *The American Scholar's* assurance of the unsearched might of man is a feat of faith in view of the actual humiliating human predicament, "with powers so vast and unweariable ranged on one side, and this little, conceited, vulnerable popinjay that a man is, bobbing up and down into every danger, on the other."

It goes without saying that one can easily overstate the case for a tragic sense in Emerson. *Experience,* for instance, is not a tragic-sounding essay. Perhaps "sense of limitation" would be more accurate; I have deliberately chosen a controversial term, in order to stress a side of Emerson often overlooked. For all his loss of millennial hope, Emerson in fact came to allow much to the will of man, as any reader of *The Conduct of Life* can see. Nor do I mean to suggest that he did not find the secret of a serene and affirmative life. The evidence is overwhelming that he did. My point is that his serenity was a not unconscious *answer* to his experience of life, rather than an inference from it (even when presented as such). It was an act of faith, forced on him by what he once called "the ghastly reality of things." Only as we sense this tension of faith and experience in him can we catch the quality of his affirmation. He *had* to ascribe more reality to his brief moments of "religious sentiment" than to the rest of life, or he could not live.

The way he did so altered sensibly, as his first excess of faith in man diminished. A gentle resignation came to settle over his thought of human nature, an elegiac recognition that life perpetually promises us a glory we can never realize. As it did so, the center of his faith traveled imperceptibly from man to the order that included him. In moments of faith, as he explained even in the midst of his essay on *Self-Reliance*, "The soul raised over passion beholds identity and eternal causation, perceives the self-existence of Truth and Right, and calms itself with knowing that all things go well." Such dogmatic optimism, always a part of his faith, became more and more its sole content as his first dream of a kingdom of Man dwindled into reasonableness.

Emerson the optimist said some shallow and callous things, as he did in his lecture on "The Tragic." To restore our sympathy with his humanity, we must glimpse the prisoner that now and then looked out of the eyes above the smile. Within, he was sovereign, a guide, redeemer and benefactor; without, he was a lecturing and publishing old gentleman. Each time his inner promise of ideal power came up against the narrow limits of his experience, the response could only be the same—a renewed surrender to the Power that planned it that way.

He did not surrender to necessity because he found it good, so much as he found it good because he surrendered. Recurrently the Good he recognizes is more conspicuous for power than for goodness, a "deaf, unimplorable, immense fate," to which all man-made distinctions of good and ill are an impertinence. In some of his poems, particularly, those that have eyes to see may watch him swept into entranced submission to "the over-god" by the compulsion of his personal problems. This is how he meets the impossible challenge of social action, in the "Ode" to Channing. So the teasing evanescence of his moments of insight into reality is submerged in "The World-Soul." He bows to the same power for a bleak consolation in his "Threnody" for his son:

> Silent rushes the swift Lord
> Through ruined systems still restored,
> Broadsowing, bleak and void to bless,
> Plants with worlds the wilderness;
> Waters with tears of ancient sorrow
> Apples of Eden ripe to-morrow.
> House and tenant go to ground,
> Lost in God, in Godhead found.

In such poems we feel the hunger for strength that sent him first to his grand doctrine of Self-Reliance, and then swung him to its polar opposite, a worship of the Beautiful Necessity.

Like all puritans, Emerson was an extremist: he had to have entire assurance, or he had none at all. Though we have a tradition of mature tragedy in our literature, American authors have typically made the same demand. Either they have risen to his transcendental trust, like Thoreau and Whitman; or they have accepted shoddy substitutes, like Norris or Sandburg or Steinbeck; or they have dropped into blackness, like Henry Adams or Jeffers. Emerson himself teetered on the edge of this drop, as did Thoreau and Whitman too, sustained by little more than their own power of belief. Since then the impulse to believe has become progressively feebler and the drop quicker and harder, until now, John Aldridge tells us, our honest writers *start* in the pit. If we are ever to have a great literature again, one would conclude, it will not be until we can break decisively with the whole extremist Emersonian pattern and find some means to face this world without either transcendence or despair.

Sherman Paul

X

Resolution at Walden

I

Walden was published in 1854, eight years before Thoreau died, some seven years after his life in the woods. His journal shows that he had proposed such a "poem" for himself as early as 1841, that its argument would be "the River, the Woods, the Ponds, the Hills, the Fields, the Swamps and Meadows, the Streets and Buildings, and the Villagers. Then Morning, Noon, and Evening, Spring, Summer, Autumn, and Winter, Night, Indian Summer, and the Mountains in the Horizon." Like *A Week on the Concord and Merrimack Rivers* (1849)—"If one would reflect," Thoreau had written in 1837, "let him embark on some placid stream, and float with the current"—*Walden* took a long time maturing, a longer time, because it was more than the stream of his reflections. The *Week* had been written out of joyousness and to memorialize his most perfect excursion in nature. *Walden,* however, was Thoreau's recollected experience, recollected not in tranquility, but in the years of what he himself called his "decay." Although one need only search the journals to find many of the events of *Walden* freshly put down, *Walden* itself reveals that Thoreau was now looking at these events with more experienced eyes: his long

From *Accent,* Vol. XIII, 1953, pp. 101–13. Copyright 1953 by *Accent.* Reprinted by permission of the author and periodical.

quarrel with society has intervened, his youthful inspiration had become more difficult to summon, the harvest of the *Week* he had hoped to bestow on the public lay in his attic, and, growing older, he was still without a vocation that others would recognize. In *Walden,* at once his victorious hymn to Nature, to her perpetual forces of life, inspiration and renewal, Thoreau defended his vocation by creating its eternal symbol.

The common moral of *Walden* is that of the virtue of simplicity; and simplicity is usually taken on the prudential level of economy with which Thoreau seemingly began the book. In terms of Thoreau's spiritual economy, however, simplicity was more than freedom from the burdens of a mortgaged life: it was an ascetic, a severe discipline, like solitude for Emerson, by which Thoreau concentrated his forces and was able to confront the facts of life without the intervening barriers of society or possessions. For simplicity, Thoreau often substituted poverty, a word which both set him apart from his materialistic neighbors and hallowed his vocation with its religious associations of renunciation and higher dedication. It was the suitable condition for the spiritual crusader: the sign in a land of traders of his profession. But it also signified his inner condition. "By poverty," he said, "*i.e.* simplicity of life and fewness of incidents, I am solidified and crystallized, as a vapor or liquid by cold. It is a singular concentration of strength and energy and flavor. Chastity is perpetual acquaintance with the All. My diffuse and vaporous life becomes as frost leaves and spiculae radiant as gems on the weeds and stubble in a winter morning." Such poverty or purity was a necessity of *his* economy. "You think," he continued, "that I am impoverishing myself by withdrawing from men, but in my solitude I have woven for myself a silken web or *chrysalis,* and, nymph-like, shall ere long burst forth a more perfect creature, fitted for a higher society. By simplicity, commonly called poverty, my life is concentrated and so becomes organized, or a κόσμος, which before was inorganic and lumpish."

This was also the hope of his paean to spring in *Walden,* to "pass from the lumpish grub in the earth to the airy and fluttering butterfly." The purpose of his experiment at Walden Pond, begun near the end of his years of undisciplined rapture—Emerson said that the vital heat of the poet begins to ebb at thirty—

was to build an organic life as consciously as he built his hut (and his book), and so retain his vital heat. "May I never," he had recorded in his journal, "let the vestal fire go out in my recesses." But there was desperation in his attempt to keep his vital heat, because it was only *vital* (or rather he felt it so) when he was maturing beyond the lumpish, grub-like existence. As well as the advocacy of the organic life which promised renewal and growth, *Walden* for Thoreau filled the immediate need of self-therapy. In the serenity and joy of his art this is often overlooked, but it is there in the journals behind the book. And the greatness of *Walden,* from this perspective at least, is the resolution Thoreau was able to fulfill through art. By creating an organic form he effected his own resolution for rebirth: by conscious endeavor he recaptured, if not the youthful ectasy of his golden age, a mature serenity.

This serenity, however, is still alert, wakeful, tense. It was a victory of discipline. "That aim in life is highest," Thoreau noted during the composition of *Walden,* "which requires the highest and finest discipline." That aim was highest, that discipline the highest vocation, because the goal and fulfillment of all transcendental callings was purity—a oneness with Nature in which the untarnished mirror of the soul reflected the fullness of being. The cost of doing without conventional life was not too great for Thoreau, considering his desire to "perceive things truly and simply." He believed that "a fatal coarseness is the result of mixing in the trivial affairs of men." And to justify his devotion to purity he wrote *Walden,* a promise of the higher society a man can make when he finds his *natural* center, a record of things and events so simple and fundamental that all lives less courageous and principled are shamed by the *realometer* it provides. Like other masterworks of its time, it has the unique strain of American romanticism: behind its insistent individualism and desire for experience, there is still more earnest conviction of the necessity of virtue.

II

In the concluding pages of *Walden,* Thoreau remarked that "in this part of the world it is considered a ground for complaint if a man's writings admit of more than one interpretation." With his contemporaries, Emerson, Hawthorne, Melville, he wanted the "volatile truth" of his words to "betray the inadequacy of the residual statement." He would have considered *Walden* a failure if it served only to communicate an eccentric's refusal to go along with society, if, taken literally, its spiritual courage was thinned to pap for tired businessmen long since beyond the point of no return. For *Walden* was *his* myth: "A fact truly and absolutely stated," he said, "is taken out of the region of common sense and acquires a mythologic or universal signficance." This was the extravagance he sought—this going beyond the bounds. For him, only the fact stated without reference to convention or institution, with only reference to the self which has tasted the world and digested it, which has been "drenched" and "saturated" with truth, is properly humanized—is properly myth. Primarily to immerse himself in truth, to merge himself with the law of Nature, and to humanize this experience by the alchemy of language, Thoreau went to Walden. There, free from external references, he could purify himself and live a sympathetic existence, alive to the currents of being. What he reported, then, would be the experience of the self in its unfolding and exploration of the "not-me." The literal record would merely remain the residual statement— no one knew better the need for concrete fact; but it would also yield a *translated* meaning.

The whole of *Walden* is an experience of the microcosmic and cosmic travels of the self. At Walden Pond, Thoreau wrote, "I have, as it were, my own sun and moon and stars, and a little world all to myself." Thoreau, of course, was a great traveller, if only a saunterer. The profession of traveller appealed to his imagination; it was, he said, the "best symbol of our life." And "Walking" was the best short statement of his way of life, of his journey to the holy land. He yearned, he wrote in 1851, "for one of those old, meandering, dry, uninhabited roads, which lead away from towns. . . ." He wanted to find a place "where you can walk and think with least obstruction, there being nothing to measure progress by; where you can pace when your breast is full, and cherish your moodiness; where you are not in false relations with men. . . ." He wanted "a road where I can travel," where "I can walk, and recover the lost child that I am without any ringing of a bell." The road he wanted led to Walden. There he regained the primal world, and lived the pristine initiation into consciousness over again. "Both place and time were changed," he said in *Walden*, "and I dwelt nearer to those parts of the universe and to those eras in history which had most attracted me."

In this effort to live out of time and space or to live in all times and places, *Walden* immediately suggests Melville's *Moby-Dick*. Melville had written another voyage of the self on which he explored reality, charted the constituents of a chaos, and raised his discovery to the universal level of archetypal experience. He had elaborated the myth of the hunter which Thoreau also employed in the chapter on "Higher Laws." "There is a period in the history of the individual, as of the race," he wrote, "when hunters are the 'best men'. . . ." Hunting, he added, "is oftenest the young man's introduction to the forest [Melville's sea], and the most original part of himself. He goes thither at first as a hunter and fisher, until at last, if he has the seeds of a better life in him, he distinguishes his proper objects. . . ." It was in in these "wild" employments of his youth that Thoreau acknowledged his "closest acquaintance with Nature." For Nature revealed herself to the hunter more readily than to "philosophers or poets even, who approach her with expectation"—or, as Melville knew, to the participant and not the observer of life. If Thoreau had long since given up hunting, he still found a sustaining link with the wild in his bean field.

There are obvious differences, of course, in the quality of these travels—each author had his spiritual torment, Melville the need for belief, Thoreau the need for recommunion. But both were projecting the drama of their selves, a drama that in both instances ended in rebirth; and the methods both employed were remarkably similar. Each abstracted himself from the conventional world, established a microcosm by which to test the conventions, and worked at a basic and heroic occupation. For example, the village stands in the same symbolic relation to Thoreau at Walden that the land does to Melville's sea; and it is the occupation in both that supplies the residual statement. In Thoreau's case, it is also a primitive concern with essentials: building his hut, planting, hoeing and harvesting his beans, fishing and naturalizing. And the nature of the occupation gives each its spiritual quality, because whaling (butchery) and colonizing (building from scratch) are projections of different visions of the universe of which only the central similarity remains—the exploration of self.

But this similarity is a sufficient signature for both; one recognizes the existential kinship. At the conclusion of *Walden* Thoreau declared: "Explore thyself . . . Be . . . the Mungo Park, the Lewis and Clark and Frobisher, of your own streams and oceans. . . ."—

> ". . . . . be
> Expert in home-cosmography."

For "there are continents and seas in the moral world to which every man is an isthmus or an inlet, yet unexplored by him, . . . [and] it is easier to sail many thousand miles through cold and storm and cannibals, in a government ship, with five hundred men and boys to assist one, than it is to explore the private sea, the Atlantic and Pacific Ocean of one's being alone." Melville at Pittsfield would have agreed that "herein are demanded the eye and the nerve." But if Melville needed the watery two-thirds of the world and the great whale for this quest, Thoreau, who had the gift of enlarging the small, needed only the pond and its pickerel. And where Melville needed the destructive forces of the sea to mirror himself, Thoreau, who had seen the place of violence in the total economy of nature, needed only the recurrence of the seasons.

III

Walden was Thoreau's quest for a reality he had lost, and for this reason it was a quest for purity. Purity meant a return to the spring (and springtime) of life, to the golden age of his youth and active senses, when the mirror of his self was not clouded by self-consciousness. *Walden,* accordingly, follows the cycle of developing consciousness, a cycle that parallels the change of the seasons. It is a recapitulation of Thoreau's development (and the artistic reason he put the experience of two years into one)—a development from the sensuous, active, external (unconscious *and* out-of-doors) summer of life, through the stages of autumnal consciousness and the withdrawal inward to the self-reflection of winter, to the promise of ecstatic rebirth in the spring. It was a matter of purification because Thoreau had reached the winter of decay at the time *Walden* was being revised for the press. With consciousness had come the knowledge of the "reptile" and "sensual" which he knew could not "be wholly expelled." "I fear," he wrote, "that it [the sensual]may enjoy a certain health of its own; that we may be well, yet not pure." For the mind's approach to God, he knew that the severest discipline was necessary; his chapter on "Higher Laws" is concerned almost entirely with the regimen of the appetites because "man flows at once to God when the channel of purity is open." The undeniable sensual energy—the "generative energy"—he had unconsciously enjoyed in the ecstasy of youth, now needed control. "The generative energy," he wrote, "which, when we are loose, dissipates and makes us unclean, when we are continent invigorates and inspires us." He was consciously using instinct for higher ends, seeking chasity by control.

In Walden Pond he saw the image of his purified self—that pristine, eternal self he hoped to possess. In 1853, while he was working on his book, he noted in his journal: "How watchful we must be to keep the crystal well that we were made, clear!—that it be not made turbid by our contact with the world, so that it will not reflect objects." The pond, he recalled, was one of the "oldest scenes stamped on my memory." He had been taken to see it when he was four years old. Now, playing his flute beside its waters, his beans, corn and potatoes replacing the damage of the years, he felt that another aspect was being prepared "for new infant eyes," that "even I have at length helped to clothe that fabulous landscape of my infant dreams. . . ." Later, he recalled his youthful reveries on its waters: "I have spent many an hour, when I was younger, floating over its surface as the zephyr willed . . . dreaming awake. . . ." But time (and woodchoppers) had ravished its shores: "My Muse may be excused," he explained, "if she is silent henceforth. How can you expect the birds to sing when their groves are cut down?" It was the confession of the Apollo who had had to serve Admetus, a confession he made again in "Walking." Visited by fewer thoughts each year, he said that "the grove in our minds is laid waste—sold to feed unnecessary fires of ambition. . . ."

But Thoreau discovered at Walden that even though the groves were cut down, the pond itself remained the same—it "best preserves its purity." "It is itself unchanged," he learns, "the same water my youthful eyes fell on; all the change is in me. . . . It is perennially young. . . ." Catching sight of his eternal self and realizing that the waste of years had only touched his shore, his empirical self, he exclaimed, "Why, here is Walden, the same woodland lake that I discovered so many years ago . . . it is the same liquid joy and happiness to itself and its Maker, ay, and it *may* be to me." The pond, so constant, clear and pure, was truly the *Walled in* pond, the undefiled soul of which the Thoreau-in-decay said, "I am its stony shore. . . ."

If Thoreau spent his youth drifting with the inspiring zephyrs on Walden's surface, he now plumbed its depths, angled for its pickerel and its bottom. For it was the purpose of *Walden* to find bottom, to affirm reality; and the reality Thoreau discovered in the soul and in the whole economy of Nature he found at the bottom of the pond. What renewed his faith was the sign of the never-dying, all-promising generative force which he symbolized when he wrote: ". . . a bright green weed is brought up on anchors even in midwinter." The hope of a renewed life, rhapso-dized in the concluding chapters of *Walden* and there symbolized in the hardy blade of grass—the green flame of life—, was the assurance he now had that "there is nothing inorganic."

And by sounding the bottom Thoreau also discovered the law of the universe and of the intellect that made possible his organic participation in the process of renewal and provided him the guarantee of its expression in natural objects. "The regularity of the bottom and its conformity to the shores and the range of the neighboring hills were so perfect," he wrote, "that a distant promontory betrayed itself in the soundings quite across the pond, and its direction could be determined by observing the opposite shore." He found, too, that the intersection of the lines of greatest length and breadth coincided with the point of greatest depth; and he suggested that this physical law might be applied to ethics. "Draw lines through the length and breadth of the aggregate of a man's particular daily behaviors and waves of life into his coves and inlets, and where they intersect will be the height or depth of his character. Perhaps we need only to know how his shores tend and his adjacent country or circumstances, to infer his depth and concealed bottom." *Walden* was just such an account of Thoreau's moral topography, and if the lines were drawn, the pond itself would be his center. For wasn't the eternal self, like the pond, " 'God's Drop' "?

The search for the bottom was conscious exploration. Here, and in the passages on fishing for pickerel and chasing the loon, Thoreau was not a naturalist but a natural historian of the intellect, using the natural facts as symbols for his quest for inspiration and thought. In "Brute Neighbors" he had asked, "Why do precisely these objects which we behold make a world?" And he had answered that "they are all beasts of burden . . . made to carry some portion of our thoughts." The natural world merely reflects ourselves. Having overcome his doubts of this central article of transcendental faith by assuring himself of the regularity of Walden's depth—that the hidden reality corresponded to its visible shores, that "Heaven is under our feet as well as over our heads"—he could trust once more his own projection of mood and thought to be reflected in its proper and corresponding object. He had noted in his journal that the poet "sees a flower or other object, and it is beautiful or affecting to him because it is a symbol of his thought, and what he indistinctly feels or perceives is matured in some other organization. The objects I behold correspond to my mood." His concern with the pond and the seasons, then, was symbolic of his soul's preoccupation. "Our moulting season . . . must be the crisis in our lives," he said; and like the loon he retired to a solitary pond to spend it. There, like the caterpillar—to use another symbol—, "by an internal industry and expansion" he cast off his "wormy coat."

IV

Thoreau went to Walden to become an unaccommodated man, to shed his lendings and to find his naked and sufficient self. Of this, the pond was the symbol. He also went to clothe himself in response to his inner needs. Building an organic life was again a conscious endeavor which was chastened by the necessity of maintaining his vital heat—the heat of body and spirit; for his purpose was not to return to nature, but to combine "the hardiness of . . . savages with the intellectualness of the civilized man." "The civilized man," he said, "is a more experienced and wiser savage," meaning, of course, that the instinctive life was most rewarding when channeled by intellectual principles. "What was *enthusiasm* in the young man," he wrote during the crisis of his life, "must become *temperament* in the mature man." The woodchopper, the animal man, must be educated to consciousness, and still retain his innocence. Properly seen in the total economy of Nature the once freely taken gift of inspiration must be earned by perceiving the law of Nature, by the tragic awareness that inspiration, like its source, has its seasons. The villagers, Thoreau wrote indignantly, "instead of going to the pond to bathe or drink, are thinking to bring its waters, which should be as sacred as the Ganges at least, to the village in a pipe, to wash their dishes with!—to earn their Walden by the turning of a cock or drawing of a plug!" The spiritual soldier had learned that after laying siege to Nature, only passivity would bring victory.

Thoreau earned his Walden by awaiting the return of spring, by sharing the organic process. Of this his hut and his bean-field became the symbols. The latter, as we have seen, helped to renew the aspect of the pond; as the work of the active self, it was rightly an alteration of the shore. And the pond, as the pure, eternal self—the "perfect forest mirror"—, was the calm surface on which these purifying activities were reflected. Thoreau labored in his bean-field because he took seriously Emerson's injunction to action in *The American Scholar*. He knew that the higher ends of the activity of the empirical self were self-consciousness, that the eternal self, the passive center, only acquired consciousness by observing the empirical self at work on the circumference. He recognized "a certain doubleness by which I can stand as remote from myself as from another." "However intense my experience," he wrote, "I am conscious of the presence of and criticism of a part of me, which, as it were, is not part of me, but spectator, sharing no experience, but taking note of it. . . ." The reward of activity, the result of this drama of selves, was self-reflection, insight. "All perception of truth is the detection of an analogy," Thoreau noted in the journal; "we reason from our hands to our head." And so through the labor of the hands, even to the point of drudgery, he was "determined to know beans." He did not need the beans for food but for sympathy with Nature; he needed to work them because, as he said, "They attached me to the earth, and so I got strength like Antaeus." His fields were also symbolic of his attempt to link the wild and the cultivated. And the "immeasurable crop" his devoted hoeing yielded came from the penetration of the earth's crust—a knowledge of the depths similar in significance to Melville's descent to the unwarped primal world. "I disturbed," Thoreau wrote, "the ashes of unchronicled nations who in primeval times lived under these heavens. . . ." In his bean-field beside Walden he was not serving Admetus, for he had found a way to delve beneath the "established order on the surface."

The prudential value of this labor came to $16.94, but the spiritual value was the realization that the Massachusetts soil could sustain the seeds of virtue—that in Thoreau's case at least, the seed had not lost its vitality and that the harvest of his example might be "a new generation of men." Later on, in the chapter on "Former Inhabitants," he again disturbed the surface by delving into the past, comparing his life at Walden to the defeated lives of its previous occupants. Here, Thoreau expressed his desire for the higher society, the ideal community in which he could wholly participate and which he hoped he was beginning. "Again, perhaps, Nature will try," he wrote, "with me for the first settler. . . . I am not aware that any man has ever built on the spot which I occupy." Like Joyce's Finnegan, he was to be the father of cities, not those reared on ancient sites, but cities growing out of the union with the earth. Looking back to Concord from the distances of past and future, Thoreau felt that *Walden* was not so much his quarrel with society, but an expiation. "Through our recovered innocence," he confessed, "we discern the innocence of our neighbors." He was willing to share his regeneration, for above the constant interplay of Walden and village, there hovered a vision of an ideal village that transcended both. In the radical sense of the word, Thoreau, who had given up the wilder pursuit of hunting for farming, was a civilizer.

When he came to build his hut—the container of his vital heat—Thoreau used second-hand materials and borrowed tools and showed his dependence on civilization. He did not abandon collective wisdom: his intention was to practice philosophy, to come directly at a conduct of life, that is, to simplify, or experience the solid satisfaction of knowing immediately the materials that made his life. He scrupulously accounts for these materials, he tells their history—where he got the boards, who used them and under what conditions. And James Collins's life in the shanty is implicitly contrasted with Thoreau's, especially in Thoreau's remark that he purified the boards by bleaching and warping them in the sun. He also acknowledged his debt for tools. He did not push his economy too far, to the verge of self-sufficiency that some believe necessary to a defense of *Walden* as social gospel. He said—and this is the only way of repaying one's social indebtedness—that he sharpened the tools by use. In a similar way, he applied the funded wisdom of man to his experiment on life. Individualist that he was, he often confirmed his experience by the experience of others: he made his use of the classics and scriptures, Indian lore and colonial history, pay their way. He was starting from scratch, but he knew that the materials were old.

The building of the hut is so thoroughly described because on the symbolic level it is the description of the building of the body for his soul. A generation that was read in Swedenborg might have been expected to see this correspondence. "It would be worth the while," Thoreau suggested, "to build still more deliberately than I did, considering, for instance, what foundation a door, a window, a cellar, a garret, have in the nature of man, and perchance never raising any superstructure until we found a better reason for it than our temporal necessities even." He was speaking the language of functionalism that Swedenborgianism had popularized; and after listing his previous shelters, he remarked that "this frame, so slightly clad, was a sort of crystallization around me, and reacted on the builder."

Thoreau built his hut as he needed it, to meet the progressing seasons of developing consciousness, a development which was as organic as the seasons. He subscribed to Emerson's use of the cycle of day and night as the symbol of the ebb and flow of inspiration and extended it to the seasons: "The day is an epitome of the year. The night is the winter, the morning and evenings are spring and fall, and the noon is the summer." In this way he also followed Emerson's "history" of consciousness. "The Greek," Emerson wrote, "was the age of observation; the Middle Age, that of fact and thought; ours, that of reflection and ideas." In *Walden,* Thoreau's development began in the summer, the season of the senses and of delicious out-of-door life. This was the period when he was in sympathetic communion with Nature, refreshed by the tonic of wildness. The chapters on "Sounds" and "Solitude" belong to this period, during which he enjoyed the atmospheric presence of Nature so essential to his inspiration. And the hut, which he began in the spring and first occupied at this time, was merely a frame through which Nature readily passed.

When the "north wind had already begun to cool the pond," Thoreau said that he first began to "inhabit my house." During the autumn season of harvest and preparation for winter, he lathed and plastered; and finally as winter approached he built his fireplace and chimney, "the most vital part of the house. . . ." By the fireside, in the period of reflection and inner life, he lingered most, communing with his self.[1] It was the time of soul-searching, when he cut through the pond's ice and saw that "its bright sanded floor [was] the same as in the summer"; and before the ice broke up he surveyed its bottom. Even in this desolate season Thoreau looked for all the signs of spring's organic promise, and in the representative anecdote of his despair, he told of Nature's sustaining power: "After a still winter night I awoke with the impression that some question had been put to me, which I had been endeavoring in vain to answer in my sleep, as what—how—when—where? But there was dawning Nature, in whom all creatures live, looking in at my broad windows with serene and satisfied face, and no questions on *her* lips. I awoke to an answered question, to Nature and daylight." Even in the winter of his discontent, Nature seemed to him to say "Forward'" and he could calmly await the inevitable golden age of spring.

v

Rebirth came with spring. In one of the best sustained analogies in transcendental writing, the chapter "Spring," Thoreau reported ecstatically the translation of the frozen sand and clay of the railroad cut into the thawing streams of life. Looking at the sand foliage—the work of an hour—he said that "I am affected as if . . . I stood in the laboratory of the Artist who made the world and me. . . ." The Artist of the world, like Thoreau and like Goethe whom he had in mind, labored "with the idea inwardly" and its correspondence, its flowering, was the leaf. Everywhere Thoreau perceived this symbol of creation, and in ascending forms from the sand, the animal body, the feathers and wings of birds, to the "airy" butterfly. "Thus it seemed," he wrote, "that this one hill-side illustrated the principle of all the operations of Nature. The Maker of this earth but patented a leaf." And the moral Thoreau drew from this illustration was the central law of his life, for it was the law of renewal: "This earth is not a mere fragment of dead history, stratum upon stratum like the leaves of a book, to be studied by geologists and antiquarians chiefly, but living poetry like the leaves of a tree, which precede flowers and fruit,—not a fossil earth, but a living earth; compared with whose great central life all animal and vegetable life is merely parasitic. Its throes will heave our exuviae from their graves." And furthermore the law applied to man and the higher society: ". . . the institutions upon it [the earth] are plastic like clay in the hands of the potter."

For Thoreau, who had found that the law of his life was the law of Life, these perceptions were the stuff of ecstasy. Reveling in the sound of the first sparrow, Thoreau wrote, "What at such a time are histories, chronologies, traditions, and all written revelations?" The spring had brought forth "the symbol of perpetual youth," the grass-blade; human life, having died down to its root, now put forth "its green blade to eternity." Walden Pond had begun to melt—"Walden was dead and is alive again." The change in the flowing sand, from excremental to spiritual, had also been accomplished in him by the discipline of purity: "The change from storm and winter to serene and mild weather, from dark and sluggish hours to bright and elastic ones." Like the dawning of inspiration this "memorable crisis" was "seemingly instantaneous at last." "Suddenly," Thoreau recorded that change, "an influx of light filled my house, though evening was at hand, and the clouds of winter still overhung it, and the eaves were dripping with sleety rain. I looked out of the window, and lo! where yesterday was cold grey ice there lay the transparent pond already calm and full of hope as in a summer evening, reflecting a summer evening sky in its bosom, though none was visible overhead, as if it had intelligence with some remote horizon. I heard a robin in the distance, the first I had heard for many a thousand years, methought, whose note I shall not forget for many a thousand more,—the same sweet and powerful song as of yore. . . . So I came in, and shut the door, and passed my first spring night in the woods."

With the coming of spring had come "the creation of Cosmos out of Chaos and the realization of the Golden Age." And with his renewal had come the vindication of his life of purity. He had recorded what he felt was nowhere recorded, "a simple and irrepressible satisfaction with the gift of life. . . ." He had suggested what the eye of the partridge symbolized to him, not merely "the purity of infancy, but a wisdom clarified by experience." He had recounted the experience of his purification so well that even the reader who accepts only the residual statement feels purified. "I do not say," he wisely wrote at the end of *Walden*, "that John or Jonathan will realize all this [the perfect summer life]; but such is the character of the morrow which mere lapse of time can never make to dawn." To affirm this eternal present, to restore, as he said in "The Service," the original of which Nature is the reflection, he fashioned *Walden* as he himself lived, after the example of the artist of the city of Kouroo. This parable unlocks the largest meaning of the book. The artist of Kouroo "was disposed to strive after perfection," Thoreau wrote; and striving, he lived in the eternity of inspiration which made the passing of dynasties, even eras, an illusion. In fashioning his staff, merely by minding his destiny and his art, he had made a new world "with full and fair proportions." The result, Thoreau knew, could not be "other than wonderful," because "the material was pure, and his art was pure. . . ."

NOTES

1. Hawthorne in "Peter Goldthwaite's Treasure" and Melville in "I and My Chimney" also made imaginative use of the house and the chimney.

XI

"One's Self I Sing"

The main item of the 1855 edition of *Leaves of Grass* was, of course, "Song of Myself," the profound and lovely comic drama of the self which is Whitman's best poem and contains in essence nearly all, yet not quite all, there is to *Leaves of Grass*. The comic spirit of the poem is of the characteristic American sort, providing expression for a realism at once naturalistic and transcendental, for the wit, gaiety, and festive energy of all good comedy, and also for meditative soliloquy, at once intensely personal and strongly generic.

One circumstance that contributes to the general spontaneity of "Song of Myself" is, in fact, Whitman's unsuccessful attempt to be an Emersonian or Wordsworthian moralist. In his preface, he wrote that "of all mankind the poet is the equable man. Not in him but off from him things are grotesque or eccentric or fail of their sanity . . . He is the arbiter of the diverse and he is the key. He is the equalizer of his age and land." Whitman tries, indeed, to install himself in his poem on this high moral ground: he will, he says, first regenerate himself by leaving the fallacious artificialities of modern life and getting back to fundamentals; then, having perfected himself as the norm, he will sum-

From *Walt Whitman Reconsidered,* 1955, pp. 58–70. Copyright 1955 by William Sloane Associates, Inc. Reprinted by permission of the publisher.

mon all the world to him to be freed of its abnormalities. But although in the poem the self remains pretty much at the center of things, Whitman finds it impossible to accept the idea that it is a norm. To the sententious prophet who "promulges" the normative self, the comic poet and ironic realist keep introducing other, disconcertingly eccentric selves.

> Who goes there? hankering, gross, mystical, nude. . . .

Whoever he is, he is not in a position to utter morality. The self in this poem *is* (to use Lawrence's phrase) "tricksy-tricksy"; it does "shy all sorts of ways" and is finally, as the poet says, "not a bit tamed," for "I too am untranslatable." So that as in all true, or high, comedy, the sententious, the too overtly insisted-on morality (if any) plays a losing game with ironical realism. In the social comedy of Molière, Congreve, or Jane Austen, moral sententiousness, like other deformities of comportment or personality, is corrected by society. But this attitude is, of course, foreign to Whitman, who has already wished to invite society to correct itself by comparing itself with him and who, furthermore, cannot even sustain this democratic inversion of an aristocratic idea. Whitman's comic poetry deflates pretensions and chides moral rigidity by opposing to them a diverse, vital, indeterminate reality.

"I resist anything better than my own diversity," says Whitman, and this is the characteristic note of "Song of Myself." Not that by referring to "Song of Myself" as a "comic" poem I wish too narrowly to limit the scope of discussion—nor do I suggest in using the term a special theory of Whitman or of American literature. I simply respond to my sense that "Song of Myself" is on the whole comic in tone and that although the poem's comic effects are of universal significance, they often take the specific form of American humor. If one finds "Song of Myself" enjoyable at all, it is because one is conscious of how much of the poem, though the feeling in many of its passages need not perhaps have been comic at all, nevertheless appeals to one, first and last, in its comic aspect. The poem is full of odd gestures and whimsical acts; it is written by a neo-Ovidian poet for whom self-metamorphosis is almost as free as free association, who can write "I am an old artillerist" or "I will go to the bank by the wood, and become undisguised and naked" as easily as he can write:

> Askers embody themselves in me and I am embodied in them,
> I project my hat, sit shame-faced, and beg.

The sense of incongruous diversity is very strong in "Song of Myself," and although one does not know how the sly beggar projecting his hat or the martial patriot is transformed into the "acme of things accomplish'd," and "encloser of things to be" who suddenly says:

> I find I incorporate gneiss, coal, long-threaded moss, fruits, grains,
>   esculent roots,
> And am stucco'd with quadrupeds and birds all over,

one is nevertheless charmed with the transformation.

Whitman conceives of the self, one might say, as James conceives of Christopher Newman in *The American*—as having the "look of being committed to nothing in particular, of standing in an attitude of general hospitality to the chances of life." In other words, the "self" who is the protagonist of Whitman's poem is a character portrayed in a recognizable American way; it illustrates the fluid, unformed personality exulting alternately in its provisional attempts to define itself and in its sense that it has no definition. The chief difference between "Song of Myself" and *The American* is, of course, the difference between the stages on which Whitman and James allow the self to act, James confining the action to his international scene and Whitman opening his stage out into an eventful universe which is a contradictory but witty collocation of the natural and the transcendent, the imperfect and the utopian, the personal and the generic—a dialectic world out of whose "dimness opposite equals advance" and in which there is "always a knot of identity" but "always distinction."

The very scope of Whitman's universe and the large freedom he assumes to move about in it allowed him to appropriate new areas of experience and thus to make of "Song of Myself" the original and influential poem it is. For one thing, this is the first American poem to invade that fruitful ground between lyric verse and prose fiction that so much of modern poetry cultivates, and one may suppose that "Song of Myself" has had at least as much effect on the novel as, let us say, *Moby Dick* or *The Golden Bowl* have had on poetry. The famous lines in Section 8 are, at any rate, both "imagistic" and novelistic:

> The little one sleeps in its cradle;
> I lift the gauze and look a long time, and silently brush away flies with
> my hand.
> The youngster and the red-faced girl turn aside up the bushy hill;
> I peeringly view them from the top.
> The suicide sprawls on the bloody floor of the bedroom;
> I witness the corpse with its dabbled hair, I note where the pistol has
> fallen.

It is probably true that more than anyone else, more than Blake or Baudelaire, Whitman made the city poetically available to literature:

> The blab of the pave, tires of carts, sluff of boot-soles, talk of the
> promenaders,
> The heavy omnibus, the driver with his interrogating thumb, the clank
> of the shod horses on the granite floor . . .

Such lines as these have been multitudinously echoed in modern prose and poetry, they have been endlessly recapitulated by the journey of the realistic movie camera up the city street. One might argue that Whitman's descriptions of the city made possible T. S. Eliot's *Waste Land.* The horror of Eliot's London, as of Baudelaire's *"cité pleine de rêves,"* is unknown in *Leaves of Grass,* but was not Whitman the first poet, so to speak, who put real typists and clerks in the imaginary city?

There can be no doubt that "Song of Myself" made sex a possible subject for American literature, and in this respect Whitman wrought a great revolution in, for example, his beautiful idyllic scene in which the "handsome and richly drest" woman imagines herself to join the "twenty-eight young men" who "bathe by the shore." In such a passage as this (as Henry Adams was to point out) American literature was moving toward the freedom and inclusiveness that came more naturally to Europeans—to Flaubert, or Chekhov, whose panoramic novelette *The Steppe* includes a similarly idyllic scene of bathing and sexuality. It is sex, too, although of an inverted kind, that allows Whitman to write the following unsurpassable lines in which love is at once so sublimely generalized and perfectly particularized:

> And [I know] that a kelson of the creation is love,
> And limitless are leaves stiff or drooping in the fields,
> And brown ants in the little wells beneath them,

And mossy scabs of the worm fence, and heap'd stones, elder, mullein
and poke-weed.

No summary view of "Song of Myself" would be complete
without reference to the elegiac tone of the concluding lines. If, as
we have been saying, Whitman's poem is remarkable for its gross
inclusive scope, his elegiac verse is a great act of discrimination
and nicety. Where else, in the generally grandiose nineteenth-
century melodrama of love and death shall we find anything like
the delicate precision of these incomparable lines?

> The last scud of day holds back for me;
> It flings my likeness after the rest and true as any, on the shadow'd
> wilds,
> It coaxes me to the vapor and the dusk.
> I depart as air, I shake my white locks at the runaway sun,
> I effuse my flesh in eddies, and drift it in lacy jags.
> I bequeathe myself to the dirt, to grow from the grass I love;
> If you want me again look for me under your bootsoles.
> You will hardly know who I am or what I mean,
> But I shall be good health to you nevertheless,
> And filter and fibre your blood.
> Failing to fetch me at first keep encouraged,
> Missing me one place, search another,
> I stop somewhere, waiting for you.

As every poet does, Whitman asks us provisionally to accept
the imagined world of his poem. It is a fantastic world in which it
is presumed that the self can become identical with all other
selves in the universe, regardless of time and space. Not without
precedent in Hindu poetry, this central metaphor is, as an artistic
device, unique in American literature, as is the extraordinary collection of small imagist poems, versified short stories, realistic
urban and rural genre paintings, inventories, homilies, philosophiz-
ings, farcical episodes, confessions, and lyric musings it encompasses
in "Song of Myself." Yet as heavily taxing our powers of provisional
credence, as inventing a highly idiosyncratic and illusory world,
"Song of Myself" invites comparison with other curious works of
the American imagination—*Moby Dick,* let us say, and *The Scarlet
Letter* and *The Wings of the Dove.* It is of the first importance at any
rate to see that Whitman's relation of the self to the rest of the
universe is a successful aesthetic or compositional device, whatever we may think of it as a moral assertion.

If we look at Whitman's implicit metaphor more closely, we see that it consists in the paradox of "identity" The opening words of *Leaves of Grass,* placed there in 1867, state the paradox:

> One's-self I sing, a simple separate person,
> Yet utter the word Democratic, the word En-Masse.

In more general terms the opening lines of "Song of Myself" state the same paradox:

> I celebrate myself and sing myself;
> And what I assume you shall assume;
> For every atom belonging to me, as good belongs to you.

Both politically and by nature man has "identity," in two senses of the word: on the one hand, he is integral in himself, unique, and separate; on the other hand, he is equal to, or even the same as, everyone else. Like the Concord transcendentalists, Whitman was easily led in prophetic moods to generalize the second term of the paradox of identity beyond the merely human world and with his ruthless equalitarianism to conceive the All, a vast cosmic democracy, placid, without episode, separation or conflict, though suffused, perhaps, with a bland illumination. More than anything else, it is this latter tendency which finally ruined Whitman as a poet, submerging as it did, his chief forte and glory—his entirely original, vividly realistic presentation of the comedy and pathos of "the simple separate person."

What finally happens is that Whitman loses his sense that his metaphor of self vs. en-masse is a *paradox,* that self and en-masse are in dialectic opposition. When this sense is lost the spontaneously eventful, flowing, and largely indeterminate universe of "Song of Myself" is replaced by a universe that is both mechanical and vaguely abstract. Whatever, in this universe, is in a state of becoming is moving toward the All, and the self becomes merely the vehicle by which the journey is made.

In some of his best as well as in some of his worst poems, Whitman actually conceives of the self as making a journey—for example, "Song of the Open Road," "Crossing Brooklyn Ferry," and "Passage to India." In others the self journeys, as it were, not forward and outward but backward and inward, back to the roots of its being, and discovers there a final mystery, or love, comradeship, or death—for example, the *Calamus* and *Sea Drift* poems.

(Notably among the latter are "Out of the Cradle Endlessly Rocking" and "As I Ebb'd with the Ocean of Life".) In "Song of Myself," however, the self is not felt to be incomplete; it has no questing odyssey to make. It stands aggressively at the center of things, "Sure as the most certain sure, plumb in the uprights, well entretied, braced in the beams." It summons the universe, "syphons" universal experience through its dilating pores, calls "anything back again when I desire it." Or the self imagines itself to be infinitely expandable and contractible (like the web of the spider in Whitman's little poem called "A Noiseless Patient Spider"), so that there is no place where at any moment it may not be, no thing or person with whom it may not merge, no act in which it may not participate. Of great importance is the fact that most of "Song of Myself" has to do not with the self searching for a final identity but with the self escaping a series of identities which threaten to destroy its lively and various spontaneity. This combination of attitudes is what gives "Song of Myself" the alternately ecstatic and gravely musing, pastoral-godlike stability one feels at the center, around which, however, the poet is able to weave the most astonishing embellishments of wit and lyric song.

This is perhaps a valid way of feeling the shifting modes of sensibility in the poem. Yet it would be wrong to attribute any clear structure to "Song of Myself." "The United States themselves are essentially the greatest poem," wrote Whitman in his preface. A Jacksonian Democrat, Whitman was not an admirer of federal unity, either in a nation or a poem. He was content to make his poem a loose congeries of states and half-settled territories. He was content that his poem should mirror that "freshness and candor of... physiognomy," that "picturesque looseness of carriage," and that "deathless attachment to freedom" which, in his preface, he attributed to his countrymen. His style would be organic; he would "speak in literature with the perfect rectitude and insouciance" of animals and growing things. Although capable of finely pictorial images, Whitman composed more by ear than by eye, and his ear being attuned to music of the looser, more variable sort, such as the Italian operas, he strung his poems together on a free melodic line and by means of motifs, voices, recapitulations, recitatives, rests, *crescendi* and *diminuendi*.

The motif of "Song of Myself" is the self taking on a bewildering variety of identities and with a truly virtuoso agility ex-
tricating itself from each one. The poem beings with the exhorta-
tion to leave the "rooms full of perfume," the "creeds and schools."
Apart from conventions,

> Apart from the pulling and hauling stands what I am,
> Stands amused, complacent, compassionating, idle, unitary.

Having put society and convention behind, "What I am" finds
itself in an Edenlike, early-morning world, wherein one easily observes the portentous dialectics of the universe:

> Urge and urge and urge,
> Always the procreant urge of the world.
> Out of the dimness opposite equals advance, always substance and in-
>   crease, always sex,
> Always a knit of identity, always distinction, always a breed of life.

But of more importance is the fact that in this idyllic world the
veil is lifted from the jaundiced eye, the cramped sensibility is set
free, the senses and pores of the body receive the joyful intelligences
dispatched to them by a friendly and providential nature. The self
appears to be the offspring of a happy union of body and soul;
sublime and delightful thoughts issue from the mind in the same
miraculous way as the grass from the ground. Death itself is seen
to be "lucky." And, in short, "what I am" can well afford to be
complacent, to be certain that it is "unitary." Nor is the feeling of
power denied to the self. It derives power from nature, as does the
horse—"affectionate, haughty, electrical"—with which the poet
compares himself. It derives power, too, from identification with
others—the "runaway slave," "the butcher-boy," the "black-
smiths," "the boatmen and clam-diggers," the "trapper," the "red
girl"—and finally with America itself.

> In me the caresser of life wherever moving, backward as well as
>   forward sluing,
> To niches aside and junior bending, not a person or object missing,
> Absorbing all to myself and for this song.

Sections 24–28, though in places rather obscure, contain the
essence of Whitman's drama of identity. The poet begins by proclaiming himself a Kosmos, and commanding us to "unscrew the
locks from the doors!/Unscrew the doors themselves from their

jambs!" so that the universe may flow through him—"through me the current and index" (that is, the undifferentiated flux and the "identities" that emerge therefrom). This proclamation announces not only the unshakable status and palpable reality but also the redemptive powers of the self. In a world which has been created by banishing social sanctions and social intelligence, what will keep man from being lost in idiocy, crime, squalor? What of that underground realm inhabited by

> . . . the deform'd, trivial, flat, foolish, despised,
> Fog in the air, beetles rolling balls of dung?

The threat of madness, crime, and obscenity is to be allayed by the curative powers of that Adamic world where wisdom consists in uttering "the pass-word primeval," "the sign of democracy." Siphoned through the haughty, electrical self or discussed frankly by persons not inhibited by prudery (the discourses seem perilously interchangeable), the crimes and obscenities will be redeemed:

> Voices indecent by me clarified and transfigur'd.

The poet then records a dreamlike idyl of auto-erotic experience, in which the parts of the body merge mysteriously with natural objects, and a great deal of diffuse and wistful love is generated. And, when dawn comes, the redemption is symbolized in these astonishing metaphors:

> Hefts of the moving world at innocent gambols silently rising, freshly
>   exuding,
> Scooting obliquely high and low.
> Something I cannot see puts upward libidinous prongs,
> Seas of bright juice suffuse heaven.

The poem then speaks anew of how the self may be distorted or destroyed. The poet's "identity" is said to be assailed and warped into other "identities" by agents referred to as "traitors," "wasters," and "marauders." Somewhat elusive in particular, these appear to have in common a quality of aggressiveness and imperiousness. They act as a radical individualist conceives society to act. They break down the self, they swagger, they assert convention, responsibility and reason, they dominate and impose passivity and furtiveness on the individual.

The beautiful, diffuse, kindly dawn is succeeded by a more formidable, a more imperious, apparition. The "dazzling and tremendous" sun leaps over the horizon and cries, "See then whether you shall be master!" The poet replies to this challenge by saying that the sunrise would indeed "kill me/If I could not now and always send sunrise out of me." The power with which the poet defeats what seeks to destroy him is asserted to be "my vision" and "my voice."

> My voice goes after what my eyes cannot reach,
> With the twirl of my tongue I encompass worlds.

In Section 26 both the metaphorical effects and the subject matter shift from the visual to the auditory. The "bravuras of birds, bustle of growing wheat, gossip of flames, clack of sticks cooking my meals"—these and myriad other sounds amplify into a symphonic orchestration. The crescendo and dying fall of the conclusion are rendered with full tone and exquisite wit.

> I hear the train'd soprano (what work, with hers, is this?)
> The orchestra whirls me wider than Uranus flies,
> It wrenches such ardors from me I did not know I possess'd them
> It sails me, I dab with bare feet, they are lick'd by the indolent waves,
> I am cut by bitter and angry hail, I lose my breath,
> Steep'd amid honey'd morphine, my windpipe throttled in fakes of death,
> At length let up again to feel the puzzle of puzzles,
> And that we call Being.

But again the poet is confronted with "Being"—that is, form or identity—and is not certain that this is the Being he wants to be. It is therefore dissipated and generalized, in Section 27, into a universal process of reincarnation.

In Section 28 there occurs the famous auto-erotic pastoral dream in which "purient provokers," like nibbling cows, "graze at the edges of me." The "provokers," conceived as symbolic of the sense of touch, arouse and madden the dreaming poet and then they all unite "to stand on a headland and worry me." After touch has "quivered" him "to a new identity"—has left him confused, vexed, self-reproachful, and isolated—he proceeds in the following sections to resume a "true," "real," or "divine" identity. This act of restoration is accomplished through love, natural piety, pastoral and cosmic meditations, symbolic fusions of self with America, allegations of the "deific" nature of democratic man, ritual celebrations, and fatherly preachments, and finally, in the last Section, by the assertion that death is also merely an extrication of the self from an identity. . . .

Calvin S. Brown

XII

The Musical Development of Symbols: Whitman

. . . We have frequently had occasion to note the difficulties of repetition or variation in literature on any extensive scale and to observe that these difficulties apply with particular force to any literary attempts at development of material by processes analogous to those of music. Extensive symbolism is the best solution which has been found, and it is not uncommon for a poet speaking through symbols to approximate closely to the methods and effects of music. However, we cannot assume musical influence in such cases unless there is clear external evidence for its existence: the natural poetic methods of handling symbols resemble musical development, and even musically ignorant poets have, on occasion, produced close musical analogies by a heightening of these methods.

Walt Whitman is a good case in point. He must have been practically a musical illiterate, for his references to music are of a uniform and magnificent banality: "The conductor beats time for his band and all the performers follow him,"—"The jay in the woods never studied the gamut, yet trills pretty well to me,"— "With music strong I come, with my cornets and my drums,"—

> I heard the violoncello, ('tis the young man's heart's complaint,)
> I hear the key'd cornet, it glides quickly in through my ears,

It shakes mad-sweet pangs through my belly and breast.
I hear the chorus, it is a grand opera,
Ah this indeed is music—this suits me.[1]

Even as a poet Whitman seems generally to have been remarkably insensitive to the possibilities (and dangers) of sound. His own characterization of his poems as a "barbaric yawp"[2] is a masterpiece of understatement for such a line as "See, dearest mother, the letter says Pete will soon be better."[3] Furthermore, the great bulk of his poetry is weakened by a formlessness which would seem to arise from an utter lack of architectonic ability. All things considered, Whitman seems offhand to offer little promise of illumination on the musical possibilities of poetry.

Nevertheless, in a few poems of medium length he attained a firm structure and real poetic distinction by a treatment of symbols closely parallel to the musical development of themes. In the darkness of his musical ignorance we can only grope for an explanation. The fact that such poems as *Crossing Brooklyn Ferry* and *When Lilacs Last in the Dooryard Bloom'd* confine themselves to a single and limited subject instead of magniloquently embracing the universe probably contributed considerably to their coherence. Furthermore, the second of these poems was the product of deeply felt personal experience,[4] and thus may well have unconsciously shaped itself in the mind of a man who seldom took the trouble consciously to organize his work. Whatever the explanation may be, only the poem itself concerns us here. . . .

Even a casual reading of *When Lilacs Last in the the Dooryard Bloom'd* shows that the entire effect is dependent on the three principal symbols of lilac, star, and bird; and that these symbols are constantly varied in application and combined both with each other and with various subsidiary symbols and ideas. A detailed examination will reveal how such an excellent and comparatively long poetic work is evolved out of such slight materials. But before beginning a consideration of the structure of the poem we may note that this symbolic treatment has the remarkable effect of universalizing the theme. The personal and historical considerations may add a certain amount of interest, but that interest is not of an essential nature. Lincoln's death on April 15 explains the choice of symbols: Venus is a conspicuous evening star; the lilacs are in bloom in Brooklyn; and the spring singing of the hermit thrush is at its height. But these facts are all unessential, for the first introduction of the symbols makes the association clear. Furthermore, Lincoln is never named in the poem, and—though Whitman would doubtless resent such a statement—he is hardly essential to it. This is true because the poem itself conveys the broader idea of grief for the death of a great man on whom the destiny of a nation hangs.

It is common knowledge that Beethoven originally dedicated his *Eroica* to Napoleon (as an apostle of freedom rather than as a conqueror), but when Napoleon assumed the title of Emperor, Beethoven tore up the title-page. The work was finally called "Heroic Symphony, composed to celebrate the memory of a great man." [5] And it has been significantly pointed out that Beethoven did not need to change a note of the music: what would do for Napoleon would do equally well for the general idea of greatness. The same principle applies to Whitman's celebration of Lincoln. Though the specific nature of such literary symbols as the lilac and the hermit thrush aids a local application, the poem is really "composed to celebrate the memory of a great man" and is universal in its application. By avoiding direct statement it goes far beyond a provincial interest in the Civil War and the war president. The poem does contain a few particularities, but, broadly speaking, it could be applied to Lee, or to the Napoleon for whom the *Eroica* was written (and who was only a *memory* when the work was published) or to Thomas à Becket with almost equal fittingness. When we consider the deliberate local particularity of the great bulk of Whitman's work this fact is startling. The explanation, however, is obvious: by using symbolic themes developed in what is essentially a musical way, Whitman achieved the universality of great music rather than the particularity of the ordinary type of *in memoriam* verse.

An examination of the poem will make the musical nature of its development clear. Section 1 introduces the lilac and star, and associates them with past and future mourning. Already, then, the real subject is announced—not the death of Lincoln, as we are in the habit of loosely saying, but the undying grief for the death of a great man. The fourth line announces the trinity which forms the structural basis of the poem, but for the moment it does not make all the symbols specific. The lilac and the "drooping star in the west" are mentioned again, but the third element is an abstraction, the "thought of him I love," which is not yet given symbolic form. The principal theme of the last movement of the *Eroica* is not announced immediately, but its way is prepared by the use of a motive which later serves as its accompaniment. In an analogous way the poet here prepares for the later introduction of the third of his symbols, the bird.

Section 2 develops the recently introduced symbol of the star. By associating it with night, referring to it as "fallen" and "disappear'd," hidden by black murk, Whitman establishes the idea of grief for departed brilliance and prepares for the later specific references to death. Likewise, in the last two lines, he reiterates the fact that the real topic is his own grief rather than the blotting out of the star.

In Section 3 he returns to the lilac and develops the physical aspect of the symbol by a description of its setting, leaves, flowers, and perfume. The echo of the "thought of him I love" (line 6) heard in "the perfume strong I love" (line 14) goes beyond a mere playing with words: it establishes a more direct connection between the thought of Lincoln and the odor of the flower. We shall see that this particular little verbal formula is later used several times for a similar purpose. The repetition of parts of the description within Section 3 ("heart-shaped leaves of rich green") does not have, for the moment, any such structural purpose, but is made for its own sake. The last line of the section extends the purpose of the symbol in its account of breaking off a sprig, but since this statement is a preparation for a later union of ideas, it is deliberately left hanging at this point.

Section 4 is entirely devoted to the announcement of the third of the principal themes, the hermit thrush singing alone in the swamp. His song is associated immediately with death and characterized as "Death's outlet song of life."

The three principal themes have now been introduced. Though Whitman is certainly following no musical model and is probably unaware of the analogy, we might say that the exposition has been completed, and the development is about to begin. A composer writing in any of the larger forms must consider not only the beauty or effectiveness of his themes in their original

statements, but also their possibilities of development. What opportunities do Whitman's symbols present? Being physical objects,
they have attributes perceptible to the senses as well as to abstract
thought. As a matter of fact, most of their symbolic development
is achieved by associating their various sensuous attributes with
abstract concepts. Therefore a variety of sensuous attributes will
permit a variety of developments. Considering the symbols from
this standpoint, we see that they are carefully selected. The lilac
has the color of leaf and flower, the pattern of heart-shaped leaves
and pointed blossoms, and an intangible, all-enveloping perfume.
The star has its light against darkness (both of night in general
and of the obscuring cloud), and it also has motion of a slow and
stately type which can be interpreted as either drooping or beckoning. And the bird has his own color, his setting in the swamp
with its dim trees and its perfume, and, above all, his song. These
various attributes of the symbols include the primary senses and,
together with associations of their settings and of abstractions for
which they come to stand, allow for rich development.

Section 5 includes the first direct mention of Lincoln's funeral, but the coffin is mentioned only at the end of a periodic sentence. Before this there is a series of visual images of plants, woods,
and fields—images which suggest the lilac and the bird without
containing any direct reference to them.

Section 6 is built on the same plan. It is ostensibly a continuation of the description of the funeral procession, but its allusions
to the symbols are more direct than those of the preceding section.
The "great cloud darkening the land" not only connects with "the
cities draped in black"; it also goes back to "the black murk that
hides the star" (line 9). Similarly the "flambeaus of the night"
make an association with the star itself, while the "dirges through
the night" suggest the song of the bird. Also, the dominant background of night is an intensification of the dimness of the swamp
and the setting of the drooping star. And finally the lilac sprig
broken off for no particular reason (as far as one could tell when
it was mentioned at the end of Section 3) is placed on the coffin.
Thus Section 6 connects the star and the bird with the funeral
procession by concealed allusions, and closes with a direct linking
of the lilac and the coffin.

In Section 7 this association is generalized. The lilac is not merely for the coffin of Lincoln, but for all coffins. Even more than for the dead it is for "sane and sacred death." This association, very necessary in later parts of the poem, is repeated and elaborated in the second division of the section. This section also contains the first appearance of a pure abstraction, the concept of death. Its reality in this poem— as compared with its artificiality in many literary works—is due to the fact that the abstraction is not thrown at the reader, but is *developed* by a combination of simple physical objects: the flower is broken—it is destined for a coffin—not for this coffin only, but for those of all the dead—and hence for death itself. Since the abstraction is built up within the poem, the author's attitude towards it can be developed at the same time, and thus there is nothing of the ordinary personification as a monster or a grim reaper. From the very first mention we have the poet (like the bird) chanting sane and sacred death and wishing to sing a song for him.

Section 8 is devoted to an intensive development of the star theme. It makes a direct connection between the previously mentioned woe and drooping of the star and the death of Lincoln. The star is also associated with the poet's earlier feeling of foreboding, and its appearance is made into a prophecy. Also, the idea of night, both as a background for the star and as a subsidiary symbol of death and grief in itself, is closely associated with that of the star. The very word *night* is reiterated in emphatic positions so that it sets the tone of the entire passage.

The next section effects a union between the themes of bird and star. This fusion is presented by a union of sense impressions enabling both symbols to be simultaneously present, for the poet hears the call of the bird as a summons, but waits to watch "the star of my departing comrade." The song of the thrush has already been something of a solace for death, and that symbolism is later to be more fully developed, but the declining star has been associated with foreboding and grief. This combination of the two symbols into a single scene, with one detaining and the other calling, thus takes on a philosophical significance: the poet hears in the distance the theoretically known idea that death is sane and sacred—is, as the bird says specifically in a later passage (line

135) "lovely and soothing death." But at the time of the death itself
(the sinking of the star) this abstract consolation is powerless to
draw him from his grief. "Philosophy easily overcomes past and
future sorrows, but present sorrows overcome philosophy."[6]

Since the three principal symbols have now received sufficient
development and interconnection for the time being, the next
three sections form an interlude in which they are kept before the
reader only by occasional allusions. Sections 10 and 11 are carefully balanced within themselves and against each other. The shift
of subject leads now to a direct statement of the author's personal
feeling—a statement more specific than that presented through
the symbols, but still reinforced by them. The transition is clearly
marked at the beginning of Section 10: the bird has been singing
of the dead, but "how shall I *warble* myself of the dead one there
I loved?" (Note the return of the "him I love" formula in these
two sections.) The real question of Section 10 involves the per-
fuming of the grave and thus makes a connection with the lilac
laid on the coffin, but the answer expands its meaning, for not
only—not merely—the lilac, but the sea-winds sweeping across the
continent and this poem itself shall be memorials.

Section 11, with its biblical question and answer, affords a
close parallel. The song of praise and the perfume of memory are
intangibles, but what shall the pictures be to adorn the burial-
house? They shall be all objects and seasons of nature and civilization, including (to expand and connect with the earlier symbols)
the pale green leaves and "floods of yellow gold of the gorgeous,
indolent, sinking sun." This last figure is a transposition to a totally
different mood and symbolism of the theme of the sinking star.

In Section 12 the same line of development is continued: all
the land is praised, both for itself and (by implication) as a continuing memorial to the man who stood by it in its hour of need.
The second part of the section is particularly remarkable in that
its pictures run through the course of a day (with what seem to be
reminiscences of Eve's morning song to Adam), thus making time
itself into a visibly apprehended thing. Furthermore, by this very
process the sun, which was developed from the symbol of the star
in the previous section, is now resumed in the form in which it was
there left, and is skilfully modulated back into its normal form
and setting.

Section 13 returns emphatically to the bird, whose song is

destined for extensive development in the next section. The verbal
return to the opening of Section 9 reestablishes the continuity of
the bird's song after the author's own chant of his hero and his
country. At this point it is well to note that, as the symbols are
interwoven into a closer texture, the free verse tends to fall into
regular patterns. The questions in Sections 10 and 11 were
strongly metrical, and the second part of Section 12 was comparatively regular. Now, with lines 100 and 101, we get a regular and
highly effective elegiac couplet:

> Sing from the swamps, the recesses, pour your chant from the bushes.
> Limitless out of the dusk, out of the cedars and pines.

The tendency towards regular metrical forms continues throughout the remainder of the poem,[7] and this passage is echoed, both
in subject and in meter, at the conclusion. The bird's song is now
specifically identified with the human song of woe, for the idea of
comfort is to be fully developed in the next section. We have
a momentary return to the exact combination of symbols used at
the end of Section 9 (except that the star is about to depart), with
the addition of the odor of the lilac. Here the three symbols can
be simultaneously presented and perceived because each is presented to a different sense: the poet can watch the star while he
hears the song of the bird and is surrounded by the mastering
odor of the lilac.

Section 14, by far the longest division of the poem, makes
specific the idea towards which the interrelated symbols have been
converging. It does this by telling straight through, in symbolical
form, the poet's reaction to the death of Lincoln. As Whitman
looked out in his imagination over the whole of the country, with
its various scenery and different pursuits, the black cloud of death
appeared, not over the star this time, but over the whole of the
nation, and with the fact of death came its thought and its sacred
knowledge. Like two comrades they went with the poet when he
fled in his grief to "the hiding receiving night, that talks not." The
thought of death seems to be a personified representation of the
involuntary grief which accompanies death; whereas the knowledge of death is that perception of its true meaning which is
expressed fully in the song of the bird. The bird here becomes not
only himself, but also the voice of nature in its comforting power,
receiving the poet (with his thought and knowledge of death), and

making explicit to him his own latent thought: "And the voice of my spirit tallied the song of the bird" (line 134). This thought is a song praising death as a soothing, delivering power, and lines 151–158 make it clear that all nature is represented in the song of the bird. In these lines, as also in the poet's flight to the night for comfort, the symbol of night undergoes a transformation parallel to that of death itself. We have already noted that night, the cloud, and darkness have formed a group of subsidiary symbols connected with the idea of death. Since the day described in Section 12 and ending with "the welcome night and the stars," this value of night has been shifting, along with the parallel idea of death, to one of peace and majesty, to the picture in line 154 of "huge and thoughtful night."

This transformation is continued in Section 15 with a return to the poet standing in the night, hearing the song of the bird and realizing that it is also the song of his own soul. As he stands there with his allegorical comrades the idea which the bird's song has expressed about Lincoln's death expands (exactly as did the significance of the lilac laid on the coffin) to an acceptance of death in general. And here, for the first time, there is a reference to the particular circumstances of Lincoln's presidency. The realization, the "knowledge of death" in the song of the bird, extends to all the slain of the war as a vision of its carnage unfolds before the poet. "My sight that was bound in my eyes unclosed," and through the experience of Lincoln's death he received comfort for all the hosts of the slain. Finally, a reconciliation between the thought and the knowledge of death is made by the realization that grief and suffering remain with the living (in their thought of the death of others), but death itself is a deliverer to those who come to know it.

This central section of the poem has been presented through one of the leading symbols as the song of the bird, but otherwise it has been an interlude employing its own symbolic characters and visions. What now remains is to return to the leading symbols, which have been greatly enriched by the episode. This is briefly and effectively done in the coda, Section 16. The phrases are frequently reminiscent of those in the opening sections of the poem, as, passing the visions, the night, the comrades, the song of the bird and his answering soul (for moments of full insight, like other things, become memories)—passing all these, the poet leaves the lilac where he found it, "in the dooryard, blooming, returning with spring." There is a summary of the principal themes and most of the subsidiary ones, the chant of the poet's soul now taking its place as a fully developed motive parallel to the three main ones, and all these things are memories, "retrievements out of the night." Here, in its last appearance, the multiple symbol of night reaches a new meaning which is a fusion of all the others. It has represented the general idea of death, the pall of grief over the land, the literal setting of the star, and the revelation of the bird. Now it embraces all these meanings simultaneously and comes to signify the total experience, from which the poet emerges with the four symbols, now combined into a single line to end the poem with the memory of that experience:

> Lilac and star and bird twined with the chant of my soul,
> There in the fragrant pines and the cedars dusk and dim.

One is tempted to speak of exposition, development, recapitulation, first and second subjects, etc., in connection with this poem. By yielding to that temptation one might easily make out some procrustean adaptation of sonata form, or of the rondo, or even of a large ABA form. The very fact, however, that there would be such a choice is sufficient proof that any identification of the structure of this poem with a musical form would be a falsification. On the other hand, some relationship with music is obvious. There is no single passage, no individual treatment of a symbol which is not in keeping with established and independent literary practise, but the degree to which these devices are employed and the fact that the entire poem depends on them for its success are, to say the least, unusual in literary works.

Finally, then, we must classify Whitman's elegy as a poem not based on any specific musical form and probably not written with any musical analogy in mind, but nevertheless conforming to certain general structural principles which are more musical than literary. The essential plan is that of three symbols separately introduced, developed both singly and in every sort of combination (with the addition of subsidiary symbols and of a fourth one of major importance—"the tallying chant of my soul"—derived from the interplay of the first three), and finally restated in much their original form, but with a great enrichment resulting from their intermediate relationships. This is clearly the circular structure of

the typical musical composition rather than the linear development of the literary work. Furthermore, the principle (though not
the structure itself) is that of sonata form: statement of related but
contrasting themes, development of these themes, and recapitulation of them in much their original form.

Also, the effect lies in the development of these themes.
Anyone called on to give a summary of the logical content of the
poem will find himself considerably embarrassed. One cannot say
what the poem is "about" except that it is about the symbols
themselves and their interrelationships—including the various
treatments of the idea of death as one of these symbols. And no
verbal summary can represent the material of the poem except in
these terms. It is clearly inadequate to say that the poem is
"about" the death of Lincoln, or death in general, except in the
same way that Beethoven's *Fifth Symphony* is—if we take the old
yarn seriously—about fate. The real subject of the poem is the
complex and beautiful interrelationship in the author's mind by
which a number of hitherto insignificant things have come to
symbolize a complex experience. It is really about its symbols and
their development, precisely as the Beethoven symphony is really
about its themes and their interrelationships. Thus this poem
approaches far more closely than do most literary works to that
condition which Schopenhauer and Pater describe as the particular glory of music—the inseparability of form and content.

NOTES

1. Whitman, *Song of Myself,* Sections 15, 13, 18, and 26, respectively.

2. *Ibid.,* Section 52.

3. "Come up from the Fields, Father," line 28.

4. See the entries in Whitman's *Specimen Days* under August 12, 1863; and under March 4 and April 16, 1865.

5. SINFONIA EROICA, composta per festeggiare il sovvenire di un grand' Uomo . . . .

6. La philosophie triomphe aisément des maux passés et des maux à venir, mais les maux présents triomphent d'elle. (La Rochefoucauld, Maxim 22)

7. For a few examples, note the dactylic hexameters of lines 119 and 124 (the latter being the first line of another elegiac couplet) and the iambic pentameters of lines 118 and 155, as well as the final couplet. Notice also that the elegiac couplet form of three of the references to the swamp with its dim cedars and pines helps to point out the repetitions of the three.

Allen Tate

XIII

Emily Dickinson

Great poetry needs no special features of difficulty to make it mysterious. When it has them, the reputation of the poet is likely to remain uncertain. This is still true of Donne, and it is true of Emily Dickinson, whose verse appeared in an age unfavorable to the use of intelligence in poetry. Her poetry is not like any other poetry of her time; it is not like any of the innumerable kinds of verse written today. In still another respect it is far removed from us. It is a poetry of ideas, and it demands of the reader a point of view—not an opinion of the New Deal or of the League of Nations, but an ingrained philosophy that is fundamental, a settled attitude that is almost extinct in this eclectic age. Yet it is not the sort of poetry of ideas which, like Pope's, requires a point of view only. It requires also, for the deepest understanding, which must go beneath the verbal excitement of the style, a highly developed sense of the specific quality of poetry—a quality that most persons accept as the accidental feature of something else that the poet thinks he has to say. This is one reason why Miss Dickinson's poetry has not been widely read.

There is another reason, and it is a part of the problem peculiar to a poetry that comes out of fundamental ideas. We lack a tradition of criticism. There were no points of critical reference

From *On The Limits of Poetry*, 1948, New York, The Swallow Press, Inc. Copyright 1948 by Allen Tate. Reprinted by permission of the author and publisher.

passed on to us from a preceding generation. I am not upholding here the so-called dead-hand of tradition, but rather a rational insight into the meaning of the present in terms of some imaginable past implicit in our own lives: we need a body of ideas that can bear upon the course of the spirit and yet remain coherent as a rational instrument. We ignore the present, which is momently translated into the past, and derive our standards from imaginative constructions of the future. The hard contingency of fact invariably breaks these standards down, leaving us the intellectual chaos which is the sore distress of American criticism. Marxian criticism has become the latest disguise of this heresy.

Still another difficulty stands between us and Miss Dickinson. It is the failure of the scholars to feel more than biographical curiosity about her. We have scholarship, but that is no substitute for a critical tradition. Miss Dickinson's value to the research scholar, who likes historical difficulty for its own sake, is slight; she is too near to possess the remoteness of literature. Perhaps her appropriate setting would be the age of Cowley or of Donne. Yet in her own historical setting she is, nevertheless, remarkable and special.

Although the intellectual climate into which she was born, in 1830, had, as all times have, the features of a transition, the period was also a major crisis culminating in the war between the States. After that war, in New England as well as in the South, spiritual crises were definitely minor until the First World War.

Yet, a generation before the war of 1861–65, the transformation of New England had begun. When Samuel Slater in 1790 thwarted the British embargo on mill-machinery by committing to memory the whole design of a cotton spinner and bringing it to Massachusetts, he planted the seed of the "Western spirit." By 1825 its growth in the East was rank enough to begin choking out the ideas and habits of living that New England along with Virginia had kept in unconscious allegiance to Europe. To the casual observer, perhaps, the New England character of 1830 was largely an eighteenth-century character. But theocracy was on the decline, and industrialism was rising—as Emerson, in an unusually lucid moment, put it, "Things are in the saddle." The energy that had built the meeting-house ran the factory.

Now the idea that moved the theocratic state is the most

interesting historically of all American ideas. It was, of course, powerful in seventeenth-century England, but in America, where the long arm of Laud could not reach, it acquired an unchecked social and political influence. The important thing to remember about the puritan theocracy is that it permeated, as it could never have done in England, a whole society. It gave final, definite meaning to life, the life of pious and impious, of learned and vulgar alike. It gave—and this is its significance for Emily Dickinson, and in only slightly lesser degree for Melville and Hawthorne—it gave an heroic proportion and a tragic mode to the experience of the individual. The history of the New England theocracy, from Apostle Eliot to Cotton Mather, is rich in gigantic intellects that broke down—or so it must appear to an outsider—in a kind of moral decadence and depravity. Socially we may not like the New England idea. Yet it had an immense, incalculable value for literature: it dramatized the human soul.

But by 1850 the great fortunes had been made (in the rum, slave, and milling industries), and New England became a museum. The whatnots groaned under the load of knickknacks, the fine china dogs and cats, the pieces of Oriental jade, the chips off the leaning tower at Pisa. There were the rare books and the cosmopolitan learning. It was all equally displayed as the evidence of a superior culture. The Gilded Age had already begun. But culture, in the true sense, was disappearing. Where the old order, formidable as it was, had held all this personal experience, this eclectic excitement, in a comprehensible whole, the new order tended to flatten it out in a common experience that was not quite in common; it exalted more and more the personal and the unique in the interior sense. Where the old-fashioned puritans got together on a rigid doctrine, and could thus be individualists in manners, the nineteenth-century New Englander, lacking a genuine religious center, began to be a social conformist. The common idea of the Redemption, for example, was replaced by the conformist idea of respectability among neighbors whose spiritual disorder, not very evident at the surface, was becoming acute. A great idea was breaking up, and society was moving towards external uniformity, which is usually the measure of the spiritual sterility inside.

At this juncture Emerson came upon the scene: the Lucifer of Concord, he had better be called hereafter, for he was the light-bearer who could see nothing but light, and was fearfully blind. He looked around and saw the uniformity of life, and called it the routine of tradition, the tyranny of the theological idea. The death of Priam put an end to the hope of Troy, but it was a slight feat of arms for the doughty Pyrrhus; Priam was an old gentleman and almost dead. So was theocracy; and Emerson killed it. In this way he accelerated a tendency that he disliked. It was a great intellectual mistake. By it Emerson unwittingly became the prophet of a piratical industrialism, a consequence of his own transcendental individualism that he could not foresee. He was hoist with his own petard.

He discredited more than any other man the puritan drama of the soul. The age that followed, from 1865 on, expired in a genteel secularism, a mildly didactic order of feeling whose ornaments were Lowell, Longfellow, and Holmes. "After Emerson had done his work," says Mr. Robert Penn Warren, "any tragic possibilities in that culture were dissipated." Hawthorne alone in his time kept pure, in the primitive terms, the primitive vision; he brings the puritan tragedy to its climax. Man, measured by a great idea outside himself, is found wanting. But for Emerson man is greater than any idea and, being himself the Over-Soul, is innately perfect; there is no struggle because—I state the Emersonian doctrine, which is very slippery, in its extreme terms— because there is no possibility of error. There is no drama in human character because there is no tragic fault. It is not surprising, then, that after Emerson New England literature tastes like a sip of cambric tea. Its center of vision has disappeared. There is Hawthorne looking back, there is Emerson looking not too clearly at anything ahead: Emily Dickinson, who has in her something of both, comes in somewhere between.

With the exception of Poe there is no other American poet whose work so steadily emerges, under pressure of certain disintegrating obsessions, from the framework of moral character. There is none of whom it is truer to say that the poet *is* the poetry. Perhaps this explains the zeal of her admirers for her biography; it explains, in part at least, the gratuitous mystery that Mrs. Bianchi, a niece of the poet and her official biographer, has made of her life. The devoted controversy that Miss Josephine Pollitt and Miss Genevieve Taggard started a few years ago with their excellent books shows the extent to which the critics feel the intimate connection of her life and work. Admiration and affection are pleased to linger over the tokens of a great life; but the solution to the Dickinson enigma is peculiarly superior to fact.

The meaning of the identity—which we merely feel—of character and poetry would be exceedingly obscure, even if we could draw up a kind of Binet correlation between the two sets of "facts." Miss Dickinson was a recluse; but her poetry is rich with a profound and varied experience. Where did she get it? Now some of the biographers, nervous in the presence of this discrepancy, are eager to find her a love affair, and I think this search is due to a modern prejudice: we believe that no virgin can know enough to write poetry. We shall never learn where she got the rich quality of her mind. The moral image that we have of Miss Dickinson stands out in every poem; it is that of a dominating spinster whose very sweetness must have been formidable. Yet her poetry constantly moves within an absolute order of truths that overwhelmed her simply because to her they were unalterably fixed. It is dangerous to assume that her "life," which to the biographers means the thwarted love affair she is supposed to have had, gave to her poetry a decisive direction. It is even more dangerous to suppose that it made her a poet.

Poets are mysterious, but a poet when all is said is not much more mysterious than a banker. The critics remain spellbound by the technical license of her verse and by the puzzle of her personal life. Personality is a legitimate interest because it is an incurable interest, but legitimate as a personal interest only; it will never give up the key to anyone's verse. Used to that end, the interest is false. "It is apparent," writes Mr. Conrad Aiken, "that Miss Dickinson became a hermit by deliberate and conscious choice"— a sensible remark that we cannot repeat too often. If it were necessary to explain her seclusion with disappointment in love, there would remain the discrepancy between what the seclusion produced and the seclusion looked at as a cause. The effect, which is her poetry, would imply the whole complex of anterior fact, which was the social and religious structure of New England.

The problem to be kept in mind is thus the meaning of her "deliberate and conscious" decision to withdraw from life to her upstairs room. This simple fact is not very important. But that it must have been her sole way of acting out her part in the history of her culture, which made, with the variations of circumstance, a single demand upon all its representatives—this is of the greatest consequence. All pity for Miss Dickinson's "starved life" is misdirected. Her life was one of the richest and deepest ever lived on this continent.

When she went upstairs and closed the door, she mastered life by rejecting it. Others in their way had done it before; still others did it later. If we suppose—which is to suppose the improbable—that the love-affair precipitated the seclusion, it was only a pretext; she would have found another. Mastery of the world by rejecting the world was the doctrine, even if it was not always the practice, of Jonathan Edwards and Cotton Mather. It is the meaning of fate in Hawthorne: his people are fated to withdraw from the world and to be destroyed. And it is one of the great themes of Henry James.

There is a moral emphasis that connects Hawthorne, James, and Miss Dickinson, and I think it is instructive. Between Hawthorne and James lies an epoch. The temptation to sin, in Hawthorne, is, in James, transformed into the temptation not to do the "decent thing." A whole world-scheme, a complete cosmic background, has shrunk to the dimensions of the individual conscience. This epoch between Hawthorne and James lies in Emerson. James found himself in the post-Emersonian world, and he could not, without violating the detachment proper to an artist, undo Emerson's work; he had that kind of intelligence which refuses to break its head against history. There was left to him only the value, the historic rôle, of rejection. He could merely escape from the physical presence of that world which, for convenience, we may call Emerson's world: he could only take his Americans to Europe upon the vain quest of something that they had lost at home. His characters, fleeing the wreckage of the puritan culture, preserved only their honor. Honor became a sort of forlorn hope struggling against the forces of "pure fact" that had got loose in the middle of the century. Honor alone is a poor weapon against nature, being too personal, finical, and proud, and James achieved a victory by refusing to engage the whole force of the enemy.

In Emily Dickinson the conflict takes place on a vaster field. The enemy to all those New Englanders was Nature, and Miss Dickinson saw into the character of this enemy more deeply than any of the others. The general symbol of Nature, for her, is Death, and her weapon against Death is the entire powerful dumb-show of the puritan theology led by Redemption and Immortality. Morally speaking, the problem for James and Miss Dickinson is similar. But her advantages were greater than his. The advantages lay in the availability to her of the puritan ideas on the theological plane.

These ideas, in her poetry, are momently assailed by the disintegrating force of Nature (appearing as Death) which, while constantly breaking them down, constantly redefines and strengthens them. The values are purified by the triumphant withdrawal from Nature, by their power to recover from Nature. The poet attains to a mastery over experience by facing its utmost implications. There is the clash of powerful opposites, and in all great poetry—for Emily Dickinson is a great poet—it issues in a tension between abstraction and sensation in which the two elements may be, of course, distinguished logically, but not really. We are shown our roots in Nature by examining our differences with Nature; we are renewed by Nature without being delivered into her hands. When it is possible for a poet to do this for us with the greatest imaginative comprehension, a possibility that the poet cannot himself create, we have the perfect literary situation. Only a few times in the history of English poetry has this situation come about, notably, the period between about 1580 and the Restoration. There was a similar age in New England from which emerged two talents of the first order—Hawthorne and Emily Dickinson.

There is an epoch between James and Miss Dickinson. But between her and Hawthorne there exists a difference of intellectual quality. She lacks almost radically the power to seize upon and understand abstractions for their own sake; she does not separate them from the sensuous illuminations that she is so marvelously adept at; like Donne, she *perceives abstraction* and *thinks sensation*. But Hawthorne was a master of ideas, within a limited range; this narrowness confined him to his own kind of life, his own society, and out of it grew his typical forms of experience, his steady, almost obsessed vision of man; it explains his depth and intensity. Yet he is always conscious of the abstract, doctrinal aspect of his mind, and when his vision of action and emotion is weak, his work becomes didactic. Now Miss Dickinson's poetry often runs into quasi-homiletic forms, but it is never didactic. Her very ignorance, her lack of formal intellectual training, preserved her from the risk that imperiled Hawthorne. She cannot reason at all. She can only *see*. It is impossible to imagine what she might have done with drama or fiction; for, not approaching the puritan temper and through it the puritan myth, through human action, she is able to grasp the terms of the myth directly and by a feat that amounts almost to anthropomorphism, to give them a luminous tension, a kind of drama, among themselves.

One of the perfect poems in English is "The Chariot," and it illustrates better than anything else she wrote the special quality of her mind. I think it will illuminate the tendency of this discussion:

> Because I could not stop for death,
> He kindly stopped for me;
> The carriage held but just ourselves
> And immortality.
>
> We slowly drove, he knew no haste,
> And I had put away
> My labor, and my leisure too,
> For his civility.
>
> We passed the school where children played,
> Their lessons scarcely done;
> We passed the fields of gazing grain,
> We passed the setting sun.
>
> We paused before a house that seemed
> A swelling of the ground;
> The roof was scarcely visible,
> The cornice but a mound.
>
> Since then 'tis centuries; but each
> Feels shorter than the day
> I first surmised the horses' heads
> Were toward eternity.

If the word great means anything in poetry, this poem is one of the greatest in the English language. The rhythm charges with movement the pattern of suspended action back of the poem. Every image is precise and, moreover, not merely beautiful, but fused with the central idea. Every image extends and intensifies every other. The third stanza especially shows Miss Dickinson's power to fuse, into a single order of perception, a heterogeneous series: the children, the grain, and the setting sun (time) have the same degree of credibility; the first subtly preparing for the last. The sharp *gazing* before *grain* instills into nature a cold vitality of which the qualitative richness has infinite depth. The content of death in the poem eludes explicit definition. He is a gentleman taking a lady out for a drive. But note the restraint that keeps the poet from carrying this so far that it becomes ludicrous and incredible; and note the subtly interfused erotic motive, which the idea of death has presented to most romantic poets, love being a symbol interchangeable with death. The terror of death is objectified through this figure of the genteel driver, who is made ironically to serve the end of Immortality. This is the heart of the poem: she has presented a typical Christian theme in its final irresolution, without making any final statements about it. There is no solution to the problem; there can be only a presentation of it in the full context of intellect and feeling. A construction of the human will, elaborated with all the abstracting powers of the mind, is put to the concrete test of experience: the idea of immortality is confronted with the fact of physical disintegration. We are not told what to think; we are told to look at the situation.

The framework of the poem is, in fact, the two abstractions, mortality and eternity, which are made to associate in equality with the images: she sees the ideas, and thinks the perceptions. She did, of course, nothing of the sort; but we must use the logical distinctions, even to the extent of paradox, if we are to form any notion of this rare quality of mind. She could not in the proper sense think at all, and unless we prefer the feeble poetry of moral ideas that flourished in New England in the eighties, we must conclude that her intellectual deficiency contributed at least negatively to her great distinction. Miss Dickinson is probably the only Anglo-American poet of her century whose work exhibits the perfect literary situation—in which is possible the fusion of sensibility and thought. Unlike her contemporaries, she never succumbed to her ideas, to easy solutions, to her private desires.

Philosophers must deal with ideas, but the trouble with most nineteenth-century poets is too much philosophy; they are nearer to being philosophers than poets, without being in the true sense either. Tennyson is a good example of this; so is Arnold in his weak moments. There have been poets like Milton and Donne, who were not spoiled for their true business by leaning on a rational system of ideas, who understood the poetic use of ideas. Tennyson tried to mix a little Huxley and a little Broad Church, without understanding either Broad Church or Huxley; the result was fatal, and what is worse, it was shallow. Miss Dickinson's ideas were deeply imbedded in her character, not taken from the latest tract. A conscious cultivation of ideas in poetry is always dangerous, and even Milton escaped ruin only by having an instinct for what in the deepest sense he understood. Even at that there is a remote quality in Milton's approach to his material, in his treatment of it; in the nineteenth century, in an imperfect literary situation where literature was confused with documentation, he might have been a pseudo-philosopher-poet. It is difficult to conceive Emily Dickinson and John Donne succumbing to rumination about "problems"; they would not have written at all.

Neither the feeling nor the style of Miss Dickinson belongs to the seventeenth century; yet between her and Donne there are remarkable ties. Their religious ideas, their abstractions, are momently toppling from the rational plane to the level of perception. The ideas, in fact, are no longer the impersonal religious symbols created anew in the heat of emotion, that we find in poets like Herbert and Vaughan. They have become, for Donne, the terms of personality; they are mingled with the miscellany of sensation. In Miss Dickinson, as in Donne, we may detect a singularly morbid concern, not for religious truth, but for personal revelation. The modern word is self-exploitation. It is egoism grown irresponsible in religion and decadent in morals. In religion it is blasphemy; in society it means usually that culture is not self-contained and sufficient, that the spiritual community is breaking up. This is, along with some other features that do not concern us here, the perfect literary situation.

II

Personal revelation of the kind that Donne and Miss Dickinson strove for, in the effort to understand their relation to the world, is a feature of all great poetry; it is probably the hidden motive for writing. It is the effort of the individual to live apart from a cultural tradition that no longer sustains him. But this culture, which I now wish to discuss a little, is indispensable: there is a great deal of shallow nonsense in modern criticism which holds that poetry—and this is a half-truth that is worse than false—is essentially revolutionary. It is only indirectly revolutionary: the intellectual and religious background of an age no longer contains the whole spirit, and the poet proceeds to examine that background in terms of immediate experience. But the background is necessary; otherwise all the arts (not only poetry) would have to rise in a vacuum. Poetry does not dispense with tradition; it probes the deficiencies of a tradition. But it must have a tradition to probe. It is too bad that Arnold did not explain his doctrine, that poetry is a criticism of life, from the viewpoint of its background: we should have been spared an era of academic misconception, in which criticism of life meant a diluted pragmatism, the criterion of which was respectability. The poet in the true sense "criticizes" his tradition, either as such, or indirectly by comparing it with something that is about to replace it; he does what the root-meaning of the verb implies—he *discerns* its real elements and thus establishes its value, by putting it to the test of experience.

What is the nature of a poet's culture? Or, to put the question properly, what is the meaning of culture for poetry? All the great poets become the material of what we popularly call culture; we study them to acquire it. It is clear that Addison was more cultivated than Shakespeare; nevertheless Shakespeare is a finer source of culture than Addison. What is the meaning of this? Plainly it is that learning has never had anything to do with culture except instrumentally: the poet must be exactly literate enough to write down fully and precisely what he has to say, but no more. The source of a poet's true culture lies back of the paraphernalia of culture, and not all the historical activity of an enlightened age can create it.

A culture cannot be consciously created. It is an available source of ideas that are imbedded in a complete and homogeneous society. The poet finds himself balanced upon the moment when such a world is about to fall, when it threatens to run out into looser and less self-sufficient impulses. This world order is assimilated, in Miss Dickinson, as medievalism was in Shakespeare, to the poetic vision; it is brought down from abstraction to personal sensibility.

In this connection it may be said that the prior conditions for great poetry, given a great talent, may be reduced to two: the thoroughness of the poet's discipline in an objective system of truth, and his lack of consciousness of such a discipline. For this discipline is a number of fundamental ideas the origin of which the poet does not know; they give form and stability to his fresh perceptions of the world; and he cannot shake them off. This is his culture, and like Tennyson's God it is nearer than hands and feet. With reasonable certainty we unearth the elements of Shakespeare's culture, and yet it is equally certain—so innocent was he of his own resources—that he would not know what our discussion is about. He appeared at the collapse of the medieval system as a rigid pattern of life, but that pattern remained in Shakespeare what Shelley called a "fixed point of reference" for his sensibility. Miss Dickinson, as we have seen, was born into the equilibrium of an old and a new order. Puritanism could not be to her what it had been to the generation of Cotton Mather—a body of absolute truths; it was an unconscious discipline timed to the pulse of her life.

The perfect literary situation: it produces, because it is rare, a special and perhaps the most distinguished kind of poet. I am not trying to invent a new critical category. Such poets are never very much alike on the surface; they show us all the varieties of poetic feeling; and like other poets they resist all classification but that of temporary convenience. But, I believe, Miss Dickinson and John Donne would have this in common: their sense of the natural world is not blunted by a too rigid system of ideas; yet the ideas, the abstractions, their education or their intellectual heritage, are not so weak as to let their immersion in nature, or their purely personal quality, get out of control. The two poles of the mind are not separately visible; we infer them from the lucid tension that may be most readily illustrated by polar activity. There is no thought as such at all; nor is there feeling; there is that unique focus of experience which is at once neither and both.

Like Miss Dickinson, Shakespeare is without opinions; his peculiar merit is also deeply involved in his failure to think about anything; his meaning is not in the content of his expression; it is in the tension of the dramatic relations of his characters. This kind of poetry is at the opposite of intellectualism. (Miss Dickinson is obscure and difficult, but that is not intellectualism.) To T. W. Higginson, the editor of *The Atlantic Monthly,* who tried to advise her, she wrote that she had no education. In any sense that Higginson could understand, it was quite true. His kind of education was the conscious cultivation of abstractions. She did not reason about the world she saw; she merely saw it. The "ideas" implicit in the world within her rose up, concentrated in her immediate perception.

That kind of world at present has for us something of the fascination of a buried city. There is none like it. When such worlds exist, when such cultures flourish, they support not only the poet but all members of society. For, from these, the poet differs only in his gift for exhibiting the structure, the internal lineaments, of his culture by threatening to tear them apart: a process that concentrates the symbolic emotions of society while it seems to attack them. The poet may hate his age; he may be an outcast like Villon; but this world is always there as the background to what he has to say. It is the lens through which he brings nature to focus and control—the clarifying medium that concentrates his personal feeling. It is ready-made; he cannot make it; with it, his poetry has a spontaneity and a certainty of direction that, without it, it would lack. No poet could have invented the ideas of "The Chariot"; only a great poet could have found their imaginative equivalents. Miss Dickinson was a deep mind writing from a deep culture, and when she came to poetry, she came infallibly.

Infallibly, at her best; for no poet has ever been perfect, nor is Emily Dickinson. Her precision of statement is due to the directness with which the abstract framework of her thought acts upon its unorganized material. The two elements of her style, considered as point of view, are immortality, or the idea of permanence, and the physical process of death or decay. Her diction has two corresponding features: words of Latin or Greek origin and, sharply opposed to these, the concrete Saxon element. It is this verbal conflict that gives to her verse its high tension; it is not a device deliberately seized upon, but a feeling for language that senses out the two fundamental components of English and their metaphysical relation: the Latin for ideas and the Saxon for perceptions—the peculiar virtue of English as a poetic language.

Like most poets Miss Dickinson often writes out of habit; the style that emerged from some deep exploration of an idea is carried on as verbal habit when she has nothing to say. She indulges herself:

> There's something quieter than sleep
> Within this inner room!
> It wears a sprig upon its breast,
> And will not tell its name.
>
> Some touch it and some kiss it,
> Some chafe its idle hand;
> It has a simple gravity
> I do not understand!
>
> While simple hearted neighbors
> Chat of the "early dead,"
> We, prone to periphrasis,
> Remark that birds have fled!

It is only a pert remark; at best a superior kind of punning—one of the worst specimens of her occasional interest in herself. But she never had the slightest interest in the public. Were four poems or five published in her lifetime? She never felt the temptation to round off a poem for public exhibition. Higginson's kindly offer to make her verse "correct" was an invitation to throw her work into the public ring—the ring of Lowell and Longfellow. He could not see that he was tampering with one of the rarest literary integrities of all time. Here was a poet who had no use for the supports of authorship—flattery and fame; she never needed money.

She had all the elements of a culture that has broken up, a culture that on the religious side takes its place in the museum of spiritual antiquities. Puritanism, as a unified version of the world, is dead; only a remnant of it in trade may be said to survive. In the history of puritanism she comes between Hawthorne and Emerson. She has Hawthorne's matter, which a too irresponsible personality tends to dilute into a form like Emerson's; she is often betrayed by words. But she is not the poet of personal sentiment; she has more to say than she can put down in any one poem.

Like Hardy and Whitman she must be read entire; like Shakespeare she never gives up her meaning in a single line.

She is therefore a perfect subject for the kind of criticism which is chiefly concerned with general ideas. She exhibits one of the permanent relations between personality and objective truth, and she deserves the special attention of our time, which lacks that kind of truth.

She has Hawthorne's intellectual toughness, a hard, definite sense of the physical world. The highest flights to God, the most extravagant metaphors of the strange and the remote, come back to a point of casuistry, to a moral dilemma of the experienced world. There is, in spite of the homiletic vein of utterance, no abstract speculation, nor is there a message to society; she speaks wholly to the individual experience. She offers to the unimaginative no riot of vicarious sensation; she has no useful maxims for men of action. Up to this point her resemblance to Emerson is slight: poetry is a sufficient form of utterance, and her devotion to it is pure. But in Emily Dickinson the puritan world is no longer self-contained; it is no longer complete; her sensibility exceeds its dimensions. She has trimmed down its supernatural proportions; it has become a morality; instead of the tragedy of the spirit there is a commentary upon it. Her poetry is a magnificent personal confession, blasphemous and, in its self-sevelation, its honesty, almost obscene. It comes out of an intellectual life towards which it feels no moral responsibility. Cotton Mather would have burnt her for a witch.

XIV

Mr. Eliot, Mr. Trilling, and Huckleberry Finn

> *In the losing battle that the plot fights with the characters, it often takes a cowardly revenge. Nearly all novels are feeble at the end. This is because the plot requires to be wound up. Why is this necessary? Why is there not a convention which allows a novelist to stop as soon as he feels muddled or bored? Alas, he has to round things off, and usually the characters go dead while he is at work, and our final impression of them is through deadness.*

> —E. M. FORSTER

The Adventures of Huckleberry Finn has not always occupied its present high place in the canon of American literature. When it was first published in 1885, the book disturbed and offended many reviewers, particularly spokesmen for the genteel tradition. In fact, a fairly accurate inventory of the narrow standards of such critics might be made simply by listing epithets they applied to Clemens' novel. They called it vulgar, rough, inelegant, irreverent, coarse, semi-obscene, trashy and vicious. So much for them. Today (we like to think) we know the true worth of the book. Everyone now agrees that *Huckleberry Finn* is a masterpiece: it is probably the one book in our literature about which highbrows and lowbrows can agree. Our most serious critics praise it. Nevertheless, a close look at what two of the best among them have recently written will

From *The American Scholar*, Vol. XXII, Autumn 1953, pp. 423–40. Copyright 1953 by *The American Scholar*. Reprinted by permission of the author and periodical.

likewise reveal, I believe, serious weaknesses in current criticism. Today the problem of evaluating the book is as much obscured by unqualified praise as it once was by parochial hostility.

I have in mind essays by Lionel Trilling and T. S. Eliot.[1] Both praise the book, but in praising it both feel obligated to say something in justification of what so many readers have felt to be its great flaw: the disappointing "ending," the episode which begins when Huck arrives at the Phelps place and Tom Sawyer reappears. There are good reasons why Mr. Trilling and Mr. Eliot should feel the need to face this issue. From the point of view of scope alone, more is involved than the mere "ending"; the episode comprises almost one-fifth of the text. The problem, in any case, is unavoidable. I have discussed *Huckleberry Finn* in courses with hundreds of college students, and I have found only a handful who did not confess their dissatisfaction with the extravagant mock rescue of Nigger Jim and the denouement itself. The same question always comes up: "What went wrong with Twain's novel?" Ernest Hemingway has an answer. After his celebrated remark to the effect that all modern American literature stems from *Huckleberry Finn,* Hemingway adds: "If you read it you must stop where the Nigger Jim is stolen from the boys. That is the real end. The rest is cheating." Even Bernard DeVoto, whose wholehearted commitment to Clemens' genius is well known, has said of the ending that "in the whole reach of the English novel there is no more abrupt or more chilling descent." Mr. Trilling and Mr. Eliot do not agree. They both attempt, and on similar grounds, to explain and defend the conclusion.

Of the two, Mr. Trilling makes the more moderate claim for Clemens' novel. He does admit that there is a "falling off" at the end; nevertheless he supports the episode as having "a certain formal aptness." Mr. Eliot's approval is without serious qualification. He allows no objections, asserts that "it is right that the mood of the end of the book should bring us back to the beginning." I mean later to discuss their views in some detail, but here it is only necessary to note that both critics see the problem as one of form. And so it is. Like many questions of form in literature, however, this one is not finally separable from a question of "content," of value, or, if you will, of moral insight. To bring *Huckleberry Finn* to a satisfactory close, Clemens had to do more than find a neat device for ending a story. His problem, though it may never have occurred to him, was to invent an action capable of placing in focus the meaning of the journey down the Mississippi.

I believe that the ending of *Huckleberry Finn* makes so many readers uneasy because they rightly sense that it jeopardizes the significance of the entire novel. To take seriously what happens at the Phelps farm is to take lightly the entire downstream journey. What is the meaning of the journey? With this question all discussion of *Huckleberry Finn* must begin. It is true that the voyage down the river has many aspects of a boy's idyl. We owe much of its hold upon our imagination to the enchanting image of the raft's unhurried drift with the current. The leisure, the absence of constraint, the beauty of the river—all these things delight us. "It's lovely to live on a raft." And the multitudinous life of the great valley we see through Huck's eyes has a fascination of its own. Then, of course, there is humor—laughter so spontaneous, so free of the bitterness present almost everywhere in American humor that readers often forget how grim a spectacle of human existence Huck contemplates. Humor in this novel flows from a bright joy of life as remote from our world as living on a raft.

Yet along with the idyllic and the epical and the funny in *Huckleberry Finn,* there is a coil of meaning which does for the disparate elements of the novel what a spring does for a watch. The meaning is not in the least obscure. It is made explicit again and again. The very words with which Clemens launches Huck and Jim upon their voyage indicate that theirs is not a boy's lark but a quest for freedom. From the electrifying moment when Huck comes back to Jackson's Island and rouses Jim with the news that a search party is on the way, we are meant to believe that Huck is enlisted in the cause of freedom. "Git up and hump yourself, Jim!" he cries. "There ain't a minute to lose. They're after us!" What particularly counts here is the *us.* No one is after Huck; no one but Jim knows he is alive. In that small word Clemens compresses the exhilarating power of Huck's instinctive humanity. His unpremeditated identification with Jim's flight from slavery is an unforgettable moment in American experience, and it may be said at once that any culmination of the journey which detracts from the urgency and dignity with which it begins will necessarily be unsatisfactory. Huck realizes this himself, and says so when, much later, he comes back to the raft after discovering that the Duke and the King have sold Jim:

> After all this long journey . . . here it was all come to nothing, every thing all busted up and ruined, because they could have the heart to serve Jim such a trick as that, and make him a slave again all his life, and amongst strangers, too, for forty dirty dollars.

Huck knows that the journey will have been a failure unless it takes Jim to freedom. It is true that we do discover, in the end, that Jim is free, but we also find out that the journey was not the means by which he finally reached freedom.

The most obvious thing wrong with the ending, then, is the flimsy contrivance by which Clemens frees Jim. In the end we not only discover that Jim has been a free man for two months, but that his freedom has been granted by old Miss Watson. If this were only a mechanical device for terminating the action, it might not call for much comment. But it is more than that: it is a significant clue to the import of the last ten chapters. Remember who Miss Watson is. She is the Widow's sister whom Huck introduces in the first pages of the novel. It is she who keeps "pecking" at Huck, who tries to teach him to spell and to pray and to keep his feet off the furniture. She is an ardent proselytizer for piety and good manners, and her greed provides the occasion for the journey in the first place. She is Jim's owner, and he decides to flee only when he realizes that she is about to break her word (she cannot resist a slave trader's offer of eight hundred dollars) and sell him down the river away from his family.

Miss Watson, in short, is the Enemy. If we except a predilection for physical violence, she exhibits all the outstanding traits of the valley society. She pronounces the polite lies of civilization that suffocate Huck's spirit. The freedom which Jim seeks, and which Huck and Jim temporarily enjoy aboard the raft, is accordingly freedom *from* everything for which Miss Watson stands. Indeed, the very intensity of the novel derives from the discordance between the aspirations of the fugitives and the respectable code for which she is a spokesman. Therefore, her regeneration, of which the deathbed freeing of Jim is the unconvincing sign, hints a resolution of the novel's essential conflict. Perhaps because this device most transparently reveals that shift in point of view which he could not avoid, and which is less easily discerned elsewhere in the concluding chapters, Clemens plays it down. He makes little attempt to account for Miss Watson's change of heart, a change particularly surprising in view of Jim's brazen escape. Had Clemens given this episode dramatic emphasis appropriate to its function, Miss Watson's bestowal of freedom upon Jim would have proclaimed what the rest of the ending acutally accomplishes—a vindication of persons and attitudes Huck and Jim had symbolically repudiated when they set forth downstream.

It may be said, and with some justice, that a reading of the ending as a virtual reversal of meanings implicit in the rest of the novel misses the point—that I have taken the final episode too seriously. I agree that Clemens certainly did not intend us to read it so solemnly. The ending, one might contend, is simply a burlesque upon Tom's taste for literary romance. Surely the tone of the episode is familiar to readers of Mark Twain. The preposterous monkey business attendant upon Jim's "rescue," the careless improvisation, the nonchalant disregard for common-sense plausibility—all these things should not surprise readers of Twain or any low comedy in the tradition of "Western humor." However, the trouble is, first, that the ending hardly comes off as burlesque: it is *too* fanciful, *too* extravagant; and it is tedious. For example, to provide a "gaudy" atmosphere for the escape, Huck and Tom catch a couple of dozen snakes. Then the snakes escape.

> No, there warn't no real scarcity of snakes about the house for a considerable spell. You'd see them dripping from the rafters and places every now and then; and they generly landed in your plate, or down the back of your neck. . . .

Even if this were *good* burlesque, which it is not, what is it doing here? It is out of keeping; the slapstick tone jars with the underlying seriousness of the voyage.

Huckleberry Finn is a masterpiece because it brings Western humor to perfection and yet transcends the narrow limits of its conventions. But the ending does not. During the final extravaganza we are forced to put aside many of the mature emotions evoked earlier by the vivid rendering of Jim's fear of capture, the tenderness of Huck's and Jim's regard for each other, and Huck's excruciating moments of wavering between honesty and respectability. None of these emotions are called forth by the anticlimactic final sequence. I do not mean to suggest that the inclusion of low comedy per se is a flaw in *Huckleberry Finn*. One does not object to the shenanigans of the rogues; there is ample precedent for the place of extravagant humor even in works of high seriousness. But here the case differs from most which come to mind: the major characters themselves are forced to play low comedy roles. Moreover, the most serious motive in the novel, Jim's yearning for freedom, is made the object of nonsense. The conclusion, in short, is farce, but the rest of the novel is not.

That Clemens reverts in the end to the conventional manner of Western low comedy is most evident in what happens to the principals. Huck and Jim become comic characters; that is a much more serious ground for dissatisfaction than the unexplained regeneration of Miss Watson. Remember that Huck has grown in stature throughout the journey. By the time he arrives at the Phelps place, he is not the boy who had been playing robbers with Tom's gang in St. Petersburg the summer before. All he has seen and felt since he parted from Tom has deepened his knowledge of human nature and of himself. Clemens makes a point of Huck's development in two scenes which occur just before he meets Tom again. The first describes Huck's final capitulation to his own sense of right and wrong: "All right, then, I'll *go* to Hell." This is the climactic moment in the ripening of his self-knowledge. Shortly afterward, when he comes upon a mob riding the Duke and the King out of town on a rail, we are given his most memorable insight into the nature of man. Although these rogues had subjected Huck to every indignity, what he sees provokes this celebrated comment:

> Well, it made me sick to see it; and I was sorry for them poor pitiful rascals, it seemed like I couldn't ever feel any hardness against them any more in the world. It was a dreadful thing to see. Human beings can be awful cruel to one another.

The sign of Huck's maturity here is neither the compassion nor the skepticism, for both had been marks of his personality from the first. Rather, the special quality of these reflections is the extraordinary combination of the two, a mature blending of his instinctive suspicion of human motives with his capacity for pity.

But at this point Tom reappears. Soon Huck has fallen almost completely under his sway once more, and we are asked to believe that the boy who felt pity for the rogues is now capable of making Jim's capture the occasion for a game. He becomes Tom's helpless accomplice, submissive and gullible. No wonder that Clemens has Huck remark, when Huck first realizes Aunt Sally has mistaken him for Tom, that "it was like being born again." Exactly. In the end, Huck regresses to the subordinate role in which he had first appeared in *The Adventures of Tom Sawyer*. Most of those traits which made him so appealing a hero now disappear. He had never, for example, found pain or misfortune amusing. At the circus, when a clown disguised as a drunk took a precarious ride on a prancing horse, the crowd loved the excitement and danger; "it warn't funny to me, though," said Huck. But now, in the end, he submits in awe to Tom's notion of what is amusing. To satisfy Tom's hunger for adventure he makes himself a party to sport which aggravates Jim's misery.

It should be added at once that Jim doesn't mind too much. The fact is that he has undergone a similar transformation. On the raft he was an individual, man enough to denounce Huck when Huck made him the victim of a practical joke. In the closing episode, however, we lose sight of Jim in the maze of farcical invention. He ceases to be a man. He allows Huck and "Mars Tom" to fill his hut with rats and snakes, "and every time a rat bit Jim he would get up and write a line in his journal whilst the ink was fresh." This creature who bleeds ink and feels no pain is something less than human. He has been made over in the image of a flat stereotype: the submissive stage-Negro. These antics divest Jim, as well as Huck, of much of his dignity and individuality.[2]

What I have been saying is that the flimsy devices of plot, the discordant farcical tone, and the disintegration of the major characters all betray the failure of the ending. These are not aspects merely of form in a technical sense, but of meaning. For that matter, I would maintain that this book has little or no formal unity independent of the joint purpose of Huck and Jim. What components of the novel, we may ask, provide the continuity which links one adventure with another? The most important is the unifying consciousness of Huck, the narrator, and the fact that we follow the same principals through the entire string of adventures. Events, moreover, occur in a temporal sequence. Then there is the river; after each adventure Huck and Jim return to the raft

and the river. Both Mr. Trilling and Mr. Eliot speak eloquently of
the river as a source of unity, and they refer to the river as a god.
Mr. Trilling says that Huck is "the servant of the river-god." Mr.
Eliot puts it this way: "The River gives the book its form.
But for the River, the book might be only a sequence of adventures with a happy ending." This seems to me an extravagant
view of the function of the neutral agency of the river. Clemens
had a knowledgeable respect for the Mississippi, and, without
sanctifying it, was able to provide excellent reasons for Huck's and
Jim's intense relation with it. It is a source of food and beauty and
terror and serenity of mind. But above all, it provides motion; it
is the means by which Huck and Jim move away from a men-
acing civilization. They return to the river to continue their
journey. The river cannot, does not, supply purpose. That purpose
is a facet of their consciousness, and without the motive of escape
from society, *Huckleberry Finn* would indeed "be only a sequence of
adventures." Mr. Eliot's remark indicates how lightly he takes the
quest for freedom. His somewhat fanciful exaggeration of the
river's role is of a piece with his negelect of the theme at the
novel's center.

That theme is heightened by the juxtaposition of sharp
images of contrasting social orders: the microcosmic community
Huck and Jim establish aboard the raft and the actual society
which exists along the Mississippi's banks. The two are separated
by the river, the road to freedom upon which Huck and Jim must
travel. Huck tells us what the river means to them when, after the
Wilks episode, he and Jim once again shove their raft into the
current: "It *did* seem so good to be free again and all by ourselves
on the big river, and nobody to bother us." The river is indifferent. But its sphere is relatively uncontaminated by the civilization they flee, and so the river allows Huck and Jim some measure
of freedom at once, the moment they set foot on Jackson's Island or
the raft. Only on the island and the raft do they have a chance to
practice that idea of brotherhood to which they are devoted.
"Other places do seem so cramped and smothery," Huck explains,
"but a raft don't. You feel mighty free and easy and comfortable
on a raft." The main thing is freedom.

On the raft the escaped slave and the white boy try to practice
their code: "What you want, above all things, on a raft, is for

everybody to be satisfied, and feel right and kind towards the others." This human credo constitutes the paramount affirmation of *The Adventures of Huckleberry Finn,* and it obliquely aims a devastating criticism at the existing social order. It is a creed which Huck and Jim bring to the river. It neither emanates from nature nor is it addressed to nature. Therefore I do not see that it means much to talk about the river as a god in this novel. The river's connection with this high aspiration for man is that it provides a means of escape, a place where the code can be tested. The truly profound meanings of the novel are generated by the impingement of the actual world of slavery, feuds, lynching, murder, and a spurious Christian morality upon the ideal of the raft. The result is a tension which somehow demands release in the novel's ending.

But Clemens was unable to effect this release and at the same time control the central theme. The unhappy truth about the ending of *Huckleberry Finn* is that the author, having revealed the tawdry nature of the culture of the great valley, yielded to its essential complacency. The general tenor of the closing scenes, to which the token regeneration of Miss Watson is merely one superficial clue, amounts to just that. In fact, this entire reading of *Huckleberry Finn* merely confirms the brilliant insight of George Santayana, who many years ago spoke of American humorists, of whom he considered Mark Twain an outstanding representative, as having only "half escaped" the genteel tradition. Santayana meant that men like Clemens were able to "point to what contradicts it in the facts; but not in order to abandon the genteel tradition, for they have nothing solid to put in its place." This seems to me the real key to the failure of *Huckleberry Finn.* Clemens had presented the contrast between the two social orders but could not, or would not, accept the tragic fact that the one he had rejected was an image of solid reality and the other an ecstatic dream. Instead he gives us the cozy reunion with Aunt Polly in a scene fairly bursting with approbation of the entire family, the Phelpses included.

Like Miss Watson, the Phelpses are almost perfect specimens of the dominant culture. They are kind to their friends and relatives; they have no taste for violence; they are people capable of devoting themselves to their spectacular dinners while they keep

Jim locked in the little hut down by the ash hopper, with its lone window boarded up. (Of course Aunt Sally visits Jim to see if he is "comfortable," and Uncle Silas comes in "to pray with him.") These people, with their comfortable Sunday-dinner conviviality and the runaway slave padlocked nearby, are reminiscent of those solid German citizens we have heard about in our time who tried to maintain a similarly *gemütlich* way of life within virtual earshot of Buchenwald. I do not mean to imply that Clemens was unaware of the shabby morality of such people. After the abortive escape of Jim, when Tom asks about him, Aunt Sally replies: "Him? . . . the runaway nigger? . . . They've got him back, safe and sound, and he's in the cabin again, on bread and water, and loaded down with chains, till he's claimed or sold!" Clemens understood people like the Phelpses, but nevertheless he was forced to rely upon them to provide his happy ending. The satisfactory outcome of Jim's quest for freedom must be attributed to the benevolence of the very people whose inhumanity first made it necessary.

But to return to the contention of Mr. Trilling and Mr. Eliot that the ending is more or less satisfactory after all. As I have said, Mr. Trilling approves of the "formal aptness" of the conclusion. He says that "some device is needed to permit Huck to return to his anonymity, to give up the role of hero," and that therefore "nothing could serve better than the mind of Tom Sawyer with its literary furnishings, its conscious romantic desire for experience and the hero's part, and its ingenious schematization of life. . . ." Though more detailed, this is essentially akin to Mr. Eliot's blunt assertion that "it is right that the mood at the end of the book should bring us back to that of the beginning." I submit that it is wrong for the end of the book to bring us back to that mood. The mood of the beginning of *Huckleberry Finn* is the mood of Huck's attempt to accommodate himself to the ways of St. Petersburg. It is the mood of the end of *The Adventures of Tom Sawyer*, when the boys had been acclaimed heroes, and when Huck was accepted as a candidate for respectability. That is the state in which we find him at the beginning of *Huckleberry Finn*. But Huck cannot stand the new way of life, and his mood gradually shifts to the mood of rebellion which dominates the novel until he meets Tom again. At first, in the second chapter, we see him eager to be accepted by the nice boys of the town. Tom leads the gang in re-enacting adventures he has culled from books, but gradually Huck's pragmatic turn of mind gets him in trouble. He has little tolerance for Tom's brand of make-believe. He irritates Tom. Tom calls him a "numbskull," and finally Huck throws up the whole business:

> So then I judged that all that stuff was only just one of Tom Sawyer's lies. I reckoned he believed in the A-rabs and the elephants, but as for me I think different. It had all the marks of a Sunday-school.

With this statement, which ends the third chapter, Huck parts company with Tom. The fact is that Huck has rejected Tom's romanticizing of experience; moreover, he has rejected it as part of the larger pattern of society's make-believe, typified by Sunday school. But if he cannot accept Tom's harmless fantasies about the A-rabs, how are we to believe that a year later Huck is capable of awe-struck submission to the far more extravagant fantasies with which Tom invests the mock rescue of Jim?

After Huck's escape from his "pap," the drift of the action, like that of the Mississippi's current, is *away* from St. Petersburg. Huck leaves Tom and the A-rabs behind, along with the Widow, Miss Watson, and all the pseudo-religious ritual in which nice boys must partake. The return, in the end, to the mood of the beginning therefore means defeat—Huck's defeat; to return to that mood *joyously* is to portray defeat in the guise of victory.

Mr. Eliot and Mr. Trilling deny this. The overriding consideration for them is form—form which seems largely to mean symmetry of structure. It is fitting, Mr. Eliot maintains, that the book should come full circle and bring Huck once more under Tom's sway. Why? Because it begins that way. But it seems to me that such structural unity is *imposed* upon the novel, and therefore is meretricious. It is a jerry-built structure, achieved only by sacrifice of characters and theme. Here the controlling principle of form apparently is unity, but unfortunately a unity much too superficially conceived. Structure, after all, is only one element—indeed, one of the more mechanical elements—of unity. A unified work must surely manifest coherence of meaning and clear development of theme, yet the ending of *Huckleberry Finn* blurs both. The eagerness of Mr. Eliot and Mr. Trilling to justify the ending is symptomatic of that absolutist impulse of our critics to find reasons, once a work has been admitted to the highest canon of literary reputability, for admiring every bit of it.

What is perhaps most striking about these judgments of Mr. Eliot's and Mr. Trilling's is that they are so patently out of harmony with the basic standards of both critics. For one thing, both men hold far more complex ideas of the nature of literary unity than their comments upon *Huckleberry Finn* would suggest. For another, both critics are essentially moralists, yet here we find them turning away from a moral issue in order to praise a dubious structural unity. Their efforts to explain away the flaw in Clemens' novel suffer from a certain narrowness surprising to anyone who knows their work. These facts suggest that we may be in the presence of a tendency in contemporary criticism which the critics themselves do not fully recognize.

Is there an explanation? How does it happen that two of our most respected critics should seem to treat so lightly the glaring lapse of moral imagination in *Huckleberry Finn?* Perhaps—and I stress the conjectural nature of what I am saying—perhaps the kind of moral issue raised by *Huckleberry Finn* is not the kind of moral issue to which today's criticism readily addresses itself. Today our critics, no less than our novelists and poets, are most sensitively attuned to moral problems which arise in the sphere of individual behavior. They are deeply aware of sin, of individual infractions of our culture's Christian ethic. But my impression is that they are, possibly because of the strength of the reaction against the mechanical sociological criticism of the thirties, less sensitive to questions of what might be called social or political morality.

By social or political morality I refer to the values implicit in a social system, values which may be quite distinct from the personal morality of any given individual within the society. Now *The Adventures of Huckleberry Finn,* like all novels, deals with the behavior of individuals. But one mark of Clemens' greatness is his deft presentation of the disparity between what people do when they behave as individuals and what they do when forced into roles imposed upon them by society. Take, for example, Aunt Sally and Uncle Silas Phelps, who consider themselves Christians, who are by impulse generous and humane, but who happen also to be staunch upholders of certain degrading and inhuman social institutions. When they are confronted with an escaped slave, the imperatives of social morality outweigh all pious professions.

The conflict between what people think they stand for and what social pressure forces them to do is central to the novel. It is present to the mind of Huck and, indeed, accounts for his most serious inner conflicts. He knows how he feels about Jim, but he also knows what he is expected to do about Jim. This division within his mind corresponds to the division of the novel's moral terrain into the areas represented by the raft on the one hand and society on the other. His victory over his "yaller dog" conscience therefore assumes heroic size: it is a victory over the prevailing morality. But the last fifth of the novel has the effect of diminishing the importance and uniqueness of Huck's victory. We are asked to assume that somehow freedom can be achieved in spite of the crippling power of what I have called the social morality. Consequently the less importance we attach to that force as it operates in the novel, the more acceptable the ending becomes.

Moreover, the idea of freedom, which Mr. Eliot and Mr. Trilling seem to slight, takes on its full significance only when we acknowledge the power which society exerts over the minds of men in the world of *Huckleberry Finn.* For freedom in this book specifically means freedom from society and its imperatives. This is not the traditional Christian conception of freedom. Huck and Jim seek freedom not from a burden of individual guilt and sin, but from social constraint. That is to say, evil in *Huckleberry Finn* is the product of civilization, and if this is indicative of Clemens' rather too simple view of human nature, nevertheless the fact is that Huck, when he can divest himself of the taint of social conditioning (as in the incantatory account of sunrise on the river), is entirely free of anxiety and guilt. The only guilt he actuallly knows arises from infractions of a social code. (The guilt he feels after playing the prank on Jim stems from his betrayal of the law of the raft.) Huck's and Jim's creed is secular. Its object is harmony among men, and so Huck is not much concerned with his own salvation. He repeatedly renounces prayer in favor of pragmatic solutions to his problems. In other words, the central insights of the novel belong to the tradition of the Enlightenment. The meaning of the quest itself is hardly reconcilable with that conception of human nature embodied in the myth of original sin. In view of the current fashion of reaffirming man's innate depravity, it is perhaps not surprising to find the virtues of *Huckleberry Finn* attributed not to its meaning but to its form.

But "if this was not the right ending for the book," Mr. Eliot asks, "what ending would have been right?" Although this question places the critic in an awkward position (he is not always equipped to rewrite what he criticizes), there are some things which may justifiably be said about the "right" ending of *Huckleberry Finn*. It may be legitimate, even if presumptuous, to indicate certain conditions which a hypothetical ending would have to satisfy if it were to be congruent with the rest of the novel. If the conclusion is not to be something merely tacked on to close the action, then its broad outline must be immanent in the body of the work.

It is surely reasonable to ask that the conclusion provide a plausible outcome to the quest. Yet freedom, in the ecstatic sense that Huck and Jim knew it aboard the raft, was hardly to be had in the Mississippi Valley in the 1840's, or, for that matter, in any other known human society. A satisfactory ending would inevitably cause the reader some frustration. That Clemens felt such disappointment to be inevitable is borne out by an examination of the novel's clear, if unconscious, symbolic pattern. Consider, for instance, the inferences to be drawn from the book's geography. The river, to whose current Huck and Jim entrust themselves, actually carries them to the heart of slave territory. Once the raft passes Cairo, the quest is virtually doomed. Until the steamboat smashes the raft, we are kept in a state of anxiety about Jim's escape. (It may be significant that at this point Clemens found himself unable to continue work on the manuscript, and put it aside for several years.) Beyond Cairo, Clemens allows the intensity of that anxiety to diminish, and it is probably no accident that the fainter it becomes, the more he falls back upon the devices of low comedy, Huck and Jim make no serious effort to turn north, and there are times (during the Wilks episode) when Clemens allows Huck to forget all about Jim. It is as if the author, anticipating the dilemma he had finally to face, instinctively dissipated the power of his major theme.

Consider, too, the circumscribed nature of the raft as a means of moving toward freedom. The raft lacks power and maneuverability. It can only move easily with the current—southward into slave country. Nor can it evade the mechanized power of the steamboat. These impotencies of the raft correspond to the innocent helplessness of its occupants. Unresisted, the rogues invade and take over the raft. Though it is the symbolic locus of the novel's central affirmations, the raft provides an uncertain and indeed precarious mode of traveling toward freedom. This seems another confirmation of Santayana's perception. To say that Clemens only half escaped the genteel tradition is not to say that he failed to note any of the creed's inadequacies, but rather that he had "nothing solid" to put in its place. The raft patently was not capable of carrying the burden of hope Clemens placed upon it. (Whether this is to be attributed to the nature of his vision or to the actual state of American society in the nineteenth century is another interesting question.) In any case, the geography of the novel, the raft's powerlessness, the goodness and vulnerability of Huck and Jim, all prefigure a conclusion quite different in tone from that which Clemens gave us. These facts constitute what Hart Crane might have called the novel's "logic of metaphor," and this logic—probably inadvertent—actually takes us to the underlying meaning of *The Adventures of Huckleberry Finn*. Through the symbols we reach a truth which the ending obscures: the quest cannot succeed.

Fortunately, Clemens broke through to this truth in the novel's last sentences:

> But I reckon I got to light out for the territory ahead of the rest, because Aunt Sally she's going to adopt me and civilize me, and I can't stand it. I been there before.

Mr. Eliot properly praises this as "the only possible concluding sentence." But one sentence can hardly be advanced, as Mr. Eliot advances this one, to support the rightness of ten chapters. Moreover, if this sentence is right, then the rest of the conclusion is wrong, for its meaning clashes with that of the final burlesque, Huck's decision to go west ahead of the inescapable advance of civilization is a confession of defeat. It means that the raft is to be abandoned. On the other hand, the jubilation of the family reunion and the proclaiming of Jim's freedom create a quite different mood. The tone, except for these last words, is one of unclouded success. I believe this is the source of the almost universal dissatisfaction with the conclusion. One can hardly forget that a bloody civil war did not resolve the issue.

Should Clemens have made Huck a tragic hero? Both Mr. Eliot and Mr. Trilling argue that that would have been a mistake, and they are very probably correct. But between the ending as we have it and tragedy in the fullest sense, there was vast room for invention. Clemens might have contrived an action which left Jim's fate as much in doubt as Huck's. Such an ending would have allowed us to assume that the principals were defeated but alive, and the quest unsuccessful but not abandoned. This, after all, would have been consonant with the symbols, the characters, and the theme as Clemens had created them—and with history.

Clemens did not acknowledge the truth his novel contained. He had taken hold of a situation in which a partial defeat was inevitable, but he was unable to—or unaware of the need to—give imaginative substance to that fact. If an illusion of success was indispensable, where was it to come from? Obviously Huck and Jim could not succeed by their own efforts. At this point Clemens, having only half escaped the genteel tradition, one of whose preeminent characteristics was an optimism undaunted by disheartening truth, returned to it. *Why* he did so is another story, having to do with his parents and his boyhood, with his own personality and his wife's, and especially with the character of his audience. But whatever the explanation, the faint-hearted ending of *The Adventures of Huckleberry Finn* remains an important datum in the record of American thought and imagination. It has been noted before, both by critics and non-professional readers. It should not be forgotten now.

To minimize the seriousness of what must be accounted a major flaw in so great a work is, in a sense, to repeat Clemens' failure of nerve. This is a disservice to criticism. Today we particularly need a criticism alert to lapses of moral vision. A measured appraisal of the failures and successes of our writers, past and present, can show us a great deal about literature and about ourselves. That is the critic's function. But he cannot perform that function if he substitutes considerations of technique for considerations of truth. Not only will such methods lead to errors of literary judgment, but beyond that, they may well encourage comparable evasions in other areas. It seems not unlikely, for instance, that the current preoccupation with matters of form is bound up with a tendency, by no means confined to literary quarters, to shy away from painful answers to complex questions of political morality. The conclusion to *The Adventures of Huckleberry Finn* shielded both Clemens and his audience from such an answer. But we ought not to be as tender-minded. For Huck Finn's besetting problem, the disparity between his best impulses and the behavior the community attempted to impose upon him, is as surely ours as it was Twain's.

NOTES

1. Mr. Eliot's essay is the introduction to the edition of *Huckleberry Finn* published by Chanticleer Press, New York, 1950. Mr. Trilling's is the introduction to an edition of the novel published by Rinehart, New York, 1948, and later reprinted in his *The Liberal Imagination*, Viking, New York, 1950.

2. For these observations on the transformation of Jim in the closing episodes, I am indebted to the excellent unpublished essay by Mr. Chadwick Hansen on the subject of Clemens and Western humor.

James M. Cox

XV

Remarks on the Sad Initiation of Huckleberry Finn

The Adventures of Huckleberry Finn is one of those rare books which are at once acceptable to the intelligentsia and to that celebrated American phenomenon, the average citizen; it is a book which even anti-literary children read and enjoy. Even if the language of the book should eventually be lost or, worse still, replaced by convenient abridgements, the memory of Huck Finn would still survive among us like some old and indestructible god. In the popular imagination, however, Huck Finn does not exist by himself, but is accompanied by Tom Sawyer, his other half. These two figures are not imagined as individuals; they are conceived as identical twins who roam about the earth stealing jam, beating up sissies, playing hooky, and raising hell in general. Furthermore, the Tom-Huck image exists in terms of Tom Sawyer; the real Huck Finn who floated down the Mississippi with Nigger Jim has been shuffled under the rather trivial aegis of the Bad Boy.

Yet there is a grim logic behind this discomforting shift, for if Huck stands uncomfortably next to Tom Sawyer at least he has been there before. Indeed he even adopted Tom Sawyer's name during those rather flat final chapters of Huckleberry Finn. After Huck reached his unknown destination, the Phelps farm, the only

From *The Sewanee Review,* Vol. LXII, 1954, pp. 389–405. Copyright 1954 by the University of the South. Reprinted by permission of the publisher.

terms on which he could exist were Tom's terms, and, driven to distraction by the hemming forces which threatened to annihilate him, he gave up his freedom to be free. In order to save himself, the fugitive played the part of Tom Sawyer and in playing it he completed his long, arduous, and disillusioning initiation. The characters, the implications, and the art of this initiation can be fully realized by beginning with the work behind *Huckleberry Finn, The Adventures of Tom Sawyer.*

The most striking aspect of *Tom Sawyer* is its almost total lack of plot in the conventional sense of that word. There is little or no transition between episodes; continuity results from appearance and reappearance of the same characters. The most obvious defense of this lack of causal sequence—plot as machinery—is that it reinforces the pervasive determinism of Tom Sawyer's world. Although Tom reacts to the daily occurrences which confront him and although he makes belated attempts to meet his fate, he is quite powerless to initiate the action.

The real unity of Tom Sawyer arises not so much from the underlying determinism as from the insistent rhythm of the novel, a rhythm based upon repetition and variation of central motives. The violence and terror which are just beneath the surface of the boy's world regularly erupt into it. After the pleasures of the schoolroom comes the dark and unknown night, bringing with it fear and death. Even on Jackson's Island, the idyllic innocence of the afternoon is overtaken by a night thunderstorm which almost rips the island apart. Often this repetition is executed in much more subtle terms, providing submerged links between the episodes. Thus in one episode Tom and Joe Harper play Robin Hood in the dark woods, pretending to kill each other. The following night, in another scene, Tom and Huck witness the brutal murder in the graveyard. This effect is repeated when Muff Potter begs Injun Joe to swear secrecy in the matter of the killing, a scene followed by the one in which the boys, who have witnessed the crime, also swear to reveal nothing of what they have seen. They attempt to make their oath "real" by creating careful rituals which they religiously enact. The innocent rituals of the children are performed with grotesque reality by the adults. The chief characters of the book sense the fundamental dangers which confront them after the sun goes down, and they fall back on ritual and superstition to protect themselves from the inscrutable powers which lurk at the edge of the clearing.

The absence of formal transition, the constant rhythm of the action, the double exposure effect arising from the superimposition of one episode upon another all coordinate to give a kind of dream structure to the novel. The presence of characters is often unexplained and their disappearance unaccounted for. Becky Thatcher and Joe Harper fade out of the action toward the end of the novel; the doctor's appearance in the graveyard remains a mystery as does his motive for hiring the grave robbers. Characters slip in and out of their identity by wearing deliberate disguises (disguise and mistaken identity are favorite devices of Mark Twain which he uses brilliantly in *Huckleberry Finn* and interestingly in *A Connecticut Yankee, The Prince and the Pauper, Tom Sawyer Detective,* and *Pudd'nhead Wilson*); episodes drift into each other; sometimes, as with the Robin Hood game, an entire episode serves as a mask for another incident. The unity of the novel can be perceived only by looking *through* one scene into another.

Adding to this rhythmic structure and reinforcing the unity is, of course, the central character of Tom. Walter Blair, a Mark Twain specialist who attempted a conventional explanation of the structure of *Tom Sawyer,* contended that the novel deals with a boy's growth, but instead of analyzing the psychology of that growth he wandered away from his fertile suggestion and divided the novel into rather useless structural units. The novel is indeed about growing up. Appearing first merely as a Bad Boy, Tom, as Mr. Blair points out, develops into a character of real interest. His humor has been much discussed, its sources have been thoroughly examined, but the psychology behind it has often been neglected. Tom's repeated death fantasies are nowhere scrutinized by the scholars who have so painstakingly provided a "background" for the novel, yet these very fantasies give Tom's character depth and complexity. Time after time the rhythm of the novel is expressed in terms of this death wish. Tom retires into solitude envisioning the mourning of the village when its inhabitants realize that he is no more. The culmination of the Jackson Island episode is the triumphal return of Tom and his two cronies to witness their own funerals. Even when death closes in on Tom and Becky in the darkness of the cave, Tom awaits it with a certain pleasure.

But there is another death, a death brutal and ghastly, lurking just beyond the boys' world and constantly impinging on it; it is the death in the graveyard and the death of Injun Joe—instead of warmth and protection this death is informed with terror. To see it as a brutal fact waiting in the adult world is to to look with wistful eyes at that other death. The cave episode, fantastic from a "realistic" point of view, is oddly appropriate because it embodies the paradox of death and isolation; it is in the cave that Tom, in the very arms of the warm shadow, manages to find the will to force his way to light and safety, but it is also in the cave that Injun Joe meets one of the most violent and horrifying deaths in our literature. The two images of death are united in the cave, and it is hardly pure coincidence that Injun Joe, the demon who has haunted Tom's dreams, lies dead at the sealed doorway of the abyss from which Tom has escaped. Tom has, albeit unconsciously, experienced what Hans Castorp more consciously experienced in the snowstorm; he has glimpsed the sheer terror at the center of his childhood image of death. His immediate return to the cave to seize the treasure suggests his inner triumph.

The discovery of the treasure, significantly hidden under Injun Joe's cross, enables Tom to enter heroically the ranks of the respectable. Of course, he has been slyly respectable all along. Even when he breaks the law he does so with the intimate knowledge that he is expected to break it. His acute dramatic sense enables him to see the part he is to play, and he is therefore constantly aware of his participation in sacred social rites. This awareness results in a kind of compulsive badness in his nature; he achieves the Frommian ideal of wanting to do what society expects him to do. As the curtain drops there is triumphant confirmation of Tom's membership in the cult of the respectable. He is even trying to sell the club to Huck, cautioning him to remain a member of society because if one is to belong to Tom Sawyer's Outlaw Gang one must, paradoxically, obey the law:

> Huck: Now Tom, hain't you always ben friendly to me? You wouldn't shet me out, would you, Tom? You wouldn't do that, now, *would* you, Tom?
>
> Tom: Huck, I wouldn't want to, and I don't want to—but what would people say? Why, they'd say, "Mph! Tom Sawyer's Gang! pretty low characters in it!" They'd mean you, Huck.

The implications of Tom's entrance into society illuminate the differences between Tom and Huck and also throw Mark Twain himself into much sharper focus. Van Wyck Brooks in his *Ordeal of Mark Twain* took the events of Twain's life and tried to see the books as repetitions of his life troubles, attempting to prove that Olivia Langdon and William Dean Howells thwarted Mark Twain's artistic development. Although his contention that Mark Twain never grew up is convincing, his approach is extremely questionable. Bernard De Voto has done much to dispel Brook's theory that Mark Twain was thwarted, and for all his windiness, De Voto has seen that Twain himself was the prude as much as Olivia Langdon or Howells. A thorough analysis of Mark Twain's work will corroborate De Voto. He actually sought out Olivia Langdon, knowing full well she was a semi-invalid and a puritan. The picture of this "bad boy" coming east to roost is fraught with irony, and certainly his complete trust in Howells' judgment can hardly be blamed on Howells. He was perfectly content with the nickname, "Youth," by which Olivia called him, and he addressed his friend Mrs. Fairbanks as "mother" while his own mother was still very much alive. One scarcely has to be a Freudian to perceive that like Tom Sawyer he sought the authority and protection of respectability. In view of Twain's own quest it is quite remarkable, yet paradoxically inevitable, that *Huckleberry Finn* ever saw the light of day.

The Adventures of Huckleberry Finn is a conscious continuation and extension of *Tom Sawyer*. As he begins his own story, Huck carefully recounts the events of his immediate past. After mentioning the discovery of gold he goes on to say:

> The Widow Douglas she took me for her son, and allowed she would sivilize me; but it was rough living in the house all the time, considering how dismal regular and decent the widow was in all her ways; and so when I couldn't stand it no longer I lit out. I got into my old rags and my sugar-hogshead again, and was free and satisfied. But Tom Sawyer he hunted me up and said he was going to start a band of robbers, and I might join if I would go back to the window and be respectable. So I went back.

Here is the argument of the entire novel—all that follows revolves around this major theme, Huck's initiation into respectable society. The tragic irony of the novel is Huck's inner awareness that membership in the cult will involve the dissolution of his character and the denial of his values.

Huck is hardly situated comfortably at the Widow Douglas' where Miss Watson plies him with frontier puritanism on the one hand and Tom Sawyer confronts him with bourgeois romanticism on the other, when his ruthless father suddenly appears demanding Huck's money which is happily drawing interest, having been shrewdly invested by Judge Thatcher. Pap's onslaught is momentarily halted by the young judge who, fresh from the East, attempts to reform the outcast drunkard. In a chapter significantly entitled "Pap Starts in on a New Life" the whole initiation and rebirth theme is launched on a tragic-comic note. The beautiful spare room in the judge's home is opened to Pap and great is the celebration by the judge's family as Pap jubilantly begins the new life, but during the night he slips out of the beautiful room, trades his new coat which they have given him for a jug of "forty-rod," and climbs back into the room, gets terribly drunk, finally falls off the porch roof into the yard—"and when they come to look at that spare room they had to take soundings before they could navigate it." After this fearful fall from respectability, Pap seizes Huck, whom he considers as property suddenly become valuable, transports him to a log hut up the river, and imprisons him. He treats Huck so violently that Huck finally stages a mock murder of himself in order to escape. This fake murder is probably the most vital and crucial incident of the entire novel. Having killed himself, Huck is "dead" throughout the entire journey down the river. He is indeed the man without identity who is reborn at almost every river bend, not because he desires a new role, but because he must re-create himself to elude the forces which close in on him from every side. The rebirth theme which began with Pap's reform becomes the driving idea behind the entire action.

Coupled with and inseparable from the theme of rebirth is the central image of death. Huck has hardly assumed the role of outcast when he meets Jim, who is also in frantic flight (interestingly enough, Jim is considered in terms of property too; his motive for escaping was fear of being sold down the river for $800.00), and the two fugitives watch the house of death float by on the swollen Mississippi. When Jim carefully covers up the face of the dead man in the house, the second major image of the novel is forged. These two images, rebirth and death, provide a frame for all succeeding episodes of the arduous initiation. As Huck and Jim move down the river, an oncoming steamboat crashes into their raft, forcing the two outcasts to swim for their lives. From this baptism Huck emerges to enter the new life at the Grangerfords under the name of George Jackson. His final act in that life is to cover the dead face of Buck Grangeford much as Jim had covered Pap's face in the house of death. When the Duke and King come aboard, their unscruplous schemes force Huck and Jim to appear in new disguises; but the image of death is never absent. It confronts Huck in the little "one-horse town" in Arkansas where Colonel Sherburn shoots the drunken Boggs in cold blood. When the townspeople lift Boggs from the street and take him to the little drug store, Huck peers in through the window to watch him die. The Peter Wilks episode involves the same central images. The Duke and the King disguise themselves as foreign kinsmen of the deceased Wilks and they force Huck to play the role of an English valet. The final scene of the episode takes place in the graveyard where the mob of townsmen has gathered to exhume the buried Wilks in an effort to discover whether the Duke and King are impostors. A flash of lightning reveals the dead man with the gold on his breast where Huck had hidden it. The man who had Huck in charge forgets his prisoner in his zeal to see corpse and gold; Huck takes full advantage of the moment and runs out of that world forever.

Finally, at the Phelps farm the initiation is completed. Huck is reborn as Tom Sawyer and this time no image of death appears. The Duke and the King are far back in his past and the wheel has indeed come full circle. Jim is imprisoned in a cabin much like the one in which Pap locked Huck; Tom Sawyer himself comes to the rescue in the role of Sid Sawyer; the entire household, though not the same as the one in which the novel began, is related to it through strong blood ties. The full import of this initiation becomes more clearly evident when the differences between Huck and Tom Sawyer are examined.

All of Tom Sawyer's world has been imported into this novel, but with the addition of Huck as narrator and protagonist and Jim as his companion, Tom's world is seen in sharp perspective. Huck and Jim may have to live in that world but they are not of it, and their very detachment creates a larger and deeper universe of which Tom Sawyer's values are but a part. True, Huck is finally overtaken by the society represented by Tom, but his heroic flight and his inner resistance give dignity to his submission. Huck is, after all, incorruptible and though his body is finally captured by the society which "wants" him so, it has not got his name affixed to it; as the novel ends, the real Huck who cannot die is ready to "light out for the territory," to continue his restless flight from "sivilization." Tom Sawyer's initiation had been routine, had merely confirmed his membership in a society to which he already latently belonged; Tom's whole attitude toward his initiators was, as I pointed out, one of self-consciousness, even affectation. Huck's initiation, on the other hand, is forced upon him; his drama is different in that it is drama, not play; everything is at stake in an elemental conflict where the values of one world are pitted against the values of another. And Huck's humor is deeper and greater because it is underlain by the pathos and tragedy of his situation.

Huck is, in the deepest sense, an outcast. Although Tom is an orphan, he at least has relatives who recognize his credentials and have adopted him. Huck has only Pap, the drunkard, the outcast himself, whose eyes shine through his tangled, greasy hair "like he was behind vines." Pap attains intense symbolic stature in his brief but violent pilgrimage:

> . . . There warn't no color in his face where his face showed; it was white; not like another man's white, but a white to make a body's flesh crawl—a tree toad white, a fish-belly white. As for his clothes—just rags, that was all.

There is in this description a supernatural quality which links Pap to Melville's whale. His ways are not so much evil as they are inscrutable; he has somehow gotten consumed by the very nature he set out to conquer and out of the dark union between himself and the River the divine Huck has sprung; Huck certainly belongs more to the river than to the society along its banks, but this in no way makes of him a Rousseauistic child of nature. His lineal descendancy from Pap removes him from the garden of innocence, but if it implies his connection with violence and terror, it also puts him in touch with deeper human forces which cannot be neatly filed under sociological headings. He has "connections" which, though they do not enable him to get ahead in an acquisitive society, give him a depth and a reality which far surpass anything Tom Sawyer has dreamed of.

Both boys fall back on a world of superstition, but Huck's rituals are naturally inherited while Tom's are appropriated from books. Tom's whole life is an imitation of the romances he has read or heard in the middle classs society of which he is a part. The drab and empty life of St. Petersburg forces Tom's mind into an irretrievable past and he pathetically attempts to revive dead chivalry in blighted prairie air. Huck's whole code is, on the contrary, part of him, and he reacts sensitively to life about him. Instead of importing life and law from outside worlds, he invests the objects and people of his world with a life of their own. The difference between Tom Sawyer and Huckleberry Finn is the difference between the primitive and the effete imagination. Tom's drive to dominate his companions, the quality which marks him a devotee at the shrine of William Jame's bitch goddess, arises from the imitative aspect of his mind. The artificial application of a foreign code demands its strict inflexibility. When Tom organizes his gang at the beginning of the novel he is helpless before the independent machinery of his code; even when the machinery obviously will not work, he insists on its use. In his desire to free Jim according to "the rules," Tom displays utter disregard for him as a human being. The ultimate irony emerges when Huck discovers Tom has known Jim was legally free all the time. This discovery explains the deep mystery to Huck who has been wondering all along why Tom Sawyer would "lower hisself" by helping a runaway slave. Through Huck's apparently innocent eyes we get an intimate glimpse into the soul of Tom Sawyer and we see an appalling relationship between Tom and Colonel Sellers, George Babbitt, and, I suppose, Willy Loman.

It is inevitable that Tom should assume Sid Sawyer's role when he reappears at the end of the novel. Sid, Tom's half brother, was the Good Boy of *Tom Sawyer;* he was the eternal prude, the darling of a puritan Sunday School. Yet for all Tom's apparent romantic revolt, his values are Sid's values and though he retains illusions of himself he shows unmistakably that he really is Sid's half-brother. In the closing chapters of the novel Tom's very words become "respectable" and "principle," "regular" and "duty."

. . . The thing for us to do is just to do our *duty,* and not worry about whether anybody *sees* us do it or not. Hain't you got no principle at all?

Huck's relationship to Tom is much more distant. True, there are times when he attempts to emulate Tom Sawyer. Even when he stages his own murder he is conscious that Tom Sawyer would think it was right proud. He sometimes treats Jim the way Tom might treat him. He puts the rattlesnake in Jim's bed and sees the terrifying results. When the two of them board the *Walter Scott,* Huck consciously plays the role of the adventurous Tom much to the dismay of Jim. After Huck and Jim become separated in the fog, Huck attempts to deceive Jim into believing that the separation is a product of Jim's fertile imagination, but Jim humiliates him in the famous passage which ends:

Dat truck dah is trash; en trash is what people is dat puts dirt on de head er dey frens en makes 'em ashamed.

Most of the time, however, Huck is living on too thin a margin to afford Tom's luxurious romances. His motives, arising from his struggle for survival, allow him to indulge in no impracticalities, but he knows the fugitive must rely on magic and superstition to propitiate the inscrutable powers which confront him. The wedding of the practical and the magical gives Huck's character a mobility in the constricting circumstances which envelop him. But all his mobility is not enough, for the forces which pursue him are as relentless as the Mississippi's current. They appear in the forms of the Duke and King, the Grangerfords and Shepherdsons and their feud, Judith Loftus, even Jim. Every living thing becomes a source of danger to the lost boy without a name. Huck's remarkable observation upon first seeing the Duke and King coming toward him at a run reveals the terror of his plight:

. . . Just as I was passing a place where a kind of a cowpath crossed the crick, here comes a couple of men tearing up the path as tight as they could foot it. I thought I was a goner, for whenever anybody was after anybody I judged it was *me*— or maybe Jim.

Because Huck completely lives his rituals, because he participates to the tips of his fingers in a struggle for survival, and because his whole world and all its values are at stake, he transcends the empty rituals of Tom Sawyer's universe and achieves mythic significance.

When he wearily walks into the Phelps yard and is once more faced with the inevitable proposition of creating himself, he feels his string playing out. At Judith Loftus', at the Grangerfords', before the King and Duke, Huck, the man without identity, had been able to choose his disguise from a vast store of verbal masks which he kept ready at hand; but at the Phelps home even his name has been chosen and he bewilderingly attempts to discover who he is. As he stands before Aunt Sally trying to solve the riddle of his identity, he feels so tight and uncomfortable that he almost wishes he were dead:

> . . . Well, I see I was up a stump—and up it good. Providence had stood by me this fur all right, but I was hard and tight aground now. I see it warn't a bit of use to try to go ahead—I'd got to throw up my hand. So I says to myself, here's another place where I got to resk the truth.

The swirl of events never allows him to "resk the truth" (the phrase itself suggests the ironic plight of Huck's position throughout the novel): Uncle Silas Phelps arrives at this precise moment and Huck finds to his delight and amazement that he is supposed to be Tom Sawyer. The very language Huck uses at this point suggests the myth behind the humor:

> By jings, I almost slumped through the floor! But there warn't no time to swap knives; the old man grabbed me by the hand and shook, and kept on shaking. . . . But if they was joyful, it warn't nothing to what I was; for it was like being born again, I was so glad to find out who I was.

There is bitter irony in Huck's assumption of Tom's name because the values of Tom Sawyer are so antithetical to the values of Huck Finn; in the final analysis, the two boys cannot exist in the same world. When Huck regains his own identity at the very end of the novel he immediately feels the compulsion to "light out for the territory" because he knows that to be Huck Finn is to be the outcast beyond the paling fences. From Mark Twain's point of view in this novel, Tom Sawyer civilization involves obedience, imitation, and is directly opposed to a dynamic and creative frontier imagination. In Tom Sawyer's triumph, the hard core of

Mark Twain's later disillusion and pessimism is already evident. Although Huck Finn may escape to the territory, the whole outline of the frontier is receding westward before the surge of small town culture, and it is indeed doomed country into which Huck must retreat.

Huck Finn cannot be reduced to historical proportions, however, even though there is much in the novel for the historian. The territory to which Huck refers is more than a diminishing area in nineteenth century America. It is a metaphoric equivalent of the broader and deeper vision which Huck and Jim represent. To be in the "territory" is not to be in heaven, for the wilderness and waste places have their perils for the sojourner, as Pap's presence fearfully testifies, but it is to escape the dehumanizing forces of the little towns; it is to be stripped of the pride encouraged by a sterile respectability and to feel absolute humility in the face of the awful unseen powers. Huck and Jim are the only real human beings in the novel—they are human because they can still feel and because they possess a heightened sensitivity to the promises and terrors of life. The characters whom they encounter, with the exception of the young and innocent, have an angularity and rigidity which mark them as grotesques. The blind spots of the eminently respectable become proving grounds for the avaricious; the pretentious righteousness of one group merely encourages the brutal sensationalism of another. Only Huck and Jim possess wholeness of spirit among the horde of fragmentary personalities which parade through the novel. The society which hotly pursues Huck and Jim knows that they possess the real secrets—that is why it so desperately wants to "own" them.

And if Tom has taken Sid's role and Huck has been forced to take Tom's in this rather discouraging progression, who is left to take Huck's place? Fifteen years later Mark Twain could not answer the question, for his imagination had been consumed by what Bernard De Voto calls the symbols of despair. There is someone, however, to take Huck's place in this novel; he is, of course, that primitive of primitives, Jim. He stands in relation to Huck in this novel much as Huck stood in relation to Tom in *Tom Sawyer,* and is in many ways the central figure of the book. It is to Jim that Huck retreats as if to a savior; he it is who mothers Huck as they travel down the big river; and he it is who, knowing secretly that Huck's Pap is dead forever, takes Huck to his own bosom to nourish him through the ordeal of being lost. Acting as Huck's foster father, Jim brings to that role a warmth and gentleness which Huck had never known under the brutal masculinity of his real father. Near the end of the novel, after Jim has accompanied and protected Huck on their perilous journey, how appropriate it is that he should be led back to the Phelps plantation, following his temporary escape with Tom, arrayed in the dress which the boys had stolen from Aunt Sally. The incident points up the ambivalent nature of Jim, emphasizing his role of motherly father to Huck. Leslie Fiedler, looking at the novel as an American myth of love, has searchingly explored this ambivalent relationship.

Jim is also one of the two great human forces in the book. By means of his truth and sincerity, the fraud and hoax of the world along the river banks are thrown into sharp relief. Probably the finest example of Jim's function as a moral norm occurs on the raft just before the King and Duke meet the country boy who unwittingly directs them into the Peter Wilks exploit. Huck awakens at daybreak one morning to see Jim grieving to himself. Jim finally tells him that a whacking sound he heard on shore reminded him of the time he disciplined his little daughter for not obeying a command. Upon repeating his command to no avail, Jim finally struck the child down, only to find that her recent attack of scarlet fever had left her deaf and dumb:

> Oh, Huck, I burst out a-crying en grab her up in my arms, en say, 'Oh, de po' little thing! De Lord God Almighty forgive po' ole Jim, kaze he never gwyne to fogive hisself as long's he live!' Oh, she was plumb deef en dumb, Huck, plum deef en dumb—en I'd ben a-treat'n her so!

Immediately after this burst of genuine remorse, the Duke and the King launch their expedition to rob the Wilks daughters of their inheritance by pretending to be Peter Wilks' foreign kinsmen. The Duke poses as a deaf mute. By employing the same device he used so successfully in *Tom Sawyer*, Twain establishes a subtle and exquisite relationship between the two episodes. Through Jim's sensitivity the entire Wilks episode is thrown into much more precise focus. Indeed, Jim is the conscience of the novel, the spiritual yardstick by which all men are measured. As the two fugitives move down the river, Huck's whole moral sense grows out of and revolves around the presence of Jim, and his ability to measure up signifies his worth. Huck's whole sense of wrong, his feeling of guilt are products of his intimate association with Jim— his companionship with the runaway slave makes possible his moral growth.

Many critics, intent on seeing Jim as a symbol of the tragic consequences of slavery, have failed to see that he is much more than this. He is that great residue of primitive, fertile force turned free at the end of the novel at the very moment Huck is captured. That Mark Twain recognized in the Negro a new American protagonist is evident not only in his creation of Jim, but in his interesting return to the whole problem of slavery in *Pudd'nhead Wilson*. Certainly Jim and Thomas à Becket Driscoll stand solidly behind Faulkner, Robert Penn Warren, and Richard Wright. Having been thrown from his secure place within the social structure, Jim will be the new fugitive which the bourgeoisie will, with a great deal of hesitation, wish to make respectable.

There is an inexorable and crushing logic inherent in the ending of *Huckleberry Finn*. T. S. Eliot, in his remarkable introductory essay to the Cressett Library edition of the novel, remarked the inevitability of the final chapters, but failed to enlarge upon the generalization. Most critics agree that the ending is much weaker than the rest of the book, as indeed it is, but often they mistakenly gauge that weakness. Certainly Tom's reappearance itself does not weaken the ending. Any comprehensive vision of the book will, it seems to me, consider Tom's presence at the end not only vital but inevitable. The flatness of the ending results from Tom's domination of the action and the style. As soon as he appears, his whole aggressive spirit bids for position, and although Mark Twain attempts to use Huck to exploit the ironies of the situation, Tom's seizure of the style damages the tenor of the novel. It is a stylistic rather than a structural flaw, a failure in taste rather than in conception.

Mark Twain's failure in taste at this particular juncture bears further consideration. *Huckleberry Finn* is without question his greatest work, and diametric opposition of Tom and Huck is eminently clear. The substitution of Tom's humor for Huck's vision indicates that Mark Twain, though aware of the two sets of values, could not keep a proper balance between them because of his fascination with Tom Sawyer. In turning over the narration to Huck Finn he had turned to the incorruptible part of himself which was not for sale and could not be bought. The opening paragraph of the novel indicates that he was not entirely unaware of what he was about:

> You don't know about me without you have read a book by the name of *The Adventures of Tom Sawyer;* but that ain't no matter. That book was made by Mr. Mark Twain, and he told the truth, mainly. There was things which he stretched, but mainly he told the truth.

"Mainly he told the truth." In this novel Mark Twain tried to tell the whole truth through Huckleberry Finn. Although Tom Sawyer makes his presence too much felt at the end of the novel, Mark Twain saw his whole truth with supreme vision. Because of the deeply human values which are at stake, neither the satire nor the humor is tainted by the scoffing disillusion and the adolescent cynicism in which he finally foundered. The unobtrusive formal perfection allows the novel to retain the primitive power and immediacy of the myth which it recreates; its impact strikes us in the profoundest areas of our consciousness, and we are reminded of the darkness and the terror and the violence which stalk the virgin forest where the American dream lies waiting, aware and unaware.

Dorothy Van Ghent

XVI

On The Portrait of a Lady

To go from Hardy's *Tess* to James's *The Portrait of a Lady* is to go
from Stonehenge to St. Peter's and from a frozen northern turnip
field, eyed hungrily by polar birds, to the Cascine gardens where
nightingales sing. Though both books concern the "campaign" of
a young woman—a campaign that, expressed most simply, is a
campaign *to live*—a greater difference of atmosphere could scarcely
be imagined nor of articulation of what it means *to live*. The gaunt
arctic birds in *Tess* have witnessed, with their "tragical eyes,"
cataclysms that no human eyes might see, but of which they retain no memory. The birds offer a symbol of Tess's world: a world
inimical to consciousness, where one should have no memory
(Tess's fatal error is to remember her own past), where the eye of
the mind should remain blank, where aesthetic and moral perceptivity is traumatic. The nightingales that sing to Isabel Archer and
her lover in the "grey Italian shade" also offer a symbol of a
world: they are the very voice of memory, of an imperishable
consciousness at once recreating and transcending its ancient, all-
human knowledge. It is to the tutelage of the European memory
that Isabel Archer passionately surrenders herself in her campaign
to live, that is, to become conscious; for, in James's world, the

highest affirmation of life is the development of the subtlest and most various consciousness. In doing so, she must—like the girl in the barbarous legend of the nightingale, who, likewise in a foreign land, read an obscene crime in the weaving of a tapestry—come into knowledge of an evil which, in its own civilized kind, is as corrupting and implacable as that in the old tale. But consciousness here, as an activity nourished by knowledge, transcends the knowledge which is its content: and this too is in an analogy with the ancient symbolic tale, where knowledge of evil is transcended, in the very doom of its reiteration, by the bird's immortal song.

The Portrait is not, like *Tess,* a tragedy, but it is as deeply informed with the tragic view of life: that tragic view whose essence is contained in the words, "He who loses his life shall find it," and "Except a corn of wheat fall into the ground and die, it abideth alone: but if it die, it bringeth forth much fruit." We associate tragic seriousness of import in a character's destiny with tension between the power of willing (which is "free") and the power of circumstances ("necessity") binding and limiting the will; and if either term of the tension seems lacking, seriousness of import fails. Apparently, no two authors could be at further antipodes than James and Hardy in the respective emphases they place on these terms. In Hardy, the protagonist's volition founders at every move on a universally mechanical, mysteriously hostile necessity; it is only in Tess's last acts, of blood sacrifice and renunciation of life, that her will appallingly asserts its freedom and that she gains her tragic greatness. In James's *Portrait,* and in his other novels as well, the protagonist appears to have an extraordinarily unhampered play of volition. This appearance of extraordinary freedom from the pressure of circumstances is largely due to the "immense deal of money" (the phrase is taken from an early page of *The Portrait*) with which James endows his world—for, in an acquisitive culture, money is the chief symbol of freedom. The vague rich gleams of money are on every cornice and sift through every vista of the world of *The Portrait,* like the muted gold backgrounds of old Persian illuminations; and the human correlative of the money is a type of character fully privileged with easy mobility upon the face of the earth and with magnificent opportunities for the cultivation of aesthetic and intellectual refinements. It is by visualizing with the greatest clarity the lustrously moneyed tones of the James uni-

verse that we make ourselves able to see the more clearly what
grave, somber shapes of illusion and guilt he organizes in this
novel. The tension between circumstances and volition, "necessity" and "freedom," is demonstrated at the uppermost levels of
material opportunity where, presumably, there is most freedom
and where therefore freedom becomes most threatening—and
where necessity wears its most insidious disguise, the disguise
of freedom.

In following the previous studies, the reader will perhaps have
been impressed with the fact that the novel as a genre has shown,
from *Don Quixote* on, a constant concern with the institutions
created by the circulation of money and with the fantasies arising
from the having of it, or, more especially, the not having it; a concern not always so direct as that of *Moll Flanders* and *Vanity Fair,*
but almost inevitably implicit at least, expressed in indirect forms
of aspiration and encitement to passion. As the definitely middle-
class literary genre, the novel purchased its roots in a money-
conscious imagination, The wealth shining on the James world is
a kind of apogee of the novel's historical concern with money,
showing itself, in *The Portrait,* as a grandly sweeping postulate of
possession: as if to say, "Here, now, is all the beautiful money, in
the most liberating quantities: what ambition, what temptation,
what errors of the will, what evil, what suffering, what salvation
still denote the proclivities of the human even in a world so
bountifully endowed?"

The "international myth"[1] that operates broadly in James's
work, and that appears, in this novel, in the typical confrontation
of American innocence and moral rigor with the tortuosities of an
older civilization, gives its own and special dimension to the
moneyed prospect. James came to maturity in a post-Civil War
America euphoric with material achievement. In terms of the
Jamesian "myth," American wealth is now able to buy up the
whole museum of Europe, all its visible "point" of art objects and
culture prestige, to take back home and set up in the front yard
(we need look no further, for historical objectification of this aspect
of the "myth," than to William Randolph Hearst's epic importation
of various priceless chunks of Europe to California). If the shadows
of the physically dispossessed—the sweat and the bone-weariness
and the manifold anonymous deprivation in which this culture-

buying power had its source—are excluded from Jame's money-gilded canvas, the shadow of spiritual dispossession is the somber shape under the money outline. We are not allowed to forget the aesthetic and moral impoverishment that spread its gross vacuum at the core of the American acquisitive dream—the greed, the obtuse or rapacious presumption, the disvaluation of values that kept pace to pace with material expansion. James's characteristic thematic contrasts, here as in other novels, are those of surface against depth, inspection against experience, buying power against living power, the American tourist's cultural balcony against the European abyss of history and memory and involved motive where he perilously or callously teeters. In *The Portrait,* the American heroine's pilgrimage in Europe becomes a fatally serious spiritual investment, an investment of the "free" self in and with the circumstantial and binding past, a discovery of the relations of the self with history, and a moral renovation of history in the freedom of the individual conscience. It is a growing of more delicate and deeper-reaching roots and a nourishment of a more complex, more troubled, more creative personal humanity. It is, in short, what is ideally meant by "civilization," as that word refers to a process that can take place in an individual.

The postulate of wealth and privilege is, in revised terms, that of the second chapter of Genesis (the story of Adam in the garden) —that of the optimum conditions which will leave the innocent soul at liberty to develop it potentialities—and, as in the archetype of the Fall of Man, the postulate is significant not as excluding knowledge of good and evil, but as presenting a rare opportunity for such knowledge. It is the bounty poured on Isabel Archer (significantly, the man who gives her the symbolical investiture of money is a man who is fatally ill; significantly, also, she is under an illusion as to the giver) that makes her "free" to determine her choice of action, and thus morally most responsible for her choice; but it is the very bounty of her fortune, also, that activates at once, as if chemically, the proclivity to evil in the world of privilege that her wealth allows her to enter—it is her money that draws Madame Merle and Osmond to her; so that her "freedom" is actualized as imprisonment, in a peculiarly ashen and claustral, because peculiarly refined, suburb of hell. Isabel's quest had, at the earliest, been a quest for happiness—the naïvely egoistic

American quest; it converts into a problem of spiritual salvation, that is, into a quest of "life"; and again the Biblical archetype shadows forth the problem. After eating of the fruit of the tree of knowledge of good and evil, how is one to regain access to the tree of life?

The great fairy tales and saints' legends have identified life with knowledge. For the fairy-tale hero, the fruit of the tree of life that is the guerdon of kingdom is the golden fleece or the golden apples that his wicked stepmother or usurping uncle have sent him in quest of; and to achieve the guerdon he must go through all tormenting knowledge—of serpents, floods, fire, ogres, enchantment, and even of his own lusts and murderous capacities. The ordeal of the heroes of saints' legends is also an ordeal of knowledge of evil, and the guerdon is life. As do these ancient tales, *The Portrait* identifies life with the most probing, dangerous, responsible awareness—identifies, as it were, the two "trees," the tree of the Fall and the tree of the Resurrection. The heroine's voluntary search for fuller consciousness leads her, in an illusion of perfect freedom to choose only "the best" in experience, to choose an evil; but it is this that, by providing insight through suffering and guilt, provides also access to life—to the fructification of consciousness that is a knowledge of human bondedness. At the very end of the book, Caspar Goodwood gives passionate voice to the illusion of special privileges of choice and of a good to be had by exclusion and separateness: he says to Isabel,

> "It would be an insult to you to assume that you care for . . . the bottomless idiocy of the world. We've nothing to do with all that; we're quite out of it . . . We can do absolutely as we please; to whom under the sun do we owe anything? What is it that holds us, what is it that has the smallest right to interfere . . . ? The world's all before us—and the world's very big."

Isabel answers at random, "The world's very small." What attitude of mind takes her back to Rome, back to old evil and old servitude, is not described; we know only that she does go back. But it is evident that she does so because the "small" necessitous world has received an extension, not in the horizontal direction of imperial mobility that Caspar Goodwood suggests, but an invisible extension in depth, within her own mind—an extension into the freedom of personal renunciation and inexhaustible responsibility.

The knowledge she has acquired has been tragic knowledge, but her story does not stop here, as it would if it were a tragedy—it goes on out of the pages of the book, to Rome, where we cannot follow it; for the knowledge has been the means to "life," and having learned to live, she must "live long," as she says. It is only the process of the learning that the portrait frame itself holds.

The title, *The Portrait,* asks the eye to see. And the handling of the book is in terms of seeing. The informing and strengthening of the eye of the mind is the theme—the ultimate knowledge, the thing finally "seen," having only the contingent importance of stimulating a more subtle and various activity of perception. The dramatization is deliberately "scenic," moving in a series of recognition scenes that are slight and low-keyed at first, or blurred and erroneous, in proportion both to the innocence of the heroine and others' skill in refined disguises and obliquities; then, toward the end, proceeding in swift and livid flashes. For in adopting as his compositional center the growth of a consciousness, James was able to use the bafflements and illusions of ignorance for his "complications," as he was able to use, more consistently than any other novelist, "recognitions" for his crises. Further, this action, moving through errors and illuminations of the inward eye, is set in a symbolic construct of things to be seen by the physical eye—paintings and sculptures, old coins and porcelain and lace and tapestries, most of all buildings: the aesthetic riches of Europe, pregnant with memory, with "histories within histories" of skills and motivations, temptations and suffering. The context of particulars offered to physical sight (and these may be settings, like English country houses or Roman ruins, or objects in the setting, like a porcelain cup or a piece of old lace draped on a mantel, or a person's face or a group of people—and the emphasis on the visual is most constant and notable not in these particulars, extensive as they are, but in the figurative language of the book, in metaphors using visual images as their vehicle) intensifies the meaning of "recognition" in those scenes where *sight* is *insight,* and provides a concrete embodiment of the ambiguities of "seeing."

In James's handling of the richly qualitative setting, it is characteristically significant that he suggests visual or scenic traits almost always in such a way that the emphasis is on *modulations of perception in the observer.* The "look" of things is a response of consciousness and varies with the observer; the "look" of things has thus the double duty of representing external stimuli, by indirection in their passage through consciousness, and of representing the observer himself. For instance, when Ralph takes Isabel through the picture gallery in the Touchett home, the "imperfect" but "genial" light of the bracketed lamps shows the pictures as "vague squares of rich colour," and the look of the pictures is Isabel's state at the moment—her eager and innately gifted sensibility and her almost complete ignorance, her conscious orientation toward an unknown "rich" mode of being that is beautiful but indeterminate. Let us take another example from late in the book. Directly after that conversation with Madame Merle when Isabel learns, with the full force of evil revelation, Madame Merle's part in her marriage, she goes out for a drive alone.

> She had long before this taken old Rome into her confidence, for in a world of ruins the ruin of her happiness seemed a less unnatural catastrophe. She rested her weariness upon things that had crumbled for centuries and yet still were upright; she dropped her secret sadness into the silence of lonely places, where its very modern quality detached itself and grew objective, so that as she sat in a sun-warmed angle on a winter's day, or stood in a mouldy church to which no one came, she could almost smile at it and think of its smallness. Small it was, in the large Roman record, and her haunting sense of the continuity of the human lot easily carried her from the less to the greater. She had become deeply, tenderly acquainted with Rome: it interfused and moderated her passion. But she had grown to think of it chiefly as the place where people had suffered. This was what came to her in the starved churches, where the marble columns, transferred from pagan ruins, seemed to offer her a companionship in endurance and the musty incense to be a compound of long-unanswered prayers.

Here the definition of visible setting—churches and marble columns and ruins, and comprehending all these, Rome—though it is full, is vague and diffuse, in the external sense of the "seen"; but in the sense that it is a setting evoked by Isabel's own deepened consciousness, it is exactly and clearly focused. It is Rome *felt*, felt as an immensity of human time, as a great human continuum of sadness and loneliness and passion and aspiration and patience; and it has this definition by virtue of Isabel's personal ordeal and her perception of its meaning. The "vague squares of rich colour" have become determinate.

The theme of "seeing" (the theme of the developing conscious-ness) is fertile with ironies and ambiguities that arise from the natural symbolism of the act of seeing, upon which so vastly many of human responses and decisions are dependent. The eye, as it registers surfaces, is an organ of aesthetic experience, in the etymological sense of the word "aesthetic," which is a word deriving from a Greek verb meaning "to perceive"—to perceive through the senses. James provides his world with innumerable fine surfaces for this kind of perception; it is a world endowed with the finest selective opportunities for the act of "seeing," for aesthetic cultivation. But our biological dependence upon the eye has made it a symbol of intellectual and moral and spiritual per-ception, forms of perception which are—by the makers of dic-tionaries—discriminated radically from aesthetic perception. Much of James's work is an exploration of the profound identity of the aesthetic and the moral. (In this he is at variance with the makers of dictionaries, but he has the companionship of Socrates' teacher Diotima, as her teaching is represented by Plato in the *Symposium*. Diotima taught that the way to spiritual good lay through the hierarchies of the "beautiful," that is, through graduations from one form of aesthetic experience to another.) Aesthetic experience proper, since it is acquired through the senses, is an experience of *feeling*. But so also moral experience, when it is not sheerly nominal and ritualistic, is an experience of *feeling*. Neither one has reality—has psychological depth—unless it is "felt" (hence James's so frequent use of phrases such as "felt life" and "the very *taste* of life," phrases that insist on the feeling-base of complete and integrated living). Furthermore, both aesthetic and moral experience are nonutilitarian. The first distinction that aestheticians usually make, in defining the aesthetic, is its distinction from the useful; when the aesthetic is converted to utility, it becomes something else, its value designation is different—as when a beautiful bowl becomes valuable not for its beauty but for its capacity to hold soup. So also the moral, when it is converted to utility, becomes something else than the moral—becomes even immoral, a parody of or a blasphemy against the moral life (in our richest cultural heritage, both Hellenic and Christian, the moral life is symbolically associated with utter loss of utility goods and even with loss of physical life—as in the Gospel passage, "Leave all that thou hast and follow me," or as in the career of Socrates, or as in Sophocles' *Antigone*). Moral and aesthetic experience have then in common their foundation in feeling and their distinction from the useful. The identity that James explores is their identity in the most capacious and most integrated—the most "civilized"—consciousness, whose sense relationships (aesthetic relationships) with the external world of scenes and objects have the same quality and the same spiritual determination as its relationships with people (moral relationships). But his exploration of that ideal identity involves cognizance of failed integration, cognizance of the many varieties of one-sidedness or one-eyedness or blindness that go by the name of the moral or the aesthetic, and of the destructive potentialities of the human consciousness when it is one-sided either way. His ironies revolve on the ideal concept of a spacious integrity of feeling: feeling, ideally, is *one*—and there is ironic situation when feeling is split into the "moral" and the "aesthetic," each denying the other and each posing as *all*.

There is comic irony in Henrietta Stackpole's moral busybodyness as she flutters and sputters through Europe obtaining feature materials for her home-town newspaper, "featuring" largely the morally culpable un-Americanism of Europeans to serve her readers as a flattering warning against indulgence in the aesthetic. Henrietta is a stock James comedy character, and she is essential. Without Henrietta's relative incapacity to "see" more than literal surfaces, the significant contrast between surface and depth, between outward and inward "seeing," between undeveloped and developed consciousness, would lose a needed demonstration. (But let us say for Henrietta that, like Horatio in *Hamlet,* she is employed by the dramatist for as many sorts of purposes as his scenes happen to demand; when a foil of obtuseness is wanted, Henrietta is there, and when a foil of good interpretive intelligence or plain charitable generosity is wanted, Henrietta is also there. She is the type of what James technically called the *ficelle,* a wholly subordinate character immensely useful to take in confidences from the principals and to serve other functions of "relief"— "relief" in that sense in which the lower level of a relievo provides perspective for the carved projections.) In Mrs. Touchett, what appears at first as the comic irony of absolute aesthetic insensitivity accompanied by a rugged moral dogmatism ("she had a little moral account-book—with columns unerringly ruled and a sharp steel clasp—which she kept with exemplary neatness") becomes at the end of the book, with her son's death, the tragic irony of that kind of ambiguous misery which is an inability to acknowledge or realize one's own suffering, when suffering is real but the channels of feeling have become nearly atrophied by lack of use. At the midday meal, when Isabel and Mrs. Touchett come together after the night of Ralph's death,

> Isabel saw her aunt not to be so dry as she appeared, and her old pity for the poor woman's inexpressiveness, her want of regret, of disappointment, came back to her. Unmistakably she would have found it a blessing to-day to be able to feel a defeat, a mistake, even a shame or two. [Isabel] wondered if [her aunt] were not even missing those enrichments of consciousness and privately trying—reaching out for some aftertaste of life, dregs of the banquet; the testimony of pain or the old recreation of remorse. On the other hand perhaps she was afraid; if she should begin to know remorse at all it might take her too far. Isabel could perceive, however, how it had come over her dimly that she had failed of something, that she saw herself in the future as an old woman without memories. Her little sharp face looked tragical.

Mrs. Touchett's habitual moralistic denial of feeling as an aesthetic indulgence has left her deserted even by herself, even by her love of her son, even by memory, even by suffering. She is stranded in a morality that is tragically without meaning.

In Madame Merle and Osmond the ironies intrinsic to James's theme receive another turn. Madame Merle first appeals to Isabel's admiration by her capacity for "feeling"—for that kind of feeling to which the term "aesthetic" has been specially adapted in common modern use: feeling for the arts, the sensuous perceptivity underlying the arts, and, by extension, feeling for the finer conventions of manners as "arts of living." (Madame Merle "knew how to feel . . . This was indeed Madame Merle's great talent, her most perfect gift.") At Gardencourt, when she is not engaged in writing letters, she paints (she "made no more of brushing in a sketch than of pulling off her gloves") or she plays the piano (she "was a brave musician") or she is "employed upon wonderful tasks of rich embroidery." (The presentation is just a bit insidious, not only because of Madame Merle's so very great plasticity in going from one art to another, but also in the style of the phrases: the suggestion of conventional fluidity in the comparison of her ease in painting with the ease of "pulling off her gloves," the word "brave"—an honorific word in certain places, but carrying here the faintest note of bravado—and the word "employed," suggesting, as it reverberates, Madame Merle's not disinterested professional aestheticism.) Her senses are active and acute; walking in the English rain, she says,

> "It never wets you and it always smells good." She declared that in England the pleasures of smell were great . . . and she used to lift the sleeve of her British overcoat and bury her nose in it, inhaling the clear, fine scent of the wood.

Just how acute her perceptions are is shown never more clearly than in that scene in which she learns of the distribution of property after Mr. Touchett's death, ocurring in Chapter 20 of Volume I. Mrs. Touchett has just told her that Ralph, because of the state of his health, had hurried away from England before the reading of the will, in which Isabel had been left half of the fortune accruing to him. With this news, Madame Merle "remained thoughtful a moment, her eyes bent on the floor," and when Isabel enters the room, Madame Merle kisses her—this being "the only allusion the visitor, in her great good taste, made . . . to her young friend's inheritance." There are no other signs than these (and the episode is typical of James's minor "recognition scenes") of just how quickly and acutely Madame Merle's senses—her perception, her intuition—have functioned in apprising her of the possibilities of exploitation now opened, and in apprising her also of the fact that Ralph is the real donor of Isabel's fortune, a fact of which Isabel herself remains ignorant until Madame Merle viciously informs her. Madame Merle's feeling for situation is so subtly educated that she needs but the slightest of tokens in order to respond. And yet, with a sensitivity educated so exquisitely and working at such high tension she is morally insensible—or almost so; not quite—for, unlike Osmond, whose damnation is in ice where the moral faculty is quite frozen, she still has the spiritual capacity of those whose damnation is in fire, the capacity to know that she is damned.

Madame Merle and Osmond use their cultivated aestheticism for utility purposes—Madame Merle, to further her ambition for place and power; Osmond, to make himself separate and envied. Their debasement of the meaning of the aesthetic becomes symbolically vicious when it shows itself in their relationships with people—with Isabel, for instance, who is for them an object of virtu that differs from other objects of virtu in that it bestows money rather than costs it. This is the evil referred to by Kant in his second Categorical Imperative: the use of persons as means—an evil to which perhaps all evil in human relationships reduces. In the case of Madame Merle and Osmond, it has a peculiar and blasphemous ugliness, inasmuch as the atmosphere of beauty in which they live—beauty of surroundings and of manners—represents the finest, freest product of civilization and is such, ideally, as to induce the most reverential feeling for people as well as for things. Isabel first appeals to Osmond as being "as smooth to his general need of her as handled ivory to the palm": it is an "aesthetic" image suggesting his fastidiousness but, ironically, suggesting at the same time his coarseness—for while ivory, like pearls, may be the more beautiful for handling, "handled ivory" might also be the head of a walking stick, and it is in some sort as a walking stick that he uses Isabel. An extension of the same figure, without the aesthetic and with only the utilitarian connotation, indicates Osmond's real degeneracy: Isabel finally realizes that she has been for him "an applied handled hung-up tool, as senseless and convenient as mere wood and iron." But the evil is not one that can be isolated or confined; it is automatically proliferative. Morally dead himself, incapable of reverence for the human quality in others, Osmond necessarily tries to duplicate his death in them, for it is by killing their volition that he can make them useful; dead, they are alone "beautiful." He urges upon Isabel the obscene suggestion that she, in turn, "use" Lord Warburton by exploiting Warburton's old love for herself in order to get him to marry Pansy; and Osmond can find no excuse for her refusal except that she has her private designs for "using" the Englishman. But it is in Osmond's use of Pansy, his daughter, that he is most subtly and horribly effective. He has made her into a work of art, the modeling materials being the least artful of childish qualities—her innocence and gentleness; and he has almost succeeded in reducing her will to an echo of his own. The quaint figure of Pansy, always only on the edge of scenes, is of great structural importance in the latter half of the book; for she shows the full measure of the abuse that Isabel resists, and it is to nourish in her whatever small germ of creative volition may remain—to salvage, really, a life—that Isabel returns to Rome and to Osmond's paralyzing ambiance.

The moral question that is raised by every character in the book is a question of the "amount of felt life" that each is able to experience, a question of how many and how various are the relationships each can, with integrity, enter into. Or, to put the matter in its basic metaphor, it is a question of how much each person is able to "see," and not only to see but to compose into creative order. The moral question, since it involves vision, feeling, and composition, is an aesthetic one as well. Madame Merle and Osmond are blind to certain relations: "I don't pretend to know what people are meant for," Madame Merle says, ". . . I only know what I can do with them." Mrs. Touchett is blind to certain others. Let us stop for a moment with Henrietta Stackpole's comic crudity of vision, for the "eye" is all-important, and the ranges of vision really begin with an eye like that of Henrietta. It is "a peculiarly open, surprised-looking eye." "The most striking point in her appearance was the remarkable fixedness of this organ."

> She fixed her eyes on [Ralph], and there was something in their character that reminded him of large polished buttons—buttons that might have fixed the elastic loops of some tense receptacle: he seemed to see the reflection of surrounding objects on the pupil. The expression of a button is not usually deemed human, but there was something in Miss Stackpole's gaze that made him, a very modest man, feel vaguely embarrassed—less inviolate, more dishonoured, than he liked.

Henrietta, with her gregariously refractive button-sight, has also "clear-cut views on most subjects . . . she knew perfectly in advance what her opinions would be." Henrietta's is the made-up consciousness, the pseudo consciousness, that is not a process but a content hopelessly once and for all given, able to refract light but not to take it in. (We can understand Henrietta's importance, caricatural as she is, by the fact that she is the primitive form of the pseudo consciousness which Madame Merle and Osmond, in their so much more sophisticated ways, exhibit: theirs too is the made-up consciousness, a rigidified content, impervious and uncreative.) The Misses Molyneux, Lord Warburton's sisters, have "eyes like the balanced basins, the circles of 'ornamental water,' set, in parterres, among the geraniums." Let us note that the figure is drawn from an "aesthetic" arrangement, that of formal gardens—and in this sense has directly opposite associations to those of Henrietta's buttons (presumably very American, very *useful* buttons). The Misses Molyneux's eyes, like Henrietta's, also merely reflect surrounding objects, and reflect more limitedly, far less mobilely; but the image is significant of certain kinds of feeling, of "seeing," that Henrietta is incapable of, and that have derived from ancient disciplines in human relationships—contemplative feeling, reverence, feeling for privacy and for grace. Extremely minor figures such as these, of the buttons and the basins, are pregnant with the extraordinarily rich, extraordinarily subtle potentialities of the theme of "seeing" as an infinitely graduated cognizance of relations between self and world.

In this book, the great range of structural significance through figurative language is due to the fact that whatever image vehicle a figure may have—even when the image is not itself a visual one—the general context is so deeply and consistently characterized by acts of "seeing" that every metaphor has this other implied extension of meaning. For example, a very intricate and extensive symbolic construct is built on a metaphor of opening doors. Henrietta, Ralph says, "walks in without knocking at the door." "She's too personal," he adds. As her eyes indiscriminately take in everything that is literally to be seen, so she walks in without knocking at the door of personality: "she thinks one's door should stand ajar." The correspondence of eyes and doors lies in the publicity Henrietta assumes (she is a journalist): her eye is public like a button, and responds as if everything else were public, as if there were no doors, as if there were nothing to be seen but what the public (the American newspaper public) might see without effort and without discomfort. In James's thematic system of surfaces and depths, "sight" is something achieved and not given, achieved in the loneliness of the individual soul and in the lucidity of darkness suffered; privacy is its necessary stamp, and it cannot be loaned or broadcast any more than can the loneliness or the suffering. "I keep a band of music in my ante-room," Ralph tells Isabel.

> "It has orders to play without stopping; it renders me two excellent services. It keeps the sounds of the world from reaching the private apartments, and it makes the world think that dancing's going on within."

The notation has its pathos through Ralph's illness. Isabel "would have liked to pass through the ante-room . . . and enter the private apartments." It is only at the end, through her own revelations of remorse and loss, that those doors open to her.

The ironic force of the metaphor of doors, as it combines with the metaphor of "seeing," has a different direction in the crucial scene in Chapter 51 of the second volume—one of the major "recognition scenes" in the book, where Isabel sees Osmond's full malignancy, a malignancy the more blighting as it takes, and sincerely takes, the form of honor, and where Osmond sees unequivocally the vivid, mysterious resistance of a life that he has not been able to convert into a tool. Isabel comes to tell him that Ralph is dying and that she must go to England. She opens the door to her husband's study without knocking.

> "Excuse me for disturbing you," she said.
> "When I come to your room I always knock," he answered, going on with his work.
> "I forgot; I had something else to think of. My cousin's dying."
> "Ah, I don't believe that," said Osmond, looking at his drawing through a magnifying glass. "He was dying when we married; he'll outlive us all."

Osmond is here engaged in an activity representative of a man of taste and a "collector"—he is making traced copies of ancient coins (the fact that it is an act of tracing, of copying, has its own significance, as has the object of his attention: coins). What he "sees" in the situation that Isabel describes to him is quite exactly what he sees in the fact that she has opened the door without knocking: a transgression of convention; and what he does not see is the right of another human being to feel, to love, to will individually. Further, what he appallingly does not see is his dependence, for the fortune Isabel has brought him, on the selfless imagination of the dying man, Ralph; or, even more appallingly (for one can scarcely suppose that Madame Merle had left him ignorant of the source of Isabel's wealth), what he does not see is any reason for the moral responsibility implied by "gratitude," a defect of vision that gives a special and hideous bleakness to his use of the word "grateful," when he tells Isabel that she has not been "grateful" for his tolerance of her esteem for Ralph. The metaphor of the "doors" thus goes through its changes, each associated with a depth or shallowness, a straightness or obliquity of vision, from Henrietta's aggressive myopia, to Ralph's reticence and insight, to Osmond's refined conventionalism and moral astigmatism.

Let us consider in certain other examples this reciprocity between theme and metaphor, insight and sight, image and eye. Isabel's native choice is creativity, a "free exploration of life," but exploration is conducted constantly—vision is amplified constantly—at the cost of renunciations. It is in the "grey depths" of the eyes of the elder Miss Molyneux, those eyes like the balanced basins of water set in parterres, that Isabel recognizes what she has had to reject in rejecting Lord Warburton: "the peace, the kindness, the honour, the possessions, a deep security and a great exclusion." Caspar Goodwood has eyes that "seemed to shine through the vizard of a helmet." He appears always as an armor-man: "she saw the different fitted parts of him as she had seen, in museums and portraits, the different fitted parts of armoured warriors—in plates of steel handsomely inlaid with gold." "He might have ridden, on a plunging steed, the whirlwind of a great war." The image is one of virility, but of passion without relation, aggressive energy without responsibility. The exclusions implied by Caspar's steel-plated embrace are as great as those implied by the honor and the peace that Lord Warburton offers; and yet Isabel's final refusal of Caspar and of sexual possession is tragic, for it is to a sterile marriage that she returns.

Architectural images, and metaphors whose vehicle (like doors and windows) is associated with architecture, subtend the most various and complex of the book's meanings; and the reason for their particular richness of significance seems to be that, of all forms that are offered to sight and interpretation, buildings are the most natural symbols of civilized life, the most diverse also as to what their fronts and interiors can imply of man's relations with himself and with the outer world. Osmond's house in Florence has an "imposing front" of a "somewhat incommunicative character."

> It was the mask, not the face of the house. It had heavy lids, but no eyes; the house in reality looked another way—looked off behind . . . The windows of the ground-floor, as you saw them from the piazza, were, in their noble proportions, extremely architectural; but their function seemed less to offer communication with the world than to defy the world to look in . . .

(One notes again here the characteristic insistence on *eyes* and *looking*.) The description, perfectly fitting an old and noble Florentine villa, exactly equates with Osmond himself, and not only Isabel's first illusional impression of him—when it is his renunciatory reserve that attracts her, an appearance suggesting those "deeper rhythms of life" that she seeks—but also her later painful knowledge of the face behind the mask, which, like the house, is affected with an obliquity of vision, "looked another way—looked off behind." The interior is full of artful images; the group of people gathered there "might have been described by a painter as composing well"; even the footboy "might, tarnished as to livery and quaint as to type, have issued from some stray sketch of old-time manners, been 'put in' by the brush of a Longhi or a Goya"; the face of little Pansy is "painted" with a "fixed and intensely sweet smile." Osmond's world, contained within his eyeless house, is "sorted, sifted, arranged" for the eye; even his daughter is one of his arrangements. It is a world bred of ancient disciplines modulating through time, selection and composition, to the purest aesthetic form.

> [Isabel] carried away an image from her visit to his hill-top . . . which put on for her a particular harmony with other supposed and divined things, histories within histories . . . It spoke of the kind of personal issue that touched her most nearly; of the choice between objects, subjects, contacts—what might she call them?—of a thin and those of a rich association . . . of a care for beauty and perfection so natural and so cultivated together that the career appeared to stretch beneath it in the disposed vistas and with the ranges of steps and terraces and fountains of a formal Italian garden. . .

The illusion is one of a depth and spaciousness and delicacy of relationships, an illusion of the civilized consciousness.

But while Osmond's world suggests depth, it is, ironically, a world of surfaces only, for Osmond has merely borrowed it. The architectural metaphor shifts significantly in the passage (Chapter 42 of Volume II) in which Isabel takes the full measure of her dwelling. "It was the house of darkness, the house of dumbness, the house of suffocation."

> She had taken all the first steps in the purest confidence, and then she had suddenly found the infinite vista of a multiplied life to be a dark, narrow alley with a dead wall at the end. Instead of leading to

the high places of happiness . . . it led rather downward and earth-
ward, into realms of restriction and depression where the sound of
other lives, easier and freer, was heard as from above . . .

"When she saw this rigid system close about her, draped though it
was in pictured tapestries . . . she seemed shut up with an odour
of mould and decay." Again the architectural image changes its
shape in that passage (quoted earlier in this essay) where Isabel
takes her knowledge and her sorrow into Rome, a Rome
of architectural ruins. Here also are depth of human time,
histories within histories," aesthetic form, but not "arranged,"
not borrowable, not to be "collected"—only to be *lived* in the
creative recognitions brought to them by a soul itself alive.
The image that accompanies Ralph through the book—"his
serenity was but the array of wild flowers niched in his ruin"—
gains meaning from the architectural images so frequent in the
Roman scenes (as, for instance, from this:

> [Isabel] had often ascended to those desolate ledges from which the
> Roman crowd used to bellow applause and where now the wild
> flowers . . . bloom in the deep crevices . . .)

Whereas Osmond's forced "arrangements" of history and art and
people are without racination, blighting and lifeless, Ralph's
"array of wild flowers" is rooted, even if precariously rooted in a
ruin; it is a life *grown,* grown in history, fertilized in the crevices of
a difficult experience. The metaphor is another version of St.
John's "Except a corn of wheat fall into the ground and die, it
abideth alone; but if it die, it bringeth forth much fruit." Isabel,
still seeking that freedom which is growth, goes back to Osmond's
claustral house, for it is there, in the ruin where Pansy has been
left, that she has placed roots, found a crevice in which to grow
straightly and freshly, found a fertilizing, civilizing relationship
between consciousness and circumstances.

NOTES

1. Discussion of James's "international myth" will be found in *The Question of Henry
James,* edited by F. W. Dupee (New York: Henry Holt & Company, Inc., 1945), and
Philip Rahv's *Image and Idea* (New York: New Directions, 1949).

XVII

Principles and Method in the Later Works of Henry James

It is commonly recognized that the reading of the later works of Henry James is an exacting task, and at least one explanation of the difficulty that has sometimes been suggested (but rarely pursued beyond the suggestion) is that it is due to a certain baffling abstractness of the famous "late" style. Those in any event who have remarked this quality of the style are likely to have remarked also the frequent occurence in James's later works of what may be called *logical* terms, expressions, and images. These are indeed not absent from James's earlier novels; but they are much more frequent, and more elaborate, in the later novels; and they do much to account for the abstract flavour of the late style as a whole. The main object of the present essay is to enquire into the signficance of this curious feature of James's late style, in the belief that to understand it will greatly help to illuminate the larger purposes and the distinctive achievements of the novels of his last period.

Instances of these "logical" terms, expressions and images are not difficult to find. In *The Ivory Tower* (to start at an advanced point and move backwards), we read that "the general hush . . .

pushed upward and still further upward the fine flower of the inferential."[1] In the same book, one character remarks to another that a particular condition "will cut down not a little your possibilities of relation," and explains that "you can't not count with a relation—I mean one that you're a party to, because a relation is exactly a *fact* of reciprocity."[2] And in another place, the young man, Gray Fielder, meditating on "the mere beastly fact of his pecuniary luck," uses the rather mysterious word *constatation* in a not readily intelligible passage: ". . . How was he going not to get sick of finding so large a part played, over the place, by the mere *constatation*, in a single voice, a huge monotone restlessly and untiringly directed, but otherwise without application, of the state of being worth dollars to inordinate amounts?"[3]

As we move back, through *The Golden Bowl* to *The Wings of the Dove* and *The Ambassadors,* the examples becomes less obscure though not less intricate. Lambert Strether, reflecting upon his changed relations with Maria Gostrey, discerns that "it was the proportions that were changed, and the proportions were, at all times, he philosophised, the very conditions of perception, the terms of thought." Maria Gostrey herself receives from Strether this special tribute to her intelligence, that "she had taken all his categories by surprise." And on that fateful expedition into the country, when Strether comes upon Chad and Madame de Vionnet in the boat, he has time, in the idyllic mood that precedes the shock of the encounter, to reflect upon the logical properties of his felicity:

> . . . The conditions had nowhere so asserted their difference from those of Woolett as they appeared to him to assert it in the little court of the Cheval Blanc while he arranged with his hostess for a comfortable climax. They were few and simple, scant and humble, but they were *the thing,* as he would have called it . . . 'The' thing was the thing that implied the greatest number of other things of the sort he had to tackle; and it was queer of course, but so it was—the implication here was complete . . .[4]

The Golden Bowl, as may be expected, yields a particularly rich crop of images of this kind. At one point, Maggie Verver's "grasp of appearances . . . was out of proportion to her view of causes"; at another, she is engaged in reducing her harrowing moral problem to a disjunctive syllogism: ". . . Unless she were in a position to plead, definitely, that she was jealous, she should be in no position to plead, decently, that she was dissatisfied. This latter condition would be a necessary implication of the former; without the former behind it, it would *have* to fall to the ground."[5] The elaborate image of the ivory tower, with which the Second Book of the novel opens, includes a characteristic example (though unfortunately not a felicitous one) of the kind of running together of logical and pictorial imagery which tends to become a favourite type of "mixed metaphor" in the late novels. The passage is worth quoting in full. It begins:

> . . . Maggie's actual reluctance to ask herself with proportionate sharp-ness why she had ceased to take comfort in the sight of [the ivory tower] represented accordingly a lapse from the ideal consistency on which her moral comfort almost at any time depended. To remain con-sistent she had always been capable of cutting down more or less her prior term.

The image is then particularised—that is, rendered less general (though still remaining logical) by restriction to the specifically moral domain; and is finally abandoned for a concrete, pictorial image:

> Moving for the first time in her life as in the darkening shadow of a false position, she reflected that she should either not have ceased to be right—that is, to be confident—or have recognised that she was wrong; though she tried to deal with herself, for a space, only as a silken-coated spaniel who has scrambled out of a pond and who rattles the water from his ears . . .

"She should either not have ceased to be right—that is, to be con-fident": in which case there would be no need to "cut down" her "prior term"—no need, that is, to modify her initial assumptions, no need therefore to think herself wrong, and consequently to lose her confidence. Or, she should "have recognised that she was wrong"—that is, have seen that a consequence *not* derivable from her "prior term" had in fact occurred; and then it *would* be neces-sary to "cut it down." The image of the silken-coated spaniel that follows is pictorial, and is drawn out rather heavy-handedly, and at such inordinate length that one can quite see how *The Mote in the Middle Distance* came to be written. The passage is useful, how-ever, for showing the kind of statement that was becoming the staple of James's writing in the later novels; and this leads one to enquire whether some light on this distinctive aspect of his late style might not be derived from his other writings of the period, in particular the Letters and the Prefaces.

The Prefaces, it turns out, give all the light one needs. There, where the subject-matter allows every freedom to James's generalising power, the logical and philosophical phraseology is at least as prominent as the sensuous and pictorial. There he speaks of "the confidence of the dramatist strong in the sense of his postulate,"[6] of "the quality involved in the given case or supplied by one's data,"[7] of the problem of artistic unity as a problem of "the order, the reason, the relation, of presented aspects"; and yields to passionate utterances about "the baseness of the *arbitrary* stroke, the touch without its reason." ("The sense of a system saves the painter from the baseness of the *arbitrary* stroke, the touch without its reason. . .").[8] The force of such phrases is, of course, best appreciated in their immediate contexts. Their most inclusive context, however, is James's theory of the art of the novel; and this revolves about three seminal principles. These are not easy to define, or even to name, in a sentence. But the key-words are "aspects," "conditions," and "(internal) relations"; and to discover the full meaning of these terms in the Jamesian critical canon is to discover at once the laws of construction (the "logic") and the view of reality (the "metaphysics") implicit in the world created in James's late novels, than which nothing perhaps is more illuminating for an understanding of their method.

II

That art concerns itself to render the world of appearances; that these appearances exist only in the consciousness, indeed, *are* the content of the consciousness, of human observers; that the world of art therefore is a beautiful representation of the appearances present to a particular consciousness under particular conditions; and the artist's (novelist's) overriding task is accordingly to exhibit in the concrete, with the greatest possible completeness and consistency, and vividness and intensity, the particular world of appearances accessible to a particular consciousness under the specific conditions created for it by the novelist: these are the elements of James's theory of art.

Nor is it difficult, once the elements have been grasped, to see how this view gives rise to those peculiar technical problems to which so many pages of the Prefaces and the Letters are devoted. Shall the story be presented through a single consciousness, with no "going behind" of any but this single centre of consciousness? Or, shall there be more than one centre of consciousness, used "alternatingly" or "successively," but always with the same rigour—always, that is, keeping the presented world fixed within the compass of that reflector, never allowing a single apprehension to slip in that could not be seen to belong by intrinsic necessity to that consciousness operating under those limitations? "To make the presented occasion," writes James in the Preface to *The Awkward Age,* "tell all its story itself, remain shut up in its own presence, and yet on that patch of staked-out ground become thoroughly interesting and remain thoroughly clear, is a process not remarkable, no doubt, so long as a very light weight is laid on it, but difficult enough to inspire great adroitness as soon as the elements to be dealt with begin at all to 'size up.'"

The "coercive charm" (as James explains in the same Preface) of this mode of conceiving and executing the fictive art is that it places the novelist under the obligation, absolutely binding, to present *exhaustively* the limiting conditions of the protagonist centre of consciousness. The conditions must be exhaustive if it is to be established what apprehensions—what perceptions, judgments, responses—in the particular situation in which it is placed are and are not logically possible to it; and, conversely, if the conditions are *not* exhaustive, the novelist will fail in one of his principal tasks, that of demonstrating apodeictically that these apprehensions and only these are accessible to this consciousness in that situation. But that "situation" is itself made up of other persons, each hedged about with his own limiting conditions; and these must also be exhaustively rendered in order that their collective limiting effect upon the centre of consciousness through which the action is being unfolded may be exhibited as necessary and inevitable. And this, the complete rendering of all the conditions, is the way in which the novelist *defines* his centre of consciousness (and consequently, as we shall see, the "aspect" or "point of view" under which the world in that particular novel is being presented); and to accomplish this is the ultimate proof of his verisimilitude, the whole business, for him, of holding the mirror up to nature. Its "beautiful difficulty" James discusses in the Preface to *The Princess Casamassima,* among other places. "Extreme and attaching always," he notes there, speaking of the special problems presented by his little Hyacinth Robinson, "the difficulty of fixing at a hundred points the place where one's impelled bonhomme may feel enough and 'know' enough—or be in the way of learning enough—for his maximum dramatic value without feeling and knowing too much for his minimum verisimilitude, his proper fusion with the fable. This is the charming, the tormenting, the eternal little matter *to be made right,* in all the weaving of silver threads and tapping on golden nails . . ."

III

If we turn our attention from the reflector to the reflected, a fresh view of James's late method presents itself. Not only is it the world of appearance, not reality, that a given centre of consciousness is conscious of; it is always the world of appearances under this or that "aspect," under this or that set of "conditions." The limiting conditions, or determinants, of the reflecting consciousness find (or create) their counterpart in the object; the particular reflection, or appearance, of the real that the given consciousness projects bears the mark of its limiting conditions or determinants.

It may be supposed that this is to say no more than that every protagonist can necessarily (and too obviously) give only a "partial" view of the world—"from his point of view," "as he sees it" are some of the common phrases. In a sense this is true; and perhaps James is doing no more than refine upon these common notions. Yet it is more, since the refinement is a matter of pursuing the method to its furthest logical limit—a process that always yields uncommon results; and in this instance the result is a method of presentation so organically, so necessarily and inescapably, *dramatic* that one searches in vain for anything comparable in the history of the novel, and turns in the end to the great dramatists for the right measure.[9]

But the common notion of the partial view will not, in any case, meet the Jamesian case. For it would not be true to say that the Jamesian centres of consciousness are "partial" in the ordinary sense—in the sense of being fatally *limited,* by this or that obvious blind spot, this or that obvious patch of stupidity or perversity or

inconsequentiality, which shuts out from their vision some portion
of the world. They see "everything," these remarkable conscious-
nesses of the late novels: "everything" is a word that frequently
recurs, to denote the excess of light, of sheer intelligibility, with
which, for them, the world is flooded. They are intensely perceptive, incessantly analytical, and marvellously articulate. They are
always lucid and ironical, never muddled or tediously portentous.
They are all possessed of a limitless curiosity and detachment,
which renders their perceptions and analyses intensely *enjoyable* to
themselves even while they burn in purgatorial fires. (Indeed, the
"enjoyment" appears to be most intense when the immediate object of their detached curiosity is their own present suffering.[10])
They are generous and fearless; earnest without being boring; delicate without loss of candour; civil and kind and good-humoured,
and never sentimental; and intent, with the strangest passionate
intentness, upon knowing themselves to the last limit of their
powers, and acting upon that knowledge with an absolute consistency—to fail in this kind of consistency being for them, it
seems, the ultimate outrage. They are indeed superior people, collectively perhaps figuring the human intelligence at its furthest
reach. They can hardly therefore be "limited" in the ordinary
sense.

Yet, even at its furthest reach, the human intelligence, as it is
human, can only see partially; for it *is*, after all, limited. But by
what, in this instance? What *could* limit such intelligences, which
seem to be as free, luminous and comprehensive as those of
angels? The answer is, by that which marks the division between
men, even the most prodigious men, and angels, what old-fashioned
moralists have called "the passions." To match the beauty and refinement of their virtues, the destructive passions in the late novels
accordingly appear in their most refined, most subtle, forms:
forms under which it is exceedingly difficult to recognise them as
destructive at all, or even dangerous; and under these forms so in-
separably bound up with the virtues that it is not at all easy to see
at what point they cease to be graces and become sins. The sins
—or, better, the virtues in their sinful aspect—can, however, be
named. The first is pride, with its attendant perversity and *hauteur*
—the damnable damning pride of an Isabel Archer, a Fleda
Vetch, a Nanda Brookenham, a Milly Theale. The next is bore-

dom, the terrible hovering *ennui* of the Prince and Charlotte in *The Golden Bowl,* of the Parisian *beau monde* in *The Ambassadors,* of Lord Mark in *The Wings of the Dove* and his well-bred friends murmuring "I say, Mark" at the luncheon parties at Lancaster Gate. Then, as a function of the boredom, there is their revulsion from stupidity and vulgarity, which in the end they hate so much more than they love truth and goodness; and this, in turn, issues in the cankerous sexuality—most fully exposed in *The Awkward Age,* but also, though more elusively, in *The Ambassadors* and *The Golden Bowl*—which ultimately finds no delight in the aspiration of the beloved after perfect knowledge and perfect goodness, but instead takes for the object of its adoration the imperfect and the incomplete, the patches of nescience and the residual mystery in the beloved. (That is why Nanda Brookenham is the type of the unmarriageable girl.) And, comprehending all these, there is the last infirmity of these noble spirits, their worship of the beautiful, that infernal aestheticism by which (James lets us know in each of his last novels) such men believe themselves saved but are in fact damned. "You've all of you here," remarks Strether in Gloriani's garden—

"You've all of you here so much visual sense that you've somehow all 'run' to it. There are moments when it strikes one that you haven't any other."

"Any moral," little Bilham explained, watching serenely, across the garden, the several *femmes du monde.* "But Miss Barrace has a moral distinction," he kindly continued; speaking for Strether's benefit no less than for her own.

"*Have* you?" Strether, scarce knowing what he was about, asked of her almost eagerly.

"Oh not a distinction"—she was mightily amused at his tone—"Mr. Bilham's too good. But I think I may say a sufficiency. Yes, a sufficiency. . . . I daresay, moreover," she pursued with an interested gravity, "that I do, that we all do here, run too much to mere eye. But how can it be helped? We're all looking at each other—and in the light of Paris one sees what things resemble. That's what the light of Paris seems always to show. It's the fault of the light of Paris—dear old light!"

"Dear old Paris!" little Bilham echoed.

"Everything, everyone shows," Miss Barrace went on.

"But for what they really are?" Strether asked.

"Oh, I like your Boston 'reallys'! But sometimes—yes."

"Dear old Paris then!" Strether resignedly sighed while for a moment they looked at each other. . . ."[11]

The Prince in *The Golden Bowl* also has a sufficiency of the moral sense—as he tells Mrs. Assingham, with disarming candour, at the very beginning of the story:

> ". . . I should be interested," she presently remarked, "to see some sense *you* don't possess."
>
> Well, he produced one on the spot. "The moral, dear Mrs. Assingham. I mean, always, as you others consider it. I've of course something that in our poor dear backward Rome sufficiently passes for it. But it's no more like yours than the tortuous stone staircase—half-ruined into the bargain!—in some castle of our *quattrocento* is like the 'lightning elevator' in one of Mr. Verver's fifteen-storey buildings. Your moral sense works by steam—it sends you up like a rocket. Ours is slow and steep and unlighted, with so many of the steps missing that—well, that it's as short, in almost any case, to turn round and come down again."
>
> "Trusting," Mrs. Assingham smiled, "to get up some other way?"
>
> "Yes—or not to have to get up at all. However," he added, "I told you that at the beginning . . ."[12]

But he finds in the end that he *has* to get up, and that his poor dear backward Roman moral sense is not after all sufficient for the purpose:

> . . . Charlotte was in pain, Charlotte was in torment, but he himself had given her reason enough for that; and, in respect to the rest of the whole matter of her obligation to follow her husband, that personage and she, Maggie, had so shuffled away every link between consequence and cause, that the intention remained, like some famous poetic line in a dead language, subject to varieties of interpretation. What renewed the obscurity was her strange image of their common offer to him, her father's and her own, of an opportunity to separate from Mrs. Verver with the due amount of form—and all the more that he was, in so pathetic a way, unable to treat himself to a quarrel with it on the score of taste. Taste in him, as a touchstone, was now all at sea; for who could say but that one of her fifty ideas, or perhaps forty-nine of them wouldn't be, exactly, that taste by itself, the taste he had always conformed to, had no importance whatever? . . .[13]

This, then, is how James's centres of consciousness in the late novels come to be "limited" after all, and therefore able to give only a "partial" view of the whole, only this or that aspect of the world of appearances. It is indeed reassuringly in accordance with the traditional practice of novelists and dramatists that the fatal limitation should be introduced by the irruption of the passions into the clear stream of intelligence. What distinguishes James from others is the *degree* of intelligence that he allows his centres of consciousness. By allowing so much, he risks at every moment the annihilation of the very possibility of destructive passion: one more turn of the screw, one feels, and they really will be angelic intelligences; and that will be the end of all story and drama.[14] James, in short, makes it all as difficult as possible for himself. Given so *much* light, what in the world (he has to ask himself) will they *not* see? Where, in such a noontide of light, *can* the shadow fall? And since they are *all* bathed in this noontide radiance, how are shadows and shadows to be differentiated? What, in each instance, are to be the "beautiful determinants" of the shadow that actually falls? And—the final and supreme problem: how shall each set of beautiful determinants beautifully determine every other set; and determine it "without remainder"—so completely, that is, as to leave not the minutest interval, not a single point at which there might be a "leak of interest"?[15] These are the difficulties in which James in the late novels is constantly rejoicing; and they are the difficulties created by and inherent in what he called "the blest operation . . . of my Dramatic Principle, my Law of successive Aspects."[16]

IV

From the law of successive aspects it is an easy passage to the last intricacy of James's theory of the fictive art, his doctrine of "internal relations." A work of art must have a beginning, a middle and an end; one thing must follow from another as "inevitably" as possible; causes (in a novel, "motivation") must be commensurate with effects, and the objective correlative adequate to the subjective content; a work of art, in short, must be an organic whole, not a mere mechanical contrivance. These are among the most important commonplaces of our current critical theory; and James in his Prefaces is affirming all this, but also much more. What he adds (as before) is his immeasurably deeper understanding of all that these critical commonplaces imply, and his incomparably exact analysis of their meaning for the practising novelist. Indeed all the most memorable things in the Prefaces are derived, in the first and last instance, from his own practice as a novelist, and for this reason his critical pronouncements there are invaluable for the understanding of the principles and method of his works, in particular the later.

Repeatedly, with variations only in the details, James lays down the fundamental condition of the fictive art. The "painter" must create a world in which nothing shall happen but by an ineluctable necessity: all that "follows" must already have been present in the conditions laid down at the beginning, so that the story is in the nature of an unfolding, an exfoliation, of all that was from the beginning "involved in" the *donnée*. The process is beautifully described in the Preface to *The Portrait of a Lady,* where James reflects upon "the whole matter of growth, in one's imagination" of such a subject as his "engaging young woman," Isabel Archer. "These are the fascinations of the fabulist's art," he writes there, "these lurking forces of expansion, these necessities of upspringing in the seed, these beautiful determinations, on the part of the idea entertained, to grow as tall as possible, to push into the light and the air and thickly flower there . . ." It follows that the necessity of the action can never be merely asserted but must always be exhibited ("The novelist who doesn't represent, and represent 'all the time,' is lost").[17] Every part of the action must always be shown to belong intrinsically to "the given case"; and this can only be shown by the most exact rendering of the given conditions, from which it may be evident to all that nothing can happen as a consequence of those conditions but what does in fact happen. The deliberate extinction of all alternatives, however desolating in life, is the vital principle of every work of art that has been fully achieved. Wherever there is a "leak," there is failure; and for the artist who has learnt the lesson of the master and cares for nothing but perfection, the distinction between partial failure and total failure is merely verbal.

But the doctrine of internal relations is not only a logical principle, which James discovered to be central to his method in the late novels. It is also a view of reality, a metaphysical principle; and it is in this character that it makes a memorable appearance at an important point in *The Ambassadors.* Strether is engaged in his great show-down with Sarah Pocock, and is pleading for recognition of Madame de Vionnet's services to Chad. "Why, when a woman's at once so charming and beneficent . . . ," he begins. But Mrs. Pocock takes him up on the ground of her Woolett metaphysic of straight and simple dichotomies: "You can sacrifice mothers and sisters to her without a blush on purpose to [make me] feel the more, and take from you the straighter, *how* you do it?" Whereupon Strether invokes in his defence another view of experience, totally distinct from Mrs. Pocock's, which she will never understand: a view that sees all reality as a tissue of implications, in which everything is internally related with everything else; in which causal sequences of the kind that direct Mrs. Pocock's thinking are never more than arbitrary and therefore false; and a single life is never long enough to make out even a fraction of what is implied by its own most significant experience. Strether replies:

> . . . I don't think there's anything I have done in such a calculated way as you describe. Everything has come as a sort of indistinguishable part of everything else. Your coming out belonged closely to my having come before you, and my having come was a result of our general state of mind. Our general state of mind had proceeded, on its side, from our quiet ignorance, our queer misconceptions and confusions—from which, since then, an inexorable tide of light seems to have floated us into our perhaps still queerer knowledge. Don't you like your brother as he is?' he went on . . .[18]

To understand the vital place of the doctrine of internal relations in James's view of reality as a whole and the world of human relations in particular is to understand also the logical place in the method of the late novels of the famous obliqueness, or indirectness, of presentation. If, for the novelist, the business of intimating (and never more than intimating) the reality beneath the appearances is the business of unfolding all that is implicit in "the given case"; if therefore personal identity (the "individual") is nothing other than that which emerges from the process of unfolding the implications of the *donnée;* and emerges, not as something distinct from the tissue of implications, but as the tissue itself —for the individual *is* the sum total of his determinants or conditions when (but only when) the full implications of those determinants have been fully understood and exhibited: if this is the fundamental logic of James's mature thinking, the method of oblique or indirect presentation may be seen as yet another instance of that high, rare consequentiality which is the characteristic expression of his genius, and not (as some have thought) a mere perversity, or the result of a "hypertrophy of sensibility," or (as one lady thought) a form of self-indulgence made possible by having Miss Bosanquet to dictate to from ten o'clock to one o'clock each day.

James's own reflections in the concluding passage of the Preface to *The Wings of the Dove* upon "his instinct everywhere for the *indirect* presentation of his main image" has, one fears, been misleading to some of his critics. James remarks there "how again and again, I go but a little way with the direct—that is, with the straight exhibition of Milly: it resorts for relief, this process, wherever it can, to some kinder, some merciful indirection . . . All of which proceeds . . . from her painter's tenderness of imagination about her, which reduces him to watching her, as it were, through the successive windows of other people's interest in her." This has sometimes been taken as a confession of sheer incapacity for the direct and the consequent evasion of directness in the late novels; and, since it is known that Milly Theale is a rendering of the beloved cousin Mary Temple, it has been taken also as a confession of the sentimentality that some readers have found in the portrayal of Milly Theale. But it is neither. The passage refers to a thoroughly deliberated, wholly intrinsic, aspect of James's late method; and so far from being a confession of weakness, it points rather to the kind of freedom of speculation upon his own practice that an artist as secure as James in the attested virtues of his method might well feel himself able to afford. An examination of the way in which the virtues of the method are attested by *The Wings of the Dove* must belong to another essay.[19]

In a well-known exchange of letters with H. G. Wells,[20] James set down an *obiter dictum* concerning the nature of art that might, at first sight, seem to imply philosophical commitments of an alarming kind. "It is art that *makes* life," he writes to Wells, "makes interest, makes importance, for our consideration and application of these things, and I know of no substitute whatever for the force and beauty of its process." One is put in mind of another famous *obiter dictum,*

> O Lady! we receive but what we give
> And in our life alone does nature live,

and one wonders how near James is to dropping into the abyss of metaphysical idealism, from which (philosophers warn us) no traveller returns.

Whatever may be the philosophical difficulties of the position, it is, at any rate, a position consistent with the logic of internal relations that James's thinking in his late period everywhere exhibits. To say that "art *makes* life" is to say that the artist at once creates the conditions in which life can be "ideally" exhibited and exhibits it thus ideally by exploring and articulating the fullest implications of "the given case." Life is made to yield its fullest, richest meanings when subjected to the artistic process; indeed, to the extent that life is significant, meaningful, *intelligible* at all, it has to that extent already been brought under the beautiful dominion of art. Art, then, *makes* life by making meaning; it "makes" meaning by discovering the full implications of the *donnée;* and it discovers these implications by creating the conditions in which they may most beautifully and instructively unfold themselves. That is how art exhibits life at its maximum intensity, at its highest reaches of "interest" and "importance" (and "amusement," in James's large sense of the word); and that is why (as James elsewhere remarks)[21] those centres of consciousness that are endowed with "the power to be finely aware and richly responsible" yield most to the attentive reader: because "their being finely aware—as Hamlet and Lear say, are finely aware—*makes* absolutely the intensity of their adventure, gives the maximum of sense to what befalls them."

To pursue the implications of the given case as far and as deep as James does in the late novels is to court, constantly, the last haunting fear that all powerfully reflective minds are heir to. It is the fear of ceasing at some point—a point wholly and heartbreakingly indeterminable—to "read out" of the given case what is really there, and instead to "read into" it some part of the contents of one's own mind. James speaks of this several times in *Notes of a Son and Brother* with a fine ironic modesty. "I have to reckon," he writes, recalling his impressions of a visit to Mr. Frank Sanborn's progressive school at Concord—

> I have to reckon with the trick of what I used irrepressibly to read into things in front of which I found myself, for gaping purposes, planted

by some unquestioned outer force: it seemed so prescribed to me, so imposed on me, to read more, as through some ever-felt claim for roundness of aspect and intensity of effect in presented matters, whatever they might be, than the conscience of the particular affair itself was perhaps developed enough to ask of it.[22]

And in another passage he speaks of his "wasteful habit or trick of a greater feeling for people's potential propriety or felicity or full expression than they seemed able to have themselves."[23] The problem, metaphysically considered, may indeed be insoluble. But the empirical solution luckily lies immediately to hand. We have only to read those late novels with the kind of attention they invite to receive all the reassurance we need that "the wasteful trick or habit" has been vindicated by its poetic fruits.

It remains to say something on the question of the sources of James's view of reality and its essential logic as these have been outlined here. It will be evident that it has affinities with the so-called idealist philosophies of the nineteenth century; and it is possible that James was even aware of the connection—if his use of the logical terms and images I drew attention to at the beginning of this essay may be taken as a sign of such an awareness. I have thought it safer, however, to proceed on the hypothesis that he did not take it from anywhere, or anybody, in particular: neither from Hegel, nor F. H. Bradley, nor from his brother William's Pragmatism,[24] nor (least of all) from his father's Swedenborgian system. He took it from the ambient air of nineteenth-century speculation, whose main current was the preoccupation with the phenomenon of self-consciousness. To this air he had been exposed from his earliest years. The animating intellectual atmosphere of his remarkable home, and the whole circle of gifted friends and relations commemorated in the pages of *Notes of a Son and Brother,* made perhaps the heaviest contribution to Henry James's philosophical development. But he must have received much also from the studies he pursued at home and abroad (and pursued rather more systematically than the circumstance of the young Jameses' desultory education would lead one to suppose) before he finally settled in England and entered upon his career as a novelist. After that, the sources of his "thought" were identically the same with the sources of his life's experience and his literary experience. James always took his thought in solution, never neat; and therefore found what he wanted, and in the form in which he best liked to receive it, in the works of his fellow-novelists and the conversation of men and women. He read such contemporary masters of his art as Balzac, Turgenev, Tolstoy, and George Eliot, as well as the humbler practitioners (W. D. Howells, for instance, Paul Bourget, Mrs. Humphrey Ward, and his dear friend Edith Wharton), with a passion of interest that stands out in marked contrast with his always languid response to the systems of systematic philosophers, his father's system not excepted. And though it is true that the conversation of the society he moved in in London was not especially rich in general ideas, owing to the dislike of the English for "criticism" and "keen analysis,"[25] it was also true that the English were not incapable of *using* ideas, of incorporating them, so to speak, into their routine day-to-day intellectual acts. There was much therefore that a mind like James's, "as receptive . . . of any scrap of enacted story or evoked picture as it was closed to the dry or abstract proposition," could learn from intercourse with them. And, interacting with all these influences, there was James's own prodigious speculative power—the power to generalise to the furthest limit the particulars of experience, and to render these, without loss of particularity, in the light of the most inclusive generality.

When it happens to be the particulars of the human condition that a man is concerned to render, his pursuit of the highest generality is also and at the same time a search for the deepest grounds of human conduct and human aspiration. He seeks to discover the most comprehensive standpoint from which the most permanent elements of human experience may be rendered most completely intelligible; and in the very pursuit of this end, finds himself committed to a particular logic and a particular metaphysic. For it is a single quest that he is engaged upon, which in its logical or philosophical aspect shows as a pursuit of the highest generality, and in its poetic aspect as a search for that which is at once the ground and the end of man's life.

In a mind like James's, however, which is "intensely watchful of its own acts and shapings," which "thinks while it feels, in order to understand, and then to generalise that feeling," no single feature of its own activities can escape its intense watchfulness. Consequently the logic of its own most comprehensive view of the condition of man becomes for it a distinct object of perception;

and it is *this* perception of the logical structure, the logical properties, of his own responses to the world that James records in
those curious terms and images that were the starting-point of the
present essay. But, finally: his perceptions of the world itself and
his perception of the logic of his perceptions of the world "happen"
simultaneously, are the parts of a single inclusive experience; and
what this shows is that in a mind like James's the philosophic,
analytic passion is all of a piece with the poetic and intuitive. In
such a mind they can only be distinguished but never divided.

NOTES

1. *The Ivory Tower,* Bk. III, Ch. V.

2. *ibid.*

3. *ibid.,* Bk. IV, Ch. I.

4. *The Ambassadors,* Bk. XI, Ch. 3. It is worth noting the difference between the
handling of the "logical" image here and that of a similar image in an earlier work
like *The Portrait of a Lady.* There Madame Merle also launches into a little disquisition
on the subject of "personal identity": "When you've lived as long as I," says Madame
Merle to Isabel, "you'll see that every human being has his shell and that you must
take the shell into account. By the shell I mean the whole envelope of circumstances.
There's no such thing as an isolated man and woman; we're each of us made up of
some cluster of appurtenances. What shall we call our 'self'? Where does it begin?
Where does it end? It overflows into everything that belongs to us—and then it flows
back again. I know a large part of myself is in the clothes I choose to wear. . . . One's
self—for other people—is one's expression of oneself; and one's house, one's furniture,
one's garments, the books one reads, the company one keeps—these things are all expressive." (Ch. XIX) Upon which follows the comment: "This was very metaphysical; not more so, however, than several observations Madame Merle had already
made. Isabel was fond of metaphysics, but was unable to accompany her friend into
this bold analysis of the human personality. . . ." It seems that the philosophical
stamina of the James characters improved as they passed out of James's middle
period into his major phase. But even here James in his own person allows himself
some charming touches: for instance, when the inflexible Mrs. Touchett's mellowing
with age is expressed as a case of stooping to the contingent: ". . . Isabel had reasons
to believe . . . that as she [Mrs. Touchett] advanced in life she made more of these
concessions to the sense of something obscurely distinct from convenience—more of
them than she independently exacted. She was learning to sacrifice consistency to
considerations of that inferior order for which the excuse must be found in the particular case." (Ch. XXI)

5. Ch. XXVI

6. Preface to *The Awkward Age.*

7. Preface to *The Princess Casamassima.*

8. Preface to *The Tragic Muse.*

9. James's notorious failure as a playwright does not reflect upon his powers as a dramatist. In his plays he was attempting to write for the theatre; and the theatre at this time happened to be dominated by a dramatic convention—the so-called "naturalistic" convention—that was to him uncongenial to a degree virtually incapacitating. A great dramatist will turn to whatever *genre* happens in his own time to offer him, by its superior vitality, freedom, and flexibility, the best opportunities for the exercise of his gift; and *The Awkward Age* is one of the great dramatic works in the English language.

10. In his Notes to *The Ivory Tower,* James makes the point explicitly in connection with his hero Gray Fielder's betrayal: ". . . . He really enjoys getting so detached from it as to be able to have it before him for observation and wonder as he does, and I must make the point very much of how this fairly soothes and relieves him . . . "

11. *The Ambassadors,* Bk. V, Ch. I.

12. *The Golden Bowl,* Ch. II.

13. *ibid.,* Ch. XLI.

14. In the Preface to *The Princess Casamassima,* James recognizes "the danger of filling too full any supposed and above all any obviously limited vessel of consciousness": ". . . If persons either tragically or comically embroiled with life allow us the comic or tragic value of their embroilment in proportion as their struggle is a measured and directed one, it is strangely true, none the less, that beyond a certain point they are spoiled for us by this carrying of a due light. They may carry too much of it for our credence, for our compassion, for our derision. They may be shown as knowing and feeling too much—not certainly for their remaining remarkable, but for their remaining 'natural' and typical, for their having the needful communities with our precious liability to fall into traps and be bewildered. It seems probable that if we were never bewildered there would never be a story to tell about us . . . ."

15. ". . . There is nothing so deplorable as a work of art with a *leak* in its interest; and there is no such leak of interest as through commonness of form. Its opposite, the *found* (because the sought-for) form is the absolute citadel and tabernacle of interest . . ." (Letter to Hugh Walpole, *Letters* ed. Percy Lubbock, Vol. II, page 246).

16. Notes to *The Ivory Tower.*

17. Preface to *The Tragic Muse.*

18. *The Ambassadors,* Bk. X, Ch. III.

19. This essay, and another on *The Golden Bowl,* have been published in *The Cambridge Journal,* August and September 1954 (Vol. VII, Nos. 11 and 12).

20. *The Letters of Henry James,* ed. Percy Lubbock, Vol. II, pp. 503–8.

21. Preface to *The Princess Casamassima.*

22. *Notes of a Son and Brother,* Ch. VII.

23. *ibid.,* Ch. II.

24. He read with admiration, however, William James's *Pragmatism* and *The Meaning of Truth,* and declared himself "lost in wonder of the extent to which I had all my life (like M. Jourdain) unconsciously pragmatized."

25. See his letter to William James, dated 8 March, 1870. (Letters, Vol. I, pp. 26–7).

XVIII

Reality in America

I

It is possible to say of V. L. Parrington that with his *Main Currents in American Thought* he has had an influence on our conception of American culture which is not equaled by that of any other writer of the last two decades. His ideas are now the accepted ones wherever the college course in American literature is given by a teacher who conceives himself to be opposed to the genteel and the academic and in alliance with the vigorous and the actual. And whenever the liberal historian of America finds occasion to take account of the national literature, as nowadays he feels it proper to do, it is Parrington who is his standard and guide. Parrington's ideas are the more firmly established because they do not have to be imposed—the teacher or the critic who presents them is likely to find that his task is merely to make articulate for his audience what it has always believed, for Parrington formulated in a classic way the suppositions about our culture which are held by the American middle class so far as that class is at all liberal in its social thought and so far as it begins to understand that literature has anything to do with society.

Parrington was not a great mind; he was not a precise

thinker or, except when measured by the low eminences that were about him, an impressive one. Separate Parrington from his informing idea of the economic and social determination of thought and what is left is a simple intelligence, notable for its generosity and enthusiasm but certainly not for its accuracy or originality. Take him even with his idea and he is, once its direction is established, rather too predictable to be continuously interesting; and, indeed, what we dignify with the name of economic and social determinism amounts in his use of it to not much more than the demonstration that most writers incline to stick to their own social class. But his best virtue was real and important—he had what we like to think of as the saving salt of the American mind, the lively sense of the practical, workaday world, of the welter of ordinary undistinguished things and people, of the tangible, quirky, unrefined elements of life. He knew what so many literary historians do not know, that emotions and ideas are the sparks that fly when the mind meets difficulties.

Yet he had after all but a limited sense of what constitutes a difficulty. Whenever he was confronted with a work of art that was complex, personal and not literal, that was not, as it were, a public document, Parrington was at a loss. Difficulties that were complicated by personality or that were expressed in the language of successful art did not seem quite real to him and he was inclined to treat them as aberrations, which is one way of saying what everybody admits, that the weakest part of Parrington's talent was his aesthetic judgment. His admirers and disciples like to imply that his errors of aesthetic judgment are merely lapses of taste, but this is not so. Despite such mistakes as his notorious praise of Cabell, to whom in a remarkable passage he compares Melville, Parrington's taste was by no means bad. His errors are the errors of understanding which arise from his assumptions about the nature of reality.

Parrington does not often deal with abstract philosophical ideas, but whenever he approaches a work of art we are made aware of the metaphysics on which his aesthetics is based. There exists, he believes, a thing called *reality;* it is one and immutable, it is wholly external, it is irreducible. Men's minds may waver, but reality is always reliable, always the same, always easily to be known. And the artist's relation to reality he conceives as a simple one. Reality being fixed and given, the artist has but to let it pass through him, he is the lens in the first diagram of an elementary book on optics: Fig. 1, Reality; Fig. 2, Artist; Fig. 1′, Work of Art. Figs. 1 and 1′ are normally in virtual correspondence with each other. Sometimes the artist spoils this ideal relation by "turning away from" reality. This results in certain fantastic works, unreal and ultimately useless. It does not occur to Parrington that there is any other relation possible between the artist and reality than this passage of reality through the transparent artist; he meets evidence of imagination and creativeness with a settled hostility the expression of which suggests that he regards them as the natural enemies of democracy.

In this view of things, reality, although it is always reliable, is always rather sober-sided, even grim. Parrington, a genial and enthusiastic man, can understand how the generosity of man's hopes and desires may leap beyond reality; he admires will in the degree that he suspects mind. To an excess of desire and energy which blinds a man to the limitations of reality he can indeed be very tender. This is one of the many meanings he gives to *romance* or *romanticism*, and in spite of himself it appeals to something in his own nature. The praise of Cabell is Parrington's response not only to Cabell's elegance—for Parrington loved elegance—but also to Cabell's insistence on the part which a beneficent self-deception may and even should play in the disappointing fact-bound life of man, particularly in the private and erotic part of his life.[1]

The second volume of *Main Currents* is called *The Romantic Revolution in America* and it is natural to expect that the word romantic should appear in it frequently. So it does, more frequently than one can count, and seldom with the same meaning, seldom with the sense that the word, although scandalously vague as it has been used by the literary historians, is still full of complicated but not wholly pointless ideas, that it involves many contrary but definable things; all too often Parrington uses the word romantic with the word romance close at hand, meaning *a* romance, in the sense that *Graustark* or *Treasure Island* is a romance, as though it signified chiefly a gay disregard of the limitations of everyday fact. Romance is refusing to heed the counsels of experience (p. iii); it is ebullience (p. iv); it is utopianism (p. iv); it is individualism (p. vi); it is self-deception (p. 59)—"romantic faith . . .

in the beneficent processes of trade and industry" (as held, we inevitably ask, by the romantic Adam Smith?); it is the love of the picturesque (p. 49); it is the dislike of innovation (p. 50) but also the love of change (p. iv); it is the sentimental (p. 192); it is patriotism, and then it is cheap (p. 235). It may be used to denote what is not classical, but chiefly it means that which ignores reality (pp. ix, 136, 143, 147, and *passim*); it is not critical (pp. 225, 235), although in speaking of Cooper and Melville, Parrington admits that criticism can sometimes spring from romanticism.

Whenever a man with whose ideas he disagrees wins from Parrington a reluctant measure of respect, the word romantic is likely to appear. He does not admire Henry Clay, yet something in Clay is not to be despised—his romanticism, although Clay's romanticism is made equivalent with his inability to "come to grips with reality." Romanticism is thus, in most of its significations, the venial sin of *Main Currents*; like carnal passion in the *Inferno*, it evokes not blame but tender sorrow. But it can also be the great and saving virtue which Parrington recognizes. It is ascribed to the transcendental reformers he so much admires; it is said to mark two of his most cherished heroes, Jefferson and Emerson: "they were both romantics and their idealism was only a different expression of a common spirit." Parrington held, we may say, at least two different views of romanticism which suggest two different views of reality. Sometimes he speaks of reality in an honorific way, meaning the substantial stuff of life, the ineluctable facts with which the mind must cope, but sometimes he speaks of it pejoratively and means the world of established social forms; and he speaks of realism in two ways: sometimes as the power of dealing intelligently with fact, sometimes as a cold and conservative resistance to idealism.

Just as for Parrington there is a saving grace and a venial sin, there is also a deadly sin, and this is turning away from reality, not in the excess of generous feeling, but in what he believes to be a deficiency of feeling, as with Hawthorne, or out of what amounts to sinful pride, as with Henry James. He tells us that there was too much realism in Hawthorne to allow him to give his faith to the transcendental reformers: "he was too much of a realist to change fashions in creeds"; "he remained cold to the revolutionary criticism that was eager to pull down the old temples to make room for nobler." It is this cold realism, keeping Hawthorne apart from his enthusiastic contemporaries, that alienates Parrington's sympathy—"Eager souls, mystics and revolutionaries, may propose to refashion the world in accordance with their dreams; but evil remains, and so long as it lurks in the secret places of the heart, utopia is only the shadow of a dream. And so while the Concord thinkers were proclaiming man to be the indubitable child of God, Hawthorne was critically examining the question of evil as it appeared in the light of his own experience. It was the central fascinating problem of his intellectual life, and in pursuit of a solution he probed curiously into the hidden, furtive recesses of the soul." Parrington's disapproval of the enterprise is unmistakable.

Now we might wonder whether Hawthorne's questioning of the naïve and often eccentric faiths of the transcendental reformers was not, on the face of it, a public service. But Parrington implies that it contributes nothing to democracy, and even that it stands in the way of the realization of democracy. If democracy depends wholly on a fighting faith, I suppose he is right. Yet society is after all something that exists at the moment as well as in the future, and if one man wants to probe curiously into the hidden furtive recesses of the contemporary soul, a broad democracy and especially one devoted to reality should allow him to do so without despising him. If what Hawthorne did was certainly nothing to build a party on, we ought perhaps to forgive him when we remember that he was only one man and that the future of mankind did not depend upon him alone. But this very fact serves only to irritate Parrington; he is put out by Hawthorne's loneliness and believes that part of Hawthorne's insufficiency as a writer comes from his failure to get around and meet people. Hawthorne could not, he tells us, establish contact with the "Yankee reality," and was scarcely aware of the "substantial world of Puritan reality that Samuel Sewall knew."

To turn from reality might mean to turn to romance, but Parrington tells us that Hawthorne was romantic "only in a narrow and very special sense." He was not interested in the world of, as it were, practical romance, in the Salem of the clipper ships; from this he turned away to create "a romance of ethics." This is not an illuminating phrase but it is a catching one, and it might be taken to mean that Hawthorne was in the tradition of, say, Shakespeare; but we quickly learn that, no, Hawthorne had entered a barren field, for although he himself lived in the present and had all the future to mold, he preferred to find many of his subjects in the past. We learn too that his romance of ethics is not admirable because it requires the hard, fine pressing of ideas, and we are told that "a romantic uninterested in adventure and afraid of sex is likely to become somewhat graveled for matter." In short, Hawthorne's mind was a thin one, and Parrington puts in evidence his use of allegory and symbol and the very severity and precision of his art to prove that he suffered from a sadly limited intellect, for so much fancy and so much art could scarcely be needed unless the writer were trying to exploit to the utmost the few poor ideas that he had.

Hawthorne, then, was "forever dealing with shadows, and he knew that he was dealing with shadows." Perhaps so, but shadows are also part of reality and one would not want a world without shadows, it would not even be a "real" world. But we must get beyond Parrington's metaphor. The fact is that Hawthorne was dealing beautifully with realities, with substantial things. The man who could raise those brilliant and serious doubts about the nature and possibility of moral perfection, the man who could keep himself aloof from the "Yankee reality" and who could dissent from the orthodoxies of dissent and tell us so much about the nature of moral zeal, is of course dealing exactly with reality.

Parrington's characteristic weakness as a historian is suggested by his title, for the culture of a nation is not truly figured in the image of the current. A culture is not a flow, nor even a confluence; the form of its existence is struggle, or at least debate—it is nothing if not a dialectic. And in any culture there are likely to be certain artists who contain a large part of the dialectic within themselves, their meaning and power lying in their contradictions; they contain within themselves, it may be said, the very essence of the culture, and the sign of this is that they do not submit to serve the ends of any one ideological group or tendency. It is a significant circumstance of American culture, and one which is susceptible of explanation, that an unusually large proportion of its notable writers of the nineteenth century were such repositories of the dialectic of their times—they contained both the yes and the no of their culture, and by that token they were prophetic of the future. Parrington said that he had not set up shop as a literary critic; but if a literary critic is simply a reader who has the ability to understand literature and to convey to others what he understands, it is not exactly a matter of free choice whether or not a cultural historian shall be a literary critic, nor is it open to him to let his virtuous political and social opinions do duty for percipience. To throw out Poe because he cannot be conveniently fitted into a theory of American culture, to speak of him as a biological sport and as a mind apart from the main current, to find his gloom to be merely personal and eccentric, "only the atrabilious wretchedness of a dipsomaniac," as Hawthorne's was "no more than the skeptical questioning of life by a nature that knew no fierce storms," to judge Melville's response to American life to be less noble than that of Bryant or of Greeley, to speak of Henry James as an escapist, as an artist similar to Whistler, a man characteristically afraid of stress—this is not merely to be mistaken in aesthetic judgment; rather it is to examine without attention and from the point of view of a limited and essentially arrogant conception of reality the documents which are in some respects the most suggestive testimony to what America was and is, and of course to get no answer from them.

Parrington lies twenty years behind us, and in the intervening time there has developed a body of opinion which is aware of his inadequacies and of the inadequacies of his coadjutors and disciples, who make up what might be called the literary academicism of liberalism. Yet Parrington still stands at the center of American thought about American culture because, as I say, he expresses the chronic American belief that there exists an opposition between reality and mind and that one must enlist oneself in the party of reality.

II

This belief in the incompatibility of mind and reality is exemplified by the doctrinaire indulgence which liberal intellectuals have always displayed toward Theodore Dreiser, an indulgence which becomes the worthier of remark when it is contrasted with the liberal severity toward Henry James. Dreiser and James: with that juxtaposition we are immediately at the dark and bloody crossroads where literature and politics meet. One does not go there gladly, but nowadays it is not exactly a matter of free choice whether one does or does not go. As for the particular juxtaposition itself, it is inevitable and it has at the present moment far more significance than the juxtaposition which once used to be made between James and Whitman. It is not hard to contrive factitious oppositions between James and Whitman, but the real difference between them is the difference between the moral mind, with its awareness of tragedy, irony, and multitudinous distinctions, and the transcendental mind, with its passionate sense of the oneness of multiplicity. James and Whitman are unlike not in quality but in kind, and in their very opposition they serve to complement each other. But the difference between James and Dreiser is not of kind, for both men addressed themselves to virtually the same social and moral fact. The difference here is one of quality, and perhaps nothing is more typical of American liberalism than the way it has responded to the respective qualities of the two men.

Few critics, I suppose, no matter what their political disposition, have ever been wholly blind to James's great gifts, or even to the grandiose moral intention of these gifts. And few critics have ever been wholly blind to Dreiser's great faults. But by liberal critics James is traditionally put to the ultimate question: of what use, of what actual political use, are his gifts and their intention? Granted that James was devoted to an extraordinary moral perceptiveness, granted too that moral perceptiveness has something to do with politics and the social life, of what possible practical value in our world of impending disaster can James's work be? And James's style, his characters, his subjects, and even his own social origin and the manner of his personal life are adduced to show that his work cannot endure the question. To James no quarter is given by American criticism in its political and liberal aspect. But in the same degree that liberal criticism is moved by political considerations to treat James with severity, it treats Dreiser with the most sympathetic indulgence. Dreiser's literary faults, it gives us to understand, are essentially social and political virtues. It was Parrington who established the formula for the liberal criticism of Dreiser by calling him a "peasant": when Dreiser thinks stupidly, it is because he has the slow stubbornness of a peasant; when he writes badly, it is because he is impatient of the sterile literary gentility of the bourgeoisie. It is as if wit, and flexibility of mind, and perception, and knowledge were to be equated with aristocracy and political reaction, while dullness and stupidity must naturally suggest a virtuous democracy, as in the old plays.

The liberal judgment of Dreiser and James goes back of politics, goes back to the cultural assumptions that make politics. We are still haunted by a kind of political fear of the intellect which Tocqueville observed in us more than a century ago. American intellectuals, when they are being consciously American or political, are remarkably quick to suggest that an art which is marked by perception and knowledge, although all very well in its way, can never get us through gross dangers and difficulties. And their misgivings become the more intense when intellect works in art as it ideally should, when its processes are vivacious and interesting and brilliant. It is then that we like to confront it with the gross dangers and difficulties and to challenge it to save us at once from disaster. When intellect in art is awkward or dull we do not put it to the test of ultimate or immediate practicality. No liberal critic asks the question of Dreiser whether *his* moral preoccupations are going to be useful in confronting the disasters that threaten us. And it is a judgment on the proper nature of mind, rather than any actual political meaning that might be drawn from the works of the two men, which accounts for the unequal justice they have received from the progressive critics. If it could be conclusively demonstrated—by, say, documents in James's handwriting—that James explicitly intended his books to be understood as pleas for co-operatives, labor unions, better housing, and more equitable taxation, the American critic in his liberal and progressive character would still be worried by James because his work shows so many of the electric qualities of mind. And if something like the opposite were proved of Dreiser, it would be brushed aside—as his doctrinaire anti-Semitism has in fact been brushed aside—because his books have the awkwardness, the chaos, the heaviness which we associate with "reality." In the American metaphysic, reality is always material reality, hard, resistant, unformed, impenetrable, and unpleasant. And that mind is alone felt to be trustworthy which most resembles this reality by most nearly reproducing the sensations it affords.

In *The Rise of American Civilization,* Professor Beard uses a significant phrase when, in the course of an ironic account of James's

the mother country than to the tang of everyday life in the new West." This is mere fantasy. Hawthorne, Thoreau, and Emerson were for the most part remarkably colloquial—they wrote, that is, much as they spoke; their prose was specifically American in quality, and, except for occasional lapses, quite direct and simple. It is Dreiser who lacks the sense of colloquial diction—that of the Middle West or any other. If we are to talk of bookishness, it is Dreiser who is bookish; he is precisely literary in the bad sense, he is full of flowers of rhetoric and shines with paste gems; at hundreds of points his diction is not only genteel but fancy. It is he who speaks of "a scene more distingué than this," or of a woman "artistic in form and feature," or of a man who, although "strong, reserved, aggressive, with an air of wealth and experience, was *soi-disant* and not particularly eager to stay at home." Colloquialism held no real charm for him and his natural tendency is always toward the "fine:"

> . . . . Moralists come and go; religionists fulminate and declare the pronouncements of God as to this; but Aphrodite still reigns. Embowered in the festal depths of the spring, set above her altars of porphyry, chalcedony, ivory and gold, see her smile the smile that is at once the texture and essence of delight, the glory and despair of the world! Dream on, oh Buddha, asleep on your lotus leaf, of an undisturbed Nirvana! Sweat, oh Jesus, your last agonizing drops over an unregenerate world! In the forests of Pan still ring the cries of the worshippers of Aphrodite! From her altars the incense of adoration ever rises! And see, the new red grapes dripping where votive hands new-press them!

Charles Jackson, the novelist, telling us in the same leaflet that Dreiser's style does not matter, remarks on how much still comes to us when we have lost by translation the stylistic brilliance of Thomas Mann or the Russians or Balzac. He is in part right. And he is right too when he says that a certain kind of conscious, supervised artistry is not appropriate to the novel of large dimensions. Yet the fact is that the great novelists have usually written very good prose, and what comes through even a bad translation is exactly the power of mind that made the well-hung sentence of the original text. In literature style is so little the mere clothing of thought—need it be insisted on at this late date?—that we may say that from the earth of the novelist's prose spring his characters, his ideas, and even his story itself.[2]

To the extent that Dreiser's style is defensible, his thought is also defensible. That is, when he thinks like a novelist, he is worth following—when by means of his rough and ungainly but no doubt cumulatively effective style he creates rough, ungainly, but effective characters and events. But when he thinks like, as we say, a philosopher, he is likely to be not only foolish but vulgar. He thinks as the modern crowd thinks when it decides to think: religion and morality are nonsense, "religionists" and moralists are fakes, tradition is a fraud, what is man but matter and impulses, mysterious "chemisms," what value has life anyway? "What, cooking, eating, coition, job holding, growing, aging, losing, winning, in so changeful and passing a scene as this, important? Bunk! It is some form of titillating illusion with about as much import to the superior forces that bring it all about as the functions and gyrations of a fly. No more. And maybe less." Thus Dreiser at sixty. And yet there is for him always the vulgarly saving suspicion that maybe, when all is said and done, there is Something Behind It All. It is much to the point of his intellectual vulgarity that Dreiser's anti-Semitism was not merely a social prejudice but an idea, a way of dealing with difficulties.

No one, I suppose, has ever represented Dreiser as a masterly intellect. It is even commonplace to say that his ideas are inconsistent or inadequate. But once that admission has been made, his ideas are hustled out of sight while his "reality" and great brooding pity are spoken of. (His pity is to be questioned: pity is to be judged by kind, not amount, and Dreiser's pity—*Jennie Gerhardt* provides the only exception—is either destructive of its object or it is self-pity.) Why has no liberal critic ever brought Dreiser's ideas to the bar of political practicality, asking what use is to be made of Dreiser's dim, awkward speculation, of his self-justification, of his lust for "beauty" and "sex" and "living" and "life itself," and of the showy nihilism which always seems to him so grand a gesture in the direction of profundity? We live, understandably enough, with the sense of urgency; our clock, like Bauderlaire's, has had the hands removed and bears the legend, "It is later than you think." But with us it is always a little too late for mind, yet never too late for honest stupidity; always a little too late for understanding, never too late for righteous, bewildered wrath; always too late for thought, never too late for naïve moralizing. We seem to like to condemn our finest but not our worst qualities by pitting them against the exigency of time.

But sometimes time is not quite so exigent as to justify all our own exigency, and in the case of Dreiser time has allowed his deficiencies to reach their logical, and fatal, conclusion. In *The Bulwark* Dreiser's characteristic ideas come full circle, and the simple, didactic life history of Solon Barnes, a Quaker business man, affirms a simple Christian faith, and a kind of practical mysticism, and the virtues of self-abnegation and self-restraint, and the belief in and submission to the hidden purposes of higher powers, those "superior forces that bring it all about"—once, in Dreiser's opinion, so brutally indifferent, now somehow benign. This is not the first occasion on which Dreiser has shown a tenderness toward religion and a responsiveness to mysticism. *Jennie Gerhardt* and the figure of the Reverend Duncan McMillan in *An American Tragedy* are forecasts of the avowals of *The Bulwark,* and Dreiser's lively interest in power of any sort led him to take account of the power implicit in the cruder forms of mystical performance. Yet these rifts in his nearly monolithic materialism cannot quite prepare us for the blank pietism of *The Bulwark,* not after we have remembered how salient in Dreiser's work has been the long surly rage against the "religionists" and the "moralists," the men who have presumed to believe that life can be given any law at all and who have dared to suppose that will or mind or faith can shape the savage and beautiful entity that Dreiser liked to call "life itself." Now for Dreiser the law may indeed be given, and it is wholly simple— the safe conduct of the personal life requires only that we follow the Inner Light according to the regimen of the Society of Friends, or according to some other godly rule. And now the smiling Aphrodite set above her altars of porphyry, chalcedony, ivory, and gold is quite forgotten, and we are told that the sad joy of cosmic acceptance goes hand in hand with sexual abstinence.

Dreiser's mood of "acceptance" in the last years of his life is not, as a personal experience, to be submitted to the tests of intellectual validity. It consists of a sensation of cosmic understanding, of an overarching sense of unity with the world in its apparent evil as well as in its obvious good. It is no more to be quarreled with, or reasoned with, than love itself—indeed, it is a kind of love, not so much of the world as of oneself in the world. Perhaps it is either the cessation of desire or the perfect balance of desires. It is what used often to be meant by "peace," and up through the nineteenth century a good many people understood its meaning. If it was Dreiser's own emotion at the end of his life, who would not be happy that he had achieved it? I am not even sure that our civilization would not be the better for more of us knowing and desiring this emotion of grave felicity. Yet granting the personal validity of the emotion, Dreiser's exposition of it fails, and is, moreover, offensive. Mr. Matthiessen has warned us of the attack that will be made on the doctrine of *The Bulwark* by "those who believe that any renewal of Christianity marks a new 'failure of nerve.'" But Dreiser's religious avowal is not a failure of nerve—it is a failure of mind and heart. We have only to set his book beside any work in which mind and heart are made to serve religion to know this at once. Ivan Karamazov's giving back his ticket of admission to the "harmony" of the universe suggests that *The Bulwark* is not morally adequate, for we dare not, as its hero does, blandly "accept" the suffering of others; and the Book of Job tells us that it does not include enough in its exploration of the problem of evil, and is not stern enough. I have said that Dreiser's religious affirmation was offensive; the offense lies in the vulgar ease of its formulation, as well as in the comfortable untroubled way in which Dreiser moved from nihilism to pietism.[3]

The Bulwark is the fruit of Dreiser's old age, but if we speak of it as a failure of thought and feeling, we cannot suppose that with age Dreiser weakened in mind and heart. The weakness was always there. And in a sense it is not Dreiser who failed but a whole way of dealing with ideas, a way in which we have all been in some degree involved. Our liberal, progressive culture tolerated Dreiser's vulgar materialism with its huge negation, its simple cry of "Bunk!," feeling that perhaps it was not quite intellectually adequate but certainly very *strong*, certainly very *real*. And now, almost as a natural consequence, it has been given, and is not unwilling to take, Dreiser's pietistic religion in all its inadequacy.

Dreiser, of course, was firmer than the intellectual culture that accepted him. He *meant* his ideas, at least so far as a man can mean ideas who is incapable of following them to their consequences. But we, when it came to his ideas, talked about his great brooding pity and shrugged the ideas off. We are still doing it.

Robert Elias, the biographer of Dreiser, tells us that "it is part of the logic of [Dreiser's] life that he should have completed *The Bulwark* at the same time that he joined the Communists." Just what kind of logic this is we learn from Mr. Elias's further statement. "When he supported left-wing movements and finally, last year, joined the Communist Party, he did so not because he had examined the details of the party line and found them satisfactory, but because he agreed with a general program that represented a means for establishing his cherished goal of greater equality among men." Whether or not Dreiser was following the logic of his own life, he was certainly following the logic of the liberal criticism that accepted him so undiscriminatingly as one of the great, significant expressions of its spirit. This is the liberal criticism, in the direct line of Parrington, which establishes the social responsibility of the writer and then goes on to say that, apart from his duty of resembling reality as much as possible, he is not really responsible for anything, not even for his ideas. The scope of reality being what it is, ideas are held to be mere "details," and, what is more, to be details which, if attended to, have the effect of diminishing reality. But ideals are different from ideas; in the liberal criticism which descends from Parrington ideals consort happily with reality and they urge us to deal impatiently with ideas—a "cherished goal" forbids that we stop to consider how we reach it, or if we may not destroy it in trying to reach it the wrong way.

NOTES

1. See, for example, how Parrington accounts for the "idealizing mind"—Melville's —by the discrepancy between "a wife in her morning kimono" and "the Helen of his dreams." Vol. II, p. 259.

2. The latest defense of Dreiser's style, that in the chapter on Dreiser in the *Literary History of the United States,* is worth noting: "Forgetful of the integrity and power of Dreiser's whole work, many critics have been distracted into a condemnation of his style. He was, like Twain and Whitman, an organic artist; he wrote what he knew —what he was. His many colloquialisms were part of the coinage of his time, and his sentimental and romantic passages were written in the language of the educational system and the popular literature of his formative years. In his style, as in his material, he was a child of his time, of his class. Self-educated, a type or model of the artist of plebeian origin in America, his language, like his subject matter, is not

marked by internal inconsistencies." No doubt Dreiser was an organic artist in the sense that he wrote what he knew and what he was, but so, I suppose, is every artist; the question for criticism comes down to *what* he knew and *what* he was. That he was a child of his time and class is also true, but this can be said of everyone without exception; the question for criticism is how he transcended the imposed limitations of his time and class. As for the defense made on the ground of his particular class, it can only be said that liberal thought has come to a strange pass when it assumes that a plebeian origin is accountable for a writer's faults through all his intellectual life.

3. This ease and comfortableness seem to mark contemporary religious conversions. Religion nowadays has the appearance of what the ideal modern house has been called, "a machine for living," and seemingly one makes up one's mind to acquire and use it not with spiritual struggle but only with a growing sense of its practicability and convenience. Compare *The Seven Storey Mountain,* which Monsignor Sheen calls "a twentieth-century form of the *Confessions* of St. Augustine," with the old, the as it were original, *Confessions* of St. Augustine.

E. M. Halliday

XIX

Hemingway's Ambiguity: Symbolism and Irony

I

One of the curious things about *The Old Man and the Sea* was the
sense of awe that it created in its author, its publisher, and
(to judge by many of the reviewers) its readers. "Don't you think
it is a strange damn story that it should affect all of us (me
especially) the way it does?"[1] wrote Hemingway to one of *Life*'s
editors. And Scribner's dust jacket responded like a good Greek
chorus, "One cannot hope to explain why the reading of this book
is so profound an experience."[2]

There has always been a certain mystery about Hemingway's
effects in his best writing. From *In Our Time* (1925), with its puz-
zling "chapters" connecting (or separating) the stories, through *For
Whom the Bell Tolls* (1940), with its oddly equivocal interpretation
of the Spanish civil war, his best has evoked a somewhat doubtful
sound from critics who nevertheless were at pains to recommend.
Something, it was felt, was being missed; or if not missed, then
sensed too vaguely for critical description. *A Farewell to Arms*
(1929), declared Edward Hope in the New York *Herald Tribune*,
was "one of those things—like the Grand Canyon—that one
doesn't care to talk about."[3] Despite such reverent throwing up

From *American Literature*, Vol. XXVIII, 1956, pp. 1-22. Copyright 1956 by Duke
University Press. Reprinted by permission of the publisher.

of hands by early critics many things were aptly observed; but the emphasis was heavily on Hemingway the realist, whose bright fidelity to the perceptible surfaces of life was accomplished through living dialogue and a prose finely engineered to the accurate rendering of sensuous experience. And the brilliance of his reflected surface together with the roughness of the things he preferred to write about—fishing, hunting, skiing, bull-fighting, boxing, horse-racing, and war—perhaps made it difficult to see one of the cardinal facts about Hemingway: that essentially he is a philosophical writer. His main interest, in representing human life through fictional forms, has consistently been to set man against the background of his world and universe, to examine the human situation from various points of view.

Not that he has a "system," for on the final questions Hemingway has always shown himself a skeptic. "It seemed like a fine philosophy," Jake Barnes says to himself at one bitter point in *The Sun Also Rises.* "In five years . . . it will seem just as silly as all the other fine philosophies I've had."[4] Like Jake, Hemingway has been "technically" a Roman Catholic, but the metaphysical doctrines of Christianity seem never to have taken a convincing hold. His most devout characters are only devoutly mystified by the universe: both Anselmo, the good old man of *For Whom the Bell Tolls,* and Santiago, of *The Old Man and the Sea,* disclaim their religiosity, and their Hail-Marys are uttered mechanically enough to evoke a chilly memory of the sleepless waiter in "A Clean, Well-Lighted Place," who prayed, "Hail nothing, full of nothing, nothing is with thee."[5] The parable of the doomed ants on the burning log, in *A Farewell to Arms,*[6] has been thought to represent Hemingway's *Weltanschauung* at its most pessimistic; but there is no reason, actually, to think that there has since been a fundamental change in his view of life. "Everything kills everything else in some way,"[7] reflects the old Cuban fisherman of the latest book; and even the small bird that rests momentarily on his fishing line may fall to the hawks before reaching land, at best must take its chance "like any man or bird or fish."[8] The world, it seems, still breaks everyone, and only the earth and the Gulf Stream abide after the vortex of human vanities has subsided forever.

Given Hemingway's suspicion of ultimate doom and his passionate fondness for being alive, it is no surprise that his philisophi-

cal preoccupation is primarily ethical. Extinction may well be the
end of all, as the writer of Ecclesiastes repeatedly remarked, but
for Hemingway and his heroes this merely emphasizes the need to
live each moment properly and skilfully, to sense judiciously the
texture of every fleeting act and perception. The focus is conduct:
"Maybe if you found out how to live in it you learned from that
what it was all about,"[9] says Jake Barnes. It is not accidental that
the French existentialists have shown a strong feeling for Hemingway's work. Like them he has been poised in his hours of despair
on the edge of nothingness, the abyss of nonmeaning which confronts most of the characters in the stories of *Winner Take Nothing*
(1933); and like them he has looked in his hours of hope to a salvation built out of individual human courage around a code, at
once rational and intuitive, of strict, often ritualistic behavior.
"*Nous sommes foutus . . . comme toujours,*" says Golz, the Loyalist
general commanding the attack with which Jordan's mission is co-
ordinated in *For Whom the Bell Tolls*. ". . . *Bon. Nous ferons notre petit
possible.*"[10] As it was for Socrates and Jeremy Taylor, although for
quite different reasons, dying well is for Hemingway the crucial
corollary to living well. So Robert Jordan fights off an impulse to
kill himself to end the anguish of a badly broken leg and avoid
possible capture. "You can do nothing for yourself but perhaps
you can do something for another,"[11] he tells himself; yet we are
to understand that he has died well not just because of his sacrifice, but because he has not abandoned the principle of fortitude.
In the image of the crucifixion which has haunted Hemingway
from "Today Is Friday" (1926) to *The Old Man and the Sea,* it is the
unique courage of the forsaken and crucified man-God that takes
his attention. "I'll tell you," says a Roman soldier in the earlier
work, "he looked pretty good to me in there today."[12] We are part
of a universe offering no assurance beyond the grave, and we are
to make what we can of life by a pragmatic ethic spun bravely out
of man himself in full and steady cognizance that the end is
darkness.

II

Undoubtedly Hemingway's preoccupation with the human predicament and a moral code that might satisfactorily control it, in
itself partly accounts for the sense of hidden significance which

many have experienced in reading him. Obscured as this preoccupation has been by his choice of particular fictional materials
and by his manner, which has always eschewed explication, it
could nevertheless almost always be felt: it was impossible to avoid
the impression that this writer was dealing with something of final
importance to us all. Like the Elizabethans whom he evidently
loves, he never lets us quite forget that death awaits every man at
some turn perhaps not far along the way. And like nobody but
Hemingway—that is, in his peculiar and distinguished manner as
an artist—he continually reminds us that (as he expressed it once
to Maxwell Perkins) it is our "performance en route"[13] that counts
for good or bad.

But what is the essence of his peculiar manner? It is a manner
of implication, clearly, as he himself has said in various notes of
self-criticism of which the figure in *Death in the Afternoon* is perhaps
the most striking: "The dignity of movement of an ice-berg is due
to only one-eighth of it being above water."[14] The question is what
mode of narrative technique he exploits in order to make the ice-
berg principle operative in his work. I do not remember seeing the
word "symbolism" in critical writing about Hemingway before
1940, nor have I seen more than one review of *The Old Man and
the Sea* that did not lean heavily on the word. The number of
exegeses that explain Hemingway as a symbolist has increased
geometrically since Malcolm Cowley suggested in 1944 that he
should be grouped not among the realists, but "with Poe and
Hawthorne and Melville: the haunted and nocturnal writers, the
men who dealt in images that were symbols of an inner world."[15]
It was a startling and pleasing suggestion. Mr. Cowley advanced
it rather tentatively and did not press his discovery very far; but
it was taken up with something like a hue and cry by other critics
who, it seemed, had been testily waiting for the scent and were
eager to get on with the hunt. Literary conversation soon began to
reflect the new trend: I recall hearing it asserted on two proximate
occasions that the sleeping bag in *For Whom the Bell Tolls* is an
"obvious" symbol of the womb; and that a ketchup bottle in "The
Killers" patently symbolizes blood. By 1949 it was no great surprise to open an issue of the *Sewanee Review* to an essay by Caroline
Gordon called "Notes on Hemingway and Kafka."[16] It would
have been surprising only if the analysis had not hinged on a comparison between the two writers as symbolists.

Is Hemingway genuinely a symbolist? I think he uses certain techniques of symbolism, but I think he does so in a very limited and closely controlled way, and that failure to recognize the controls leads—already has led—to distortions of his meaning and misappreciations of his narrative art. As a sample, Miss Gordon's essay is instructive on this point. Starting calmly, as her title suggests, with the assumption that Hemingway is a symbolist, she proceeds to compare him, not very favorably, with Kafka. And it turns out that Hemingway's trouble is simple—he is not *enough* of a symbolist: "this plane of action is for him a slippery substratum glimpsed intermittently. It does not underlie the Naturalistic plane of action solidly, or over-arch it grandly, as Kafka's Symbolism does."[17]

But this is mistaking an artistic discipline for a fault. Hemingway has not attempted Kafka's kind of symbolism and fallen short: it is something foreign to Hemingway's art. The Kafka story used by Miss Gordon as the basis for her comparison is "The Hunter Gracchus," a carefully elaborated allegory revolving around the life of Christ—that is to say, there are two distinct and parallel narrative lines, the primary, which operates within the confines of a more or less realistic world, and the secondary, which operates within the realm of religious myth and in this case is assumed by the author to be a prior possession on the part of the reader. Incidentally, Miss Gordon forces her comparison from both sides, claiming for Kafka, as something he shares with Hemingway, "a surface which is strictly Naturalistic in detail."[18] But this claim must rest on a curious understanding of the phrase "in detail" since the story on the "Naturalistic" level offers, among other attractions, a corpse that is mysteriously still alive, and a German-speaking dove the size of a rooster.

Hemingway, as far as I know, has never written an allegory—notwithstanding the bright interpretations of *The Old Man and the Sea* that illuminated cocktail parties a few years ago when it was published in *Life*—and for a very good reason. In successful allegory, the story on the primary level is dominated by the story on the secondary level, and if the allegorical meaning is to be kept clear, its naturalistic counterpart must pay for it by surrendering realistic probability in one way or another. A strain is imposed on the whole narrative mechanism, for mere connotative symbolism will not do to carry the allegory: there must be a denotative equation, part for part, between symbols and things symbolized in order to identify the actors and action on the allegorical level. The extreme difficulty of satisfactorily conducting the dual action throughout a prolonged narrative is classically illustrated by *The Faerie Queene* and by *The Pilgrim's Progress*. The allegorist who admires realism is constantly pulled in two directions at once, and is very lucky when he can prevent one or the other of his meanings from unbalancing him.

Still, Hemingway has used the symbolism of association to convey by implication his essential meaning from the time of his earliest American publication. It may well be that this was inevitable for a writer starting out with Hemingway's determination to communicate, as he put it (in *Death in the Afternoon*) "what really happened in action; what the actual things were which produced the emotion that you experienced."[19] Nothing could more clearly differentiate Hemingway's kind of realism from Zolaesque naturalistic description than this early statement of intent. Everything is to depend on judicious discrimination of objective details: *what really happened* is not by any means everything that happened; it is only "the actual things . . . which produced the emotion that you experienced." As a matter of fact "produced" is a little too strict, as Hemingway demonstrates again and again in *The Sun Also Rises* and *A Farewell to Arms*, where he depends heavily on the technique of objective epitome—a symbolist technique, if you like—to convey the subjective conditions of his characters. The details selected are not so much those which *produce* the emotion as those which epitomize it; it is the action of the story which has produced the emotion. Thus at the crisis of *The Sun Also Rises*, when Jake Barnes presents Brett to Pedro Romero—a Pandarism for which he is obliged to hate himself— his agonized feelings are not discussed, but are nevertheless most poignantly suggested by the perceptions he reports:

> When I came back and looked in the café, twenty minutes later, Brett and Pedro Romero were gone. The coffee-glasses and our three empty cognac-glasses were on the table. A waiter came with a cloth and picked up the glasses and mopped off the table.[20]

In *A Farewell to Arms*, Frederic Henry goes dully out for breakfast from the Swiss maternity hospital where Catherine Barkley is fighting for life in ominously abnormal labor:

Outside along the street were the refuse cans from the houses waiting for the collector. A dog was nosing at one of the cans.

"What do you want?" I asked and looked in the can to see if there was anything I could pull out for him; there was nothing on top but coffeegrounds, dust and some dead flowers.

"There isn't anything, dog," I said.[21]

There is, of course, a large sense, germane to all good fiction, in which Hemingway may be said to be symbolic in his narrative method: the sense which indicates his typical creation of key characters who are representative on several levels. We thus find Jake Barnes's war-wound impotence a kind of metaphor for the whole atmosphere of sterility and frustration which is the *ambiance* of *The Sun Also Rises;* we find Catherine Barkley's naïve simplicity and warmth the right epitome for the idea and ideal of normal civilian home life to which Frederic Henry deserts; we find the old Cuban fisherman in some way representative of the whole human race in its natural struggle for survival. But the recent criticism of Hemingway as symbolist goes far beyond such palpable observations as these, and in considering the fundamental character of his narrative technique I wish to turn attention to more ingenious if not esoteric explications.

Professor Carlos Baker, in *Hemingway: The Writer as Artist* (1952), has established himself as the leading oracle of Hemingway's symbolism. His book is, I think, the most valuable piece of extended Hemingway criticism that we yet have, and to a large extent its contribution is one of new insights into the symbolist aspect of his subject's narrative method. He is sweeping: "From the first Hemingway has been dedicated as a writer to the rendering of Wahrheit, the precise and at least partly naturalistic rendering of things as they are and were. Yet under all his brilliant surfaces lies the controlling Dichtung, the symbolic underpainting which gives so remarkable a sense of depth and vitality to what otherwise might be flat two-dimensional portraiture."[22] This may fairly be said to represent Mr. Baker's major thesis, and he develops and supports it with remarkable energy and skill. I do not wish to disparage his over-all effort—he is often very enlightening—but I do wish to argue that he has been rather carried away by his thesis, and that therein he eminently typifies the new symbolist criticism of Hemingway which in its enthusiasm slights or ignores other basic aspects of Hemingway's technique.

Mr. Baker's chapter on *A Farewell to Arms* is an original piece of criticism, and it solidly illustrates his approach. He finds that the essential meaning of this novel is conveyed by two master symbols, the Mountain and the Plain, which organize the "Dichtung" around "two poles": "By a process of accrual and coagulations, the images tend to build round the opposed concepts of Home and Not-Home. . . . The Home-concept, for example, is associated with the mountains; with dry-cold weather; with peace and quiet; with love, dignity, health, happiness, and the good life; and with worship or at least the consciousness of God. The Not-Home concept is associated with low-lying plains; with rain and fog; with obscenity, indignity, disease, suffering, nervousness, war and death; and with irreligion."[23] It is in terms of these antipodal concepts that Mr. Baker analyzes the semantic structure of *A Farewell to Arms,* a structure which he finds effective chiefly because of the adroit and subtle development of the correspondingly antipodal symbols, the Mountain and the Plain. He argues that from the first page of the story these are set up in their significant antithesis, that they are the key to the relationships among several of the leading characters, and that the central action—Frederic Henry's desertion from the Italian Army to join Catherine Barkley, the British nurse—can be fully appreciated only on this symbolic basis. *"A Farewell to Arms,"* he concludes, "is entirely and even exclusively acceptable as a naturalistic narrative of what happened. To read it only as such, however, is to miss the controlling symbolism: the deep central antithesis between the image of life and home (the mountain) and the image of war and death (the plain)."[24]

Clearly there is some truth in this. The "deep central antithesis" cannot be denied, I would think, by anyone with an acceptable understanding of the book. The question at issue is one of technique; to what extent, and how precisely, is the central antithesis in fact engineered around the Mountain and the Plain as symbols?

One thing is noticeable immediately: as in virtually all of Hemingway, anything that can possibly be construed to operate symbolically does no violence whatsover to the naturalism (or realism) of the story on the primary level. Nothing could be a more natural—or more traditional—symbol of purity, of escape from the commonplace, in short of elevation, than mountains. If thousands of people have read the passages in *A Farewell to Arms* which associate the mountains "with dry-cold weather; with peace and quiet; with love, dignity, health, happiness and the good life" without taking them to be "symbolic" it is presumably because these associations are almost second nature for all of us. Certainly this seems to be true of Frederic Henry: it is most doubtful that in the course of the novel he is ever to be imagined as consciously regarding the mountains as a symbol. This of course does not prove that Hemingway did not regard them as such, or that the full understanding of this novel as an art structure does not perhaps require the symbolic equation, *mountain* equals *life and home*. It does, however, point differentially to another type of symbolism, where the character in question is shown to be clearly aware of the trope, as when Catherine Barkley says she hates rain because "sometimes I see me dead in it,"[25] or when Frederic Henry says of his plunge into the Tagliamento, "Anger was washed away in the river along with any obligation."[26]

But Mr. Baker has claimed a most exact detailed use by Hemingway of the Mountain-Plain symbolism, and his ingenious interpretation deserves closer attention. Like many other critics he is an intense admirer of the novel's opening paragraph, which, he says, "does much more than start the book. It helps to establish the dominant mood (which is one of doom), plants a series of important images for future symbolic cultivation, and subtly compels the reader into the position of detached observer."[27] He proceeds to a close analysis of this paragraph:

> The second sentence, which draws attention from the mountainous background to the bed of the river in the middle distance, produces a sense of clearness, dryness, whiteness, and sunniness which is to grow very subtly under the artist's hands until it merges with one of the novel's two dominant symbols, the mountain-image. The other major symbol is the plain. Throughout the sub-structure of the book it is opposed to the mountain-image. Down this plain the river flows. Across it, on the dusty road among the trees, pass the men-at-war, faceless and voiceless and unidentified against the background of the spreading plain.[28]

This is highly specific, and we are entitled to examine it minutely. Mr. Baker says the river is "in the middle distance" in the direction of the mountains with the image of which, as he sees it, the symbolic images of the river are to merge into one great symbol. But is the river really in the middle distance? The narrator tells us he can see not only its boulders but its *pebbles,* "dry and white in the sun." The river must, of course, flow from the mountains, but in the perspective seen from the house occupied by Frederic Henry, it would appear to be very close at hand— closer than the plain, and quite in contrast to the distant mountains. And this raises the question of whether the clearness, dryness, whiteness, and sunniness offered by the river are in fact artfully intended to be associated with the mountain-image and what it is held to symbolize; or, disregarding the question of intent, whether they do in fact so operate in the artistic structure. Why must the river images be disassociated from the images of the plain across which the river, naturally, flows? Because the river images are of a kind which, if they work as symbols, are incongruent with what Mr. Baker has decided the Plain stands for; they must instead be allocated to the Mountain. This is so important to his thesis that the river shifts gracefully, but without textual support, into "the middle distance," closer to the mountains.

And what of the soldiers on the road? Since they must be firmly associated with the Plain ("war and death"), it is against that background that Mr. Baker sees them in Hemingway's opening paragraph—it would not do to see them against the background of the river, with its Mountain images. But let us look again at the paragraph.

> In the late summer of that year we lived in a house in a village that looked across the river and the plain to the mountains. In the bed of the river there were pebbles and boulders, dry and white in the sun, and the water was clear and swiftly moving and blue in the channels. Troops went by the house and down the road and the dust they raised powdered the leaves of the trees.

Mr. Baker says the road is across the river, as of course it would have to be if we are to see the figures of the soldiers against the background of the plain. Hemingway does not say the road is across the river. Indeed, everything indicates the opposite arrangement: a house on a road running along the near side of the river, across which the plain stretches out to the mountains. "Sometimes in the dark," begins the third paragraph of the novel, "we heard the troops marching under the window. . . ." The truth is that a strong part of Mr. Baker's initially persuasive exegesis of the opening paragraph of *A Farewell to Arms* hangs on a reading that the written words will not support. This is not to deny that the paragraph establishes a mood of doom by its somber tone and the epitomic symbols of dust and falling leaves: what I am questioning is the over-all symbolic organization of the novel's structure in terms of the Mountain and the Plain, which Mr. Baker argues as a prime illustration of his unequivocal judgment of Hemingway as symbolist artist.

As a matter of fact, the plain presented in the opening pages of *A Farewell to Arms* is as troublesome as the river when it comes to supporting Mr. Baker's interpretation. There are plains in many countries that could well serve as symbols of emptiness, desolation, disaster, and death—we have some in the American West. But this does not appear to be that sort of plain: quite the contrary. "The plain," Frederic Henry narrates in the opening words of the second paragraph, "was rich with crops; there were many orchards of fruit trees. . . ." Mr. Baker tells us neither how these images of fertility and fruition are to fit in with "rain and fog; with obscenity, indignity, disease, suffering, nervousness, war and death," nor how we should symbolically interpret the conclusion of the sentence, ". . . and beyond the plain the mountains were brown and bare." One can easily grant that as the novel unfolds the impression of war itself grows steadily more saturated with a sense of doomsday qualities: that was an essential part of Hemingway's theme. But to what degree is this impression heightened by the use of the Plain as symbol? The simple exigencies of history prevent exclusive association of the war with the plain as opposed to the mountains, as the narrator indicates on the first page: "There was fighting in the mountains and at night we could see flashes from the artillery." Yet if Mr. Baker is right we would expect to find, despite this difficulty, a salient artistic emphasis of the Plain in symbolic association with all those images which his interpretation sets against those coalescing around the Mountain symbol.

Mr. Baker makes much of the fact that Frederic Henry, during his leave, fails to take advantage of the offer of his friend the chaplain and go to the high mountain country of the Abruzzi, "where the roads were frozen and hard as iron, where it was clear

cold and dry and the snow was dry and powdery. . . . I had gone
to no such place but to the smoke of cafés and nights when the
room whirled and you needed to look at the wall to make it stop,
nights in bed, drunk, when you knew that that was all there
was."[29] Here, Mr. Baker claims, "the mountain-image gets further
backing from another lowland contrast."[30] Granting the familiar
association here of mountain-country with certain delectable and
longed-for experiences, one would like to see, in support of the
Mountain-Plain explication, a clearer identification of the contrasting, soldier-on-leave experiences, with the lowland or plain.
And while wondering about this, one reads on in *A Farewell to
Arms* and soon finds Frederic Henry and Catherine Barkley in
Milan, where Henry is recuperating from his wound. They are
having a wonderful time. They are in love, have frequent opportunities to be alone together in the hospital room, go often to the
races, dine at the town's best restaurants, and in general lead an
existence that makes the most pleasant contrast imaginable to the
dismal life at the front. "We had a lovely time that summer,"[31]
says the hero. What has happened here to the Mountain-Plain
machinery? It does not seem to be operating; or perhaps it is
operating in reverse, since Milan is definitely in the plain. Mr.
Baker passes over these pages of the novel rather quickly, remarking that Catherine here "moves into association with ideas of
home, love and happiness."[32] He seems to be aware of the
difficulty, although he does not mention it as such: "She does not
really [*sic*] reach the center of the mountain-image until, on the
heels of Frederick's harrowing lowland experiences during the retreat from Caporetto, the lovers move to Switzerland. Catherine
is the first to go, and Henry follows her there as if she were the
genius of the mountains, beckoning him on."[33]

This is romantically pleasant, but inaccurate. Catherine does
not go to Switzerland, but to the Italian resort village of Stresa, on
Lake Maggiore. Stresa, moreover, although surrounded by mountains, is itself distinctly lowland: you can pedal a bicycle from
Milan or Turin without leaving nearly flat country. Still, it can be
allowed that the lovers are not free of the contaminating shadow
of war until they have escaped up the lake to Switzerland and
established themselves in their little chalet above Montreux. Here,
again, the associations all of us are likely to make with high-

mountain living assert themselves—clear, cold air; magnificent views; white snow; peace and quiet—and the hero and heroine are shown to be happily aware of these. The rain, however, which they both come to regard as an omen of disaster, grants no immunity to the mountain; it refuses to preserve a unilateral symbolic association with the plain. Mr. Baker knows this, but does not discus the extent to which it obscures his neat Mountain-Plain antithesis, making the point instead that "the March rains and the approaching need for a good lying-in hospital have driven the young couple down from their magic mountain" to "the lowlands"[34] of Lausanne. Here again observation is fuzzy to the point of distortion: Lausanne happens to stand on a series of steep hills and is an extraordinarily poor specimen of a City of the Plain. This is clear, incidentally, without reference to an atlas, since there are several allusions to the hills and steep streets of Lausanne in the novel itself.[35] But Mr. Baker is caught up in his symbolic apparatus, and if one symbol of death (rain) has failed to stay where it belongs in his scheme (on the plain) he still is persuaded to see the topography of Switzerland in a light that will not darken his thesis.

What all this illustrates, it seems to me, is that Mr. Baker has allowed an excellent insight into Hemingway's imagery and acute sense of natural metonymy to turn into an interesting but greatly overelaborated critical gimmick. It is undeniable that in the midst of the darkling plain of struggle and flight which was the war in Italy, Frederic Henry thinks of the Swiss Alps as a neutral refuge of peace and happiness—surely millions must have lifted their eyes to those mountains with like thoughts during both World Wars. But in so far as this is symbolism it belongs to our race and culture; and if it is to be sophisticated into a precise scheme of aristic implication revolving around two distinct polar symbols, the signals transmitted from artist to reader must be more clearly semaphored than anything Mr. Baker has been able to point to accurately. I do not believe this is derogatory to Hemingway. Sensitive as always to those parts of experience that are suggestive and connotative, he used the mountain metaphor which is part of our figurative heritage to deepen the thematic contrast in *A Farewell to Arms,* between war and not-war. But nowhere did he violate realism for the sake of this metaphor; nor did he, as I read the novel, set up the artificially rigid and unrealistic contrast be-

tween the Mountain and the Plain which Mr. Baker's analysis
requires.

Mr. Baker himself has summed up the sequel to his investigation of *A Farewell to Arms*. "Once the reader has become aware
of what Hemingway is doing in those parts of his work which lie
below the surface, he is likely to find symbols operating everywhere. . . ."[36] Mr. Baker does find them everywhere, and they not
infrequently trip him into strangely vulnerable judgments. Finding
an unprecedented display of symbolism in *Across the River and into
the Trees* (1950), for instance, he is willing to accord that disappointing novel a richly favorable verdict: "a prose poem, with
a remarkably complex emotional structure, on the theme of the
three ages of man. . . . If *A Farewell to Arms* was his *Romeo
and Juliet* . . . this . . . could perhaps be called a lesser kind
of *Winter's Tale* or *Tempest*."[37]

III

But we are not interested so much in the narrative technique of
Hemingway's weakest work as we are in what happens in his best.
To see symbolism as the master device of the earlier novels and
short stories tends to obscure another and more characteristic type
of ambiguity which makes his best work great fiction in the tacit
mode. I mean Hemingway's irony. The extent to which the ironic
method has packed his fiction with substrata of meaning has not
yet, I think, been adequately appreciated in published criticism.
And it needs to be appreciated; for irony as a literary device is
singularly suited to the view of life which Hemingway has consistently dramatized now for a quarter of our century in such manner
as to distinguish him as a writer.

If you look at Hemingway's earliest American publication in
a medium of general circulation you are struck by this irony
of view and method, just as it is strikingly there in *The Old Man and
the Sea*. "Champs d'Honneur" was the title of one of six short
poems printed in *Poetry* for January, 1923:

> Soldiers never do die well;
>   Crosses mark the places—
> Wooden crosses where they fell,
>   Stuck above their faces.
> Soldiers pitch and cough and twitch—

> All the world roars red and black;
> Soldiers smother in a ditch,
> Choking through the whole attack.[38]

One of the most interesting things about this is the strong ironic tension set up between the title and the verse itself; the harsh incongruity between the traditional notion of the soldier's heroic death and the grim reality. A tough irony of situation is also the keynote of *In Our Time* (1925), not only as clue to the individual meanings of most of the stories that make up the book, but as the very principle upon which it was composed. Many readers have tried to puzzle out a nice relationship between each story and the narrative fragment, numbered as a "chapter," which precedes it. But the principle in fact was irrelevance; what Hemingway did was to take the numbered sketches of *in our time* (Paris, 1924) and intersperse them with the longer stories to give a powerfully ironic effect of spurious order supporting the book's subject: modern civil disruption and violence seen against the timeless background of everyday human cross-purposes.

The ironic gap between expectation and fulfilment, pretense and fact, intention and action, the message sent and the message received, the way things are thought or ought to be and the way things are—this has been Hemingway's great theme from the beginning; and it has called for an ironic method to do it artistic justice. All of his work thus far published deserves study with special attention to this method.

I do not think, for example, that a reader must understand the symbolic pattern Mr. Baker claims for *A Farewell to Arms* in order to get the main point of the story; but unless he understands the irony of Catherine Barkley's death he surely has missed it completely. Long before this denouement, however, irony has drawn a chiaroscuro highlighting the meaning of the book. There is from the beginning the curious disproportion between Frederic Henry's lot in the army and his frame of mind. A noncombatant, he lives in comfortable houses, eats and drinks well, makes frequent visits to a brothel maintained exclusively for officers, and has extensive leaves urged on him by a sympathetic commanding officer. Despite such pleasures he is malcontent; and the more this fact emerges the more it becomes evident that his mood is a reflection not of his personal fortune, but of the whole dismal panorama of civilization disjointed by war. His manner of narration is already ironical: "At the start of the winter came the permanent rain and with the rain came the cholera. But it was checked and in the end only seven thousand died of it in the army."[39] Healthy in body, the hero is afflicted by a paralysis of the will, a torpor brought on by too many months of living close to the war; and this is the reason for his paradoxical failure to visit the home of his friend the chaplain while he is on leave: "I myself felt as badly as he did and could not understand why I had not gone. It was what I had wanted to do. . . ."[40] Even the one constructive effort he has been regularly capable of, the performance of his duty as an ambulance officer, has begun to seem absurdly inconsequential to him: when he returns from leave he finds that his absence apparently has made no difference whatever.

As the war wears on, its grotesqueries receive more attention; it begins to be felt, indeed, that they are perhaps after all indigenous to life itself, and only emphasized by war. Henry is given a protective St. Anthony by the heroine: "After I was wounded I never found him. Some one probably got it at one of the dressing stations."[41] The ambulance unit which he commands makes elaborate preparations to receive wounded soldiers during a forthcoming attack: while they are waiting—and eating cheese and spaghetti—in a dugout, an enemy shell lands squarely on top of them, thus making Lt. Henry himself part of the first load of wounded going to the rear. For this, he learns, he is to receive a bronze medal; his friend Rinaldi hopes it may be silver.

The episode in Milan, so recalcitrant to Mr. Baker's symbolist scheme, has an integral function in the ironic structure of the narrative. Recuperating far behind the lines, the hero becomes part of the incongruously pleasant civilian scene which always—to the incredulous and bitter astonishment of most combat soldiers— goes on while men die at the front. Yet to add a further ironic twist to this, there is Hemingway's satirical portrait of Ettore, the American-Italian who is a "legitimate hero" in the Italian Army. Not only does he see the social life of wartime Milan as perfectly normal, but it is clear that his view of the war as a whole is the reverse of Henry's: "Believe me, they're fine to have," he says, exhibiting his wound stripes. "I'd rather have them than medals. Believe me, boy, when you get three you've got something."[42]

Back at the front for only two days, Henry finds himself mixed up in the nightmarish retreat from Caporetto. Hemingway's famous description of this debacle is a stringent comment on the bewildering stupidity and chaos of war, but he takes the occasion to inject again a shot of special irony. With one ambulance mired to the hubs on a rainsoaked back road, Lt. Henry shoots a sergeant who, in his anxiety to keep up with the retreat, tries to get away on foot instead of staying to cut brush for the spinning wheels. The sergeant is only wounded, but he is quickly dispatched, with Henry's acquiescence, by Bonello, one of the ambulance drivers. "All my life I've wanted to kill a sergeant,"[43] Bonello says proudly; but a few hours later he too deserts, to let himself be captured by the enemy. The climax of this grim comedy is of course Frederic Henry's own desertion. Threatened with military justice akin to that he so summarily had dealt the sergeant, he dives into the Tagliamento River; and his sarcastic remarks on his would-be executioners ring with hyperironic overtones against the baffle of the earlier incident:

> I saw how their minds worked; if they had minds and if they worked. They were all young men and they were saving their country. . . . The questioners had that beautiful detachment and devotion to stern justice of men dealing in death without being in any danger of it.[44]

There are many other ironic strokes in *A Farewell to Arms,* but it is this series, identifying the activities of war with all that is brutal and meaningless in human life, that gives the novel its predominantly ironic texture. The catastrophe, Catherine Barkley's shocking death, has the ambivalent effect of partly canceling this identification while at the same time violently reinforcing the total effect of irony. It is as if the author had said, "Do not imagine that the kind of cruelty and disruption I have shown you are confined to war: they are the conditions of life itself." It is thus only at the end that the full ironic ambiguity of the title springs into view.

The title of Hemingway's other great war novel is likewise an index of its strongly ironic theme. It was strange how many reviewers and critics underweighed the epigraph from Donne and the meaningful paradox of the whole sentence furnishing the title: "And therefore never send to know for whom the bell tolls: it tolls for thee." Appraisals from both Right and Left accused Hemingway of having gone over to the other side, while certain critics less politically biased found that his theme was confused or that it had backfired. "At the center of *For Whom the Bell Tolls*," wrote Maxwell Geismar, "there is a basic confusion of Hemingway's intention. The novel attempts to be a constructive statement on human life. Yet Hemingway's underlying sense of destruction often contradicts this."[45]

But Hemingway was not confused. As always, he wanted to show something true about human life (not necessarily something "constructive"); and he had come to take a more complex view of humanity at war than he projected in *A Farewell to Arms*. "A plague on both your houses"—the prevailing mood of Frederic Henry—has been replaced by Robert Jordan's unillusioned sense of the community of the human predicament. No man is an island, it turns out; but the storms that sweep the human continent are of such force, and the quakes that rack its surface so disruptive, that none of use can depend on better fortune than that of Jordan, who died making his own small and paradoxical effort to maintain its integrity. His affiliation with the Loyalists is no simple partisan allegiance; and to extend and support the hero's explicit awareness of the inevitable contradictions of his position, Hemingway poses a series of situations pregnant with irony.

Outstanding is Pilar's account of the start of "the movement" in Pablo's home town, with its unflinching report of the steadily mounting sadism which infused the execution of the local Fascists. There is a remarkable tone to this report, as if Pilar were at confession, anxious to tell the whole truth and omitting not even the most shameful details, yet seeking at the same time to make it understood how these grisly acts could have occurred among normally decent Spanish peasants. She tells how, at first, many of the peasants were sickened by Pablo's plan to flail the Fascists down between a double line of men leading to the edge of a steep cliff. But within the ironic frame of the entire episode, in relation to the book, there are lesser ironies: for it is the cowardly behavior of the Fascists themselves that brings these peasants to a pitch of mob hatred and violence equal to Pablo's inveterate cruelty.

Throughout all this the reader is never allowed to forget that it is the Loyalists who are committing the atrocities described, and that the leaders of the massacre are the very people with whom

Jordan is now allied. Robert Penn Warren cites the irony of this, but he suggests that *For Whom the Bell Tolls* is not Hemingway's best novel "primarily because . . . Hemingway does not accept the limitations of his premises . . . the irony . . . runs counter to the ostensible surface direction of the story."[46] So it does—but this is the nature of irony; and this is why it is so valuable to Hemingway in his intense effort to dramatize fully the implications of Donne's epigraph in relation to the ironical self-destruction which is civilized warfare. It is a mistake to think of *For Whom the Bell Tolls* as a document of social optimism in its intent, as opposed to the dark pessimism of Hemingway's earlier books. The darkness is relieved, deliberately, only by a faint existentialist glimmer: the general human enterprise seems very likely to end in failure, but each of us must do what he can—"*Nous ferons notre petit possible.*"

It is to this end that the irony of the Loyalist massacre of the Fascists, which early in the book sets the theme of human sacrifice in a highly critical perspective, is complemented by the irony of the denouement. For the central action—the blowing of the bridge —which is responsible for the deaths of El Sordo, Anselmo, Fernando, and, indeed, Robert Jordan, is rendered a strategic failure by the loose tongues of their comrades behind the lines.

To these two fundamental veins of irony many scenes provide tributary support: three may be cited as exemplary. There is the one in which Jordan reads the letters found in the pockets of a Fascist cavalryman he has just shot, and discovers he is from a Spanish town that Jordan knows well:

> How many is that you have killed? he asked himself. I don't know. Do you think you have a right to kill any one? No. But I have to. . . . But you like the people of Navarra better than those of any other part of Spain. Yes. And you kill them. Yes. . . . Don't you know it is wrong to kill? Yes. But you do it? Yes. And you still believe absolutely that your cause is right? Yes.[47]

This irony of Jordan's self-conscious ambivalence is heightened by juxtapositions of which he knows nothing. In the midst of El Sordo's great last fight, we are suddenly given a decidedly sympathetic portrait of Lt. Berrendo, second in command of the Fascist cavalry. Julian, his best friend, has just been killed by Sordo, and Captain Mora, the blustering officer in command, is shouting blasphemies at the hilltop in an effort (which carries its own small irony, in view of his imminent death) to prove that no one is left alive up there. Later, after Mora has become El Sordo's "Comrade Voyager," Berrendo reluctantly has his troopers decapitate the dead guerrillas for "proof and identification," and the Fascists start back towards their headquarters:

> Then he thought of Julian, dead on the hill, dead now, tied across a horse there in the first troop, and as he rode down into the dark pine forest, leaving the sunlight behind him on the hill, riding now in the quiet dark of the forest, he started to say a prayer for him again.[48]

At this point Anselmo, watching from a hillside, sees them ride past; and on his way back to the guerrilla cave he crosses El Sordo's hilltop where he finds the headless bodies of his comrades: ". . . as he walked he prayed for the souls of Sordo and of all his band. It was the first time he had prayed since the start of the movement."[49] The episode thus ends in ironic equilibrium, with both sides petitioning Heaven. But we have not yet seen our last of Lt. Berrendo. It is he who looms in the sights of Robert Jordan's machine gun in the last paragraph of the story, lending the finale an ironic depth that protects it from false heroics. For these two young soldiers, preponderant as our sympathy may be for one rather than the other, the same bell tolls. The novel is Hemingway's fullest work so far in scope and artistic realization, and to its fulfilment the ambiguity of irony contributes an essential part.

IV

It would be foolish to argue that the work of any first-rate writer owes its success exclusively or even predominantly to any one narrative artifice. Hemingway has used techniques of symbolism and techniques of irony and used them well; what we want in criticism is an even view of his use of these and other artistic resources that does not exaggerate one at the expense of others. A point deserving great attention and emphasis about this writer is his devotion to the implicit rather than the explicit mode: and both symbolism and irony truly serve this artistic purpose. Hemingway, in fact, stirs thought as to the interrelationship of these two kinds of ambiguity. It is remarkable how often they operate together in his stories: an ironic fact, perception, or event on the primary level may epitomize an irony in a broader context, and thus doubly deserve selection and accurate report by the narrator. As an illustration of his early effort to communicate "what really happened in action," Hemingway tells in *Death in the Afternoon* how he worked on the problem of accurately depicting a certain bullfight incident:

> ... walking in the night I tried to remember what it was that seemed just out of my remembering and that was the thing that I had really seen and, finally, remembering all around it, I got it. When he stood up, his face white and dirty and the silk of his breeches opened from waist to knee, it was the dirtiness of the rented breeches, the dirtiness of his slit underwear and the clean, clean, unbearably clean whiteness of the thighbone that I had seen, and it was that which was important.[50]

Clearly, it was the startling irony of the contrast that struck Hemingway here as "important"; but certainly (if not so clearly) there is also the symbolic suggestion of another contrast going far beyond the physical—the ironically pathetic gap, perhaps, between the matador's professional failure and his untouched inner pride which is the subject of "The Undefeated."

In a fictional narrative the double operation, ironic and symbolic, can often be seen more sharply: take *The Old Man and the Sea,* where in effect the same subject is dramatized. The old fisherman's physical triumph in catching the great fish is ironically cut down—or transmuted—into spiritual triumph by the marauding sharks who leave him with only the skeleton of the largest marlin ever seen in Cuba. Without working out the metaphor in precise terms it can be said that the irony of the event itself would hardly be so effective without the broadening and deepening of its implication through symbolic suggestion.

It may be true that all perceptions are reducible finally to perceptions of likeness or perceptions of difference. Perhaps this offers a clue to the effectiveness of both symbolism and irony for a writer who, like Hemingway, makes it his life's business to tell a truth, as he once put it, "truer . . . than anything factual can be."[51] With all his famous skill in writing with his eye upon the object, he understood from the beginning that it was only the object in relationship to other objects and to the observer that really counted: significance is, in short, a matter of likeness and difference. This is to speak broadly; and to apply the generalization to symbolism and irony requires a good deal of qualification. Yet symbolism does depend essentially on likeness, and irony on difference; and as artistic tools both are means of interpreting imaginatively, and with the flexibility of implication, a complex reality. Symbolism signifies through a harmony, irony through a discord; symbolism consolidates, irony complicates; symbolism synthesizes, irony analyzes.

For all of this, I would not like to see Hemingway go down in new literary histories as either "a symbolist" or (less likely, if somewhat more appropriately) "an ironist." Taken at face value the denomination "symbolist" has meanings in the common language of criticism that are quite inapplicable to him. But beyond this, Hemingway uses symbolism, as I have tried to show, with a severe restraint that in his good work always staunchly protects his realism. So likewise does he use irony. It is the ambiguity of life itself that Hemingway has sought to render, and if irony has served him peculiarly well it is because he sees life as inescapably ironic. But if we must classify him let us do him justice: with all his skilful use of artistic ambiguity, he remains the great *realist* of twentieth-century American fiction.

NOTES

1. Quoted in *Time,* LX, No. 9, 48 (Sept. 1, 1952).
2. *The Old Man and the Sea* (New York, 1952).
3. Quoted on the flyleaf of *A Farewell to Arms,* Bantam Edition (New York, 1954).
4. *The Sun Also Rises* (New York, 1926), p. 153
5. *The Short Stories of Ernest Hemingway* (New York, 1938), p. 481.
6. *A Farewell to Arms* (New York, 1932), p. 350.
7. *The Old Man and the Sea,* p. 117.
8. *Ibid.,* p. 61.
9. *The Sun Also Rises,* p. 153.
10. *For Whom the Bell Tolls* (New York, 1940), pp. 428, 430.
11. *Ibid.,* p. 466.
12. *The Short Stories,* p. 457.
13. Quoted by Perkins in *Scribner's Magazine,* LXXXI, 4 (March, 1927).
14. *Death in the Afternoon* (New York, 1932), p. 192.
15. Introduction to *The Portable Hemingway* (New York, 1944), p. vii.
16. *Sewanee Review,* LVII, 214–26 (Spring, 1949).
17. *Ibid.,* p. 226.

18. *Ibid.,* p. 222.

19. *Death in the Afternoon,* p. 2.

20. *The Sun Also Rises,* p. 194.

21. *A Farewell to Arms,* p. 336.

22. Carlos Baker, *Hemingway: The Writer as Artist* (Princeton, 1952), p. 289.

23. *Ibid.,* pp. 101, 102.

24. *Ibid.,* pp. 108, 109.

25. *A Farewell to Arms,* p. 135.

26. *Ibid.,* p. 248.

27. Baker, *op. cit.,* p. 94.

28. *Ibid.,* pp. 94–5.

29. *A Farewell to Arms,* p. 13.

30. Baker, *op. cit.,* p. 102.

31. *A Farewell to Arms,* p. 119.

32. Baker, *op. cit.,* p. 104.

33. *Ibid.*

34. *Ibid.,* pp. 104, 108.

35. See, for instance, pp. 328, 331, 334.

36. Baker, *op. cit.,* p. 117.

37. *Ibid.,* pp. 264, 287.

38. *Poetry,* XXI, 195 (Jan., 1923).

39. *A Farewell to Arms,* p. 4.

40. *Ibid.,* p. 13.

41. *Ibid.,* p. 47.

42. *Ibid.,* p. 130.

43. *Ibid.,* p. 222.

44. *Ibid.,* pp. 240, 241.

45. *Writers in Crisis* (Boston, 1942), p. 81.

46. Introduction to *A Farewell to Arms* (New York, 1949), p. xxv.

47. *For Whom the Bell Tolls,* pp. 303–4.

48. *Ibid.,* p. 326.

49. *Ibid.,* p. 327.

50. *Death in the Afternoon,* p. 20.

51. Introduction to *Men at War* (New York, 1952), p. xi.

Frederick J. Hoffman

XX

No Beginning and No End: Hemingway and Death

In her novel *Death Comes for the Archbishop* Willa Cather has several observations about human death and the circumstances in which it takes place. On one occasion a Father Lucero receives his last sacrament, after confession: "The ceremony calmed the tormented man, and he lay quiet with his hands folded on his breast." This ceremony is significant not only for him but for those who attend him in his last moments: "Watching beside a death-bed was not a hardship for them, but a privilege,—in the case of a dying priest it was a distinction." In those days, Miss Cather says (she is speaking of the early nineteenth century and of the south-western United States),

> death had a solemn social importance. It was not regarded as a moment when certain bodily organs ceased to function, but as a dramatic climax, a moment when the soul made its entrance into the next world, passing in full consciousness through a lowly door to an unimaginable scene. Among the watchers there was always the hope that the dying man might reveal something of what he alone could see; that his countenance, if not his lips, would speak, and on his features would fall some light or shadow from beyond . . .[1]

From *Essays in Criticism*, Vol. III, 1953, pp. 73–84. Copyright 1953 by Frederick J. Hoffman. Reprinted by permission of the author and periodical. Part of this essay appears in Mr. Hoffman's book, *The Twenties*, published by The Viking Press, Inc.

These words, published two years before Hemingway's *A Farewell to Arms* (1929), have a source and an orientation radically different from Hemingway's. *Death Comes for the Archbishop* celebrates the triumph of a simple and serene faith over the hardships of terrain and society; elsewhere Miss Cather has spoken of her rejection of the modern world: she will have nothing to do with its crassness, its vulgarity and its violence. In 1936, looking back upon her first introduction to the widow of James T. Fields, she spoke of the passing of that gracious life in the home at 148 Charles Street. The house had since been replaced by a garage, its stark vulgarity superseding the "softly lighted drawing-room, and the dining-table where Learning and Talent met, enjoying good food and good wit and rare vintages, looking confidently forward to the growth of their country in the finer amenities of life."[2] Somehow, "The world broke in two in 1922 or thereabouts . . ." and she thought it not unlikely that the first World War had been at least partially responsible. Despite the fact that it had proved a source of renewal for one of her heroes, Claude Wheeler of *One of Ours* (1922), it was nevertheless blamed for having radically altered twentieth-century tastes, habits and points of view. She was not explicit about this, only vaguely resentful; she did not try to explain why the change had taken place, but rather retreated from the world which had suffered it, retiring to a place where traditional securities were still an important means of defining and governing human behaviour.

To Miss Cather the modern world was one in which death and life had lost what she thought was a peculiarly precious and meaningful relationship. The extreme form of imbalance between death and life is caused by violence; but there are, of course, forms and degrees of violence. The most widely disparate forms are violence caused by "strong emotion" and that made possible by efficient technological means. Of the first Miss Cather feels that the securities have their own emotional means of combating it; but there is no real way out of the agony, the shock, the meaninglessness of the second. The hero of *One of Ours,* though he died in combat, carried his glory and his illusion intact to his grave: "'He died believing his own country better than it is, and France better than any country can ever be'."[3] We can scarcely hope to find in

Miss Cather's work a proper explanation of the loss of such illusions. The very feeling of disillusionment was beyond the capacity of a person who could so readily move out of the world in which that feeling dominated.

One of the most radical changes in modern literary sensibility can be described as the symbolic injury. The circumstances in which such an injury occurs are almost invariably violent, and the violence, while not entirely unexpected, comes as a surprise, as a shock, to the person injured. There are some evidences of security even here, though these are quite superficial, not at the heart of the experience. The hero may be with soldiers whom he knows, with whom he talks, and eats an improvised meal. Beyond this scene, there are the love and the religion he has left, which should give him some feeling of security. About him there are many threatening noises, and these bear promise of violent injury or death. If one of them should come near, to actualize the danger, that is an accident; but the accident is the result, not of mere chance, but of impersonal misfortune impersonally caused. The injury, when it comes, is a form of death whether the victim survives it or not. Hemingway once spoke of his own injury, on the night of July 8th, 1918, as a death (it is important too that the injury should occur at night). "I died then," he is reported by Malcolm Cowley as having said, "I felt my soul or something coming right out of my body, like you'd pull a silk handkerchief out of a pocket by one corner. It flew around and then came back and went in again and I wasn't dead anymore!"[4] According to Ezra Pound's version, told to John Peale Bishop, Hemingway "had lain four days under the débris of the trench" before he was rescued; this, adds Bishop, "is one day longer underground than Lazarus."[5] Though the facts of this account may not be true, they do have a symbolic meaning: Hemingway's "awareness of death," his experience of it, had led to a form of rebirth, had 'separated' him from his (as well as from Nick Adams's) American past, from the Middle West. The experience of the wound and the circumstances in which it had happened radically altered Hemingway's entire view of the world he re-entered. He had therefore to find a different perspective from which to view and judge that world.

The most important consequence of a traumatic shock is that the experience which has caused it is recalled again and again. It is not that the victim enjoys the experience and so wishes it repeated, but rather that initially it has thrown him entirely off guard and he has therefore been unable to adjust to it. The more violent, the less expected, the experience has been, the more liable it is to such compulsive repetition, which is in all seriousness a long and painful means of reaching a stage of complete adjustment. A deep injury to the body suggests a comparably severe injury to the psychic nature. The injured man will not rest until he has found what is to him a meaningful and original pattern of adjustment. The shock often has other effects: for one, it may upset his confidence in the past—his own past and the social past of which he has been a part. The experience is itself almost equivalent to a death; since this is true, what follows will amount to a new and a different life. The man who survives violence is often quite remarkably different from the man who has never experienced it.

The symbolic wound has affected a large share of Hemingway's fiction. Its distinguishing features are the shock of the actual experience, the sudden cutting away from past experience and securities (which do survive, but only in fragmentary form), the mystery and impersonality of its source, the anger, fear, and helplessness that are part of the reaction to it. The wound is "unreasonable"; that is, the victim cannot satisfactorily or reasonably understand why "it has happened to *him*." It gives him a profound distrust of those who—remote from the experience itself—try to formulate explanations or assurances concerning it. They are obviously "faking"; they don't know what they are talking about; if they had had any experience like it, they would not talk at all, and they would most certainly not try to speak of dignity or glory or sacrifice, because these words are almost invariably betrayed when tested by reality. But some definition of a man's life is necessary if he is to care about surviving, and this definition is hard to formulate when so many useful words and expressions have defaulted.

The memory of the war haunts Hemingway's earliest fiction; many of the stories of Nick Adams's youth in *In Our Time* are given in terms of his author's own experience with violence. The securities provided by Nick's father and mother and by the natural setting are never free of the tortured comment which the

sketches of war and violence offer. In fact, these sketches act as a
sombre, brooding supervisory deity in the affairs of Nick Adams.
His father's assurances may have been adequate before the injury
occurred, but they are no longer capable of exorcizing the nightmarish spirit which returns after each of the Adams stories.
"There was no end and no beginning" in the Greek retreat described in "Chapter Two" of *In Our Time,* a sketch immediately
after the story "Indian Camp," in which there have been both
beginning *and* end; the emotional response to birth and death is
governed by Nick's own ability to accept the security of his father's
competence as a doctor and of the quiet natural setting of the
early morning: ". . . sitting in the stern of the boat with his father
rowing, he felt quite sure that he would never die."[6] The "absolutely perfect barricade" of "Chapter Four" and the garden wall
of "Chapter Three" both lead to "perfect" deaths, containing in
them elements of shock and accident and managed as they are
through ingenuity and skill, with a total lack of emotion or passion. "It was simply priceless," and "we were frightfully put out
when we heard the flank had gone and we had to fall back."
These remarks are a form of compulsive repetition; in placing
them in the context of *In Our Time,* Hemingway skilfully explains
the meaning of his title: in our time, he says in effect, a return to
the past of Nick's boyhood is never free of the shock and the
wound. Almost everything that happens to Nick Adams in the
stories seems accounted for simply; he has a way of adjusting to
the horror that penetrates his world from "the outside," or he can
get away from it—he can "get out of this town" or just "not think
about it." But in "Chapter Six" of *In Our Time* Nick himself experiences "the wound": "Nick sat against the wall of the church
where they had dragged him to be clear of machine-gun fire in
the street. Both legs stuck out awkwardly. He had been hit in the
spine." He talks to Rinaldi, who "lay face downward against the
wall," about the end of his commitment to the war, about his having paid his debt, and about his "separate peace."[7] All of *In Our
Time* is an early testimony to the powerful influence of "the unreasonable wound." The most important meaning of that book is
not its portrayal of a placid boyhood but the exercise of a sensibility profoundly changed by violence. Even the sparse symbolism
employed in the book contributes to that impression: the garden

wall, the "absolutely perfect obstacle," and the wall of the church
are alike in underscoring the helplessness of the war's circumstance; the rain falls grimly upon the refugees as they make their
way out of Adrianople, and upon the six cabinet ministers who
are shot against the wall of a hospital. At the end, we see not Nick
Adams but the war, not tradition and the church but the wall and
the rain; Nick's position against the wall of the church is an important sign of his initiation into the reality of the "outside"; a
wall usually suggests protection, but "in our time" it has become
an object to prevent safety and security.

A *Farewell to Arms* contains the fullest account of this kind of
death. Lieutenant Henry's wound is itself received in terms
roughly similar to those of Hemingway's actual experience. Very
important too are certain facts of the novel's war setting. Gorizia,
the "nice" town, with its hospitals, its cafés, its two brothels (one
reserved for the officers), its artillery "up side streets." The two
important ministers to the faith and security of the soldiers are the
priest and Rinaldi, the surgeon. Dominating the town are the
artillery pieces, which in the summer are "covered with green
branches" to disguise them as part of the landscape. In the mountains, at the front, they are hidden from view, and only the 'round
puffs' of smoke can be seen: "You saw the flash, then heard the
crack, then saw the smoke ball distort and thin in the wind."[8]
The guns, the surgeon and the brothels all act to reduce life at the
front to its secular minimum; in these circumstances the priest is
always "five against one," as Rinaldi says. It is hard, therefore, for
the priest's advice to be taken seriously; his remarks are not quite
like the patriotic phrases of the battle police, but they are heard
by Lieutenant Henry with embarrassment, and sometimes with
boredom. The most crucial of all Hemingway's explorations of the
military condition is his description of the retreat from Caporetto
(Book Three). The retreat begins in an orderly enough fashion,
but as it proceeds the sense of order dissolves. It becomes "unreasonable"; Italians fire on Italians; Germans break through the
lines; the *carabinieri* suspect impartially and kill the innocent. In
the landscape of unreason of which this section of the novel gives a
brilliant description, Lieutenant Henry loses all sense of personal
dedication to his fellow soldiers, abandons his feeling of responsibility to the army, and breaks out of the trap the war has laid for

him. From then on he links his fate with only a few persons, and they serve his emotional needs and protect him from dangers.

All of this does not, however, save him from ultimate defeat; it is important to see this defeat in terms of the "unreasonable wound" received earlier. The death of Catherine Barkley, however remote its setting from that of the war, is placed in sharp equation with the defeating and confusing terror of the war itself. The long, slow, almost monotonous life of waiting in Switzerland is designed to intensify the terror and bitterness of the final scene. The two deaths of that scene are an excruciating addition to the evidence of impersonal cruelty the novel as a whole provides. The child is stillborn and the mother dies in her attempt to give him life. Here there is no priest to speak of God and love; there is only the death and the rain outside on the walk back to the hotel. More important, Catherine's death is another example of the "unreasonable wound," more pathetic really because it defeats a plan to which Lieutenant Henry has irrevocably committed himself.

A Farewell to Arms affords a remarkably complete view of the "modern death" about which Miss Cather had been so critical. Superficially, Lieutenant Henry may be said to have had an "honourable choice" of two equally persuasive and practicable modes of action. Actually, the choices are neither persuasive nor practicable. The war itself gives only one kind of answer to the question posed by those living at its centre: the shock, the surprise, the helpless anger are present three times in the novel—when Lieutenant Henry is wounded, at the end of the retreat, and in Catherine's death in Switzerland. The setting of the war—of the guns hidden in the mountains and dealing impersonally in death—dominates Hemingway's fiction throughout the postwar decade. To this spectre priest, surgeon and other men of skill or good intention pay a futile and desperate heed, but adjustment to the violent and incalculable death which is its gift cannot be made with the help of any of them.

With the feeling that he must understand and honestly account for this condition, Hemingway came to Paris early in the 1920s to learn how to write; he found that the greatest difficulty, "aside from knowing truly what you really felt, rather than what you were supposed to feel, and had been taught to feel, was to put down what really happened in action; . . ." He wanted to begin with "the simplest things, and one of the simplest things of all and the most fundamental is violent death." The only place to see that happen, "now that the wars were over, was in the bullring . . ."[9] The consequences of this interest are testified to both in *Death in the Afternoon* (1932) and in *The Sun Also Rises* (1926). In the total design of the bullfight, as in its details of risk, grace, danger and death, Hemingway seems to have found the perfect palliative to the bewilderment and terror felt by the victims of the "unreasonable wound." The key to Hemingway's interest in the bullfight seems to be the artificial nature of its design; quite aside from the very real danger of death that it poses for the matador, it is true that he creates, manipulates, and controls that danger. It is the only art, he said in *Death in the Afternoon*, "in which the artist is in danger of death and in which the degree of brilliance in the performance is left to the fighter's honour."[10] Here there was nothing unreasonable; there were no surprises, no tragedies that could not be explained as the result of fear, ignorance, or mere gracelessness. Within the limitations imposed by usage and circumstance (tradition and "present danger"), it was possible to evaluate courage and virtue, "purity of line" and "grace under pressure." The bullfight had a simplified past and a continuous, ritualized present. It was above all possible to measure, to gauge, human emotions within a set of brilliantly formed "calculated risks." There is no doubt, also, that Hemingway was attracted to the simplicity of the matador-heroes, to their lack of sophistication, and to their constant preoccupation with the concrete details of their own task and craft. This simplicity of dedication—that is, among those fighters who were "the real thing"—when circumstances were right and when acts of grace and courage were sympathetically seen and understood, led to what for Hemingway was a meaningful ritual for his time, the most meaningful he was able to find during the first postwar decade.

The strength of his interest in Spain and in the bullfights is fully seen in the novel, *The Sun Also Rises*. This novel is a brilliant improvisation of a moral point of view, largely because of that interest. That the *corrida* was a specious resolution of postwar ills and that it could not, because of its artificiality, really take the place of religion or become a substitute tradition does not necessarily nullify its importance. The bullfight contributes both a criticism and a corrective to the persons involved in the atmosphere of postwar life. It is an ideal measure of that group's inadequacy; and, in the end, it profoundly influences certain persons and certain actions. The bullfight marked an ideal unity of specific detail with formal tradition, a unity lacking in the lives of the expatriates. The past had in the former case preserved a matador's naivety, his purity and his "honour"; the requirements of the fight itself meant that he had always to renew his caution, his skill and his courage, with each new appearance in the ring. While the procedures were largely fixed by tradition, there was nothing lifeless or mechanical or meaningless in any of them. The motion, the emotion and the action all formed a single figure that could be seen and shared by those who had understanding. In every detail this artificial pattern of behaviour, this aesthetic ordering of human risk and emotion, contrasts sharply with the lives of Jake Barnes and his friends.

The Sun Also Rises, in its attention to them, itemizes with an earnest exhaustiveness the consequences of "the unreasonable wound." That the wound should in this case have deprived Jake Barnes of his virility is at least in one sense an example of literary and moral economy. The sterility and perversion described in several of Hemingway's stories are intended as one insight into the postwar situation. In making Jake Barnes impotent through an "accident," Hemingway offers a comparable observation, while at the same time providing a pathos and terror like that of the last scenes of *A Farewell to Arms.* Jake tries for a constant limitation of his behaviour and judgment. He must always in his own personal and private life hold himself back, subdue his resentment and his anger, by excluding all "romantic effusion" and all abstract reasoning from his attitude, and thus face his death-in-life with all the courage and grace that are his to command. In this struggle for balance, Robert Cohn is an ever-present danger—a danger not unlike that risked by the "honest" matador who is tempted to give in to the "decadence" of his art. Whatever either Jake Barnes or Lady Brett does must fail to achieve an entirely satisfactory adjustment, except when it touches upon the world and art of the matador. Brett's release of Romero at the end is a fine, positive moral act, the only kind of which she is capable.

It is important to judge this novel on its own terms. Jake's private heroism and courage are admirable when put within the context of what Hemingway has described as "the real thing" in the bullfight. In the Paris scenes of the novel, this context is lacking and Hemingway here gives us the fullest description of the postwar equivalent of the landscape of unreason. The three acts of the bullfight are in themselves a quite artificial pattern, an adventitious ordering of human emotion and act, but there is no other. "The sun also ariseth, and the sun goeth down, and hasteth to the place where he arose. . . ."

From 1924 to 1932 Hemingway gave us in his writing the most compelling evidence of his concern over the 'unreasonable wound', his repeated efforts to review it and its consequences, to find a kind of balance between the inner terror caused by it and the outward need to survive. Since he could not call upon religion to provide that balance, he had to discover it in a context both secular and traditional. He has never since described the moral condition of postwar man with quite the same precision. Harry Morgan's dying is forced self-consciously into a social reference; Robert Jordan's heroics are too excessively and too deliberately placed within a context of affirmation; too much is made of his sacrifice and too little of himself. *For Whom the Bell Tolls* was, for Hemingway, an extremely important stage in the development of his point of view. In the 1920s he could not turn either to politics or to religion; but in the 1930s he found, in the Spanish Civil War, an ideal union of violence and meaning. Jordan's situation and his task both call for danger, almost certain death and an intimate life with Spaniards, a people whom Hemingway admired above all others. The death of Jordan is different from the wound suffered by Lieutenant Henry in every particular: it is not unexpected; Jordan is not unprepared for it; most important of all, it is given a specious meaning by Jordan's love for Maria and by his dedication to a cause. Hemingway found—to his own satisfaction at least—a significant and sufficient reason for violence and death, outside the bullring.

When we come to *Across the River and into the Trees* (1950), we discover an almost obsessive preoccupation with wounds and death. Since Hemingway had found in the 1930s and 1940s a meaning for the violence, a reason for the wound, the concern of his Colonel Cantwell with death becomes both sentimental and retrospective. The kneecap he had lost in the Italian war is now part of the land and has helped to make that land "sacred." He would like to be buried near it. Anyway, he reflects, after death you are of some use, "a sort of mulch, and even the bones will be of some use."[11] He can have no affection save for those who had fought in that first war, "where it all made sense," those "who had been there and had received the castigation that everyone receives who goes there long enough."[12] In this novel death is expected, and laborious preparations of feeling are made for it; love is pure and romantic, and the expectation of death adds a flavour of sentiment to it: food, drink, sights and savours provide the details of the sentiment. The Colonel does not die of violence or shock or even of treachery or the misfire of stratagem. Nor does he die Robert Jordan's kind of death; he is pathetic and not patently heroic, and the meaning of his career is buried in a mass of bitter and resentful reflection. He dies of a heart attack, for which the entire novel has provided a tedious preparation.

Among other distinctions, Hemingway can claim that of having honestly attempted an explanation of a form of death to which the twentieth century is peculiarly heir. It is a death that comes as a violent disruption of life. It is unreasonable (that is, it is not properly "motivated," cannot be understood in terms of any ordinary system of motivation). It puts traditional securities to shame, since they cannot satisfactorily keep pace with its indiscriminate destructiveness. It demands a new form of resourcefulness and courage, and—in Hemingway's case—a new type of moral improvisation. The sudden and violent injury inflicted impersonally upon its victim by efficient guns or planes too remote from him to "hold him any special grudge" is the symbol of this type of death and of the death-in-life which is its consequence.

The problem of this death remains unsolved. "We died on the wrong page of the almanac," says the narrator of Randall Jarrell's poem, "Losses," who then reflects upon a kind of death even more impersonalized than that suffered in the Italian retreat of *A Farewell to Arms*. "When we died they said, 'Our casualities were low.'" The individual death is absorbed into a statistical estimate, and it involves the kind of ironical official notice that Hemingway uses at the end of chapter two of *A Farewell to Arms*: "At the start of the winter came the permanent rain and with the rain came the cholera. But it was checked and in the end only seven thousand died of it in the army."[13] Jarrell's poem underscores the persistence of this "unreasonable wound" in modern morality and literature. It was Hemingway's task to describe its circumstance and to give it its first and most incisive literary statement and judgment.

NOTES

1. *Death Comes for the Archbishop*, New York, 1927, p. 194.

2. *Not Under Forty*, New York, 1936, p. 73.

3. *One of Ours*, New York, p. 458.

4. "A Portrait of Mister Papa," in *Ernest Hemingway: The Man and His Work*, ed. J. K. M. McCaffery, New York, 1950, p. 47. First published *Life*, January 10th, 1949.

5. "The Missing All," in *ibid.*, p. 302. First published, *The Virginia Quarterly Review*, Winter 1937.

6. "In Our Time," in *The Viking Portable Hemingway*, edited by Malcolm Cowley, New York, 1944, p. 376. First published, 1925.

7. *The Viking Portable Hemingway*, p. 387.

8. *A Farewell to Arms*, New York, 1929, p. 192.

9. *Death in the Afternoon*, New York, 1932, p. 2.

10. *Ibid.*, p. 91.

11. *Across the River and into the Trees*, New York, 1950, p. 35.

12. *Ibid.*, pp. 60 and 71.

13. *A Farewell to Arms*, p. 4.

R. W. B. Lewis

XXI

The Hero in the New World: William Faulkner's The Bear[1]

If, as several of Faulkner's most enlightened observers have suggested, the novels and stories preceding *Go Down Moses* possess an atmosphere like that of the Old Testament, then *The Bear* may be regarded as Faulkner's first sustained venture towards the more hopeful and liberated world after the Incarnation. It is also of course a story about the South in the 1880's, when the frontier was rapidly disappearing. And it is another American *bildungsroman,* another tale of a boy growing up in America, with all the special obstacles to moral maturity which our culture has erected and which comprise the drama for many another sad or lucky protagonist of fiction. We must not forget that *The Bear* is grounded in these historic and locally traditional elements. But we should say at the outset that in it we meet Faulkner's first full-fledged hero— and that he is a young man who quite deliberately takes up carpentering because

> if the Nazarene had found carpentering good for the life and ends He had assumed and elected to serve, it would be all right too for Isaac McCaslin.

The Bear is a canticle or chant relating the birth, the baptism and the early trials of Isaac McCaslin; it is ceremonious in style, and

From *The Kenyon Review,* Vol. XIII, 1951, pp. 641–60. Copyright 1951 by *The Kenyon Review.* Reprinted by permission of the author and periodical. Another version of this essay appears in Mr. Lewis's *The Picaresque Saint,* published in 1959 by the J. B. Lippincott Co.

it is not lacking in dimly seen miraculous events. We get moreover *an* incarnation, if not *the* Incarnation: or at least we get a reincarnation; and we witness an act of atonement which may conceivably flower into a redemption.

Consequently *The Bear* is a pivotal work. Change is of its essence. Our notion about it is reinforced when we encounter the same reanimated human will at work and a still larger conviction of human freedom in the novel which followed it, *Intruder in the Dust*. In both stories, but much more spectacularly and indeed much more visibly in *The Bear*, what is positive in human nature and in the moral structure of the world envelops and surrounds what is evil; which is to say, more significantly, that the corrupting and the destructive and the desperate in human experience become known to us in their opposition and even their subordination to the creative and the soul-preserving. This presents us with just the sort of dramatic clarity that seems otherwise denied to writers for almost a century. The highest reaches of modern literature, in fact, have taken the form of an ultimate and vibrant duplicity, the best account of our times that honest genius has been empowered to construct—with every virtue and every value rendered instantly suspect by the ironic co-existence of its opposite: Ahab and Starbuck, and all their fellows, in a never-ending exchange of the reader's allegiance. We have known these splendid discords and artful confusions in the early novels of William Faulkner: which is why *The Bear* appears as pivotal; although it is as likely to appear merely old-fashioned, and to be regretted—the way *Billy Budd* is sometimes regretted—as a regression to lucidity.

It is true, and worth pausing over for a moment, that in those earlier novels as well a not entirely dissimilar ethical distribution can be alleged. *As I Lay Dying*, for example, and *Light in August* have been compared to Jacobean drama; presumably with the thought that they are projections of worlds wherein what is human or decent or pure flickers uncertainly in a darkness charged with violence and horror; the horror and the darkness being the norm, and the measure of such pitiful virtue as stirs feebly to combat them. But even there, something more ancient and enduring, something more substantial than the central tragic characters and their wicked propensities flows through them and reaffirms itself at the end as it flows on into the future. And this is what, with a wry face, we have to call life itself. The grimace is due to the form in which life re-exerts itself: a new set of false teeth, in *As I Lay Dying,* a new wife for Anse Bundren: "a kind of duck-shaped woman all dressed up, with them kind of hard-looking pop eyes like she was daring ere a man to say nothing"; an illegitimate child, which Dewey Dell has not found the medical means to get rid of. Life in *Light in August* is personified on the first and the last pages by Lena Grove, moving calmly and with animal obstinacy across a stage littered elsewhere with depravity and death, carrying in her womb her own bastard child, to be born on the other side of town. But it would scarcely be honest to describe either novel as a drama of the triumph of life: the design in each case is, if anything, a tension between creative and destructive possibilities.

In *The Bear,* however, the balance is tipped. What we discover first, along with young Ike McCaslin, and what determines his and our subsequent judgments is an archetypal or ideal human personality. It is something composed of a cluster of virtues unambiguously present from the beginning, as qualities to be striven for, prizes to be won: proving their efficacy in the mastery of self and the conquest of temptation—pity and humility and courage and pride and the will to endure and the rest. Their names recur with musical regularity, like the burden of a song. And together they are what we may call the honorable: something Roman and a trifle stiff, but independent of the fluctuation of moral fashions in the city. It is the honorable which permeates the wilderness, scene of the main action and home of the main actors in the story. And like Old Ben, the bear, patriarch of the wilderness, embodying the virtues in some undefined and magical way, the honorable exists as an ethical reality before the story opens, "before the boy was born": as a glimpse of immortality. It is an ideal prior to civilization, but it is not an uncivilized ideal and has nothing to do with noble savagery; it is prior exactly insofar as it is ideal, not so much older as timeless; and taking the humanly recognizable shape of a ritual pattern of behavior. The narrative image of that pattern is "the yearly rendez-vous," "the yearly pageant-rite of the old bear's furious immortality": the annual duel between the skilled hunters and the shaggy, tremendous, indomitable Old Ben. It is a duel enacted within a solid set of conventions and rules, faultlessly observed on both sides. This is the ritual by participation in which the young hero, Isaac McCaslin, becomes reborn and baptized, receives the sacramental blessing and accomplishes his moral liberation. It is the substance of the first half of the story; in a sense I will suggest later, it is the whole of the story; the rest of the book tells us how a properly baptized and educated hero may act when confronted with evil.

But it is evident that in order to explain these remarks and to see more deeply into the total experience, we must examine the experience in its only exact and living form. We must, that is, look more closely at the story's structure.

II

The difficulty of any Faulkner story lies in the order of its telling. He has always provided us with lots of action; and if his unconventional arrangement of incidents sometimes suggests an antic shuffle through a fateful crazy-house, it does at least avoid the other extreme in modern fiction: it never dissolves into atmosphere and "situation." What *happens* in a Faulkner story is more important than anything else; but it is the last thing we understand— we are let in on it gradually, from many different viewpoints and at different times. *The Bear* has a plot relatively simpler than, say, *The Sound and the Fury:* but here also Faulkner has played weird tricks with chronology. In particular, he has concluded his narrative with an episode that occurs at a moment earlier in conventional time than one of the chief episodes which precede it in the telling. If we follow the events in the life of Isaac McCaslin rather than the numerical sequence of the sections, we discover this personal history:

(Sections One, Two, Three) A boy named Ike McCaslin grows up in Mississippi, during the years after the Civil War. Every year from the time he is ten, he goes bear-hunting in the still untracked wilderness north of the town, along with his cousin Cass and some of the town's leading citizens—all highly skilled hunters. He gradually acquires some of the skill of the older men, and the virtues that are the product of so severe and masculine a life. There is one bear, greater and older than any of the others, who engages the hunters in an annual duel. He is called Old Ben. When the boy is sixteen, Old Ben is killed by one of the men and a huge mongrel dog.

(Section Five) After Old Ben's death, the boy, now eighteen, comes back once to the wilderness, but the old hunting-lodge is gone, the group of hunters broken up, and tourists have begun to invade and transform the forest. He encounters Boon Hogganbeck, the man who had killed Old Ben, and finds him reduced to hysteria.

(Section Four) At the age of twenty-one, Ike inherits the land and money that have been passed down through his father (known as Uncle Buck) from his grandfather, Carrothers McCaslin. Ike decides to give up this inheritance, since he had previously discovered that it is tainted at the source by the misdeeds of his grandfather. The latter had seduced and had a child by a negress slave, Tomasina, who may well have been his own daughter also. Such a combination of incest and miscegenation represents for Ike an image of the evil condition of the South—and of humanity in general from the beginning of time. Ike determines not to compromise with this condition. He continues to live a simple, somewhat Christ-like existence. He takes up carpentering and marries the daughter of his partner. He has no children.

Thus the "real life" equivalent of the career of Ike McCaslin; but we must keep in mind, during the remarks that follow, that we come upon the incidents of his twenty-first year and of his later years *before* we are told about the return to the woods, at eighteen, in the fifth section.

André Gide, when he was writing *The Counterfeiters*, confided to his journal an ambition to render the events of his novel *légèrement déformés*, so that the reader's interest might be aroused in the effort to restore the originals: the reader becoming thereby the author's collaborator. Faulkner's motive may be much the same; his so-called contempt for the reader (and others have made the point) has the effect anyhow of involving the reader nearly to the extent of devouring him. Certainly no other American writer engages his readers so strenuously; and there is no doubt that, except for those who fear and resent him on quite other grounds, the readers of Faulkner do or can derive immense aesthetic pleasure in that participation with him that verges on the creative. Homer and Virgil (not to mention Conrad, or the Russians) ask no less of us. *The Odyssey,* for example, indicates importance by the chronological order of presentation, and we can only assess the famous wanderings of Odysseus when we notice that they are not given us directly but as they issue much later from the memory of a gifted liar: much, though Ike is no liar, as the revelations of evil exist primarily in the young man's memory. And in the *Aeneid* of

Virgil (a poet much closer to Faulkner), the last event in the poem occurs many centuries before some of the events already described in it. Here of course the grandiose history of the ages to come appears explicitly as a prophecy, and almost as a dream: but I am willing to suggest that such may also be the nature of the fourth section in *The Bear*.

Before we get that far, however, a few mechanical observations may be helpful. It is worth seeing that the fourth section has the same purely formal organization and is roughly the same in length as the first three combined: this suggests, rightly, that it has the function of counter-weight. Both of these two large parts begin at a certain moment in Ike's life (16 and 21 respectively), retreat to an earlier period and circle back through their starting-points. The recurring insistence of Faulkner upon his hero's age is too striking to be overlooked: a whispering connivance, like a plea: "He was sixteen then . . . then he was sixteen." Ike's age is the chief structural element; and his sixteenth year was the *annus mirabilis:* the story flows through that year on three distinct occasions, as though only by this means could the contradictory richness of its experience be made apparent.

This aspect of the structure can be presented graphically, while not forgetting the many warnings against draining away Faulkner's vitality in cold schemas.

The graph suggests, at least, the very considerable artfulness that governs Faulkner's temporal re-arrangements; if we have survived the shock of the initial disorder, we can admire the elegance and symmetry in the redistribution. The solid lines are of course the sustained narrative, and the broken lines the more rapid shifts in time: even these, however, not so much sudden leaps across the years as a fading backward of memory or a surge forward of imagination. But while we are aware of strong currents carrying us forward and backward in *The Bear,* we must also acknowledge the corollary impression that time is motionless, and everything is occurring simultaneously. This effect Faulkner achieves by bringing in past events as they are returned to in present memory: by parentheses, and by parentheses within those parentheses, like one memory jogging another. He achieves it too, in his narrative order, by the triple journey through the sixteenth year. *The Bear* thus constitutes (as the graph may dimly show)a unique conjunction of time and eternity: if we accept the word of Boethius, who distinguished between them as between a flowing-away and a standing-still.

The story begins in Ike's sixteenth year. It would have to, because it is Ike's story, and it is only then that his history ceases to be mysterious; it is only then that he completes the ritual of his initiation. Till that moment he had grasped the importance but not fully the meaning of the experience.

> It seemed to him there was a fatality in it. It seemed to him that something, he didn't know what, was beginning; had already begun. It was like the last act on a set stage. It was the beginning of the end of something, he didn't know what except that he would not grieve. He would be humble and proud that he had been found worthy to be a part of it or even just to see it too.

The drama he is engaged in is the drama of death and birth, and this is what he is disciplined to perceive as the story returns, in part three, to the great year: the death of Old Ben, of Sam Fathers, of Lion—and of the wilderness as wilderness and the companionship Ike had known there; and the birth of Isaac McCaslin as the reincarnation of those dead and the witness of that world. We might almost say that Old Ben dies in child-birth; he has many features in common with the "terrible mother" of many heroic myths; and the name of Sam Fathers is in no way accidental. It requires only the slightest twist of the tongue to convert the story's title into "The Birth."

Then, finally, we find out in the fourth section, if we submit ourselves to its spell, that it is in his sixteenth year also, on a December night after the last bear-hunt, that Ike solves the riddle of his family's history. That section begins with the sentence, ominously uncapitalized: "then he was twenty-one;" and the defining occasion of most of it is a conversation between Ike and his cousin Cass Edmonds in the plantation commissary on what appears to be Ike's twenty-first birthday; but, while the entire span of Ike's eighty-year-long life is touched on, it is specifically the discoveries of his sixteenth year that account for the intensity of Ike's speech and the resoluteness of his decision to give up his inheritance. With the conversation as foreground, those discoveries pass through Ike's memory like shadows on the wall behind—shadows themselves engaged in ghostly conversation; for they appear as remembered entries in the commissary ledgers, written in a question-and-answer manner. The very language of the entries—made several decades earlier by Ike's uncle and father, and agonizingly pieced together by Ike five years before the present moment—has the sparseness and the foreshortened quality of a memory.

> Uncle Buck: "Eunice Bought by Father in New Orleans 1807 650 dolars. Marrid to Thucydus 1809 Drowned in Crick Cristmas Day 1832."
> Uncle Buddy: "June 21th 1833 Drowned herself."
> Uncle Buck: "23 Jun 1833 Who in hell ever heard of a niger drownding herself."
> Uncle Buddy: "Aug. 13th Drownd herself."

The motivation for Eunice's suicide is revealed to us through its implications, in the shape it assumes in Ike's oddly mythopoetic imagination. It is up to us, participants in the hunt, to discover that Eunice had been the mistress of the grandfather, Carrothers

McCaslin, and bought by him and married to "Thucydus" when she was pregnant with the child Tomasina; and that Eunice drowned herself when she realized that her daughter was pregnant by her lover. For Ike, the tragic event has the fixed formality of legend:

> He seemed to see her actually walking into the icy creek on that Christmas day six months before her daughter's and her lover's (*Her first lover's,* he thought. *Her first*) child was born, solitary, inflexible, griefless, ceremonial, in formal and succinct repudiation of grief and despair, who had already had to repudiate belief and hope.

The first essential link between the first three and the fourth sections is the literal near-simultaneity of the death of Old Ben and the discovery of mixed blood in the McCaslin clan. But the relationship is a good deal more organic than that; the fourth section of *The Bear* ought not to be taken (as I am afraid it sometimes is taken) as merely the further adventures of Isaac McCaslin. We appreciate the harmony of the parts when we begin to describe the two different moments in ancient formulae: the birth into virtue and the vision of evil. For only a person adequately baptized is capable of having the vision at all; and only the grace bestowed at the baptism enables the initiate to withstand the evil when it is encountered. The action in Section Four is made possible by the experience preceding it: the ritual in the wilderness *contains* the decision in the commissary.

And this leads us into a somewhat more complex view of the relationship. For it is quite exact to say that the whole of the fourth section is contained within the sections which have the wilderness as their setting: this is the unmistakable effect accomplished when Faulkner concludes the story with a short section which returns to the forest, returns to the life of Ike before he is twenty-one, returns to the atmosphere and the rhythms of the hunting world. The fifth section reverts too to the style—relatively straightforward, though highly orchestrated and charged with autumnal splendor—of the first, second and third: picking up that style where it had been left almost sixty pages before, and so enveloping and containing the style in between. The difference is shown by quoting the last lines of section four and the first of

section five—breaking in anywhere on the endlessly flowing
sentence of the former:

> and on their wedding night she had cried and he thought she was
> crying now at first, into the tossed and wadded pillow, the voice
> coming from somewhere between the pillow and the cacchinations:
> 'And that's all. That's all from me. If this don't get you that son you
> talk about, it won't be mine': lying on her side, her back to the empty
> rented room, laughing and laughing.
>
> He went back to the camp one more time before the lumber com-
> pany moved in and began to cut the timber. Major de Spain himself
> never saw it again.

Faulkner has even gone to the extreme of employing the single
inverted comma in the conversations of the fourth section: the
conventional sign of the speech contained within the speech—as
against the double comma elsewhere. It is the sort of device that
is peculiarly trying for those not already persuaded by Faulkner;
but it is another instance of his anxiety that we should recognize
the mode of existence of this moment in the experience.

For what we are given in the fourth section is essentially not
a narrative of past events, but a vision of the future. We can
justify its appearance between the third and the fiifth sections—
between, that is, episodes of Ike's sixteenth and his eighteenth
years—by thinking of it as a dream; perhaps, though this is not
necessary, a dream in the year between. It is a true dream to be
sure, issuing securely from the gate of horn, but passing before our
eyes events which, at this moment of perception, exist only in a
state of possibility. A condition of potentiality, as of something not
yet fully realized, is carried in the prose itself. We are struck at
once by the decrease in visibility: on an immeasurably vast setting,
actions and dialogue have curiously hazy outlines; sentences spray
out in all directions, rarely reaching (within our hearing) their
probable periods. Everything is unfinished, incomplete. But the
experience is not a *mere* possibility, in the sense that its opposite is
equally possible; for we have to reckon here with Faulkner's
implicit theories of time and destiny, according to which all events
are pre-determined and so can be said to exist and to be seen as
taking place simultaneously. To see them this way is to assume the

divine viewpoint, as Mme. Magny has observed; divine also, as she does not go on to say, because Faulkner manages—in *The Bear* anyhow—to detect a modicum of human liberty within the grand design: as though not discontent with the ancient and irresolvable paradox of fixity and freedom. Thus the events are certain, but they are not yet; and so they are not clearly to be distinguished by a human perception fully competent only with the past.

Something like this fourth section is probably as close as contemporary fiction can come to that moment in the traditional career of the hero when he descends into the dark underworld, encounters his ancestry and has a vision of the future. We have become skeptical of prophecy; we no longer project spiritual darkness in such simple geographic terms. But here, as Ike see his inevitable moral decision and its determination in the vast sweep of human history, we partake again of that transfiguring moment narrated already by Homer in *Odyssey* XI and by Virgil in *Aeneid* VI.

III

It is a very long way from Mississippi to ancient Rome and Greece, and no doubt it is time now to remember the national and provincial boundaries within which Ike's initiation is undertaken. For like *Moby Dick*, *The Bear* is most in tune with primary and perennial rhythms of experience when it is most explicitly American. The content of its story is drawn from that imaginary world inhabited also by many of the heroes of Hawthorne and Melville, and much more recently of F. Scott Fitzgerald. And if we close in more sharply on the particular portion of America that provides the image for its dramatic scene (as, in *The Divine Comedy*, we must remember Florence as well as Italy in general), we recognize the most significant prototype of *The Bear* in *Huckleberry Finn*. Both are narratives of boys growing up in the 19th Century southwest; but the essence of the analogy lies, of course, in their common sense of the kinship between white and black, in their common identification of slavery as a kind of original sin, in their common reversal of the conventional morality that legitimizes social injustice. Faulkner, characteristically, carries the inter-racial kinship literally into the blood streams: Ike and Tennie's Jim are cousins in fact as well as brothers in the spirit of humanity; and also characteristically, Faulkner intrudes a lecture on social legislation, with a warning to the national government up north to keep its hands off the problems of the south—while Mark Twain never exposes Huck Finn to the danger of a pretentious awareness of his own virtue. But both novelists, while telling again the most familiar of stories, confront their heroes with the trials peculiar to the southerner before and just after the Civil War: especially, the challenge of negro slavery.

The central poetic insight, however, which Faulkner shares with Mark Twain and many another American writer is something larger: it is an insight into the fertile and ambiguous possibility of moral freedom in the new world. In the Mississippi wilderness of the eighteen-seventies and -eighties, Faulkner has projected another compelling image, so striking elsewhere in American fiction, of the ethically undefined: undefined, that is—like the river in *Huckleberry Finn* and the sea in *Moby Dick*—only in the sense of not yet fixed in the implicitly hypocritical conventions of "civilized" life. The frontier, as Turner and Constance Rourke were the first to make clear, was the major physical source of this uniquely American idea: the idea, I mean, of a new, unspoiled area in which a genuine and radical moral freedom could once again be exercised—as once, long ago, it had been, in the garden of Eden; and Faulkner locates his image in time at the very moment when the frontier was disappearing. Insofar as *The Bear* is a story about death, it is about the death of the frontier-world; and to a very limited degree it may be regarded as a narrative enactment of the historic development elaborated in Turner's famous essay. But to say so without qualification would be to ascribe to Faulkner a view of innocence quite the opposite of that finally revealed in *The Bear;* and it would be to forget how often Faulkner, like Hawthorne and Melville, has engaged in the ritual slaughter of the animal innocent.

A part of the history Ike McCaslin rehearses for Cass Edmonds seems to echo the comfortable story optimistic Americans were telling each other a century ago.

> [God] made the earth first and peopled it with dumb creatures, and then He created man to be His overseer on the earth and to hold suzerainty over the earth and the animals on it in His name, not to hold for himself and his descendants inviolable title forever . . . . and all the fee He asked was pity and humility and endurance. . . . He

watched it. And let me say it. Dispossessed of Eden. Dispossessed
of Canaan and those who . . . devoured their ravished substance
ravished in turn again and then snarled in what you call the old
world's worthless twilight over the old world's gnawed bones, blasphemous in His name until He used a simple egg to discover to them a
new world where a nation of people could be founded in humility and
pity and sufferance and pride of one to another.

Such an identification of the new world as a divinely offered
second chance for humanity, after the first opportunity had been
so thoroughly muffed, can be matched in countless editorials and
orations: especially during the generation before the Civil War.
But Faulkner's hero is examining the myth to see where it went
wrong; and he concludes, not that the new world is devoid of evil,
but that evil was brought into it with the first settlers, "as though
in the sailfuls of the old world's tainted wind which drove the
ships." It was the evil of slavery; and beneath it and responsible
for it, the sin of spiritual pride. Ike McCaslin is the first of Faulkner's
characters to understand American history.

He can do so because he is free—or rather, because he has
achieved freedom. He is even, we may say, innocent: but in a
crucially new sense. For the quality of innocence undergoes a
profound dialectical transformation in *The Bear*. The nature of the
dialectic is indicated very forcefully in the opening sentences:

> There was a man and a dog too this time. Two beasts counting Old
> Ben, the bear, and two men, counting Boon Hogganbeck, in whom
> some of the same blood ran which ran in Sam Fathers, even though
> Boon's was a plebeian strain of it and only Sam and Old Ben and the
> mongrel Lion were taintless and incorruptible.

Taintless, in a new sense, for Lion is a mongrel and Sam (we know
this also from "A Justice") is the half-breed offspring of a negress
slave and a Chickasaw Indian. But in the moral world of *The Bear*
a primary purity, fundamentally materialistic and suggested by
the physical purity of the land, is transcended as a dangerous
illusion; and for it there is substituted a purity and a freedom
much tougher and far more durable. This innocence is an achievement, not merely a gift; it is gained through discipline and
submission, it is announced in a ritual. This innocence is nothing
else than conscience itself.

Now conscience is the mark of maturity; and, exactly because of the historical illusion so tenaciously clung to, conscience has been something not often reached without the intervention of tragedy, in the American literature of education: consider Donatello and Billy Budd and Jay Gatsby. Isaac's achievement is the achievement of his creator, working an astonishing alchemical change on specifically American materials: converting not only history into art, but illusion into reality, and converting qualities like innocence from a lower to a higher order of value. In order to see the magnitude of this change—of the transmutation of values on which the story rests—we must move into a somewhat more expansive vocabulary than we have employed so far.

Faulkner himself is most willing, too willing perhaps, that we should recognize the universal design into which his southern saga fits; he plants, if anything, too many clues to his wider ranges of meaning. Nonetheless *The Bear* is his masterpiece in this respect: it is his most successful attempt to accommodate to each other in a single narrative the various accounts of themselves that the world and man can give. The fusion has been strained and uneven heretofore; but now it is as though Faulkner, the artist, had like his hero Ike discovered the unity of meaning. And so, while grounded historically and built out of the moral dilemmas which the history gave rise to, *The Bear* no less impressively reflects a timeless psychic drama. It is indeed a treasure-chest for psychologists in criticism (among whom I do not very warmly count myself), for object after object that are known to be recurring symbols in the dream legends of the unconscious are scattered throughout the story: the forest, the tree, the rifle, the bear, and a score of others. The great adventure in which these objects play such a prominent part is quite plainly that transformation of character which is like a second birth, and which some psychologists refer to as the return to the womb; as Faulkner is careful we should see: "It seemed to [Ike] that at the age of ten he was witnessing his own birth." "The birth of the hero," Carl Jung concludes from his survey of world-mythology, "is not that of an ordinary mortal, but is a re-birth from the mother-spouse . . . because only through her does he share in immortality." The second mother is often an animal, Jung assures us, and may be one normally thought of as male: like Hiawatha's mother who first appeared as the Great Bear of the Mountains. Ike first shares in Old Ben's "furious immortality"

during that extraordinary episode, like a dream in color, when he
penetrates the heart of the forest, finds the (sacred) tree, manifests
his submission by abandoning first his gun and then his watch and
his compass: until, stripped of hostility and outside of time, he
stands in the presence of the wilderness god. It is a liberating experience, as the return to the womb (or any well-organized education) is supposed to be. But final freedom comes only with the
death of the parents: for Ike, of Sam Fathers and Old Ben; and then
he is prepared to meet the challenge of maturity. Traditionally in
this phase of the psychic journey, the hero moves, in the words of
Joseph Campbell, "in a dream landscape of curiously fluid, ambiguous forms, where he must survive a succession of trials." It is
an apt description of the fourth section.

Yet if Old Ben does have some of the qualities of the "terrible
mother" in the myth of the hero, he is at the same time the embodiment of the courage and chivalry and the will to endure
which are shaping elements in the honorable. He is "not
malevolent, just big"; and if in one of the most extraordinary
verbal achievements in modern literature we hear of "the legend"
about him: "corncribs broken . . . shoats and grown pigs and even
calves carried bodily into the woods and devoured . . . dogs
mangled and slain . . . a corridor of wreckage and destruction"—
still, Old Ben emerges from this epic portrait by way of a comparison with Priam, King of Troy. Priam, we remember, was the
ruler of the old citadel and was destroyed with it; but one warrior
survived him, Aeneas, his nephew and we may say his foster-child,
who after many trials established a new kingdom in a new country. I do not say that all this is packed into Faulkner's single
allusion; but I suggest that we are closer to the archetypal image
reproduced in *The Bear* if we think of it as a pattern of redemption
in terms of the ultimate forces in the world (like the *Aeneid*), rather
than a dream projection mirroring interior psychic conflicts. And
in identifying the pattern, we do well to look carefully at the
nature and use of *power* within it.

Power is often symbolized, in the heroic myth, by the character of the hero's "magic weapon," and the use to which he puts
it: and we can contemplate a significant range from the great bow
of Odysseus, with which he ruthlessly slays a houseful of political
and domestic rivals, to St. Martin of Tours, telling the pagan

Emperor that "Armed only with the Cross, in the forefront of the enemy, I will fear no evil." Aeneas enters his supreme battle wearing a shield on which is engraved the histories and the triumphs to come of the Roman people; it is a recorded destiny which renders him invulnerable to the mightiest of the Latins. In *Moby Dick,* Ahab forges a tremendous harpoon for the final hunt (in a scene consciously modelled on similar moments in Homer and Virgil), and he baptizes it "Not in the name of the father, but in the name of the devil"—the book's secret motto, Melville said later: the secret source of Ahab's strength; and the harpoon is the instrument of his own violent death. For Isaac McCaslin there is the rifle, and much is made of it. First, a rifle too large for him, a man's weapon in a boy's hands, which he can no more handle than can Telemachus his father's bow; and then at ten years, the year of his first communion with Old Ben, he receives "his own gun . . . a new breech-loader, a Christmas gift." "He would own it and shoot it for almost seventy years." The imagery of the gun is diffused through the story; it becomes one of the central unifying symbols. Ike has two occasions on which he might use his rifle against Old Ben: the first time, he abandons it in order to present himself in evident humility to the bear; the second time, he throws it away and risks his life in the charitable act of rescuing the little fyce.

This, I believe, is the essential symbolic movement of the story (it was the conclusion, in the original short version of *The Bear*), and it is not surprising that this, of all incidents, is remembered and re-examined in the fourth section when Ike is expressing his insight into history and his own historic role. For what we comprehend at last in *The Bear* is the transmutation of power into charity. No loss of power is effected; but it suffers a rich sea-change, it comes under the control of moral understanding; grace enters into it. More concretely: Ike does not give up his gun altogether; on the contrary, we have swift previews of him in later years as the greatest hunter in Yoknapatawpha County; but he uses his power with restraint and fidelity, and for a life lived as closely as possible to the source of his moral energy. It is what he gains from that source that makes the life possible and makes Ike what he is: a Christ-like person with some ineradicable southern biases. It is a dimensional increase of perception, and through this also Ike is uniquely capable of reading the past correctly. The total change at work in *The Bear* may thus, in these various respects, be compared to the transition from the pagan to the Christian era, if not from the Old to the New Testament.

History became readable, according to most apologists, when meaning was put into it at the moment of the Incarnation. Now what has been most striking in Faulkner's earlier novels has been just that endless, hopeless fumbling in the past, that obsessive struggle for its meaning by constant re-arrangements of its content: which seem the only resource of a person or a people from whom the gift of illumination has been so far withheld. From this point of view, the repeated attacks of Quentin Compson on the history of his country may be fruitfully contrasted with the disciplined exposition of Isaac McCaslin, and Quentin's suicide with Ike's honorable long career. This is not to say that Ike is intended to represent Christ in a second coming, but only that Ike moves in a world of light—a light still meagre but definite; a new world in which values have been confirmed by being raised to a higher power; not the new world beyond the frontier—that is precisely what is transcended—but a world so perpetually new that Ike sometimes seems to be its only living inhabitant. It is worth insisting that the life of Christ is not under any circumstances a subject for fiction: not at all because it would be irreverent, but because within the limits of literature it would be impossible. But *The Bear* does as much as literature may with propriety try to do: it enacts for us, by means of human individuals in a local habitation, the miracle of moral regeneration.

NOTES

1. The longest and richest component in the collection of stories about the McCaslin family, *Go Down Moses* (1942).

Alfred Kazin

XXII

The Stillness of Light in August

Light in August begins unforgettably with a pregnant young woman from Alabama sitting beside a road in Mississippi, her feet in a ditch, her shoes in her hand, watching a wagon that is mounting the hill toward her with a noise that carries for a half-mile "across the hot still pinewiney silence of the August afternoon." She has been on the road for a month, riding in a long succession of farm wagons or walking the hot dusty roads with her shoes in her hand, trying to get to Jefferson. There, she firmly expects, she will find her lover working in a planing mill and ready to marry her, and there—that is the big city—she will put her shoes on at last.

This opening chapter, so dry and loving in its pastoral humor, centering on the picture of Lena and her precious burden being carried in one wagon or another, by one farmer after another, to her hoped-for destination in a husband, ends sharply on the outskirts of Jefferson, from which she can see smoke going up from a burning house. It is the house of Joanna Burden, who has just been murdered by Joe Christmas. And the images that have been crowding us with the dust and the heat of the unend-

Reprinted from *Twelve Original Essays on Great American Novels,* Charles Shapiro, Ed., by permission of the Wayne State University Press. Copyright 1957 by Wayne State University Press.

ing road—with Lena continually amazed at how far a body can
go, the serenity of the deserted young woman whose face is "calm
as a stone, but not hard," the "sharp and brittle crack and clatter"
of the "wagon's weathered and ungreased wood and metal," the
identical and anonymous wagons, the mules plodding in a steady
and unflagging hypnosis, the drowsy heat of the afternoon; with
Lena's faded blue dress, her palm leaf fan, her small cloth bundle
in which she carries thirty-five cents in nickels and dimes; with the
shoes that she takes off and carries in her hand as soon as she feels
the dust of the road beneath her feet—all provide us with that
foundation in the local and the provincial, the earth and the road
which man must travel on it, against which are set images of fire
and murder, of aimless wandering and of flight, embodied in the
figure who soon enters the book and dominates it in his remorseless gray anonymity. Joe Christmas does not even have a name of
his own, only a mocking label stuck on him at the orphanage
where he was deposited one Christmas eve. "Joe Christmas" is
worse than any real name could be, for it indicates not only that
he has no background, no roots, no name of his own, but that he
is regarded as a *tabula rasa,* a white sheet of paper on which anyone can write out an identity for him and make him believe it.

It is the contrast of Lena Grove and Joe Christmas, of the
country girl and the American wanderer, who is a stranger even
to himself, the ultimate personification in modern loneliness, that
frames the book—literally so, since Lena Grove begins and ends
it, while Joe Christmas's agony and crucifixion are enacted as
within a circle round which he runs in an effort to catch up with
himself. When he finds that he cannot run out of this circle and
stands still at last in order to die, the book comes back to Lena
Grove and ends on her ritualistic procession up the road with her
baby and Byron Bunch—Faulkner's version of the Holy Family.
By the time we have finished *Light in August,* we have come to feel
that the real greatness of Faulkner in this book (and indeed of his
extraordinary compassion) lies in the amazing depth which he
brings to this contrast of which American writers are so fond,
particularly in Southern writing, between the natural and the
urban, between Lena Grove's simplicity and the forces personified
by Joe Christmas's walking all smooth city pavements with the
same isolation and indifference, eating at the coldly smooth

wooden counter, and murder. Faulkner even leads up to a strange
and tortured fantasy of Joe Christmas as Lena Grove's still unnamed son. There is virtually an annunication to Lena, in the
moving last phase of the book when Lena, delivered of her child
just as Joe Christmas is running for his life, hears Mrs. Hines,
Christmas's grandmother, calling the baby "Joey"—he who is a
"nigger" murderer, and whom Lena has never seen. The reader
comes to this with a shock, only because of Faulkner's reckless,
desperate eagerness to wrest all the possible implications from his
material, to think it out interminably, since there is no end to all
one's possible meditations round and round the human cycle. One
of the conflicts of which the book is made—between life and anti-
life, between the spirit of birth and the murderous abstractions
and obsessions which drive most of the characters—is in Faulkner
himself, in his attempt to will his painful material into a kind of
harmony that it does not really possess.

But in any event, it is Lena who opens the book, Lena's world,
Lena's patience, that set the ideal behind the book—that world of
the permanent and the natural which Joe Christmas seeks all his life
without knowing that he does, and seeking it, will run full tilt into
the ground. "Light in August" is itself a country saying: Light as
a mare or a cow is light after delivery. And it is this world of Lena
Grove from Doane's Mill—the tiny hamlet which was too small
for any post-office list; yet even Lena, living in the backwoods,
had not seen it until her parents died—with the sound of the
wagon wheel taking her away from it, that remains in the book
not merely a world that Faulkner celebrates but a mythic source
of strength. As indeed it is. For it is this intense sense of itself, it is
this superb registering of country sights and sounds as the stillness
is broken by the creaking and lumbering wagon coming up the
hill, that is the secret of Southern writing. In his attachment to the
irretrievable, in his obstinate feeling for the earth, the good
Southern writer makes so much writing in America seem as
shallow as if it had been composed by a young instructor in
English sitting in his study surrounded by manuals on the great
novels. Albert Camus, talking appreciatively about Southern
novelists, once remarked to a friend of mine that what he liked
about their books was "the dust and the heat." And to the man
from North Africa, with his memories of that blazing world de-

scribed in *Noces,* that world into which Paris can never enter,
Faulkner's sense of local color must be especially moving. But after
all, it is this sense of place that is the great thing about all American writing. It is the "mossy scabs of the worm fence, heap'd
stones, elder, mullein and poke-weed" in *Song of Myself;* the landscape that in *Walden* seems always to be reflected in water; the
strong native sense of the here and now that is the basis of Emerson's
aesthetic; the edge of the world seen from Hemingway's Michigan
woods; "reading the river" in *Life on the Mississippi* and *Huckleberry
Finn;* the "snow, the real snow" seen only beyond Chicago that
Scott Fitzgerald described so rapturously in his memories of Mid-
westerners in Eastern colleges going home for Christmas. And if
we ask what is so remarkable about that sense of place which is,
after all, essential to imaginative writing, the answer is that we
Americans are in fact just the opposite of the homogeneous mass
we are always trying to be, and that what distinguishes American
writing is exactly the fact that we are strangers to each other and
that each writer describes his own world to strangers living in the
same land with himself.

Now of all parts of the United States the South is certainly
the strangest to the others; it is, in fact—or used to be—a separate
nation. And almost all the good Southern writers have this sense
of local color to an extreme, for to the same degree that the South
is what it is because of its rural background, its "backwardness,"
its isolation, its comparatively homogeneous white population, to
this same extent does the American need to value and venerate
one's own region or place as the only escape from American big-
ness, American smoothness, American abstractness, American
slogans, the juggernaut of American progress, find (at least it used
to find) its deepest expression in the South. Even poverty, which
in America certainly is a disgrace, becomes in Southern writing a
sign of the natural man (Huckleberry Finn) or the earth-mother
(Lena Grove). And, as so often happens in Southern writing—for
the sensitive Southerners are likely to feel that they are lost in the
modern industrial world and, in mourning their traditional home-
land, to see the immediate world around them as damned—
Faulkner's pictures of the impersonal modern world, the opposite
of Lena's sacred grove, are lurid. As Lena is all fertility, the others
are all barrenness. Destruction, fire, obsession, inhumanity,

anonymity, the "frictionsmooth" wooden counter at which Joe Christmas eats, the hard cold eyes of Bobbie the prostitute and Mame the madam and Max the pimp: these against the images of locality, the farmers in their faded and patched but clean overalls, and of time, the wagon along the road and the "heelgnawed porch" of the country store around which the farmers sit. As soon as we get to Jefferson, we catch the typical dialectic of life and anti-life, the contrast of birth and destruction on which the book is founded, in the fact that the slow patient rhythms of Lena, the wagon, the road, are immediately followed by the whine of the saw in the planning mill, the reiteration of *smooth*. The world is narrowing down to the contest between the good Christian laborer, Byron Bunch, the very essence of the common ordinary good man, and those who, like Lena's seducer, have either taken on a name which is not their own, "Brown," a name too conventional even to be *his* name, or who, like Joe Christmas, have no name to begin with.

This contrast is familiar enough in Southern opinion, and one can find the same horror of miscegenation, of uprooting, of the city man's anonymity, in any expression of Southern agrarianism. But Faulkner does not stop at the abstraction of the alien: he carries it on, he carries it out, to astonishing lengths. And it is this intensity of conception that makes the portrait of Joe Christmas compelling rather than believable, makes him a source of wonder, of horror, yet above all of pity, rather than of pleasure in the creation of a real human being. For Joe Christmas remains, as he is born, an abstraction; from the moment he appears, "there was something definitely rootless about him, as though no town nor city was his, no street, no walls, no square of earth his home." He comes to work in the only clothes he has, a serge suit and a white shirt; and Byron Bunch, watching him, knows that Joe Christmas "carried his knowledge with him always as though it were a banner, with a quality ruthless, lonely, and almost proud." So from the moment Joe Christmas appears, he is seen as what others say about him, he is only a thought in other people's minds. More than this, he is looked at always from a distance, as if he were not quite human, which in many ways he is not.

We see Joe Christmas from a distance, and this distance is the actual space between him and his fellows. It is also the distance between the name "Joe Christmas," which is clownish, and the actual suffering of someone who has to live up to the non-humanity of his name, to the obsession (founded on hearsay, not on actual evidence) that his father had "some" Negro blood in him. Joe Christmas, then, is really "Man" trying to discover the particular kind of man he is. He is an abstraction created by the racist mania of his grandfather, a former preacher whose tormented life is spent insisting that Negroes are guilty in the eyes of God and must serve white men. When his daughter ran away with a "Mexican" circus hand, Doc Hines not merely killed the man, and, after his daughter died in childbirth on Christmas Eve, left the baby on the steps of an orphanage, but later took a job as a janitor in the orphanage in order to make sure that his "nigger" grandson would never be allowed to contaminate anyone. This obsessiveness about race goes hand in hand with a Calvinist obsession of the elect and of the hopeless sinfulness of others, an obsession which is found both in Joe Christmas's rigidly doctrinaire foster-father, Calvin MacEachern, and in his future mistress, Joanna Burden, a descendant of New Hampshire Puritans who remains in the South though she is the sworn enemy of its ways. All these obsessions about purity and guilt are, Faulkner indicates, the remnants of an inhuman religion that has added bigotry and arrogance to the curse of slavery. They are the symbols of a church that has lost its spiritual function, and that has been deserted by the Reverend Gail Hightower, who spends his days in endless reveries of the South's irretrievable glory. The obsessions are all summed up in the fate of Joe Christmas, who is trying to become *someone*, a human being, to find the integrity that is so ripely present in Lena Grove. Lena does not have to try; her symbol is the wheel on the road. Joe Christmas's is flight: flight on the same road, but flight toward himself, which he cannot reach, and away from hatred of himself, which he cannot escape. Only his pursuers catch up with him, to murder and to castrate him.

Joe Christmas is an abstraction seeking to become a human being. In the race-mad South, many a Negro—and Mexican, and Jew—is turned into an abstraction. But this man is *born* an abstraction and is seeking to become a person. He is an orphan, brought up in a foundling home, who in earliest childhood is watched by his own grandfather as if he were a caged beast. He is then bribed by the dietitian, whom he has heard making love with the interne, as if he knew enough to betray her. He is adopted by a farmer who re-names him, lectures him, starves him, beats him for not memorizing the Catechism. He is robbed and beaten by the pimp of the prostitute with whom he has fallen in love. He is constantly treated by his Negrophile mistress, Joanna Burden, as if his own personality were of no account and is beseeched in her sexual transports as "Negro." And finally, after being starved, betrayed, flogged, beaten, pursued by bloodhounds, he is castrated. The essential picture behind Joe Christmas is that of his grandfather carrying him to the orphanage and then from it in a savage parody of loving care. Joe Christmas is nothing but the man things are done to, the man who has no free will of his own, who is constantly seeking a moment of rest ("When have I ever eaten in peace?") and who looks for an identity by deliberately provoking responses that will let him be *someone,* if only as a white man among Negroes, or as someone calling himself a Negro in an effort to shock the white prostitute he has just slept with. His passivity, his ability to lend himself to situations and to people who will "carry" him for awhile, is immense and pitiful.

Joe Christmas is the most solitary character in American fiction, the most extreme phase conceivable of American loneliness. He is never seen full face, but always as a silhouette, a dark shadow haunting others, a shadow upon the road he constantly runs—a foreshadowing of his crucifixion, which, so terrible and concentrated is his suffering, already haunts the lives of others like a black shadow. For, almost *because* he does not look it, he becomes the "Negro," or the thought of, the obsession with, Negroes in the minds of those who, looking at Joe Christmas, can think of nothing else. And Joanna Burden, whose abolitionist grandfather was murdered in the South, whose whole life has been an obstinate carrying-on, deep inside Mississippi, of her family's coldly abstract espousal of Negroes, shows us how much of an abstraction Joe Christmas is when she makes love crying to him "Negro! Negro!" Whether the "Negro" represents the white man's guilt or the white man's fear, he is always a thought in the white's mind—and in the South, an obsession. So Joanna Burden, who befriends him, and Doc Hines, who hates him, come to see in him the cause of guilt that is finally the image of guilt. "I thought," Joanna says to her lover,

> of all the children coming forever and ever into the world, white, with the black shadow already falling upon them before they draw breath. And I seemed to see the black shadow in the shape of a cross. And it seemed like the white babies were struggling, even before they drew breath, to escape from the shadow that was not only upon them but beneath them, too, flung out like their arms were flung out, as if they were nailed to the cross.

And she quotes her father: "In order to rise, you must raise the shadow with you. But you can never lift it to your level. I see that now, which I did not see until I came down here. But escape it you cannot. The curse of the black race is God's curse. But the curse of the white race is the black man who will be forever God's chosen own because He once cursed Him." The grounds of this obsession, then, can be a compassion for the Negro that is as profound as hatred, and equally removed from brotherhood. This compassion seems to me the essence of Faulkner's approach to Joe Christmas, and the triumph of the book is Faulkner's ability to keep his leading character a shadow, and yet to make us feel all his suffering. Compare Joe Christmas with the types of the Northerner, the city man, the "stranger" in Southern writing, to say nothing of the Negro, and you realize that where so many neo-orthodox Southern literary critics are hysterically fearful of the "stranger," Faulkner, by a tremendous and moving act of imagination, has found in Joe Christmas the incarnation of "man" —that is, of modern man, reduced entirely to his unsupported and inexplicable human feelings. There are no gods in Faulkner's world; there are only men—some are entirely subject to circumstances, some protest against them, some are even moved to change them. The hero of *A Fable* is of the last; Joe Christmas is of the first. He is human to us because of the experience he undergoes, but his passivity is so great that he is finally a body castrated, a mere corpse on a dissection table—or someone whose body has been turned into the host, material for a ritual, so that his last agony will earn him the respect he never earned while he was alive. He is not, like the Christ of *A Fable*, a man who gives new meaning to life; like Benjy in *The Sound and the Fury,* he is an incarnation of human suffering, unable to speak—except in the tremendous action near the end of the book when he stops running from his pursuers and waits for them, and attains in this first moment of selfhood, the martyrdom that ends it.

We see Joe Christmas always from a distance. The distance from ourselves to him seems to me the key to the book, for it explains why Joe exists for us principally as a man who is described, not seen. He is so far away that we cannot see him; he is reported to us. And this distance is filled with the stillness of a continuous meditation. *Light in August* tells a story of violence, but the book itself is curiously soundless, for it is full of people thinking to themselves about events past. As soon as Lena Grove arrives in Jefferson, at the end of the first chapter, the story of Joe Christmas comes to us through flashbacks, through talk by the other men at the planing mill, through a whole chapter of summary biography, through rumors and gossip by the townspeople, and at the very end, when Joe Christmas's whole story is put together for us, by Gavin Stevens's telling a stranger about the grandparents. Almost everything we learn about Joe Christmas comes to us in the form of hearsay, accusation, the tortured memories of others; even his death is told as an incident in the life of his murderer, Percy Grimm. All these reports about the stranger sufficiently suggest his alienation. But in themselves they also create that stillness, that depth of meditation into which all the characters are plunged.

This meditation begins in Joe Christmas himself, who in his distance from other men is constantly trying to think himself back to life, and who, without knowing exactly how his ordeal began— and certainly not why—finds himself like a caged animal going over and over the same ground. We hear him talking to himself, and we follow his slow and puzzled efforts to understand the effect of his actions upon others. We see him as a child in the orphanage, eating the toothpaste, frightening the dietitian out of her wits because he is staring straight at her, trying to understand what she is accusing him of. We watch him walking the path between his cabin and Joanna Burden's house for his meals, thinking out everything he finds between the four walls of her kitchen. Finally we watch him running, and thinking deliriously in his flight, until, in that magnificent and piercing scene near the end of his flight, he falls asleep as he runs. The pressure of thought, the torture of thought, is overwhelming—and useless, since Joe Christmas does not know who he is, and so cannot locate the first cause of his misery. But still he thinks, he broods, he watches, he waits. And it is this brooding silence in him, fixed in attention over he does not know what, that explains why he is so often described in the book as looking like a man in prayer—even like a "monk." There is a strange and disturbing stillness about him that eases him, more swiftly than most men, into the stillness of non-being.

The stillness of the book has, of course, an immense reverberation within it. Describing Doc Hines, Faulkner notes about him "a quality of outworn violence like a scent, an odor," and the actual violence of Joe Christmas is always felt about him even when he sits rigidly still at counters like a man in prayer. When Joe's back history is run off in the rapid newsreel style of Dos Passos, one feels not only his personal insignificance, but the just-leashed violence of American life of which Joe is, in his way, completely the creature:

> He stepped from the dark porch, into the moonlight, and with his bloody head and his empty stomach hot, savage, and courageous with whiskey, he entered the street which was to run for fifteen years.
> The whiskey died away in time and was renewed and died again, but the street ran on. From that night the thousand streets ran as one street, with imperceptible corners and changes of scene, broken by intervals of begged and stolen rides, on trains and trucks, and on country wagons with he at twenty and twentyfive and thirty sitting on the seat with his still, hard face and the clothes (even when soiled and worn) of a city man and the driver of the wagon not knowing who or what the passenger was and not daring to ask.

Yet it is a stillness of thought that generally pervades the book, in the form of enormous meditations by which Faulkner tries to lift his material into place. The stillness is interrupted by shooting, burning, beating, the barking of bloodhounds and Percy Grimm's mutilation of Joe Christmas, which interrupt like the sound which nails must make when they are driven into wood through human flesh. Yet, just behind this obvious figure of the Roman soldier torturing Christ, there is a pastoral world. As Irving Howe has noted, the arrangement of the book "resembles an early Renaissance painting—in the foreground a bleeding martyr, far to the rear a scene of bucolic peacefulness, with women quietly working in the fields." Despite its violence, *Light in August* is one of the few American novels that remind one of the humanized and tranquil landscape in European novels. Its stillness is rooted in the peaceful and timeless world which Lena Grove personifies and in which she has her being. It is the stillness of the personal darkness inside which Joe Christmas lives. But this stillness is also the sickly, after-dark silence of the Reverend Gail Hightower sitting in his study, with his stale clothes and stale thoughts, going over and over the tragedy of his life, his grandfather's "glorious" death, his wife's desertion and suicide—and finally and typically summing it all up into a stale round of human illusion and defeat. Faulkner wishes us to understand that Hightower finally cuts the gordian knot of his thoughts when he delivers Lena's baby and is finally struck down by Percy Grimm as he stands between him and Joe Christmas. But Hightower, whether brooding out upon the street from behind the study window, or sitting behind the green lamp in his parlor when he receives Byron Bunch, his only visitor, enlarges the stillness, increases its weight, by personifying what is immediately present in the book, and throughout Faulkner's novels—the Southern effort to explain, to justify, and through some consummation in violent physical action even to lighten, the burden of this obsession with the past.

Hightower, by general consent, is one of the failures of the book: he is too vague, too drooping, too formless, in a word too much the creature of defeat and of obsession, to compel our interest or our belief. But this is so partly because Hightower is both a surrogate figure for Faulkner's meditations and a kind of scapegoat on whom Faulkner can discharge his exasperation with Southern nostalgia and the endless searching in the labyrinths of the past for the explanation of the Southern defeat and of the hold it keeps on the descendants of the Confederate aristocracy. Hightower is a failure because Faulkner both uses and parodies him. Because of the absurdly literal symbolism of his name, his constant watchful position behind the green lamp, his useless reveries, he is never on the same scale as the other characters, who are equally obsessed by the past, but who function on the plane of some positive action. Hightower not only lives by his thoughts; he has no life but his thoughts. We miss in him the life-like element of violence (the only possible end to characters so entirely formed of

reverie) that we find in Joanna Burden's degeneration, in Joe
Christmas's hatred, in Percy Grimm's fanaticism, in Doc Hines's
mania. Hightower, acting in various sections of the book as a foreground observer, brings to them not merely a stillness but a dead-
ness which intervenes between us and the other characters. This
shapeless, ghostly body of thought has its symbolic place in the
mind of Hightower. For just as his life is over, and he has no
function but to brood, so Faulkner has signified in Hightower that
wholly retrospective, watchful concern, not with the past but with
their bondage to the past, that seems to me the essence of what
Faulkner's characers are always thinking about.

Joe Christmas, Joanna Burden, Gail Hightower—each of
these is the prisoner of his own history, and is trying to come to
terms with this servitude in his own mind. That none of them can
ever lift himself out of the circumstances that enclose him, Faulkner
sees as the condition of man. Man is engulfed in events that are
always too much for him. Hightower, listening to Byron Bunch
make plans for Lena's confinement, thinks: "It is because so much
happens. Too much happens. That's it. Man performs, engenders,
so much more than he can or should have to bear. That's how he
finds out that he can bear anything. That's it. That's what is so
terrible. That he can bear anything, anything." Endurance, as we
know, is the key word in Faulkner's system of values. At least this
was so up to *A Fable*. There, Faulkner himself has told us, the
highest value is represented not by the young Jewish pilot officer
who said, "This is terrible. I refuse to accept it, even if I must refuse
life to do so"; not by the old French quartermaster general who
said, "This is terrible, but we can weep and bear it"; but by the
English battalion runner who said, "This is terrible, I'm going to
do something about it." *Light in August* does not arrive at this step.
Man never thinks of changing the world; it is all he can do to get
a grip on it, to understand some part of what has happened
to him and to endure all of it. Any release that occurs is a purely
individual one, as when Hightower finally frees himself, in the one
profoundly unselfish act of his life, by delivering Lena's baby. In
the freshness of the early morning, after Lena has given birth,
Hightower feels that he is in touch with the earth again—the
symbol throughout the book of rightness, authenticity, peace. But
the earth is not his life, as it is Lena Grove's. Man's highest aim

in this book is to meet his destiny without everlasting self-concern. Yet this profoundly tragic cast to *Light in August,* so much like a Hardy novel in the implacable pattern that unrolls against a country background and in the inarticulate stillness of its leading characters, is matched by Faulkner's ironic awareness that man, even in his endless brooding over the event, can never stop, that the event is nothing compared with the speculation that follows and in a sense replaces it. One of the most revealing phrases in Faulkner's rhetoric is: "not that"—it is not peace, not an end, that his people ever want. The violence may be "outworn," but it is the human passion. He describes his chorus, the townspeople, scurrying around Joanna Burden's house after her murder, looking "for someone to crucify":

> But there wasn't anybody. She had lived such a quiet life, attended so to her own affairs, that she bequeathed to the town in which she had been born and lived and died a foreigner, an outlander, a kind of heritage of astonishment and outrage, for which, even though she had supplied them at last with an emotional barbecue, a Roman holiday almost, they would never forgive her and let her be dead in peace and quiet. Not that. Peace is not that often. So they moiled and clotted, believing that the flames, the blood, the body that had died three years ago and had just now begun to live again, cried out for vengeance, not believing that the rapt infury of the flames and the immobility of the body were both affirmations of an attained bourne beyond the hurt and harm of man. Not that.

We can never let the event go, for that would mean an end to the human history that is lived in retrospection. Just as Faulkner's language is full of words, like "avatar" and "outrage," which are really private symbols left over from his unceasing meditation, and just as his style is formed from the fierce inner pressure of problems which give no solution, so the actual texture of *Light in August* suggests, in the tension and repetition of certain verbal motifs, that man can never quite say what the event originally meant, or what he is to think of it now. Language never quite comes up to the meaning of events. To adapt Faulkner's phrase, it is not that, or that. The townspeople exist in *Light in August,* as in so many Faulkner novels, to ask questions whose very function is to deny the possibility of an answer. Faulkner's grim sarcastic asides show that he views language as in some basic sense unavailing. The astounding repetition of certain key phrases and verbal rhythms in his work signifies his return back and back on the question.

Call the event history, call it the Fall: man is forever engaged in meditating, not the past itself, for that would bring knowledge, but man's guilt, for that may bring freedom. Guilt, not history, is the nightmare from which all of Faulkner's deepest characters are trying to escape. The guilt arises from man's endless complicity in his own history, as when the innocent, gravely staring child that Joe Christmas was, ate her toothpaste and listened to the dietitian making love. Hightower is guilty because his sickly, foolish nostalgia for his grandfather's one day of glory made him unavailable to his own wife, who committed suicide; Joanna Burden feels so guilty that she has remained an alien in the Southern town in which she was born, accepting her isolation as the price of her identification both with her Abolitionist forebears, who were shot down in the South, and with the Negroes, on whom a curse must have been laid. Even Doc Hines and Percy Grimm murder in order to "clean" life of the stain that Negroes have put on it, for as the Negroes were cursed by God, so they have cursed life, and the maniac "saviors" of Southern racial purity have to save their hallowed country from contagion. But just as no one of them can really distinguish the hate they feel for others from self-accusation, so no one can say with whom guilt began, where the ultimate human crime was committed. The paths which lead back to the human past are endless through the human brain, and sitting at his study window after he has gained new self-respect by delivering Lena's baby and by standing up to Percy Grimm, the dying Hightower still ruminates, goes over and over the past, as "the final copper light of afternoon fades" and "the world hangs in a green suspension in color and texture like through colored glass." The everlasting reverie begins again, but now the wheel of life that brought Lena Grove to Jefferson begins to slow down, runs into sand, "the axle, the vehicle, the power which propels it not yet aware." These memories are endless, and the style in which they are described is over-colored in a way that shows how static action often becomes in Faulkner's work, how much it serves as the raw material for reflection, which is why he can lavish so many Joycean compound words on objects which do not seem to move of their own accord, but to be rallying points in Faulkner's tortured concern with guilt.

Guilt is endless; in the labyrinths of the mind, there is turning, but no deliverance. Like T. S. Eliot, Faulkner is a favorite today because he takes his stand on human guilt; this is the side of ourselves that we can recognize, and curiously, stand by; for in this alone, as we feel, is the possibility of our freedom. When men feel so wretchedly small before their own past, they must be guilty. So runs the legend. This is the argument behind Faulkner's novel: of the God who made Yoknapatawpha County. In the beginning, life was free and good and natural; but something inexplicable, a curse, was put on it. Perhaps the curse is nothing more than man's effort to get the better of events that are "too much for us"; the evil lies in arrogance. Doc Hines hears God addressing him personally, ordering him to act for Him. Calvin MacEachern, Joe Christmas's adopted father, starves and beats him because he cannot memorize portions of the catechism on order. "He asked that the child's stubborn heart be softened and that the sin of disobedience be forgiven him also, through the advocacy of the man whom he had flouted and disobeyed, requesting that Almighty be as magnanimous as himself, and by and through and because of conscious grace." Even Joanna Burden tries to play God to her Negro charges. *Light in August* is one of the sharpest criticisms of Calvinism ever written, but unlike so many Southern writers on Puritanism, Faulkner knows that the same religion is found in Doc Hines and Joanna Burden. The guilt that is the mainstay of their faith is embodied in the assumption of excessive authority by fathers, lawgivers, teachers, ministers. Everyone wants to play God to the orphan Joe Christmas. In Faulkner's eyes, life is an ironic and tragic affair that is beyond human rule and misrule; but Calvinists like Doc Hines and Calvin MacEachern, or the children of Calvinists like Joanna Burden, even murdering simon-pure "patriots" like Percy Grimm, take life in their hands, they dominate, and they murder. Joe Christmas is their favorite charge; he is the man "things are done to." His final ignominy comes when his mistress, Joanna Burden, regarding him in her new phase as a Negro charge to be "brought up," tells him that she wants him to go to school so that he can become a lawyer. And it is at this point that he breaks. It is this point that has always been the signature of the everlasting victim. Other men are the law-givers; the law is passed out to him, through him, inflicted on him. And so finally he murders and dies, a pure victim, shot, castrated, treated like a thing. It is the final ignominy. But in the very unattainability of his suffering, in its inexpressibility, is the key to his healing power over others. For where life exists so much in the relation of master to man, of the elect to the sinner, the only possible consummation man can ever reach, for Joe Christmas as for Uncle Tom, is in the final consistency of his suffering, in a fate so extreme that it becomes a single human word which men can read. This is what Faulkner means in that exalted passage after Joe Christmas's immolation:

> . . . when they saw what Grimm was doing one of the men gave a choked cry and stumbled back into the wall and began to vomit. Then Grimm too sprang back, flinging behind him the bloody butcher knife. "Now you'll let white women alone, even in hell," he said. But the man on the floor had not moved. He just lay there, with his eyes open and empty of everything save consciousness, and with something, a shadow, about his mouth. For a long moment he looked up at them with peaceful and unfathomable and unbearable eyes. Then his face, body, all, seemed to collapse, to fall in upon itself, and from out the slashed garments about his hips and loins the pent black blood seemed to rush like a released breath. It seemed to rush out of his pale body like the rush of sparks from a rising rocket; upon that black blast the man seemed to rise soaring into their memories forever and ever. They are not to lose it, in whatever peaceful valleys, beside whatever placid and reassuring streams of old age, in the mirroring faces of whatever children they will contemplate old disasters and newer hopes. It will be there, musing, quiet, steadfast, not fading and not particularly threatful, but of itself alone serene, of itself alone triumphant.

Joe Christmas has attained the stillness that will finally allow us to see him. Of sufferings alone is he made, and in this sense, and in this sense alone, is he a figure whose condition is so total that he reminds us of Christ in the sense of Christ's integrality. That tortured and would-be Christian philosopher, Simone Weil, understood this when she found in *malheur,* affliction, that it could become so much in itself that she felt riven to the universe by bonds of pain. The arch-victim may not be a "martyr," as students of modern totalitarianism have noticed, but there is a kind of suffering in our time which is so extreme that it becomes an integral *fact* of the human condition. Father Zossima bowed down to Dmitri Karamazov because of all the affliction he would undergo. So marvelous is Faulkner's compassion, he can visualize in the man who was nothing but a victim, the shadow thrown from the Cross of Christ, who was nothing, as it were, but Himself. Men are men because events are always "too much" for them; Joe Christmas became one with his life in that extreme moment when even he had no longer to search out the past. The figure on the Cross is the most tremendous interventive symbol in history; the castrated man on the floor has only one free power in his life—to stop running at last and to face his murderer. Faulkner intends no parody; he is moved by the likeness of totality to totality. But neither is he a Christian. There is no redemption; there is not even in *A Fable*— but there man has the courage to redeem circumstances by denying their fatality. In *Light in August* the past is not merely exigent; it is even malicious, the spirit of pure bad luck, a god-like force that confronts man at every turn with everything he has been, and so seems to mock and to oppose him. This is called "The Player": Lena's seducer, "Brown," still running away from her at the last, sends a Negro boy to the sheriff for the reward money he has earned in informing on Joe Christmas, but knows despairingly that he will never see the money.

> 'He wont do it. He cant do it. I know he cant find him, cant get it, bring it back.' He called no names, thought no names. It seemed to him now that they were all just shapes like chessmen—the negro, the sheriff, the money, all—unpredictable and without reason moved here and there by an Opponent who could read his moves before he made them and who created spontaneous rules which he and not the Opponent, must follow.

This is the Opponent that Joe Christmas decides finally not to elude again, the "Player" who moves Percy Grimm unerringly from position to position:

> He was beside the ditch now. He stopped, motionless in midstride. Above the blunt, cold rake of the automatic his face had that serene, unearthly luminousness of angels in church windows. He was moving again almost before he had stopped, with that lean, swift, blind obedience to whatever Player moved him on the Board. He ran to the ditch.

All things are fated; man is in any place because the Player moved him there. Our past sets up the positions into which we fall. This is why Joe Christmas's grandmother, Mrs. Hines, utters the most significant lines in the book when, at the end, she pitifully cries out:

"I am not saying that he never did what they say he did. Ought not
to suffer for it like he made them that loved and lost suffer. But if folks
could maybe just let him for one day. Like it hadn't happened yet. Like
the world never had anything against him yet. Then it could be like he
had just went on a trip and grew man grown and come back. If
it could be like that for just one day."

And it is in these terms that we come to understand why Joe
Christmas, in running away from a past that he cannot escape
seems constantly to be looking back as he runs. Not only is no one
free of his past; he even has, at the most critical moments, the
sense not of moving at all, but of being silently lifted from position
to position. It is because of this curious effect of immobility in
Faulkner's characters as they run (as if they were held up in the
air by wires), that Faulkner can lavish such idle poetic largesse
upon them: can see in a Percy Grimm that "serene, unearthly
luminousness of angels in church windows," and at various points
throughout the book emphasize Joe Christmas's rigid likeness to
a man in prayer. Even the countrymen in overalls move at one
point "with almost the air of monks in a cloister." The reason is
that all these characters are lost in contemplation as they are
moved here and there by the Player. There is no free action for
anyone: everyone is carried, as Lena Grove was carried to Jefferson in a whole succession of farm wagons, by the fate that was and
so shall be.

Faulkner's world is grim—a world in which the Past exerts
an irresistible force, but against which there is no supernatural
sanction, no redeeming belief. He believes in original sin, but not
in divine love, and he is endlessly bemused by the human effort to
read fate or to avoid it. The highest reach of his belief is the effort
to become "a saint without God" (Albert Camus), but this is a
point not yet tried for in *Light in August*. Correspondingly, there
is great power in his work, but little color, and *Light in August*,
for all its brilliance, somehow wears the lack-luster look of the
year in which it was published, 1932. It is a grim book, and the
countryside described in it already has the pinched, rotted look
that one sees in so many depression novels about the South. The
greatest fault of the book is its overschematic, intellectualized cast.
Although Faulkner himself has lived more like Joe Christmas than

like the Sartorises, he is socially far from the world of Joe Christmas and Lena Grove, and there are tell-tale signs in the novel that
it is written *down*—for Faulkner, too much from his head down,
and about people whom he tends to generalize and to overpraise,
as if he saw them only as symbols rather than as entirely complex
beings. And it is a simple fact that the opening of *Light in August*
is so beautiful that nothing else quite comes up to it.

On the other hand, it is one of Faulkner's greatest books, and
although it does not have the blazing directness of *The Sound and
the Fury* (a book written more directly out of Faulkner's own experience), it has much of the creative audacity which is Faulkner's
highest ideal in art. With this book, published in 1932, Faulkner
completed a period of extraordinary fertility. He was only thirty-
five; since 1929, he had published, in rapid order, *Sartoris, The
Sound and the Fury, As I Lay Dying, Sanctuary,* and *Light in
August.* It was a period of tremendous creative power. When he
was recently in Japan, Faulkner said of this time:—"I think there's
a period in a writer's life when he, well, simply for lack of any
other word, is fertile and he just produces. Later on, his blood
slows, his bones get a little more brittle, his muscles get a little
stiff, he gets perhaps other interests, but I think there's one time in
his life when he writes at the top of his talent plus his speed, too.
Later the speed slows; the talent doesn't necessarily have to fade
at the same time. But there's a time in his life, one matchless time,
when they are matched completely. The speed, and the power
and the talent, they're all there and then he is . . . 'hot.' "

Light in August comes out of that "one matchless time." The
only possible objection one can have to the book is the number of
implications which Faulkner tries to bring out of his material—for
just as the characters' own lives are "set" for them to mull over, so
Faulkner constantly mulls over them, wringing a poetry that has
grandeur but also an intensity of contemplation that is sometimes
more furious in expression than meaningful in content. If we see
Faulkner's narrative method as essentially recollective, in the form
of individual meditation over past events, we can recognize the
advantage he has over most "naturalistic" writers and we understand why Faulkner refers to himself as a "poet." For what makes
the portrait of Joe Christmas so astonishing is the energy of imagination lavished upon it, the consistency of texture that derives

from the poet's sense that he has not only to *show,* in the modern realistic sense, but to *say*—that is, to tell a story which follows from his contemplation of the world, and which preserves, in the nobility of its style and in the serene independence of its technique, the human victory over circumstances.

It is this that makes us hear Faulkner's own voice throughout the book, that allows him to pull off the tremendous feat of making us believe in a character who in many ways is not a human being at all—but struggling to become one. And this, after all, is the great problem of the novelist today. Joe Christmas is an incarnation not only of the "race problem" in America, but of the condition of man. More and more, not merely the American novel, but all serious contemporary novels, are concerned with men who are not real enough to themselves to be seriously in conflict with other men. Their conflicts, as we say, are "internal"; for they are seeking to become *someone.* Joe Christmas lives a life that is not only solitary but detached. He lives in society physically, but actually he is concerned only with the process of self-discovery, or of self-naming, even of self-legalization. This is a fate which, as we know, can be as arduous and deadly as that of the classic heroes. But in Joe Christmas's case, there is no conflict from positions of strength, no engagement between man and man— only the search of the "stranger," *l'etranger,* to become man.

Roy Harvey Pearce

XXIII

The Poet as Person

In 1920 William Carlos Williams, publishing a collection of self-consciously experimental poems under the title "Kora in Hell: Improvisations," began his volume with a long rambling preface on the state of the world and American letters. He came to the conclusion that the proper credo for the true poet was this: "There is nothing in literature but change and change is mockery. I'll write whatever I damn please, whenever I damn please and as I damn please and it'll be good if the authentic spirit of change is on it." His desire was that the poet discover and rediscover his world exclusively in terms of himself. As he wrote, "It is in the continual and violent refreshing of the idea [of discovery of self] that love and good writing have their security." And poets who looked elsewhere than into the violence of the self for a means of discovering the spirit of change in the world, were to be anathematized: "Our prize poems are especially to be damned not because of superficial bad workmanship, but because they are re-hash, repetition—just as Eliot's more exquisite work is rehash, repetition in another way of Verlaine, Baudelaire, Maeterlinck—conscious or unconscious—just as were Pound's early paraphrases from Yeats and his constant later cribbing from the Renaissance,

From *The Yale Review*, Vol. XLI, March 1952, No. 3. Copyright 1952 by Yale University Press. Reprinted by permission of author and publisher.

Provence and the modern French: Men content with the connotations of their masters."

It was, in fact, the "connotations of their masters" that Williams feared would somehow destroy the connotations of the self. And it was such connotations that he felt his friend Pound was teaching as the only means by which American poets might discipline themselves out of their moribund Victorianism. All this Pound cheerfully admitted in a series of letters he sent Williams on receiving a copy of "Kora in Hell." Justifying himself, he said that he had "sweated like a nigger to break up the clutch of the old . . . Harper's etc. That [he had] tried to enlighten . . . Chicago, so as to make a place for the real thing. That [he had] sent over French models, which [had] given six hundred people a means of telling something nearer the truth than they would have done senza."

We may reduce the question that Pound and Williams debated to this: How could the twentieth-century American tell the truth in poetry? For Williams it was by letting nothing interfere with the poet's need to know himself primarily as an individuated, violently individuated, self. For Pound it was by going to school to other poets and learning thereby to delimit and to give precise form to that need—as it were, to put an end to the violence of the self.

But the problem is only an aspect of a far larger one: the eternal problem of community, of finding a moral and social order which men can accept, while yet remaining sufficiently differentiated and egocentric to be aware that the acceptance is an individual matter. It is the problem of constructing a society in which men can remain individuals and at the same time share values, ideas, and beliefs, in which they can realize themselves as somehow at once different and alike, separate and together, democratic and en masse.

We are told by our social scientists that we participate in society doubly, so to speak, as individuated and as socialized selves, and that the struggle to survive as whole men is the struggle to make one kind of participation coördinate with the other. Calling the elements in this double participation culture and personality, the anthropologist Edward Sapir wrote:

"The interests connected by the terms culture and personality are necessary for intelligent and helpful growth because each is based on a distinctive kind of imaginative participation by the observer in the life around him. The observer may dramatize such behavior as he takes note of it in terms of a set of values, a conscience which is beyond self and to which he must conform, actually or imaginatively, if he is to preserve his place in the world of authority or impersonal social necessity. Or, on the other hand, he may feel the behavior as self-expressive, as defining the reality of individual consciousness against the mass of environing social determinants. Observations coming within the framework of the former of these two kinds of participation constitute our knowledge of culture. Those which come within the framework of the latter constitute our knowledge of personality. One is as subjective or objective as the other, for both are essentially modes of projection of personal experience into the analysis of social phenomena."

This puts the matter at its most general, as is fitting for the social scientist, but it also, I think, achieves, through its very generalization, a perspective which will let us see that our poetry, being the intensest kind of "imaginative participation" in the life around us, must also tend to express, on the one hand, our sense of personality, and, on the other, our sense of culture. If our social scientists have become aware of the culture-personality split primarily because our society is so constituted as to make them aware of it, then our poets, by virtue of being poets operating according to the canons of *their* mode of knowledge, will be even more intensely aware of it, and even more intensely committed to it. But if our social scientists posit an ideal society wherein the demands of culture and personality are exactly reciprocal, our poets cannot; for they live not by positing generalities but by realizing particulars. Being artists, not scientists, they cannot speak in terms of that which is abstractly and generally desirable. They must speak of what is and of what they desire, whether psychologically or metaphysically, in terms of what they have empirically. If what they see in the world around them manifests a split between personality and culture, if all forms of culture seem alien to the modern personality as it discovers and reveals itself, and if the choice of one cancels out the choice of the other, then they must try to discover the kind of a community (or,

strictly speaking, substitute for a community) that is possible when
they have chosen one or the other. Which is to say, they must discover what it is to need a sense of community and not to have it.
Thus they must write their poems and let us know fully what one
or the other choice comes to.

What I want to get at from this perspective of sociological
generalization is this: that Pound and Williams, in making their
separate choices, were willy-nilly—as men in some sense limited by
the language and values-in-language which their world gave them
—touching at the heart of our cultural crisis; that, as poets, they
asked the right and necessary questions. For them a sense of
community—and the ability to write poetry in and to a community—had to be searched for, had to be discovered. For Pound the
possibility of community (again, strictly speaking, of a substitute
kind) lay in a source ultimately outside the individual poet's sensibility, in authoritative models, and he proceeded to shape his
sensibility in accordance with those models. In short, he gave primary devotion to culture. Williams, on the other hand, found the
possibility of community in his own radically individuated sensibility and made it his business either to deny the usefulness of
models or to make them into something genuinely his own; he
insisted that they have no meaning except as the poet gives them
meaning. He gave primary devotion to personality.

It is this latter devotion, especially as it appears in the work
of Wallace Stevens, William Carlos Williams, and E. E. Cummings, that is my main interest in this essay. Not that these are
the only poets who have chosen this course; there are many more
—from Imagists to Activists, from a Marianne Moore through a
Theodore Roethke; and I write with all of them in mind. Taken
all in all, their work makes up, if not a school, at least a strain in
our poetry, a strain so clear and vibrant that it lets us know surely
and certainly one way that the poet works in our world—and, beyond that, one way that our world makes the poet work.

But we must remember that the greater number of our poets
have chosen the other course; they have chosen to celebrate
culture—as in our society and its search for a sense of community,
more of us have followed the way to authority which guarantees
order and runs the risk of denying the self, than the way to free
and full selfhood which runs the risk of denying order and achiev-

ing only chaos or isolation—the violence of change, as Williams put it. Thus before we look more closely at that minor strain in our poetry which centers on personality, we must glance hastily, by way of recall, at that major strain which centers on culture.

The most obvious instance besides Pound himself is, of course, T. S. Eliot. The history of Eliot's enterprise, it is now obvious, has been that of seeking an adequate culture—artistic and moral and political. He began by writing small poems of objective description, which were yet more than descriptive because they were cast in an ironic evaluative form; "Sweeney among the Nightingales" is a characteristic example. Here the situation of one of our bourgeoisie is found negatively meaningful by being contrasted with a larger, alien kind of order. The very texture of the poem depends not upon our perception of the situation as it is objectively, in and of itself—but rather historically, in relation to something larger, more stable than itself; the situation is worth looking at only in relation to this larger order which it reflects in a bitter and dumb irony.

So it is, on a much larger scale, with "The Waste Land." The obscurity of this poem derives from Eliot's dependence upon authorities nominally extraneous to the situation of the poem; yet we must feel the order immanent in these authorities if we are to know the disorder, twentieth-century disorder, which is the subject of the poem. The poet continually makes us aware of what he is not, not of what he is, by means of such fragments of folklore, myth, and his literary heritage as he can shore against his ruins. "Shore against his ruins" is precise, I think; for insofar as Eliot's poet-protagonist is to have a self, it is literally a self shored up—held together by forces derived from something outside, not from something within.

"Ash Wednesday" moves towards the positive, certainly. But it is positive denial and discipline: "Teach us to care and not to care"—which I take it means to know, even to love, the world for what it is, so as to be able to renounce it fully. The structure of "Ash Wednesday" depends upon a continual, if only implicit, reference to received Christian doctrine. The ruins of the self begin to be reconstituted into a whole; yet the principle of reconstitution is the will of God and not of the individual. The perceptions that the poet registers for us are his only secondarily. First they are those of what he takes to be universal Christendom; his secondary perceptions make uniform sense only as they are those of this universal Christendom.

The poems which make up "Four Quartets" record this seeking of order most fully and most brilliantly; likewise they push this seeking to its logical end. The task is, within the structure of time, to achieve the timeless. There is still, but much more subtly than in "The Waste Land," the dependence upon history and tradition and myth for points of reference around which the poems may be organized. The perceiving self still values most what he is not, not what he is. He comes to know what he is not, in terms of the material qualities which mark his earthly nature: air, earth, water, fire. These qualities are held together, as I have noted, by something which is outside of man; he can know what that something is only by denying, insofar as he can, his material nature. Thus in "The Dry Salvages":

> . . . to apprehend
> The point of intersection of the timeless
> With time, is an occupation for the saint—
> No occupation either, but something given
> And taken, in a lifetime's death in love,
> Ardour and selflessness and self-surrender.
> For most of us, there is only the unattended
> Moment, the moment in and out of time . . .

"hints and guesses. . . . Hints followed by guesses": this is the lot of the modern self. One presumes that the guesses are possible because they are based on a certainty that there are saints. And saints are part of a larger order to which one must appeal to find his place in the world—if one is so disposed, to write poetry; "Four Quartets," we remember, is also a series of poems about language, the mystery of the Word. It is not out of context, I think, to recall Eliot's pronouncement in "Tradition and the Individual Talent": "What happens [to the poet] is a continual surrender of himself as he is at the moment to something which is more valuable. The progress of the artist is a continual self-sacrifice, a continual extinction of personality."

Eliot, of course, has been the great example for our poets, though there are others. One thinks of Ransom and Tate and of all the young men who have gone to school to them. The kind of order differs, certainly; but the conviction that there is order somewhere—in the past, or in tradition, or in formal religion—is there. And for our purposes it is important to note that the older Southerners were by no means influenced by their reading of Eliot into writing the kind of poetry that they wrote and continue to write. Their own cultural situation, as the history of the Agrarian-Fugitive movement shows, directed them to a search for models of order; their discovery that Eliot's search was like theirs only served to authenticate and to verify their own need and their own procedure and to make it possible for them to go to school to Eliot.

But the tendency to search for an order and an authority alien to the modern world is not confined to poets such as these. It is the product of too deep a need in our society to be so. Thus it seems to me that Robert Frost is, in his own way, a poet whose work is equally characterized by devotion to culture. Frost achieves his celebrated individualism, what on first glance may seem to be a devotion to personality, simply by refusing to have anything to do with a modern world which, so his poems report, lacks a principle capable of supporting any kind of individualism. His is an individualism out of a nineteenth-century agrarian America, a Transcendentalism which has barked its shins on evil and has come to be skilled at avoiding or facing it where it is most easily identifiable, in the New England mountains. Frost strikes us as an individualist because he will have none of our more usual kinds of authority. Yet we must be sure to note that he will have none of the modern self either. Seeking to find a personality, yet turning away from whatever there is of personality in his own time, he has found—for us as his readers—only culture.

Recently, putting Job in the twentieth century, Frost has made him complain to God:

> We don't know where we are, or who we are,
> Don't know one another; don't know You;
> Don't know what time it is. . . .

Starting from a position something like this, Eliot finally located himself in the world of Christian orthodoxy. Frost will have none of that. Yet he has found a place and a condition in which he can know himself well enough to be a whole poet and write whole poems. With the farm, country, and mountain settings of his

longer poems, with the simple and direct relationship set up between man and the natural world in his lyrics, he is able to record
a sense of community and self-awareness as satisfying, in its way,
as Eliot's. But that sense is achieved only by virtue of such a
setting and such a relationship. The principle of order is immanent in a sensibility most fully aware of life in the country, life
apart from centralization, industrialization, and urbanization. Because in our world culture and personality are not consonant,
Frost has withdrawn (not retreated) to a place where they can be
consonant, where he can write as an individual living in a community; and our memory, however acquired, of that sense of community is such that we can follow him, or his poems.

The community which is in Frost's poems does not rise
directly out of the world we find about us; for it is a community
limited, restricted, apart from our workaday concerns. Thus the
poems must embody for us something superimposed, a culture
sought for so as to give order to, even to create, a modern personality which has no proper culture of its own. Frost's poems, above
all because they are such beautifully adequate poems, make a figure somewhat too neat and ordered for those of us who go to
them to see what we might be, under conditions alien to our own,
if we were not what we are. If Frost can write (in "New Hampshire") "Me for the hills where I don't have to choose," we must
feel that he has nonetheless chosen, chosen to work out his poems
in terms of a set of relationships which derive from the past and
from an agrarian, individualistic tradition which can function in
the present only as a superimposed culture. If, like Eliot, he satisfies us most because his verses seem completely to control and
judge a portion of our world, so too, like Eliot, he achieves that
control and is enabled to make that judgment only by virtue of
withdrawing from our world. In effect, his verses, like Eliot's,
manifest a denial of the irreducibly private and idiosyncratic and
a holding-fast to a principle of order which, as it must enforce
that denial, makes withdrawal inevitable.

At once the complement to and the polar opposite of such a
denial is, of course, an affirmation of the irreducibly private and
idiosyncratic in man, and thus of personality. The choice for the
poet, so far as I can understand it, has tended towards the either/or.
This very extremity of choice, indeed, has set its mark on, perhaps

made possible, the writing of poetry in our generation; for ours is, if nothing else, an extreme poetry. The situation is worth remarking here, because we haven't been sufficiently aware that the choice existed in all its extremity, that poets have chosen compulsively, and, most important, that some have chosen personality, with *its* affirmations and denials. We can see then, in the work of three of our poets of "established" reputation, the evidence of this choice and all that it implies for practice and achievement in our poetry. These three are William Carlos Williams, who celebrates perception; E. E. Cummings, who celebrates emotion; and Wallace Stevens, who celebrates creative imagination—all celebrations stemming from a sense of the personality as simple, separate, and immediately doomed when lost in the mass.

Celebration of the perceiving self has been for some thirty years William Carlos Williams' stock-in-trade. There is, for example, this celebrated piece:

> so much depends
> upon
>
> a red wheel
> barrow
>
> glazed with rain
> water
>
> beside the white
> chickens

This says, if I may run the risk of making indirect that which depends for its quality upon directness: So much depends upon our continuing clear and coherent perception of such a little scene; so much depends, because we depend upon seeing objects thus; what is important is the perceptive act; it is a way we have of taking possession of our world without destroying it. The bare claim of the first line literally "depends" upon the effectiveness of what follows; the generalization comes alive only if the instance is fresh and strong, forever new. Always in Williams' work the procedure is to discover other things, other selves—and to discover them sharply and precisely and separately; then to discover that the paradox of relatedness is in non-relatedness.

The bulk of Williams' poems over the past thirty years has been such small poems as the one I have quoted, poems in which the personality has realized itself by appropriating esthetically part of its world—a world of things and events, big and little, in a doctor's life. There has been no search for a highest authority, but rather for a community of perceiving selves. When Williams has occasionally written about authority from above—for example, in the much-anthologized "The Yachts"—he has imaged it as something fearful and monstrous and destructive, yet beautiful, and so all the more dangerous.

The form and movement of his poems reflect the sentiments. Or can one say that they make the sentiments? Williams characteristically begins with a natural situation and sticks to it as hard as he can, searching out its every immediate quality. If the situation bodies forth a "meaning" larger than itself, that meaning is made literally to force itself on the poet's sensibility, so that he can register it in his poems as being, in all its uniqueness, integral to his own full and clear knowledge of the world. The meaning is immanent in the perceptive act, in the separateness and uniqueness of the subject-object relationship.

This is the structural principle of the poems, realized most fully in the long work which Williams has just completed: "Paterson." He attached this note to the section of the poem published in 1946: "This is the first part of a long poem in four parts—that a man in himself is a city, beginning, seeking, achieving and concluding his life in ways which the various aspects of a city may embody—if imaginatively conceived—any city, all the details of which may be made to voice his most intimate convictions." The poem is a portrait of the poet-protagonist wandering over his city, meditating upon it, recalling its history and his life in it, and fusing what he sees, meditates upon, and recalls into one continuing image. What unifies the poem is the poet who is at its center; structurally it moves by a kind of associationism; the poet is gifted with an eloquent and lyrical recall. He discovers not so much that he is a city, but that by virtue of being a poet he has made the city himself. It is the self, his and others', which he discovers in all its possible fullness, and discovering, celebrates. If there is to be a community, it is a community of infinitely different, infinitely varied selves. In the form of his poem, as well as in its sentiments, Williams manifests a fear of any kind of order which would make those selves deny any part of their being. Order itself is denied—

unless it be the order of living, discovering, and dying. Order becomes process; so that whatever form there is in Williams' poem is one deriving from a sense of the process which constitutes the life-principle for each man and object in his world.

For Williams the poet's job is to work with language; and language is of separate and unique things which must be perceived for what they are and so saluted. Language must be saved from itself, from the death-drive which is in the necessity to communicate by abstracting and destroying the particular. The poet's job is a large one, not to be subordinated to any authority; for only he can discover the uniqueness of the self and through that discovery give life to language. In the words of the fairly recent "Convivio":

> We forget sometimes that no matter what
> our quarrels we are the same brotherhood:
> the rain falling or the rain withheld,
> —berated by women, barroom smells
> or breath of Persian roses! our wealth
> is words. And when we go down to defeat,
> before the words, it is still within and
> the concern of, first, the brotherhood.
> Which should quiet us, warm and arm us
> besides to attack, always attack—but to
> reserve our worst blows for the enemy, those
> who despise the word, flout it, stem
> leaves and root; the liars who decree laws
> with no purpose other than to make a screen
> of them for larceny, murder—for our
> murder, we who salute the word and would
> have it clean, full of sharp movement.

Devotion to the word—"clean, full of sharp movement"—and all that such devotion implies has been the way of another poet who in yet another way is marked by obsession with personality. This is E. E. Cummings. Saluting him in 1946, Williams wrote, "I think of cummings as Robinson Crusoe at the moment when he first saw the print of a naked human foot in the sand. That . . . implied a new language—and a readjustment of conscience." And further, "cummings is the living presence of the drive to make all our convictions evident by penetrating through their costumes to the living flesh of the matter." Williams and Cummings are by no means poets teaching in the same school.

But they are devoted to what is, in the last analysis, the same cause.

In an essay called, appropriately enough, "Technique as Joy," Theodore Spencer thus described Cummings' cause: "There is no doubt about what Mr. Cummings stands for. He has said it again and again. He is for the individual human being against mechanical regimentation, for the living Now—in flower, bird, mountain and man; he is for 'the remembrance of miracle . . . by somebody who can love and be continually reborn.' He hates standardization, communism, all planning and ordering that kills the sensuous and emotional awareness by which people are kept alive.

> my specialty is living said
> a man (who could not earn his bread
> because he would not sell his head)."

Cummings' mode is the lyric; for his concern is to make us aware of awareness, of the act of living and feeling all the riches of our world; and not the least of these riches is ourselves. His characteristic strategy is to wrench the common and the ordinary from the context which would abstract it into negativeness and to make it positive. For him, what is most common and most ordinary is, of course, man and his experience of living.

His earlier poems, say those published before 1938, shock us into awareness primarily by their typographical misbehavior; poems are set up on a page so as to force us to attend to the quality of an individual experience as it is occurring. Another way of forcing awareness in these poems is by going to nominally "unpoetic" subject matters and exhibiting the poetry immanent in them. So there are poems on violent love, self-consciously tough-tender—many of these; and in straining for effect, Cummings is too often like a Bret Harte come to the Village. What saves the poems, when they are saved, is Cummings' good humor, his knowledge that only the most sacred things of the self can be kidded and still remain sacred. The end of the poems is to register joy, any kind of joy; and the source of joy is always in the uniqueness of the self. So, in general, the earlier poems are attempts to define maximally individuated experience in such a way as to show that its only end is realization of self. The poems range from this:

```
                                        i will be
        M o ving in the Street of her
        bodyfee l inga ro undMe the traffic of
        lovely;muscles-sinke x p i r i n g S
               uddenl
        Y               totouch
                            the curvedship of
                                            Her-

        . . . . KIss . . .
```

to this

```
        since feeling is first
        who pays any attention
        to the syntax of things
        will never wholly kiss you
```

and this:

```
        I'd rather learn from one bird how to sing
        than teach ten thousand stars how not to dance.
```

In his more recent poetry Cummings has worked to refine this technique by trying literally to rescue abstract language from the abstractness that deadens it. He had wrenched words out of the regular grammatical and syntactical functions, more closely to associate them with the men and women whose experience they are to represent:

```
        my father moved through dooms of love
        through sames of am through haves of give,
        singing each morning out of each night
        my father moved through depths of height
```

for example, or this:

```
        all ignorance toboggans into know
        and trudges up to ignorance again:
        but winter's not forever, even snow
        melts; and if spring should spoil the game, what then?
```

or this:

```
        when faces called flowers float out of the ground
        and breathing is wishing and wishing is having—
        but keeping is downward and doubting and never
        —it's april (yes, april; my darling) it's spring!
        yes the pretty birds frolic as spry as can fly
        yes the little fish gambol as glad as can be
        (yes the mountains are dancing together)
```

Here language has somehow been restored to the feeling self from which it has been too long absent. This is Cummings' achievement, this is how he has chosen personality in preference to culture.

His choice continues to make him speak loudly and to follow out its fullest implications. He is now, I suppose, a self-admitted philosophical anarchist, an unreconstructed Bohemian. "The Enormous Room" and "Eimi" only point to something which the poems realize. Recently Cummings has written a preface to a collection of Krazy Kat comic strips. Krazy, he finds, represents the highest of our realities; for she is all love, loving most of all Ignatz Mouse, even though he continually heaves bricks at her. The villain of the piece, for Cummings, is Offisa Pup—who in trying to protect Krazy from Ignatz only succeeds in setting up abstract authority. But, then, Offisa Pup is always defeated; and Krazy's love, if it does not conquer Ignatz, at least conquers Krazy herself, and in a dim way even conquers Offisa Pup. So love conquers all, because the self, conquering nothing, gives all. Cummings' lyricism is absolute, because it is a lyricism which celebrates personality as purely and directly as possible.

The most commanding of modern American poets who celebrate personality is Wallace Stevens. He is, in his own way, a philosophical poet; and striving to be as inclusive and exact as a philosophical poet must be, he demands most of his poetry and his audience. For, from the beginning, he has poetized about what he has called reality and the imagination—which is to say, the world we live in and our selves, considered as interacting forces. His problem has been: What is the relation of one to the other? And he has treated it literally as a problem. As a result, his recent poems, instead of celebrating the self, have been concerned with studying it. And he has by now evolved a kind of informal, rhetorically-stated philosophic position on the problem. The development is long and complex; his production has been voluminous; I shall be able only to note its high points.

What is central in Stevens' earliest poems (those published before 1935) is an awareness of the texture of reality (in Stevens' sense of the thing-in-itself) as a factor at once for the enriching and for the limiting of the experience of the self. Here he is akin to Williams. The driving concern of these early poems is with the sensuously flowing aspect of reality as we come to know, to partake of, and thus to inform it and be informed by it. These are specifically poems of the creative imagination, of the creative self. On the one hand, Stevens writes lyrics, in which the self is, as it were, caught in the act of experiencing and organizing the world, thus giving it meaning; on the other hand, he writes dramatic poems, in which men and women puzzle over the limitations that their selfhood imposes on them and try to comprehend their relations to the world outside. Thus there is a poem like "Peter Quince at the Clavier," which ends:

> Beauty is momentary in the mind—
> The fitful tracing of a portal;
> But in the flesh it is immortal.

And there is a poem like "Sunday Morning" the argument of which turns on the predicament of a sensitive woman who is disturbed by her awareness of a "holy hush of ancient sacrifice" in which she cannot participate. She tries to break through the limits of her bright warm world and to achieve realization of the world of received religion and of the authority which might be outside herself. But she cannot; she can only know what her sensitive self will let her know. Stevens does not let her, and many another like her in his earlier poetry, deny reality or authority outside herself. He makes her accept its possibility; yet he will not let her know it unless she somehow makes it by and through herself.

Since the middle 'thirties Stevens' subject has been this problem of finding a sense of authority which is generated in significant part by the personality (for him, the creative imagination) and of facing frankly the inadequacy of such culture or cultures as are available to modern man. His poems through the 'forties continually speak of the need for such a sense and of the part which poetry should play in achieving it. One poem from "The Man with the Blue Guitar" ends with what might be taken as the text of this essay:

> Poetry
>
> Exceeding music must take the place
> Of empty heaven and its hymns,
>
> Ourselves in poetry must take their place
> Even in the chattering of your guitar.

He sees clearly that the question of the role of the self is not simply one of realization but of belief, not simply of awareness but of understanding the fundamental role of awareness in making knowledge possible. In another poem of this period, he writes:

> The prologues are over. It is a question, now,
> Of final belief. So, say that final belief
> Must be in a fiction. It is time to choose.

Further, this belief must somehow be in the self, in that

> . . . impossible possible philosopher's man,
> The man who has had the time to think enough,
> The central man, the human globe, responsive
> As a mirror with a voice, the man of glass,
> Who in a million diamonds sums us up.

Personality must dominate.

And Stevens' latest poems, those in his last two volumes, have been devoted to defining the fiction in which we must believe and the role of the self in generating that fiction. If the fiction is to be authoritative for us, it is to be so because it results from a man's meditating his private relation to reality, because it is a product of the imaginative self giving shape to reality, because only it will allow for the primacy of existence of an infinite number of selves. Poetry, Stevens concluded in a lecture a few years ago, is the product of a violence within which protects us from the violence without. One recalls Williams and his talk about the quality of "continual and violent refreshing" which characterizes worthwhile poetry.

The two poems in which Stevens has most fully treated this problem are "Notes toward a Supreme Fiction" and "Esthétique du Mal." These are explicitly philosophical poems, poems of ideas. But they are also poems of the imaginative, artistic self. For imaginative experience is shown to be the only means we have of initiating the inquiry by which we arrive at philosophical ideas and to be, moreover, the only means we have of realizing and believing in those ideas. Thus the poetry is at once an expression and an exposition of a philosophical attitude. Since the authenticity of that attitude depends on an origin in imaginative experience, it depends on the sensibility of the poet, on the self—a self divorced, ideally, from any kind of external authority. The place

of dialectic is taken by rhetoric; for rhetoric is of the self and
dialectic of authority. Stevens has said that when he writes "poet,"
he means "any man of imagination." Presumably, all good men
must be men of imagination, knowing the world in acts of imagination—in poems.

   The Supreme Fiction which is generated and realized thus
will compel belief because it will be a product of the act of the
believer. This Supreme Fiction has the following attributes:
abstractness, change, good, and evil. For these are qualities which
we discover in all our imaginative experience of reality; these are
qualities which we can know imaginatively and so must believe
in. The poems in which the qualities are elucidated are long and
difficult. They are elegantly worded, discursive, modulating from
perceived idea to perceived idea, cast in a language which registers
as precisely as possible the imaginative qualities of the perceptions
out of which they are made. Beginning with the notion of a radically free self and an utterly alien reality, Stevens has created an
object for a kind of religious belief, a God of four attributes, a
God literally made (so far as He is known) by the self, a God who
is literally a fiction. To return to the central generalization of this
essay, he has celebrated the creative imagination in such a way as
to define culture in terms of personality and to deny culture any
existence except as a fiction—however compelling, however
supreme.

   The very end of "Esthétique du Mal" reads thus:

> . . . out of what one sees and hears and out
> Of what one feels, who could have thought to make
> So many selves, so many sensuous worlds,
> As if the air, the mid-day air, was swarming
> With the metaphysical changes that occur
> Merely in living as and where we live.

This, with its insistence on sees, hears, feels, changes, living, is at
the opposite pole from and complementary to Eliot's

> . . . to apprehend
> The point of intersection of the timeless
> With time, is an occupation for the saint—
> No occupation either, but something given
> And taken, in a lifetime's death in love,
> Ardour and selflessness and self-surrender.

> For most of us, there is only the unattended
> Moment, the moment in and out of time . . .

The two passages read together tell us a great deal about our world, our society, and ourselves—in all, about our present discontents. I suggest that we must "use" the two passages— and all that leads up to and follows from them—in a way analagous to that in which we use concepts like culture and personality; for the poetry fills out and realizes the concepts, as the concepts generalize and make operative the poetry. And I suggest further that, as with the concepts, we cannot really understand the one passage of poetry and the place it has in our lives unless we understand the other. A poetry whose strength is manifest in a denial of the radically free self makes final sense to men living in this world only in relation to a poetry whose strength is manifest in an affirmation of that self. In the end we must come from Eliot and Stevens, as from culture and personality, to ourselves in our world. Then, if we look about carefully, we shall discover that with Eliot and Stevens, as with culture and personality, we have already been there.

TECHNOLOGY IS AWESOME!

101 INCREDIBLE THINGS EVERY KID SHOULD KNOW

ALICE HARMAN

ARCTURUS

This edition published in 2019
by Arcturus Publishing Limited
26/27 Bickels Yard, 151–153 Bermondsey Street,
London SE1 3HA

Author: Alice Harman
Designer: Sarah Fountain

Picture credits: p2m and p65t: Library of Congress; p2r, p19t, p19b:
EKSO Bionics; p7b: US Air Force; p8: Gravity Industries; p9b: Gravity
Industries; p18: Lulu Kyriacou; p22l: ARAIG; p33t: Lorrie LeJeune/
MIT; p38: SpecialEffect; p39t: Fred Davison/Quadstick; p39b:
Microsoft; p47t: Imperial College London; p62: Cmglee; p65b: Ammar
shaker; p66: Stratolaunch; p71b: Steve Nicklas/NOAA Ship Collection;
p77t: U.S. Air Force/Volkmar Wentzel; p91b: © Ecocapsule Holding;
p99bl and p99br: mimica; p100 and p101: Studio Roosegaarde; p108
and p100: Natural Machines; p115b: ICON/New Story; p118l and
p119: John Romanishin, MIT CSAIL: PI Rus Distributed Robotics
Laboratory. All other images by Shutterstock.

ISBN: 978-1-78888-491-4
CH006566NT
Supplier 29, Date 0519, Print run 7964

Printed in China

What is STEM?

STEM is a world-wide initiative that
aims to cultivate an interest in
Science, Technology, Engineering,
and Mathematics, in an effort
to promote these disciplines to
as wide a variety of students as
possible.